FORMAL DESCRIPTION TECHNIQUES

First International Conference on
Formal Description Techniques
Stirling, Scotland, 6-9 September, 1988

(FORTE 88)

organised by
University of Stirling, Scotland

NORTH-HOLLAND
AMSTERDAM • NEW YORK • OXFORD • TOKYO

FORMAL DESCRIPTION TECHNIQUES

Proceedings of the First International Conference on
Formal Description Techniques
Stirling, Scotland, 6-9 September, 1988

edited by

Kenneth J. TURNER

Professor of Computing Science
University of Stirling,
Stirling, Scotland

1989

NORTH-HOLLAND
AMSTERDAM • NEW YORK • OXFORD • TOKYO

© Elsevier Science Publishers B.V., 1989

All rights reserved. No part of this publication may be reproduced, stored in a retrieval system or transmitted in any form or by any means, electronic, mechanical, photocopying, recording or otherwise, without the prior written permission of the publishers, Elsevier Science Publishers B.V. (Physical Sciences and Engineering Division), P.O. Box 103, 1000 AC Amsterdam, The Netherlands.

Special regulations for readers in the USA – This publication has been registered with the Copyright Clearance Center Inc. (CCC), Salem, Massachusetts. Information can be obtained from the CCC about conditions under which photocopies of parts of this publication may be made in the USA. All other copyright questions, including photocopying outside of the USA, should be referred to the copyright owner, Elsevier Science Publishers B.V., unless otherwise specified.

No responsibility is assumed by the Publisher for any injury and/or damage to persons or property as a matter of products liability, negligence or otherwise, or from any use or operation of any methods, products, instructions or ideas contained in the material herein.

pp. 91-106, 107-120, 121-134, 295-310: Work for a Government Agency, not subject to copyright.

ISBN: 0 444 87126 8

Published by:

ELSEVIER SCIENCE PUBLISHERS B.V.
P.O. Box 103
1000 AC Amsterdam
The Netherlands

Sole distributors for the U.S.A. and Canada:

ELSEVIER SCIENCE PUBLISHING COMPANY, INC.
655 Avenue of the Americas
New York, N.Y. 10010
U.S.A.

Library of Congress Cataloging-in-Publication Data

```
International Conference on Formal Description
   Techniques (1st : 1988 : Stirling, Scotland)
   Formal description techniques.

   Bibliography: p.
   1. Electronic digital computers--Programming--
Congresses.  2. Formal languages--Congresses.  I. Turner,
Kenneth J.  II. Title.
QA76.6.I545  1988         005.1           88-29139
ISBN 0-444-87126-8
```

PRINTED IN THE NETHERLANDS

Preface

It is evidence of the growing maturity of a subject when it spawns a new Conference. Various Conferences in recent years have dealt with formal languages for specification, verification, and design of communications systems. However, FORTE 88 is the first Conference devoted exclusively to the FDTs *(Formal Description Techniques)* Estelle, LOTOS, and SDL. The FORTE 88 Conference was timed to coincide with the last stage of standardisation of these languages. As they achieved stability and international acceptance it seemed appropriate to bring them to a wider audience.

Some eight years in elapsed time and hundreds of years in manpower have gone into developing the FDTs. At times the path to standardisation has been hard. Formal languages and formal methods are still the subject of intense ongoing research, so standardisation has required care in selecting the best of current work. Those not involved in FDT standardisation have found it difficult to understand the new approach which FDTs bring. The FDTs may have seemed abstruse, the effort to become familiar with them may have appeared too great. However, as knowledge of the FDTs continues to grow and as experience in writing formal descriptions accumulates, more people are becoming convinced of their value. The barrier to be overcome is educational, not technological nor intellectual.

The main emphasis of the FORTE 88 Conference was therefore on creating awareness and understanding. The Conference included introductions to the FDTs, advice sessions for those needing help with FDTs, demonstrations of software tools for FDTs, and reports on practical experience in using FDTs. Although the FDT introductions are not included in these Proceedings, ample tutorial material is to be found in the FDT standards themselves and in the literature. The Bibliography suggests a few introductory texts.

The FDTs have sometimes been portrayed as being in competition with each other. However, detailed study of the FDTs reveals that they have their own individual strengths and weaknesses. There will never be a universal FDT any more than there will never be a universal programming language. It will take some years — and events like FORTE 88 — for a clear picture to emerge of which FDTs should be used for what applications and with what objectives. Although the FDTs were conceived to help with specification and design of communications systems, their applicability is bound to be much wider. As international standards they will reach a very large range of users and applications.

It is my hope that FORTE 88 will help to encourage the use of FDTs, and will be the first of a long and successful series of Conferences.

Kenneth J. Turner
September, 1988

Contents

Preface v
Contents vii
Acknowledgements xi
Committee Members and Invited Speakers xiii
Referees xv
Bibliography xvii

Software Tools - Papers

An Approach to providing Support Tools for Formal Specification 1
    J. J. Masterson, K. P. Ishaq, A. T. Hockley, *British Telecom, Ipswich, U.K.*

ESTIM - The Estelle Simulator Prototype of the Esprit SEDOS Project 15
    P. de Saqui-Sannes, J.-P. Courtiat, *LAAS du CNRS, Toulouse, France*

A LOTOS to PARLOG Translator 31
    D. R. Gilbert, *Imperial College, London, U.K.*

Transforming LOTOS Specifications with LOLA - The Parameterised Expansion .. 45
    J. Quemada, S. Pavón, A. Fernández, *ETSI Telecomunicación, Madrid, Spain*

Software Tools - Demonstrations

SDT - The SDL Design Tool 55
    M. Atlevi, *Telelogic Europe, Brussels, Belgium*

LOTTE - A LOTOS Tool Environment 61
    W. H. P. van Hulzen, *Dr. Neher Laboratories, Leidschendam, Netherlands*

SPIDER - Service and Protocol Interactive Development Environment 67
    S. G. Johnston, *Hewlett-Packard Laboratories, Bristol, U.K.*

A LISP-Based LOTOS Environment 73
    G. Karjoth, *IBM Research Laboratory, Zurich, Switzerland*

From LOTOS to C 79
    J. A. Mañas, T. de Miguel-More, *ETSI Telecomunicación, Madrid, Spain*

EWS - An Integrated Workstation for the Design and the Automatic Generation .. 85
of Distributed Software
    J.-M. Ayache, J. Dufau, *Verilog, Toulouse, France*, M. Huybrechts, *Expert Software Systems, Ghent, Belgium*, E. Mattera, *Marben, Paris, France*

Object-Oriented Design with FDTs

An Object-Oriented Model for Estelle 91
    R. Sijelmassi, P. Gaudette, *National Bureau of Standards, Gaithersburg, U.S.A.*

Specification of Object-Oriented Systems in LOTOS 107
    T. Mayr, *Institut für Angewandte Informatik, Vienna, Austria*

An Object-Oriented Model for ASN.1 121
    P. Gaudette, S. Trus, S. Collins, *National Bureau of Standards, Gaithersburg, U.S.A.*

Language Issues arising from Practical Use

Modelling OSI in SDL 135
    F. Belina, *Telelogic, Malmö, Sweden*, D. Hogrefe, *University of Hamburg, West Germany*, S. Trigila, *Fondazione Ugo Bordoni, Rome, Italy*

Graphical Views of Process-Orientated Specifications 143
    D. W. Bustard, A. C. Winstanley, *Queen's University of Belfast, Northern Ireland*, M. T. Norris, R. A. Orr, S. Patel, *British Telecom, Ipswich, U.K.*

Non-Determinism and SDL 157
    D. Hogrefe, *University of Hamburg, West Germany*, A. Sarma, *Research Institute of the Deutsche Bundespost, Darmstadt, West Germany*

Theoretical Aspects of Analysis

The Boyer-Moore Theorem-Prover and LOTOS 169
    S. S. Aujla, *British Telecom, Ipswich, U.K.*, M. Fletcher, *University of Oxford, U.K.*

Using Estelle for Verification - An Experience with the T.70 Teletex 185
Transport Protocol
    M. Phalippou, R. Groz, *CNET, Lannion, France*

Squiggles - A Tool for the Analysis of LOTOS Specifications 201
    T. Bolognesi, M. Caneve, *CNUCE, Pisa, Italy*

Transformation from LOTOS Specifications to Galileo Nets 217
   S. M. Rodriguez, *Alcatel, Madrid, Spain*, G. L. Serrano, *ETSI Telecomunicación, Madrid, Spain*

Experience in writing Formal Descriptions

Specifying ROSE in LOTOS 231
   D. Freestone, S. S. Aujla, *British Telecom, Ipswich, U.K.*

On the Use of LOTOS for the Formal Description of a Transport Protocol 247
   J. van de Lagemaat, G. Scollo, *University of Twente, Enschede, Netherlands*

The Application of LOTOS for the Formal Description of the ISO Session Layer .. 263
   M. van Sinderen, I. Ajubi, *University of Twente, Enschede, Netherlands*,
   F. Caneschi, *TECSIEL, Pisa, Italy*

LOTOS-Supported System Development 279
   K. Bogaards, *University of Twente, Enschede, Netherlands*

Practical Aspects of Analysis

Application of Formal Description Techniques to Conformance Evaluation 295
   J.-P. Favreau, R. J. Linn, P. Gaudette, *National Bureau of Standards, Gaithersburg, U.S.A.*

Derivation of Useful Execution Trees from LOTOS by using an Interpreter 311
   R. Guillemot, L. Logrippo, *University of Ottawa, Canada*

SDS - A LOTOS-Based Tool for Symbolic Debugging 327
   F. Costa, D. Nardi, R. Rinaldi, *Olivetti, Ivrea, Italy*

Validation of the Ferry-Clip Local Testing System using an Estelle-C Compiler ... 337
   S. T. Vuong, W. Y. L. Chan, *University of British Columbia, Vancouver, Canada*

Acknowledgements

A Conference on the scale of FORTE 88 demanded the time and enthusiasm of many people. Prominent among these was Elspeth Cusack, Conference Vice-Chair, who was extremely helpful with practical and moral support. Programme Committee members also contributed extensively to the preparation and runing of the Conference. Among the Local Organising Committee, Julie Husbands, Anne McNeill, and Sam Nelson deserve special mention for their hard work.

The Conference was fortunate to have a number of leading FDT experts give invited presentations. Many others gave of their time to referee papers. And, of course, a Conference could not exist without the support of those giving papers.

Several organisations kindly sponsored the Conference. The Research and Technology Executive of British Telecom gave financial and practical help. Equipment for demonstrations of software tools was loaned by Apollo Computer (U.K.) Ltd. and by SUN Microsystems (U.K.) Ltd.

I am grateful to the people mentioned above and to everyone else involved for making the FORTE 88 Conference successful.

Kenneth J. Turner
Conference Chair

Committee Members and Invited Speakers

Conference Chair

Ken Turner	*University of Stirling, U.K.*	(Chair)
Elspeth Cusack	*British Telecom, Ipswich, U.K.*	(Vice-Chair)

Programme Committee

Tommaso Bolognesi	*CNUCE, Pisa, Italy*
Ed Brinksma	*University of Twente, Enschede, Netherlands*
Elspeth Cusack	*British Telecom, Ipswich, U.K.*
Dieter Hogrefe	*University of Hamburg, West Germany*
Günter Karjoth	*IBM Research Laboratory, Zurich, Switzerland*
Bill McCrum	*Department of Communications, Ottawa, Canada*
Jan de Meer	*GMD-Fokus, Berlin, West Germany*
Elie Najm	*INRIA, Rocquencourt, France*
Juan Quemada	*ETSI Telecomunicación, Madrid, Spain*
Richard Tenney	*University of Massachusetts, Boston, U.S.A.*
Ken Turner	*University of Stirling, U.K.*

Invited Speakers

Ferenc Belina	*Telelogic, Malmö, Sweden*
Tommaso Bolognesi	*CNUCE, Pisa, Italy*
André Danthine	*University of Liège, Belgium*
Ove Færgemand	*TFL, Hørsholm, Denmark*
Richard Tenney	*University of Massachusetts, Boston, U.S.A.*
Chris Vissers	*University of Twente, Enschede, Netherlands*

Referees

R. B. Alderden	*University of Twente, Enschede, Netherlands*
S. S. Aujla	*British Telecom, Ipswich, U.K.*
P. Azema	*LAAS du CNRS, Toulouse, France*
F. Belina	*Telelogic, Malmö, Sweden*
J. Berrocal	*ETSI Telecomunicación, Madrid, Spain*
S. Black	*Hewlett-Packard Laboratories, Bristol, U.K.*
D. Blyth	*Incord Ltd., Wimbourne, U.K.*
G. von Bochmann	*University of Montréal, Canada*
T. Bolognesi	*CNUCE, Pisa, Italy*
R. E. Booth	*British Telecom, Ipswich, U.K.*
E. Brinksma	*University of Twente, Enschede, Netherlands*
S. Budkowski	*Bull S. A., Louveciennes, France*
V. Chari	*Marben, Paris, France*
E. L. Cusack	*British Telecom, Ipswich, U.K.*
P. Dembinski	*Bull S. A., Louveciennes, France*
M. Diss	*Hewlett-Packard Laboratories, Bristol, U.K.*
P. van Eijk	*University of Twente, Enschede, Netherlands*
W. Fischer	*University of Stüttgart, West Germany*
D. Freestone	*British Telecom, Ipswich, U.K.*
G. le Gall	*CNET, Lannion, France*
D. R. Gilbert	*Imperial College, London, U.K.*
D. Hogrefe	*University of Hamburg, West Germany*
W. H. P. van Hulzen	*Dr. Neher Laboratories, Leidschendam, Netherlands*
G. Karjoth	*IBM Research Laboratory, Zurich, Switzerland*
L. Logrippo	*University of Ottawa, Canada*
J. A. Mañas	*ETSI Telecomunicación, Madrid, Spain*
J. de Meer	*GMD-Fokus, Berlin, West Germany*
T. de Miguel-More	*ETSI Telecomunicación, Madrid, Spain*
E. Najm	*INRIA, Rocquencourt, France*
R. Neely	*STC Technology Ltd., Stevenage, U.K.*
M. T. Norris	*British Telecom, Ipswich, U.K.*
F. Orava	*Swedish Institute of Computer Science, Stockholm, Sweden*
A. J. Payne	*British Telecom, Ipswich, U.K.*
D. Pitt	*University of Surrey, Guildford, U.K.*
B. F. Potter	*STC Technology Ltd., Harlow, U.K.*
J. Quemada	*ETSI Telecomunicación, Madrid, Spain*
R. Reed	*GEC Telecommunications Ltd., Coventry, U.K.*
O. Rees	*ANSA Project, Cambridge, U.K.*
S. Rudkin	*British Telecom, Ipswich, U.K.*

G. Scollo	*University of Twente, Enschede, Netherlands*
M. van Sinderen	*University of Twente, Enschede, Netherlands*
C. R. Smith	*GEC Hirst Research Centre, Wembley, U.K.*
R. L. Tenney	*University of Massachusetts, Boston, U.S.A.*
P. A. J. Tilanus	*Dr. Neher Laboratories, Leidschendam, Netherlands*
D. R. Till	*Kings College, London, U.K.*
E. Vazquez	*ETSI Telecomunicación, Madrid, Spain*
G. Wheeler	*Telecom Australia, Victoria, Australia*
M. C. Wilbur-Ham	*Telecom Australia, Victoria, Australia*

Bibliography

The following short list gives references to the FDT standards as well as to some introductory material.

Bolognesi, T. and Brinksma, E.: *Introduction to the ISO Specification Language LOTOS*, Computer Networks and ISDN Systems, *14* (1), pp. 25–29, North-Holland, Amsterdam, 1988

Budkowski, S. and Dembinski, P.: *An Introduction to Estelle: A Specification Language for Distributed Systems*, Computer Networks and ISDN Systems, *14* (1), pp. 3–24, North-Holland, Amsterdam, 1988

CCITT: *Specification and Description Language*, Z.100, International Consultative Committee for Telephony and Telegraphy, Geneva, March 1988

ISO: *Information Processing Systems - Open Systems Interconnection - Estelle, A Formal Description Technique based on an Extended State Transition Model*, DIS 9074, International Organisation for Standardisation, Geneva, July 1987

ISO: *Information Processing Systems - Open Systems Interconnection - LOTOS, A Formal Description Technique based on the Temporal Ordering of Observational Behaviour*, DIS 8807, International Organisation for Standardisation, Geneva, July 1987

ISO: *Guidelines for the Application of Estelle, LOTOS, and SDL*, JTC1/SC21/N2549, International Organisation for Standardisation, Geneva, March 1988

Saracco, R. and Tilanus, P. A. J.: *CCITT SDL: Overview of the Language and its Applications*, Computer Networks and ISDN Systems, *13* (2), pp. 65–74, North-Holland, Amsterdam, 1987

An Approach to Providing Support Tools for Formal Specification

J J Masterson, K P Ishaq and A T Hockley

Human Factors Division,
British Telecom Research Laboratories,
Martlesham Heath,
Ipswich,
Suffolk.

Formal Description Techniques can improve the design and implementation of computer systems through ensuring that the problem space is analysed thoroughly. However, the very precision of the techniques makes them demanding to use, requiring high levels of abstract reasoning. This deters many potential users, whose objectives are to produce a specification, rather than becoming involved in the intricacies of the method. A solution to these difficulties can be provided by the provision of software tools to support the specification process. This paper presents an approach to the production of support tools, based upon the application of Knowledge Based Systems techniques and Human Factors principles. The products of the research programme are very encouraging, offering the possibility of going well beyond the assistance that can be provided through conventional software tools.

1. Introduction

Formal Description Techniques (FDT), being based upon mathematical concepts, offer great benefits in the design of computer and communication systems. There are now a number of formal techniques available for the specification task. However, these techniques have not been taken up to the full extent possible and informal techniques, including natural language, are still widely used. The prevalence of such approaches, in spite of the acknowledged problems in terms of accuracy and conflicting interpretations, result from their accessibility. Support tools may offer a way of introducing FDTs to a wider audience.

The work presented in this paper is a 'snapshot' of a research programme that was begun in 1986. Since that time we have investigated the provision of support for three FDTs: the Vienna Development Method (VDM), Z and LOTOS, in collaboration with two other divisions of British Telecom Research Laboratories. For the first two techniques we have completed prototype systems and work is underway towards providing support for LOTOS. We believe that our approach is different to that of other tool builders, both in the scope of activities our tools will support and in terms of the human interface. We are seeking to construct complete, interactive, environments in which the user can concentrate upon the specification task, with the system handling peripheral activities, for example housekeeping. To achieve this we are using Knowledge Based Systems (KBS) techniques, coupled with user-centred design (Monk, 1985), and using Prolog as a development language.

This paper seeks to illustrate the way that the research has developed and present the results of the work so far. To achieve this the three projects will be outlined, although the VDM work will be referred to only briefly, a description being available elsewhere (Masterson et al, 1988). However, before presenting the results we need to look at the underlying framework of our activities, beginning with an examination of the need for tools in this area.

2. Tool Support

Consultation with potential users of FDTs reveals that the lack of support tools is seen as a major barrier to their use. It takes time to become familiar with an FDT, and support tools may reduce the learning time, thereby aiding their introduction. Tools can aid the specifier in a number of ways, including: Editing facilities (eg structure editors), Syntax checkers, Specification animators, Aids for refinement and Assistance with proofs (eg use of theorem provers). The main areas found suitable for tool support have been syntax checkers (eg van der Vegte, 1987) and specification animators (eg Stepney and Lord, 1987). The general view on structure editors is that they are unsatisfactory - restricting the user to an unacceptable degree. The other areas have received very little attention.

Those using formal specification techniques, being involved in other aspects of the design and implementation process are unlikely to use an FDT continuously. Like any other occasional user of a technique, the formal specifier needs tools which are easy to learn and easy to use, otherwise they will be rejected by the potential users - even those experienced in computer usage.

3. Usability through KBS Techniques

Knowledge Based Systems are programs which can solve problems that would be computationally expensive or impossible using conventional techniques. The use of the KBS approach allows a concentration upon specific aspects of the problem area, which can be connected together to produce the overall problem solving behaviour and therefore provides a methodology for an incremental approach to producing a working system. KBS use domain knowledge - descriptions, relationships or procedures in an application area, rather than high level reasoning strategies.

The concentration upon the features of a domain that can assist in problem solving requires that the specification portion needed for the development of KBSs is prolonged, when compared to conventional programs. The process, known as 'Knowledge Acquisition' (KA), generally requires prolonged contact between an analyst (the Knowledge Engineer) and a person who has a good knowledge of the domain (the Expert). This process is aimed at identifying the important characteristics of the domain, the scope of the KBS component and the heuristics that will prove useful. Knowledge Acquisition has been a major component of the research we have performed, being used to establish the aspects of formal specification that we could encode and providing the basic facts and heuristics necessary.

4. The Formal Description Domain

Our work on providing support for formal specification began with an analysis of VDM, moving on to Z and more recently LOTOS. Consequently our view of the domain has been strongly influenced by our experience with these FDTs and may not be applicable to other FDTs. VDM is a fairly old technique, based on set theory and mathematical logic, which was developed by IBM Vienna in the 1970's as an aid to the creation of formally provable programs (see Jones, 1980). Z is more recent, having first been introduced in 1979, is founded in predicate logic, and is now widely used. LOTOS has only recently been developed (ISO/DIS8807, 1987) and is rather different to the earlier techniques, allowing the user to readily specify concurrency. This is achieved through the use of a process algebra derived from CCS (Milner, 1980) and CSP (Hoare, 1985). Although there are differences in the techniques, particularly between LOTOS and the others, there are similarities in the way that the specifier will approach the task. An individual writing a specification in any of these FDTs goes through an iterative cycle in which the problem space is explored and represented within the specification language. Initially the conception of the problem space is fairly vague and is refined through trying to express it clearly.

This kind of human reasoning (see Curtis, 1986) is difficult to replicate within a computer program, even one which adopts a KBS approach. Consequently we decided in our first venture into this area that the program would provide assistance to the VDM specifier and concentrated upon the 'housekeeping' knowledge involved in creating a specification. These concerns include syntax, data typing and the purpose of refinement - the making of the specification less abstract. Our experience has shown that the application of such domain knowledge can help to provide a useful support tool, as is being demonstrated by our work on VDM and Z. The new challenges presented by LOTOS, coupled with a greater familiarity with the domain, have led us to take a more fundamental approach to this FDT, as detailed in a later section.

5. Design Philosophy

Our design strategy is essentially user centred, looking to produce tools which are in keeping with the approach of the formal specifier. This strategy is implicit in the Knowledge Engineering work of the earlier projects (VDM and Z) and made explicit in the current research on LOTOS. The outstanding requirement for the design of a formal specification tool is to provide a working environment which is flexible and reduces the cognitive strain involved in producing the specification. This objective can be partly satisfied through the provision of a good interface, with icons, menus and the mouse as major characteristics (see Shneiderman, 1987). In addition the KBS components can take control of many aspects of the specification task leaving the specifier free to concentrate upon the part of the task only he can do.

6. Work for Intelligent Support Tools

The work aimed at creating support tools for formal specification has undergone a development path from a single implementation to produce a wider perspective. We began with the pragmatic objective of building a system which would demonstrate that KBS support for the task was possible. The production of the Intelligent VDM Assistant (IVA) program succeeded in this objective and provided a better understanding of the domain. The work to produce the Z Environment (ZEN) benefited in many ways from the earlier prototype, allowing a much more satisfactory design than would have otherwise been possible.

The Knowledge Acquisition process has also been modified over time, taking on some of the characteristics of conventional user-centred design. The IVA program was built with the assistance of a single expert, whereas ZEN benefited from the experience of several. The research that will contribute to a LOTOS tool is proceeding through a survey of users and potential users. This change of emphasis is reflected in the sections that follow, with the VDM and Z work being mainly concerned with the implementation issues. The section on the LOTOS work, in contrast, is mainly concerned with the domain knowledge, although with some reference to the architectural implications.

6.1 The Intelligent VDM Assistant

IVA is a prototype interactive environment for the creation of formal specifications, through the Vienna Development Method (VDM). Support for specification was provided in a number of ways. For example, all conditions to be used in the specification could be entered through a natural language form - reducing chances of error through greater comprehensibility. However, the user could input directly in VDM syntax if he wished or combine it with natural language. The system also performs all housekeeping tasks involved in moving from one level of abstraction to another - driven by user supplied data types appropriate to the new level.

IVA was developed through a process of rapid prototyping within a three month period, and involved less than six man-months of programming effort. The system was written in Prolog 2 and runs on an IBM AT compatible. To achieve the objective of delivering a working prototype in three months, restrictions were placed on the scope of the support that could be provided. Although the system is limited, it could be extended to provide full support. However, we have progessed to other FDTs, putting what has been learned directly into the development of the environment to support Z (see Masterson et al, 1988 for a full system description of IVA).

6.2 The Z Environment

The work on ZEN was begun at the request of the Standards Division of BTRL who are involved in the specification of distributed computer systems. They have a need to demonstrate that their specifications are correct and were interested in a tool that would support the task, particularly the provision of an animator. Work began in 1987 to investigate the structure of Z and to see if the

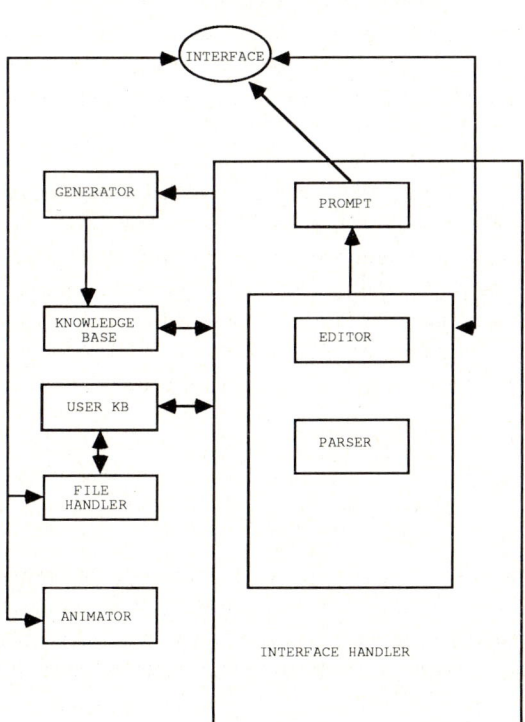

Figure 1: ZEN Overall Architecture

experience of the VDM assistant could be applied to this technique. The similarities between Z and VDM meant that progress was fairly rapid and work on a prototype began at the beginning of 1988.

To provide more advanced facilities than were possible in the earlier system, development took place on a Sun workstation using BIM Prolog, interfaced with the SunView windows and graphics environment. The prototype consists of two seperate parts: an environment for creating the specification and an animator. There follows a description of the system to give an indication of the nature of the support environment that will eventually be produced.

6.2.1 General Architecture

The general architecture of the system consists of five major components, two knowledge bases and a 'File Handler' (see Fig 1). The latter is used to save and recall a Z specification that is being

Figure 2: The ZEN Main Screen

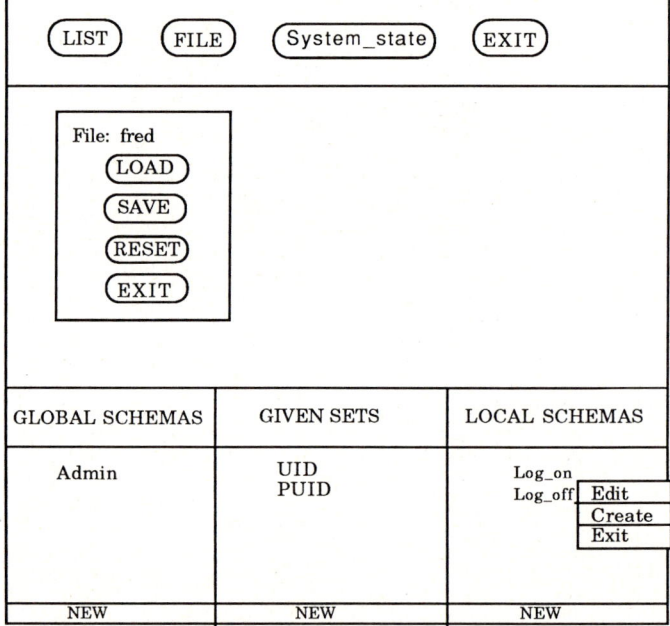

worked on, with an active specification being stored in the 'User Knowledge Base'. The domain knowledge relating to specifying in Z is contained in the main Knowledge Base in a production rule form, for use by the procedural components, described in the following sections.

a. Interface Module

The interface is structured to allow the user a high degree of flexibility. The main screen is split into three parts (see Fig 2). The first portion is a panel containing a number of buttons - each button allowing the user to carry out a particular task. The second portion of the screen is a scratch area - to display any pop-up menus, feedback to the user, or any information passed from the user to the system, such as the definition of schemas (convenient groupings of predicates). The final portion of the screen gives the user a general view of the Z specification defined so far. This itself is split into three windows - given sets, state schemas and operational schemas.

b. Generator

The generator maps the Z specification into Prolog assertions which are used as data for animation and listing the specification. Schemas are entered by the user through a schema frame (see Fig 3).

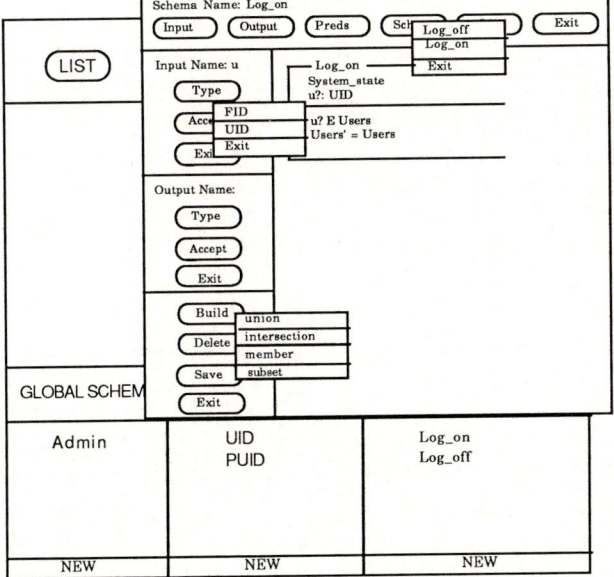

Figure 3: The Schema Frame

The user types in the schema name and the input and output variables. The variable type is defined through a menu selection - all types declared so far forming the menu options. A 'New' option in the menu allows the user to define a new type. A schema is also declared within another schema through a menu selection - the menu consisting of all the schemas defined so far.

c. Parser

The parser allows the user to define predicates in Z through menu options. When defining a predicate, a menu will appear of all the possible options that the user can apply at a particular stage of the predicate definition. This approach reduces errors by only presenting the user with the options that are useful at a particular time. For example let us suppose that the user has defined the following predicate so far:

p union

where *p* is defined as a *set*, then the next menu that will be displayed will only contain all the possible sets that have been defined in the specification.

d. Animation

This module allows the user to check the validity of the specification by testing it against a data set of values. The Animator is implemented as a production system, with all changes to values being asserted into the data base. The Animator module allows the user to test the validity of a specific schema. This involves determining the truth value of all the predicates of the schema and then those in the System state. Testing the truth value of a predicate involves having values for variables defined in the Z specification and having an internal representation for each Z operator.

Access to the Animator is through a windowed interface which displays the schema to be animated, the animation trace and error messages (see Fig 4). The user can examine one schema at a time, either single stepping through the predicates or getting a result for the schema as a whole. The single step providing output, like the following, for each predicate:

Predicate: u? member Users
Call: Sue member {Ann,Fred,Tom,Dick}
Result: false

The user has control over the input variables to a schema and can also change the internal database through the use of an editor which is activated through the Database button. This opens an editing window, as illustrated in Fig 4.

Figure 4: The Animator

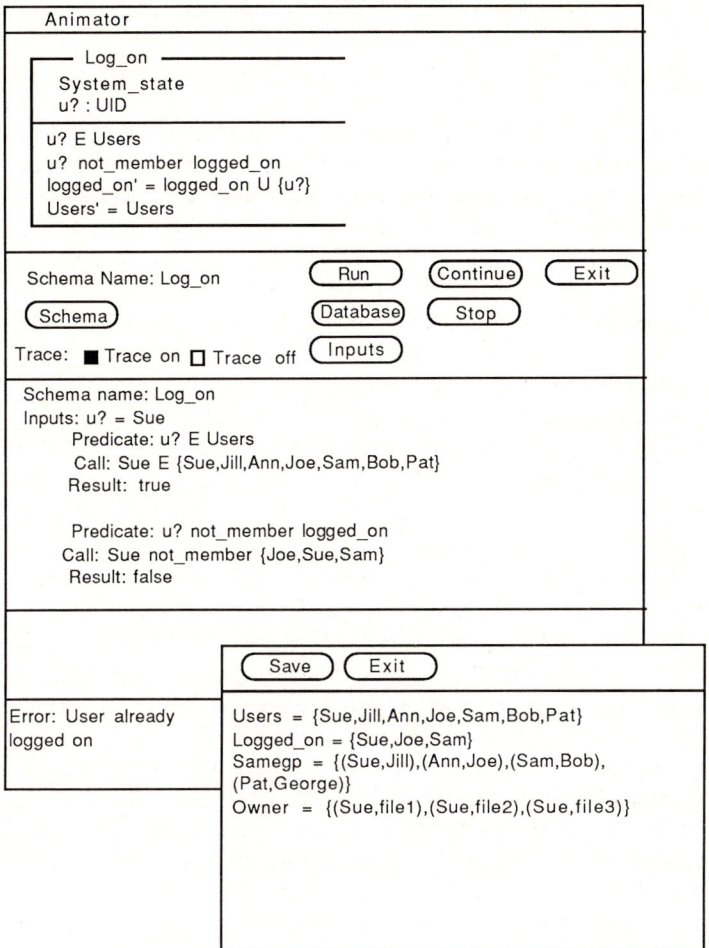

e. Editor

The editor module is in the course of development and will enable the user to create and modify a Z specification - to add or delete variables, change type definitions and input predicates. The effects of any edits will be propagated to the rest of the specification, as they may lead to invalidation. For example, by editing the following predicate:

p? union Users

the deletion of *p* will invalidate the union operator. The inconsistencies in the specification caused by editing are tackled using edit agendas, which keep track of all the edits the user has to complete to make the specification consistent.

6.3 LOTOS

For LOTOS we have refined our Knowledge Acquisition methodology to take a more fundamental view. Familiarity with the FDT was gained through informal interviews with two experts working in our Standards division, supported by a four day course. This was followed by a telephone survey of attenders of an introductory course on LOTOS, in order to identify areas of LOTOS expertise in BT. This confirmed that despite the high level of interest in LOTOS, its user base is restricted within BT. Many people are clearly waiting for a LOTOS methodology before committing themselves to it.

Those surveyed were interested in tools as a conventional aid to producing a LOTOS specification and also as an aid to gaining an understanding of other writers' specifications. The latter is of particular importance as a vehicle for standards' specification. Finally, tools to support good style are desirable. This is because LOTOS is particularly flexible in allowing users many different ways of representing the same thing. This flexibility offers power at the expense of giving enough rope to hang oneself convincingly. A comprehensive LOTOS tool should encourage the user to develop specifications which are as clear and simple to interpret as possible.

6.3.1 Interviews with LOTOS Experts

Two LOTOS experts were identified during a preliminary survey of people interested in LOTOS. They had 18 months and 4 months experience of LOTOS respectively, and had worked on a range of specification problems, including one specification produced together. Both were interviewed for approximately 2 hours. In the first stage of each interview, the expert was asked about his experience with LOTOS, particular attention being paid to the way in which he had structured the task of writing the specification.

The expert was also given a LOTOS specification, and asked to work out what it did, while providing a commentary on what he was looking at, and why. The final stage of the interview was to question the subjects directly about the features that they would like to see in tools.

6.3.1 Writing Specifications

The first step identified by both of the experts interviewed was to understand the system that they were trying to describe, and hence build up a model of the description. The next step was to identify elements of the model which could best be represented as separate processes. The identity and level of these processes is determined by producing what the experts consider to be an appropriate separation of concerns - with similar events being grouped into single processes. A major aim of the specifier is to identify a structuring of the problem space which facilitates such a grouping. However there is a need to achieve a balance which contributes to elegance and economy throughout the specification. The processes are then elaborated; any sub-processes, together with the locations and types of synchronisations being decided. Only when the basic structure of the process descriptions has been completed did the expert attempt to assemble the processes into the top level behaviour description. There will typically be many iterations within this and the previous phase.

Only when the basic backbone of the process algebra was complete did the experts seriously think about the datatyping. They feel that the process algebra is by far the most volatile part of a specification, and that time spent on datatyping in the early stages is time wasted. They prefer to minimise the datatyping wherever possible, inducing the requirements for this part of the specification from what has already been written in the process algebra. The final step is another iteration of the whole procedure, in which changes may be made to any or all of it. Typically these changes will be small.

6.3.3 Assessing Specifications

There were two concerns in assessing specifications - factual errors and style. Factual errors are induced by a process of self animation, bearing in mind real world constraints, and common errors. As a general matter of policy, both experts favoured a style which minimised the use of datatyping, unless this would lead to an exceptional lack of clarity. Also favoured was a minimum of levels, with specifications which involved more than 2 levels of embedding thought to be bad style. An important consideration in choosing the top level processes therefore is to choose processes that will lead to a minimum number of gates.

The experts heavily favoured a "constraint based" approach. By this they meant structuring the specification so that the general "normal case" was expressed as the first process, with exceptions being represented by following synchronisations. The advantages claimed for this were that it made it easy to see what was going on, as the the general case was made clear and specific, and also that it was easier to add additional constraints should the need arise.

There was more diversity of opinion over the use of operators. The more experienced expert disliked the interrupt operator, and preferred to use parallel operators with boolean guards. The less experienced expert liked the clarity he felt the interrupt offered. Both preferred to use simple synchronisations, favouring a general parallel synchronisation or interleaving, rather than synchronising on specific gates only.

6.3.4 Tools for LOTOS

The general objectives of tools for formal specification still apply to LOTOS. A user requires an environment in which they are able to perform the iterative design process, unencumbered by detailed considerations. Consequently, the eventual LOTOS tool is likely to retain the windowed interface and have similarities with the Z system described earlier. However, some features of that system, such as using menu-driven dialogue for specifying behaviour descriptions are unlikely to prove appropriate. The LOTOS specifier does not worry about data typing when writing the process part of the specification and consequently there would be no information on which to constrain the generation of the menus. However, other constraints upon the consistency of the specification, for example around the interleaving operator can be encoded.

The features which we are considering as useful for a LOTOS support tool are as follows:

- Accessible representation of the specification: graphics, cross referencing of gates.

- Syntactic aids: process templates, bracketing guide, interleaving consistency.

- Re-organising the specification easily - a highly flexible editor representation.

- Data type aid: inferring possible ADT from process structure.

- Library aid: browsing, summarising data type properties.

- Animator: including lookahead and multiple process.

- Temporal logic.

These requirements are not unique to the users we have talked to and work is already underway to satisfy them (eg GLOTOS for graphical representation: ISO/TC97 1987). Indeed, our own work is being conducted with other groups who are exploring some of these issues (see Bustard et al, 1988). Currently we are exploring an architecture for providing editing facilities in which the underlying representation and interface supports the user in re-organising the specification. It is likely that the LOTOS specification will be held within a network structure and mechanisms provided to restructure the network. However, the survey work and the implementation issues are still being researched and no firm decisions have yet been taken.

7. Discussion

The work shows promise as a vehicle for exploring support for formal specification and providing useful tools. The specification methods available prove complex to use and difficult to learn. Many potential users appear to be put off by the length of time that it takes before they can become competent and really assess the true benefits of these methods. The provision of a support environment can enhance learning by reducing the errors that can be made and giving rapid feedback on those that remain. Moreover, the cognitive load on any user is reduced, through the system taking away the need to worry about the simpler aspects of the task, such as maintaining consistency in the specification.

These systems are not merely for the novice, but have benefits for the experienced user. When producing a specification on paper, the user must retain a memory of what has been specified and what remains to be done. Human cognitive limitations restrict the size of specification to a level that can be maintained in an individual's head (maybe with the assistance of notes). The complex software systems which are now commonplace require large specifications, beyond what is feasible with manual methods. However, it is just such projects that can most benefit from formal specification. The use of a support environment can extend the 'power' of the individual through more effective use of their intelligence, thereby helping to express the promise offered by formal specification techniques.

Large developments also require team, rather than individual effort. Again, the use of a support environment can facilitate these ways of working, managing the relationships between the work of people and providing a uniform representation of the specification which is accessible to all. The communication aspects are facilitated by the use of animators and could also be aided by integrating textual descriptions. We are considering whether it might be possible to generate part of the text automatically from the specification.

8. Conclusion

The different projects outlined here are serving to aid our understanding of formal specification and the user needs. The abstract nature of formal specification makes it unlikely that fully knowledge based approaches will be applied to this area in the foreseeable future. However, there are considerable benefits that can accrue from even limited support. We are hoping to extend the use of KBS assistance to other parts of the specification process, including requirements specification and the proof process. It may be a long time before a computer program can conduct specification tasks unaided, but in the meantime many benefits can gained from the use of KBS support tools.

Bibliography

Bustard, D. W. et al. "Graphical Views of Process-Orientated Specifications", *this volume*.

Curtis, B. (ed), "Human Factors in Software Development", IEEE Computer Press/North Holland, 1986.

Hoare, C. A. R. "Communicating Sequential Processes", Prentice-Hall, 1985.

ISO/DIS8807 "Information Processing Systems - Open Systems Interconnection - LOTOS - A Formal Description Technique Based on the Temporal Ordering of Observational Behaviour", 1987.

ISO/TC 97/SC 21/WG1. "Graphical Representations for LOTOS: Objectives and Potential Requirements", October 1987.

Jones, B. 'Software Development: A Rigorous Approach', Prentice-Hall, 1980.

Masterson, J. J., Ishaq, K., Patel, S., Norris, M. T. and Orr, R. A. "Intelligent Tools for Formal Specification, Proceedings of the IEE/BCS Second Conference on Software Engineering, Liverpool, 1988.

Milner, A. J. "A Calculus of Communicating Systems", Springer-Verlag, 1980.

Monk, A. (ed) 'Fundamentals of Human-Computer Interaction', Academic Press, 1985.

Shneiderman, B. Designing the User Interface: Strategies for Effective Human-Computer Interaction', Addison-Wesley, 1987.

Stepney, S. and Lord, S. P. "Formal Specification of an Access Control System, Software-Practice and Experience, Vol. 17(8), Sept. 1987.

ESTIM: THE ESTELLE SIMULATOR PROTOTYPE
OF THE ESPRIT-SEDOS PROJECT

P. de SAQUI-SANNES and J-P. COURTIAT

LAAS/CNRS
7 Avenue du Colonel Roche
31077 Toulouse Cedex, France
E.mail : pdss@laas.laas.fr , courtiat@laas.laas.fr

ESTIM is the Estelle simulator prototyped at LAAS/CNRS within the framework of the ESPRIT/SEDOS project. The paper is organized as follows: first, a convenient subset of Estelle is identified for simulation purposes. Then, the simulator kernel is presented as well as the main capabilities of the user interface. Finally, the use of ESTIM is described by means of the simulation of the Abracadabra protocol.

1. INTRODUCTION

Within the scope of the European ESPRIT program, the SEDOS (Software Environment for the Design of Open distributed Systems) project [Diaz 85] has promoted the use of two Formal Descriptions Techniques (FDTs) - Estelle [Estelle 87] and LOTOS [LOTOS 87] - being standardized within ISO. The objective of this project was the production of trial specifications, the assessment of verification techniques and the prototyping of a consistent set of tools supporting the different design phases of complex OSI protocols and services [Diaz 86].

ESTIM (Estelle SimulaTor based on an Interpretative Machine) is the SEDOS prototype developed at LAAS/CNRS for simulating Estelle specifications. The current release is available on SUN 3 workstations (under UNIX 4.2 BSD) and BULL SPS7/SPS9 machines (under SPIX).

The aim of this paper is to describe the main points dealing with the design, implementation and use of ESTIM. In the first section, a convenient subset of the Estelle language is identified for simulation purposes. In the second section, the ESTIM kernel is detailed together with its relationship with the Estelle formal global model defined at LAAS for Estelle. In the third section, the main tool capabilities are discussed from a user's point of view. Finally, a simulation of the Abracadabra protocol is presented.

2. The subset of Estelle supported by ESTIM

2.1. Position with regard to ISO Estelle

This paper assumes a knowledge of the Estelle FDT. Those interested in the main Estelle concepts may refer to several tutorial papers [Estelle 87, Linn 85, Budkowski 87, Courtiat 87c, Diaz 87b].

In the following, we analyze and evaluate the features offered in Estelle for expressing parallelism among module instances. This analysis leads us to consider a convenient subset of Estelle for simulation purposes. This subset is further extended to support the Rendez-Vous mechanism proposed in [Courtiat 87 b]. Finally, a particular semantics of the "delay" clause is considered; this semantics is derived from that of time proposed in Time Petri Nets and is consistent with the constraints defined in the Estelle DIS for time progression.

2.1.1. Parallelism semantics

The behaviour within one system is regulated by the "parent/child" priority principle and by the "process" or "activity" attributes assigned to each module definition nested within the considered system. Using the "process" and "activity" attributes for a module (and therefore for all its instances) allows to distinguish two possible forms of execution:
 - a *synchronous parallel execution*, synchronized by the "parent/child" priority (case of the "process" attribute);
 - a *non deterministic execution*, always preserving the "parent/child" priority (case of the "activity" attribute).

The global behaviour of an Estelle specification is characterized by the set of the valid transition firing sequences. The latter are obtained in the general case (i.e., the case of a specification structured into several system modules) from the *global situation graph* [Dembinski 86, Budkowski 87, Estelle 87]. A global situation characterizes the global state of the specification as well as the set of the transitions which are preselected in each system in order to be fired at a later stage; thus nothing can prevent a preselected transition from being fired, this being a direct consequence from the fact that systems behave asynchronously.

The consideration of a systemprocess instance in an Estelle specification makes it possible to define a permanent and implicit synchronization without value passing among transitions belonging to the different module instances of the considered systemprocess instance. This global synchronization for the whole systemprocess instance seems, from the authors' point of view, both unrealistic (in particular such a synchronization mechanism is difficult to implement in a monoprocessor system as well as in a multiprocessor one) and not very useful for OSI protocol description, as it is implicit and may lead to generating overspecifications. This implicit synchronization mechanism prevents furthermore from introducing, within the systemprocess instance, an explicit synchronization mechanism which appears to be very useful for representing the abstract interactions between a service provider and service users [Courtiat 87b, Afnor 88]. These rationales led us to rule out the systemprocess concept in ESTIM as well as, consequently, the process concept [Saqui 87].

For some hierarchy of module instances, there may exist several valid system instance configurations with respect to the Estelle nesting principles, each one representing a particular implementation scheme. The way of structuring an OSI system [Zimmermann 80] into asynchronous Estelle system instances (with attributes "systemactivity" or "systemprocess") depends indeed on the particular software and/or hardware division of the OSI system. This choice is completely justified if the purpose of the description is to produce an implementation prototype, but may lead to undesirable overspecifications if the purpose is to produce a formal description of an OSI architecture [Courtiat 87a].

Let us therefore consider a specification SPEX where several systemactivity instance configurations are possible. With the concern of not modifying the Estelle language itself, one way for avoiding the overspecification introduced by the particular system configuration selected, would be to impose few restrictions (hopefully light) in the use of some Estelle features, in such a way to ensure that the non deterministic firing of the specification transitions (case where SPEX is attributed by "systemactivity") does represent an asynchronous parallelism among the module instances which are not in a "ascendant/descendant" relationship; this non deterministic behaviour for the whole specification will furthermore express the behaviour of any systemactivity instance configuration valid for SPEX. These restrictions may be expressed as a sufficient condition, which has to be

satisfied by an Estelle specification (introduced and proved in [Courtiat 88]); this sufficient condition relies on the two following points:
- there is no priority clause associated with any transition having a "when" clause;
- once initialized (see the "init" statement) and attached (see the "attach" statement), these module instances are autonomous with respect to their parent module instance; in particular, any decision of "detach" or "release" is local to these module instances and depends on the interactions they receive from the lower layer service (PDUs from the peer entity or interactions generated by the service).

One may note that the proposed sufficient condition is realistic, as it takes into account a dynamic module instance configuration and imposes a description style corresponding to the user requirements when substructuring a protocol entity into elementary components; in particular, most of the Estelle specifications produced within the ESPRIT/SEDOS project satisfy this condition directly, e.g. the specification of the ISO Presentation service [Ayoub 87], the CCITT T70 recommendation of the Transport protocol [Chari 87], a significant subset of the ISO FTAM protocol [Gilot 87] and the description of the ISO Session protocol [Mondain 87].

Taking further into account the fact that the "systemprocess" concept is not supported for the reasons invoked previously, ESTIM implements a non deterministic transition firing rule. The valid firing sequences expressing the global behaviour of the specification may therefore be directly obtained from the specification global state graph. This approach is consistent with the semantics of parallelism as expressed in the Petri net field [Genrich 79, Diaz 82, Courtiat 84, Billington 85] and in the models commonly used for protocol modeling and verification [Brand 83].

Finally, one should point out, that the proposed approach is quite suitable for verification purposes. In the case of validation [Azema 85,Billington 88,Blumer 86, Richier 87, Vuong 86] a global state graph does not expend so fast as a global situation graph [Dembinski 86]; in the case of a simulation, the user is only required to select (among all the firable transitions) the next transition to be fired. Conversely, the other approach (case of a specification composed of several systemactivity module instances) requires preselection of one transition by distinct system as well as selection of the next transition to be fired among those that have been preselected [Saqui 87, Courtiat 88].

2.1.2. "Delay" clause semantics

In Estelle a "delay" clause may be associated with a transition. This "delay" clause is useful for modeling time-outs, which have to be specified in most protocols. Two times representing respectively the minimum time during which the transition must be delayed and the maximum time during which it may be delayed are specified in a "delay" clause.

As stated in paragraph 5.3.5 of the Estelle DIS [Estelle 87], "The computational model for Estelle is intentionaly formulated in time-independent terms; one of the principal assumptions of this model is that nothing is known about the execution time of a transition in a module instance. Knowledge of execution speeds is considered implementation dependent".

A particular semantics of the "delay" clause is implemented in ESTIM based on the semantics of Time Petri nets [Merlin 76,Berthomieu 83]. The starting point of this semantics is the assumption that the firing time of a transition is very short with respect to the time values expressed in the "delay" clause; it is then possible to consider that the firing time is equal to zero. This approach, consistent with the assumptions dealing with time progression in Estelle, makes it possible to update the time evolution at the level of the global model, something which is very interesting to model protocol time-outs; furthermore the time evolution does not directly depend on the number of transitions fired nor on the speed of the processors involved in the implementation [Dembinski 87].

2.2. Enhancing Estelle with a rendez-vous mechanism

Furthermore, ESTIM implements the rendez-vous mechanism proposed for Estelle in [Courtiat 87a, Afnor 88]. The rendez-vous has been introduced to allow representation in a more abstract way of the interactions between adjacent layer protocol entities [Courtiat 88]; its usefulness has been demonstrated on the Abracadabra protocol (see section 4) as well as on several OSI protocols (e.g. the Transport and Session protocols).

The proposed mechanism, extensively formalized in [Courtiat 87b], may be seen as a generalization of the CSP rendez-vous [Hoare 78] to the case of a dynamic instance configuration (dynamic module instances and dynamic links between module instances). It introduces new clauses (called synchronization clauses) which permits to express an explicit synchronization with value passing between two transitions of two distinct module instances; the notation used for expressing the synchronization clauses refers to the one introduced in [Hoare 78]: "IP?interaction" for a synchronization in reception on some interaction point IP and "IP!interaction" for a synchronization in emission. Since the synchronization requests are located at the level of the transition guards, deadlocks are avoided; moreover, the rendez-vous is consistent with the assumptions about the Estelle transition atomicity.

3. THE ESTIM KERNEL

3.1. The formal basis

The global model of an Estelle specification introduced in this section is the formal basis of the ESTIM kernel. This global model is fully consistent with the semantics defined in the Estelle DIS [Estelle 87] and takes into account all features specific to Estelle, particularly those dealing with the dynamic architecture of the module and interaction point instances.

The intuition behind this global model, is that all module instances having the same generic behaviour (characterized by some couple (b_i, h_j) where b_i is a module body identifier and h_j a module header identifier) are represented by the same Colored Extended State Machine, each particular instance being identified during its lifetime by a colored token, called reference. The global model may then be obtained by composition of the Colored Extended State Machines.

It is shown in [Courtiat 86] that the global state set S of an Estelle specification may be defined as (a subset of) the Cartesian product

[M × PARENT × CONNECTED × ATTACHED × MARKING × ENV × STORE × DFTI]

where :

- the space M represents all the possible module instance configurations

$(M = [X \rightarrow [[BODY \times HEADER] + \{unused\}]])$,

where X denotes the primitive set of all the potential module references which may be considered in the specification, and where BODY (respectively HEADER) denotes the set of the module body (respectively header) identifiers; let μ be a typical member of M : (μ x) <> unused denotes the type of module instance x (i.e. the pair (b_i, h_j)), (μ x) = unused indicates that currently reference x does not identify any module instance;

- the space PARENT represents all the possible module instance architectures

$$(PARENT = [X \rightarrow [X + \{\bot\}]]);$$

let π be a typical member of PARENT: (π x) identifies the current parent module instance of module instance x, if any ($\bot$ denotes undefined);

- the space CONNECTED represents all the possible interaction point instance "connection" configuration

$$(CONNECTED = [IPI \rightarrow [IPI + \{\bot\}]]),$$

where IPI = [IP $\times$ X] denotes the set of all the potential interaction point instances (an interaction point instance ipi = (ip,x) denotes interaction ip under the particular context of module instance x); let c be a typical member of CONNECTED): (c ipi) identifies the interaction point instance to which ipi is currently connected, if any;

- the space ATTACHED represents all the possible interaction point instance "attachment" configuration

$$(ATTACHED = [IPI \rightarrow [IPI + \{\bot\}]]);$$

let a be a typical member of ATTACHED: (a ipi) identifies the lower level interaction point instance to which ipi is currently attached, if any;

- the space MARKING represents all the possible "marking" functions

$$(MARKING = [X \rightarrow [P + \{\bot\}]]),$$

where P denotes the set of all the major states of the specification; let m be a typical member of MARKING: (m x) identifies the current major state of module instance x, if any;

- the space ENV represents all the possible "environment" functions

$$(ENV = [IDI \rightarrow [LOC + \{unbound\}]]),$$

where IDI denotes the set of all the potential identifier instances of the specification (an identifier represents either a variable identifier or an interaction point identifier declared in the specification) and where LOC denotes the primitive set of all the available memory locations; let e be a typical member of ENV: (e (id,x)) identifies the current memory location associated with identifier id of module instance x, if any;

- the space STORE represents all the possible "store" functions

$$(STORE = [LOC \rightarrow [SV + \{unused\}]]);$$

let σ be a typical member of STORE): (σ l) identifies the current value of l, if memory location l is currently allocated to a module instance ((σ l) = unused in the opposite case);

- the space DFTI represents all the possible "dynamic firing time interval" functions

$$(DFTI = [[T \times X] \rightarrow [[N \times [N + \{\infty\}]] + \{\bot\}]],$$

where T denotes the set of all the transitions of the specification; let τ be a typical member of DFTI: (τ (t,x)) represents the current dynamic firing time interval associated with transition t, if t is enabled under the context of module instance x.

Starting from that definition of the global state $s = (\mu,\pi,c,a,m,e,\sigma,\tau)$ of an Estelle specification, it is possible to define the denotational semantics [Gordon 79b] of all the statements and expressions specific to Estelle as "init", "connect", "attach", "output"... It is also possible to define in a lambda calculus based formalism the transition enabling and firing conditions as well as the transition firing rules. The corresponding functions are presented in [Courtiat 86] and also directly implemented in the ESTIM kernel [Saqui 87].

3.2. Prototyping ESTIM in ML

3.2.1. Rapid prototyping in the ML programming environment

The ESTIM tool has been prototyped in ML [ML 85], a functional programming language developed within the framework of the LCF project at Edinburgh [Gordon 79a]. The most interesting features of ML are as follows:
 - a strong typing mechanism which allows the definition of concrete data types as well as abstract ones with their associated operators;
 - the handling of data structures described at a high level of abstraction, e.g. mathematical functions;
 - the function polymorphism, i.e. the ML interpreter supports generic functions whose parameter type is inferred at function call.

The code size of the current release of ESTIM is about 5000 ML lines:

part of program	ML sources lines
Basic types and functions	1200
Expression evaluator	500
Declaration evaluator	350
Command interpreter	950
Transition selection	150
Transition firing rule	700
User interface	1200

3.2.2. Definition of an ML abstract syntax for ESTELLE

The development methodology of the ESTIM kernel is similar to the one commonly used for writing an interpreter in a prototyping language. First an ML abstract syntax of the Estelle language has been defined; this syntax is the support of the specification abstract tree provided in input of ESTIM. The abstract syntax introduced in [Saqui 87] is consistent with the latest version of the Estelle BNF [Estelle 87]. In particular, the ML type definition associated with the abstract tree root is as follows:

```
type ESTELLE =        % this is an ML type definition              %
       spec of         % "spec" is the new type constructor          %
                       % 'string'predefined string type              %
                       % other types are defined completely in [Saqui 87] %
       string #        % specification identifier                    %
       declaration #   % specification declaration part              %
       initialization # % specification initialization part          %
       transition  ;;  % specification transition part               %
```

Translating automatically an Estelle specification into its ML abstract form requires the development of a parser, e.g. by using the interface existing between ML and YACC. Prototyping ESTIM within the scope of the SEDOS project has led to choosing another solution: a "ML code generator" [Lenotre 87] has been written in C; it translates the specification "intermediate form" output by an Estelle compiler [Chari 86] into the convenient ML form, hence it builds the specification abstract tree.

3.3. INTERPRETATION OF THE SPECIFICATION ABSTRACT TREE

3.3.1. Static initialization of a specification

While traversing depth first the abstract tree of a specification, the ESTIM interpreter creates the generic architecture that is necessary to the dynamic module instanciations; the abstract representation of these modules is the basis of the ML implementation of the specification generic architecture. The evaluation of statement "init" (which creates a new module instance) consists of an incremental interpretation of the abstract subtree associated with the module body to be instanciated.

Several tools have already been developed for languages which support the static features of Estelle [Bochman 87, Jard 85, Richier 87]. Note that our approach (i.e. interpreting a generic architecture based on an ML abstract syntax) is interesting because it allows to support the dynamic features of Estelle in a quite natural way; on the contrary, one could be faced with potential code duplication problems by following a compilation approach and using a development language not able to support the concept of genericity, e.g. Pascal.

When the static initialization is completed, i.e. when both the top level declarations and the root initialization part have been evaluated, the interpreter returns the initial global state of the specification. The ML implementation of the 8-tuple of functions which characterize the specification global state s is derived from the formal definition introduced in section 3.1; nevertheless, in order to improve the running time performances of the tool, the store is now handled by means of ML pointers instead of mathematical functions [Saqui 87]. It should also be noted that simulating an Estelle specification by ESTIM is completely independent of the machine on which the interpreter is running; hence, ESTIM is a simulator of Estelle specifications as opposed to a debugger which runs the code produced by a compiler.

3.3.2. Role of the interpreter while running a simulation

The simulation starts as soon as the specification static initialization is completed. It consists of an exchange of information between the interpreter and the user; according to the semantics of a specification attributed by "systemactivity" (see section 1.2), the interpreter is invoked each time a firable transition has been selected; then, the specification enters a new global state whose components may be displayed to the user.

Although the interpreter is not intended to handle the interactive driving of a simulation, it reports each significant event which may occur during transition firing, for instance the dynamic creation of new module instances. In order to turn ESTIM into an efficient tool for studying the Estelle language as well as for following the dynamic evolution of the specification, it is possible to trace systematically the evaluation of the statements specific to Estelle ("init", "connect", ...).

Moreover, ESTIM performs a dynamic checking while running the specification; for instance, a warning message is displayed when an interaction is sent to a non connected interaction point characterizing therefore a potentially incorrect use of the "output" statement.

In the same way, an error is reported when the expression evaluator attempts to access an unassigned variable, for instance when evaluating a "provided" clause. Nevertheless, such an error does not lead necessarily to a simulation failure.

3.4. Time scheduling in ESTIM

3.4.1. Global handling of a logical time

The "delay" clause semantics supported by ESTIM is consistent with the assumptions stated in the DIS about time progression ("time progresses as the computation does" and "this progression is uniform with respect to delay values of the transitions involved") but it is more restrictive than these sole assumptions. It is based on the semantics of Time Petri Nets [Merlin 76], and starts from the extra assumption that the firing of a transition (which cannot be expressed in Estelle) is very short with respect to the values specified in any "delay" clause, such that it is possible to consider this transition firing time equal to 0. The proposed semantics, formalized in [Courtiat 86], does not require any additional external information and has the advantage of being widely accepted (tools are available for verification purposes [Berthomieu 83]) and very suitable for protocol modelling.

Scheduling a virtual time is very convenient in a simulation framework; it allows to observe a protocol mechanism as a logical sequence of events without taking into account actual delays which would slow down the simulation [Jard 88]. On the other hand, it seems unrealistic to ask the user to choose a transition selection time that is inherent in the algorithm implemented in the simulator but completely independent of the Estelle specification.

3.4.2 Transition firing rule and time progression in ESTIM

Transitions are selected with regard to the following properties:
        - a transition is enabled iff its clause "from", "when" and "provided" are satisfied simultaneously;
        - an enabled transition is firable as soon as its earliest dynamic firing time (see the function τ in section 3.1) is less than or equal to the minimum of the latest dynamic firing times among the specification transition set;
        - finally, the firable transitions considered are the ready-to-be-fired ones, with respect to the priority mechanisms defined in [Estelle 87].

As explained in section 3.1.2, the transition firing rule implemented in ESTIM considers both a zero transition selection time and a zero transition firing time. A step by step simulation scheme is given below (no rendez-vous mechanism is used within the considered specification) :

```
(* The specification static initialization is completed;                              *)
(* Time has progressed; the dynamic firing time (Tmin,Tmax) has been computed         *)
(* Moreover, the ready-to-be-fired transitions have been selected                     *)
while not end_of_simulation do
   begin
        let t be the ready-to-be-fired transition chosen by the user;
        (* def(t) denotes the dynamic earliest firing time associated with t *)
        theta <-- random (deft (t), Tmax);   progress_time(theta);
        evaluate the statement block of t;   update marking, if a clause "to" is used in t;
        update transition dynamic firing time; (* see the function detailed below *)
        select enabled transitions; compute the new firing interval (Tmin,Tmax);
        progress_time (Tmin); (* global time progression within the specification *)
        select the ready-to-be-fired transitions among the firable ones
   end;
```

From the algorithm above, it appears that time progression depends on both the latest fired transition and the next one to be fired chosen by the user.

On the other hand, the algorithm given below is run after any transition firing in order to update the transition dynamic firing interval (dfti(t) denotes the dynamic firing time associated with transition t; sfti(t) denotes the static firing time associated to t, i.e. the transition "delay" clause values, if any):
      let t be the last transition to have been fired ; let t' be any one of the transitions;
        if t' was not enabled in the previous specification global state
           and it is enabled in the current specification global state
        then dfti(t') <-- sfti(t')
        else if t' was enabled previously and keeps enabled in the current state
           then if t' = t then dfti(t') <-- sfti(t') else dfti(t') is not updated
           else (* t' is not enabled *) dfti(t') is undefined.

4. USING THE ESTIM TOOL

4.1. ESTIM user interface

4.1.1. User access to the simulation environment

The simulation environment is accessed by the user from two entry points:
      1) "genestim" invokes the Estelle compiler (see section 3.2.2) ; it first performs specification parsing and static type-checking; then, if the specification is both syntactically and semantically compatible with the subset of Estelle supported by ESTIM, "genestim" translates the source text into an ML abstract form. This ML object is saved in a text file provided as input to the ESTIM interpreter.
      2) "estim" invokes the ESTIM simulator which interprets the ML abstract tree (see section 3.3); then, it returns the control to the user interface whose main capabilities concern access to the specification global state components as well as driving of transition firing.

4.1.2. Overview of user interface

The command language of the simulator user interface has been defined in [Saqui 87]. Simulation driving is performed interactively outside the "closed world" of an Estelle specification; therefore, our approach is different from tools (e.g. [Jard 88 88],[Richier 87]) which require either an Estelle-like description of an observer module inside the specification or a dedicated language preliminary description of the scenarios to be checked. A criticicsm of an external simulation driver is related to the description of the specification identifiers (variables,...). Such a problem did not appear while using ESTIM; indeed, each object handled by the interpreter is identified unambiguously by a pair (id,x) where x denotes the ML `name` of the instance which owns the object known as id in the Estelle source; moreover, note that ESTIM creates a new module instance reference each time a primitive "init" is evaluated.

4.1.3. Access to the specification global state

Protocol simulation is assessed to be more efficient than implementation prototype debugging as soon as it make possible control over the mechanisms involved in the protocol under study. Therefore, display commands have been defined [Saqui 87] for providing access to all specification global state components and in particular:

- the specification architecture: the instance tree (functions μ and π) as well as the connections and the attachments between the interaction points (functions c and a); it is therefore possible to observe the dynamic evolution of the architecture;
- the module instance marking (i.e. the instance major state represented by function m);
- the value of the variables and constants (functions e and σ);
- the interactions stored in the queues associated with the interaction points (also represented by functions e and σ); interactions are displayed with the value of their parameters.
- the dynamic firing time interval associated with the enabled transition instances having a "delay" clause in their guard (function τ).

4.1.4. Transition firing

Four transition firing modes are available:

1) the step by step mode:

Since non deterministic behaviours may be expressed in Estelle, it is necessary to provide the user with a way to select one transition among the firable transitions; he may look at the current state of the specification, for instance in order to follow the interaction exchange between the protocol entities. The "UNDO" command cancels the previous transition firing(s) and restores the previous global state; this mode therefore provides a "manual" capability for exploring parts of the global state graph.

2) the random mode:

Using this mode, the user is asked a number of transitions to be fired before the simulation control is returned to him. This full random exploration of the global state graph is adapted when the specification must be runned as far as possible, e.g. until the specification enters a deadlock state; the protocol error may then be found by accessing the components of the current global state and by displaying the list of transitions which have been fired as well as the ones which have not yet been fired.

3) the user-controlled automatic mode

The non determinism in selection of transitions may be disabled to ensure "fairness" properties concerning the selection of module instances which own firable transitions. In particular, module instances may be chosen by using a round-robin politics. On the other hand, the user may privilege the firing of input transitions (i.e. transitions whose "when" clause is not empty) in order to observe interaction exchanges.

4) the "exec" mode:

The user attempts to fire a transition sequence previously stored in a file; an error is reported if the first transition of this sequence is not firable in the specification current state.

Irrespective of the chosen firing mode, a command is provided to display the percentage of transitions which have been fired within each module instance; these statistics give a rapid overview of the way the specification has been explored since the beginning of the simulation.

Moreover, facilities are offered for defining the subset of instances whose transition firing is needed, at a given time, to investigate the simulated protocol behaviour. For instance, when a connection request has been fired, it may be convenient to "inhibit" the user which has sent this request until the peer user accepts the connection (cf. section 4).

4.2. Enhancing Estelle for simulation purposes

In this section, it is shown how Estelle may be enhanced with simulation options which rely on the use of qualifying comments. Qualifying comments are used commonly for inserting compiling options in e.g. a Pascal or a C program. In a simulation framework, qualifying comments appear to be a good compromise between the need for minimizing the changes of the specification source and the one for offering simulation options as well as trace facilities. A qualifying comment consists in a ML text line, more precisely a new production of the Estelle abstract syntax (see section 2.2.2), which will be illustrated in the sequel:

4.2.1. Tracing a simulation session

An Estelle specification may be seen as a closed world since no mean of communication with the outside world is provided to the module instances. For instance, the Pascal statements related to the file management system are not supported by Estelle. ESTIM allows for the display of a trace message as well as variable values during transition firing.

```
from A
to   B
delay (tmin,tmax)
begin
     (*$ message `the time-out has elapsed` *); { Back quotes are string delimiters in ML }
     ...
end;
```

4.2.2. Setting breakpoints inside a transition

Breakpoints may be inserted in any transition block by using the qualifying comment (*$ bp *). This extension is constrained by the principle of transition atomicity in Estelle; indeed, the interpretation of the abstract statement "bp" gives access to both display and help commands of the user interface without allowing any modification of the specification global state.

4.2.3. Disabling the priority mechanism

Both the previous simulation options improve the user-friendliness of ESTIM without modifying (semantically speaking) the interpretation of the specification. On the other hand, ESTIM offers an option (*$ PRIO_OFF *) which disables the Estelle priority mechanisms. ESTIM provides therefore a means of supporting both the ISO definition of a "systemactivity" attributed specification [Estelle 87] as well as an Estelle* specification [Courtiat 88].

5. APPLICATION: THE ABRACADABRA PROTOCOL

The "Abracadabra" protocol is an adhoc protocol specified jointly by ISO and CCITT to help users understand FDTs. This protocol relies on a connection-less lower layer service and provides a connection oriented service allowing two users to exchange SDUs in a full duplex mode. The protocol is simple and easy to understand and presents many common features with OSI connection oriented protocols [FDTA 87].

The formal specification whose architecture is given in Fig.1 considers a static module instance configuration and describes the protocol behaviour for one Abracadabra connection established between two users UA and UB. The communication between UA and protocol entity A (respectively between UB and B) is expressed by means of the rendez-vous mechanism of Estelle* [Courtiat 88] in order to handle correctly the Abracadabra service primitives and to express backpressure flow control. The communication between A (respectively B) and the lower layer service is expressed by the classical FIFO queues of Estelle, since this service is connection-less and consequently neither service primitive collision situations nor backpressure flow control have to be considered.

A simulation of the Abracadabra protocol will be demonstrated at the Conference.

6. CONCLUSION

ESTIM implements all the dynamic features as well as the non-determinism of the current version of Estelle; on the other hand, it supports only the structuring principle that corresponds to a non deterministic interleaved execution between module instances. ESTIM implements futhermore the rendez-vous mechanism proposed by LAAS, hence contributes to the promotion of a FDT compatible with the requirements of ISO protocol descriptions.

ESTIM has been operational since June 1987, and the first public demonstration took place in Brussels during the last ESPRIT Week Conference (September 1987). The effectiveness of our rapid prototyping approach has been pointed out while simulating several Estelle protocol descriptions, e.g. the T70 Transport protocol description - about 1500 Estelle source lines. Moreover, ESTIM has been used successfully by students involved in the development of real-case Estelle specifications.

An extension of the rendez-vous mechanism currently supported by ESTIM is being investigated in order to express conveniently a broadcast mechanism (rendez-vous among several transitions and not only two as presently).

Other current developments of ESTIM deal with the applicability of verification techniques to an Estelle specification. An interface between ESTIM and PIPN [Azema 85], a Predicate/Transition Net verificator prototyped in Prolog at LAAS, is under study.

Finally, the flexibility of the ML written interpreter makes it possible to enhance Estelle with primitive data types handled frequently in the field of protocols. Integrating type description based on the Abstract Syntax Notation 1 [ASN1 87] is being investigated in order to facilitate Estelle specifications of OSI upper layer protocols.

REFERENCES

[Afnor 88]   "Proposition of a Rendez-Vous mechanism for Estelle", Contribution to ISO/IEC JTC1/SC21 meeting, WG1 N575, February 1988.

[ASN1 87]   "Specification of Abstract Syntax Notation One (ASN.1)", ISO-DIS 8824, August 1987.

[Ayoub 87]   M. AYOUB DIT AYADI, "Estelle Presentation Service Specification", SEDOS report 107, October 1987.

[Azema 85]   P. AZEMA, G. PAPANAGIOTAKIS, "Protocol Analysis by using Predicate Nets", 5th Workshop on Protocol Specification, Testing and Verification, Moissac-Toulouse, June 1985.

[Berthomieu 83] B. BERTHOMIEU, M.MENASCHE, "An Enumerative Approach for Analysing Time Petri Nets", Proceedings of IFIP Congress, Paris, September 1983.

[Billington 85] J. BILLINGTON, M.C. WILBUR-HAM, M.Y. BERAMAN, "Automated Protocol Verification", 5th IFIP Workshop on Protocol Specification, Testing and Verification, Moissac, June 1985, North-Holland.

[Billington 88] J. BILLINGTON, G.R. WHEELER, M.C. WILBUR-HAM, "PROTEAN: A High-level Petri Net Tool for the Specification and Verification of Communication Protocols", IEEE Transactions on Software Engineering, VOL.14, N°3, March 1988.

[Blumer 86] T.P. BLUMER, D.P. SIDHU, "Mechanical verification and automatic implementation of communication protocols", IEEE Transaction on Software Engineering, August 1986.

[Bochmann 87] G.V. BOCHMANN, "Usage of protocol development tools: the result of a survey", 7th IFIP Symposium on Protocol Specification, Testing and Verification, Zurich, May 1987.

[Brand 83] D. BRAND, P. ZAFIROPOULO, "On communicating finite-state machines", Journal of the ACM, April 1983.

[Budkowski 87] S. BUDKOWSKI, P. DEMBINSKI, "An introduction to Estelle: a specification language for distributed systems", Computer Networks and ISDN Systems, VOL.14, N°1, 1987.

[Chari 86] V. CHARI, J-F. LENOTRE, E. MARIANI, E. MATTERA, "Estelle Compiler specification", SEDOS report 80, November 1986.

[Chari 87] V. CHARI, "Contribution to joint ISO-CCITT Document(Q48.2)" SEDOS report 103, October 1987.

[Courtiat 84] J-P. COURTIAT, J-M. AYACHE, B. ALGAYRES, "Petri nets are good for protocols", Computer Communication Review, VOL.14, N°2, 1984.

[Courtiat 86] J-P COURTIAT"A Petri Net Based Semantics for Estelle" SEDOS report 052, May 1986 - revised version, SEDOS report 109, October 1987.

[Courtiat 87a] J-P. COURTIAT, "How could Estelle become a better FDT?", 7th IFIP Symposium on Protocol Specification, Testing and Verification, Zurich, May 1987.

[Courtiat 87b] J-P. COURTIAT, "Proposition of a rendez-vous mechanism for Estelle", SEDOS report 110, October 1987.

[Courtiat 87c] J-P. COURTIAT, P. DEMBINSKI, R. GROZ, C. JARD, "Estelle: An ISO language for distributed algorithms and protocols", Technology and Science of Informatics, VOL6, N°5, 1987.

[Courtiat 88] J-P. COURTIAT, "Estelle* : a powerful dialect of Estelle for OSI protocol description", 8th IFIP Symposium on Protocol Specification, Testing and Verification, Atlantic City, June 1988.

[Dembinski 86] P. DEMBINSKI, "Estelle semantics", SEDOS report 054, June 1986.

[Dembinski 87] P. DEMBINSKI, S. BUDKOWSKI, "Simulating Estelle specifications with time parameters", 7th IFIP Symposium on Protocol Specification, Testing and Verification, Zurich, May 1987.

[Diaz 82] M. DIAZ, "Modelling and Analysis of Communication and Cooperation Protocols using Petri Nets based Models", Tutorial paper, Computer Networks, VOL.6, N°6, December 1982.

[Diaz 85] M. DIAZ, CH. VISSERS, J-P. ANSART, "SEDOS, Software Environment for the Design of Open distributed Systems", ESPRIT Week, Brussels, September 1985.

[Diaz 86] M. DIAZ, J-P. COURTIAT, P. DEMBINSKI, E. BRINKSMA, "Formal description techniques in SEDOS", ESPRIT Week, Brussels, September 1986, North Holland, DGXIII Editors, 1987.

[Diaz 87a] M. DIAZ, C. VISSERS, S. BUDKOWSKI, "Estelle and LOTOS Software Environment for the Design of Open Distributed Systems", Proceedings of the 4th Annual ESPRIT Conference, Brussels, September 1987, North Holland.

[Diaz 87b] M. DIAZ, "ESTELLE, une technique de description formelle de protocoles" (ESTELLE, a Formal Description Technique for protocols), 9ièmes Journées Francophones sur l'Informatique, Liège, January 1987.

[Estelle 87] "Estelle, a formal description technique based on an extended state transition model", ISO DIS 9074, June 1987.

[FDTA 87] ISO/SC21/WG1/FDT-A, "Guidelines for the application of Estelle, LOTOS and SDL, Project/97.21.9/Q48.2 CCITT/SG/X/Q7, August 1987.

[Genrich 79] H.J GENRICH, K. LAUTENBACH, "The Analysis of Distributed Systems by means of Predicate/ Transition Nets", Lecture Notes on Computer Science - Springer Verlag.

[Gilot 87] T.GILOT, J. TOUTAIN, "FTAM protocol description in Estelle", SEDOS report 102, October 1987.

[Gordon 79a] M. GORDON, A. MILNER, C. WADSWORTH, "Edinburgh LCF", Lecture Notes on Computer Science, Springer Verlag.

[Gordon 79b] M.GORDON, "The Denotational Description of Programming Languages", Lecture Notes on Computer Science, Springer Verlag.

[Hoare 78] C.A.R. Hoare "Communicating Sequential Processes", Communications of the ACM, August 1978.

[Jard 85] C. JARD, J-F. MONIN, R. GROZ, "Experience in implementing Estelle - X250 (a CCITT subset of Estelle) in VEDA, 5th IFIP Workshop on Protocol Specification, Testing and Verification, Moissac, June 1985, North-Holland.

[Jard 88] C. JARD, J-F. MONIN, R. GROZ, "Development of Véda, a Prototyping Tool for Distributed Algorithms", IEEE Transactions on Software Engineering, VOL.14, N°3, March 1988.

[Lenotre 87] J-F. LENOTRE, "The Estelle to ML Generator Reference Document", SEDOS report 116, October 1987.

[Linn 85] R.J. LINN, "The features and facilities of Estelle", 5th IFIP Workshop on Protocol Specification, Testing and Verification, Moissac, June 1985, North-Holland.

[LOTOS 87] "LOTOS, A formal Description Technique Based on the Temporal Ordering of Observational Behaviour", ISO DIS 8807, July 1987.

[ML 85]   "The ML Handbook", INRIA ("FORMEL" project), November 1985.

[Merlin 76]   P.M. MERLIN, D.J. FABER, "Recoverability of communication protocols, Implication of a theoritical approach", IEEE Transactions on Communications, September 1976.

[Mondain 87]   P. MONDAIN-MONVAL, "ISO Session Protocol in Estelle", SEDOS Report 106, November 1987.

[Richier 87]   J-L. RICHIER and al, "Verification in XESAR of the sliding window protocol", 7th IFIP Symposium on Protocol Specification, Testing and Verification.

[Saqui 87]   P. de SAQUI-SANNES, J.P COURTIAT, "ESTIM: An interpreter for the simulation of Estelle descriptions",SEDOS report 115, November 1987.

[Vuong 86]   S.T. VUONG, D.D HUI, D.D. COWAN, "VALIRA - a tool for validation via reachability analysis", 6th IFIP Workshop on Protocol Specification, Testing and Verification, Montreal, June 1986, North-Holland.

[Zimmermann 80]   H. ZIMMERMANN, "OSI Reference Model: the ISO model of architecture for Open Distributed Systems Interconnection", IEEE Transactions on Communications, April 1980.

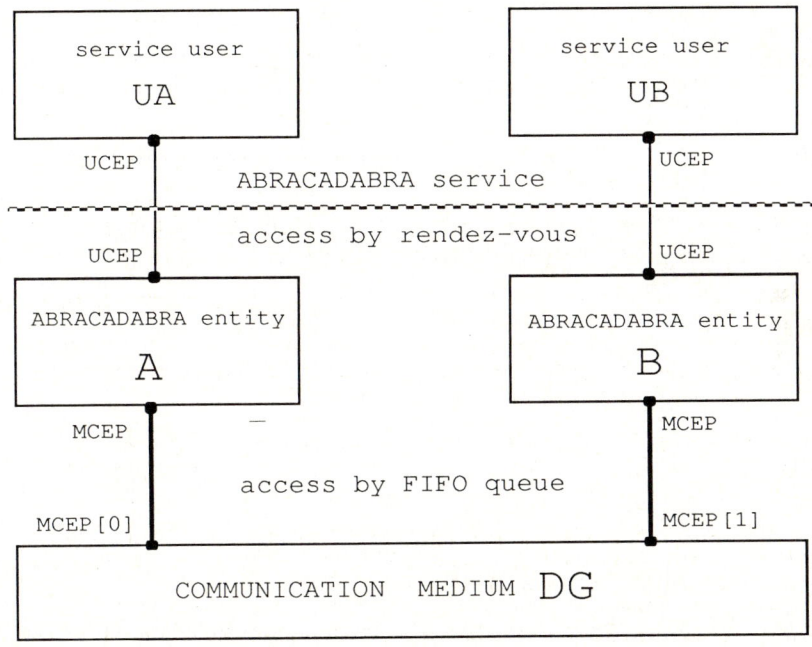

Fig. 1. Architecture of the Abracadabra protocol Estelle description

A LOTOS to PARLOG Translator

David Gilbert

PARLOG Group
Imperial College
London SW7 2BZ
U.K.

email: drg@doc.ic.ac.uk

A translator from a subset LOTOS into PARLOG is described, and the process of its development charted. The use of the software is described, and comments made on the difficulties of implementing a direct translator from LOTOS specifications into executable code.

1. Introduction

The specification of communicating systems has become an important task as the ability to construct such systems has evolved. One class of such systems in particular, namely that of computer networks, has become a subject for such specifications since the role of communications and information interchange is vital to the functioning of new generation technology.

However, the ability to specify highly concurrent systems in a formal manner does not guarantee that the path to the construction of such systems from their specifications is either clear or automatic. This paper describes an attempt to construct an automatic translator from specifications in a formal description language into executable code. The formal language selected as a source was LOTOS [ISO87] and the target was the parallel logic programming language PARLOG [Gregory87].

2. LOTOS as a Formal Description Technique.

LOTOS is a process algebra based language developed by the International Standards Organisation (ISO) as a Formal Description Technique (FDT) to specify OSI protocols and services. It has been accepted as an international standard and will be one of the three techniques which can be used in the the description of the OSI model. The language is based on concepts introduced in CCS [Milner80] for the definition of the dynamic behaviour of processes, and also incorporates an abstract data type language, ACT-ONE [Ehrig83]. This paper reports implementation work performed with the dynamic part of LOTOS, and does not deal with the implementation of ACT-ONE. Tutorials on LOTOS may be found in [ISO87, Bolognesi87].

3. Routes to implementing LOTOS.

LOTOS could be implemented by

(i) extending a simulator to produce an interpreter or even a compiler for the language [van Eijk88];

(ii) using traditional compiler methods to produce executable machine code from the LOTOS source code;

(iii) prototyping an implementation of LOTOS using an existing computer language.

The first method might be implementable in a short time, but the resulting interpreter could well be quite inefficient due to the slow speeds of execution of interpreters in general. There are difficulties involved in the second, because the formalism on which LOTOS is based has little relation to the traditional von-Neumann machine architecture. We chose the last route, and selected PARLOG as the target language due to its ability to express concurrency and the possibility of executing PARLOG code on a multi-processor or distributed system. It might well be that such an implementation would result in inefficient programs which execute very slowly. This technique would, however, allow the testing of protocols in conditions simulating those of the intended application, providing a tool to assist the designers of specifications to discover whether the specification had the intended result. Hopefully this interface between specification and implementation via rapid prototyping would result in a more efficient software production cycle.

4. PARLOG

PARLOG is a committed choice parallel logic programming language, and can explicitly express both OR and stream-AND parallelism as well as non-determinism. Unlike Prolog, it does not possess the ability to backtrack, due to its committed choice nature, which is implemented by the use of guards. PARLOG programs can be written without regard to the underlying hardware on which they are to be run; hence they may be executed on whatever machine the language has been implemented, either monoprocessor, multiprocessor or a distributed system. The language is fully described in [Gregory87], and tutorial material can be found in [Gilbert87]; only a minimal description of the language will be given here.

The syntax of PARLOG, given in the table below, is similar to the emerging standard for Prolog, with the addition of explicit sequential operators, a guard operator, and mode declarations.

Table 1 PARLOG syntax.

Symbol	Meaning
<-	logical implication
&	sequential-AND
,	parallel-AND
;	sequential-OR
.	parallel-OR
:	guard operator
?	input mode annotation
^	output mode annotation

Mode declarations are used to specify communication constraints on shared variables, which are declared to be either **?** ("input") or **^** ("output"), thus acting as communication channels. These declarations are made once for each relation, and each argument of the relation is annotated:

        `mode name(a1?,..,ak^,..).`

Messages sent along these channels are incrementally constructed from partially determined data structures, usually consisting of lists of terms acting as message streams.

A PARLOG procedure is a collection of clauses with the same name n and arity k, and is referred to in this paper as n/k. The general form of a PARLOG clause is:
<head> <- <guard> : <body> <or-op>
Note that <head> is in the form $name(a_1,...,a_k)$, where *name* is the relation name, and $a_1,...,a_k$ its arguments. The logical implication symbol is '<-' and ':' the guard operator. Both the guard and the body can be a conjunction of calls, or empty, and the calls are separated by the sequential-AND or parallel-AND operators. A clause is a candidate for evaluation if both input matching in the head and the evaluation of the guard succeeds, whereas in a non-candidate clause either of these fail. A clause can be suspended if either the input matching or guard evaluation suspend waiting for an input variable to become instantiated. A suspended call may eventually become either candidate or non-candidate. Note that no output bindings are made until committal has been made to the clause (ie the guard conditions are satisfied), and committal may be made to only one clause of a procedure.

The naive form of communication in PARLOG is that of asynchronous producer and synchronous consumer, with channels acting as unbounded buffers. However synchronous communication can be expressed in PARLOG using the co-operative construction of binding terms. The producer sends a stream (an incrementally constructed list) of tuples, each of which contains two arguments, one the data item to be sent and the other a variable; the use of a sequential-AND operator then forces the producer to wait until the consumer instantiates the variable to an agreed message. We illustrate this using the tuple '+' to encapsulate the message, with the first argument the message item itself, and the second argument the synchronisation tuple[1]:
Item + Reply
We then implement synchronous send and receive in PARLOG by the following programs:

Example 1 Synchronous communication in PARLOG.

mode synch_send(item?,tupleˆ).
synch_send(Item,Item+Reply)<- data(Reply).

mode synch_receive(tuple?,itemˆ).
synch_receive(Item+Reply,Item)<- Reply=ok.

Note that *data/1* suspends until its argument is ground (ie the top level functor of a data-structure is instantiated). Thus the query *?data(X)* suspends, and *?data([H|T])* succeeds. The call to =/2 in *synch_receive/2* instantiates the **Reply** variable to **ok**. These programs can be composed as follows:
? synch_send(item , Msg) , synch_receive(Msg , X).
and may be thought of as roughly equivalent to the LOTOS behaviour expression
g ! item || g ? X

5. Source-to-source translation.

The method used to translate one high level computer language into another may be broadly described by the label "source-to-source translation". LOTOS is very similar to a conventional computer language in its overall design, and is thus a candidate for such a translation process.

One technique that can be used to effect source-to-source translation is *compiler-like translation*. This consists of the derivation from algorithm A in language L, of an algorithm A´ in language L´, each distinct component of A´ being semantically equivalent to the corresponding component in A. In its most low-level form, constructs from the original language are mapped directly into constructs in the target language. One of the advantages of this method is that a "building-block"

---

[1] Note that '+' is infix operator with arity 2

approach to translation can be used. Little or no "intelligence" is required of the translator process once the low level components have been successfully mapped from A to A´. Implementation of the translator itself as a computer program is thus facilitated. For the reasons given above, we employed compiler-like translation as the method of implementing LOTOS specifications in PARLOG.

An initial examination of the syntax and semantics of LOTOS and PARLOG suggests that there might exist some ready similarities between the two languages. However, detailed investigation revealed that a naive approach of mapping operators from the former language directly to those of PARLOG would not be possible [Gilbert87b]. A description of early work undertaken to create constructs in PARLOG which behave like LOTOS constructs is reported in [Gilbert86], and is summarised in [Gilbert87b]. This work was performed, however, using an early definition of LOTOS which does not permit multi-way synchronisation [ISO/BSI86]. We describe in more detail the actual implementation aspects of that work and reports on the experience gained with the new draft standard for LOTOS [ISO87] which does permit multi-way synchronisation.

6. Development of the translator

Only the "dynamic" part of LOTOS was considered for translation into PARLOG, that is the aspects based on CCS [Milner80]. However, PARLOG does possess 'implicit' types (lists, tuples, strings and integers), enabling the interaction between the ADT and the dynamic part of LOTOS and in the areas of "sort-checking" and synchronisation conditions to be incorporated into our translator to an extent[2].

The translator was developed by first building the 'primitive building blocks', ie atomic actions, and also more complex behaviour expressions including choice and parallel operators.

6.1. Processes in LOTOS and PARLOG.

LOTOS processes are represented as PARLOG processes in the translator. The latter are coded as recursively defined predicates (mutual or self recursion) and possess many of the properties of LOTOS process definitions, including the ability to import and export parameters, and to express recursion. Parameter lists in LOTOS process abstractions may take the form of gate and value parameters as two import lists, and an export list categorised by sorts.

In order to express the facility for communication with the environment, a fourth (output) argument needs to be included in the PARLOG predicate which allows a stream of synchronisation messages (offers) to be exported. These messages are in effect *event offers*. The mode template of the PARLOG process representing the LOTOS process *name* is:

        mode `name(gates?,val-params?,exports^,offers^).`

6.2. Event offers

The basic building block of a LOTOS specification is the *atomic event* which is used to express the synchronised interaction between communicating processes. Thus the atomic event is the first item in the repertoire of LOTOS that requires the attention of the designer of a translation system. Closely associated with atomic events are event gates, or *interaction points*, referred to in the literature on LOTOS as abstract resources shared by processes [ISO87]. The most important properties of atomic events are that they are indivisible, are capable of synchronous communication and are parameterised by gate-names.

The three kinds of synchronisation in which LOTOS atomic events can participate are *value matching*, *value passing* and *value generation*. An additional constraint which may be applied to synchronisation is that of *selection-predicates*; if used, synchronisation can only occur if the

---

[2] Type checking in PARLOG is performed at run-time, using both pattern matching and the relations *list/1*, *atom/1* and *number/1*.

predicate in each partner evaluates to **true**.

6.2.1. Using one-to-one synchronisation.

The technique of cooperative construction of binding terms is used (see above) to enforce synchronous communication, but has been adapted to permit encoding of the synchronisation classes of LOTOS. The signal tuple employed may be either *send/5* or *receive/5*:

```
send(Gate,Value,Sort,Condition,Reply).
receive(Gate,Value,Sort,Condition,Reply).
```

`Gate` and `Sort` are constants, `Value` corresponds to a LOTOS *value expression* in *send/5* and is a variable in *receive/5* at time of transmission. `Condition` is a boolean expression in each case, and `Reply` is the synchronisation variable.

Although LOTOS does not always refer explicitly to the sort in an expression such as

$$g!x$$

the following alternative description can be used:

$$g!x \, \textbf{ofsort} \, \text{message-sort}$$

with the implication that the value part of *all* communications possesses a sort, which if apparently absent must nevertheless be presumed to be of a *default sort*. The translator can insert a default sort **true** if required. If the ADT part of LOTOS were to be treated by the translator, a table of sort declarations would enable the sorts of the value in `g!x` to be determined during the translation process.

Similarly, since the selection predicate is optional, it must always be included in the tuple. If not present in the LOTOS specification, the translator can insert **true** as a condition.

6.2.2. Value matching

An example, *value matching*, is presented below:

Example 2 Value matching.

```
mode match( signal1?, signal2?, result1^, result2^).

match(   send(Gate,Val1,Sort,Condition1,Out1),
         send(Gate,Val2,Sort,Condition2,Out2))<-
    Val1 =:= Val2&
    call(Condition1) & call(Condition2):
    Out1 = ok, Out2 = ok.
```

Note that in this case the Gate and Sort names must be identical. We assume in this example that the Sort is Nat, so that the value expressions Val1 and Val2 are evaluated for equality by the predicate =:=/2. A more complex test of equality could be made if sorts other than Nat were allowed. Both Conditions must be evaluated to **true** using PARLOG's *call/1* before commitment is made to the clause.

6.2.3. Value passing

For the implementation of *value passing* we base our code on the following outline:

Example 3 Value passing.

```
match(    send(Gate,Val1,Sort,Condition1,Out1),
       receive(Gate,Val2,Sort,Condition2,Out2))<-
  Val2 is  Val1&
  call(Condition1) & call(Condition2):
  Out1 = ok, Out2 = ok.
```

Note that in, as in value matching, the Gate names and Sorts must be the same, but Val2 is ground to the value of Val1, using the predicate is/2. The Conditions are then evaluated to **true** before commitment to the body of the clause[3].

6.2.4. Value Generation

A detailed discussion of this is to be found in [Gilbert86], with reference to the older semantics of the parallel operator which permitted 1:1 synchronisation only. The outline code is:

Example 4 Value generation.

```
match( receive(Gate,Val1,Sort,Condition1,Out1),
       receive(Gate,Val2,Sort,Condition2,Out1))<-
       randomise(Val,Condition1,Condition2,Num):
       Val1 = Num,  Val2 = Num,
  Out1 = ok,  Out2 = ok.
```

Note that this relation generates a random number which satisfies both Conditions, and thus again assumes Sort to be Nat.

6.2.5. The parallel operator.

The semantics of LOTOS's parallel operators differ widely from that of PARLOG. Hence the parallel operators are mapped into a *par* program, written in PARLOG, which emulates their behaviour. Each PARLOG process representing a LOTOS behaviour expression produces a stream of synchronisation signals which are available to an environment, usually represented as a *par* process. Every *par* process consumes two streams of synchronisation signals (produced either by processes representing behaviour expressions, or by other *par* processes), and produces a stream of synchronisation signals.

The mode declaration of the *par* program is:

mode par(in-1?,in-2?,selected-gates?,hidden-gates?,out-stream^).

6.2.6. The parallel operator and multi-way synchronisation.

The code for the parallel operator and synchronisation has to be considerably more complex when value generation is considered along with multi-way communication.

The latest draft standard for LOTOS [ISO87], differs from that used in the original development of the translator [ISO/BSI86], and permits multi-way synchronisation in the use of the parallel operator. This semantics, coupled with 'value generation' and the use of predicates permits a constraint-oriented style of specification. This style, however, introduces aspects of undecidability and implies that the route from specification to implementation is very difficult if not impossible. An example in LOTOS, the solution to which is effectively undecidable, would

---

[3] In order to preserve clause safety and prevent the binding of a variable in an input position in the guard, the code used in the translator makes a *copy* of Val2 and Condition2 before performing the other guard tests.

be [van Eijk88]

```
choice x,y :int []  [3x↑2 + y↑5 = 0 ] -> g;B
```

Constraint-oriented specification is used in the description of multi-partner negotiation for value generation according with restriction by predicates:

```
g?x:nat [x<100]  ||  g?y:nat [y>0]  ||  g?z:nat [z*z > 200]
```

If, on the other hand, the style of specification is oriented towards implementation, and the use of multi-way communication avoided, the implementation of the specifications is much easier. A more detailed discussion of specification styles and their effect on implementability can be found in [van Eijk88].

The new semantics of the parallel operator are implemented in PARLOG as processes which manipulate the streams produced by processes and perform synchronisation across all streams involved. The code is complex, and is under development at present.

6.3. The inactive process: stop

The completely inactive process in LOTOS, **stop**, cannot perform any event. It can be represented in PARLOG by a call suspending on a variable which will never become bound.

6.4. Selection and hiding

Selection is performed by *par/2*, in that only signals naming common gates (or all gates in the case of |||) are considered for synchronisation. Hiding is performed by the multi-way communication predicate, in that signals to gates named as hidden are not made available to the outer environment.

6.5. Action prefix and enable operators

Action prefix is represented as the sequential-AND operator in PARLOG, as is the enable operator. Value passing is not permitted for the latter operator since the ADT part of LOTOS has not yet been incorporated into the translator.

6.6. The choice operator

The choice operator in LOTOS does not map directly into the or-parallel operator of PARLOG, since no output can be made in a guard in PARLOG before commitment to a clause. Instead, choice is represented as a list of possible offers contained within signals produced by processes. Thus the LOTOS expression:

```
        a ! 3 ; exit [] b ? x : nat  [ x < 5] ; exit
```

would produce a choice list in the message tuple of the form:

```
message([send(a,3,nat,true),receive(b,X,nat,less(X,5))],Result,Ok)
```

The LOTOS choice operator was not fully implemented in the translator with respect of the environment's interaction with the process offering the choice. Although provision has been made in the design of the **signal** predicate for choices to be sent to the *par* process and a reply to be received indicating the successful signal, this facility has not been incorporated into the code generator. In order to implement the full semantics of the choice operator, all behaviour expressions must initially offer one synchronisation message, and if it is selected, the remainder may be offered. Due to the properties of PARLOG guards, no output bindings can be made unless committal has been made to the whole clause. PARLOG representations of behaviour expressions would consist of two predicates, the first offering an initial signal, and the next offering the rest.

This would present difficulties if one process invokes others and the choice is offered at lower levels of the instantiation process.

6.6.1. Guarded expressions

Guarded expressions are implemented by PARLOG guards; when used in combination with the choice operator they are mapped onto guard conditions and OR-parallel search in PARLOG.

6.6.2. Internal events

Internal events are implemented as synchronisation signals which are always satisfied in the match procedure, but leave the corresponding matching signal to be retried for matching against subsequent signals. In this way, the use of internal events and the choice operator in LOTOS to describe combinations of deterministic and non-deterministic choice can be mapped into PARLOG.

6.6.3. Disable

The disable operator was originally not implemented, and expansion of disable expressions into those containing choice and sequential operators was employed. However, the present translator makes use of PARLOG's three argument metacall *call/3* [Clark86], to implement LOTOS's disable operator. This metacall is derived from *call/1*, a metalevel programming facility similar to that of Prolog and Lisp.

In its simple form the **call/1** predicate has mode declaration `call(goal?)`. The logical reading of *?call(goal)* is the same as that of *?goal*. A call with a variable as a goal suspends until the variable is instantiated to a term denoting a PARLOG clause body (a relation call or conjunction). A program can thus evaluate calls which are determined at run-time.

The PARLOG system predicate *call/3* has mode `call(Call?, Status^, Control?)`. *Control* is a stream of messages which can be used by a supervisor or monitor program to control the evaluation of the Goal. The acceptable messages on the control stream are: **stop**, **suspend** and **continue**. The Status argument, a variable at the time of the call, is instantiated by the call to a stream of messages reporting key states in the evaluation of the call. The last message will be one of: **failed**, **succeeded** or **stopped**, indicating the form of termination; **stopped** indicating premature termination due to an input **control** message on the **Control** stream.

We use this predicate to implement `[>/2` in our system by adapting *call/3* to output the message **started** on the status stream when the reduction of a call has started:

Example 5 PARLOG Disrupt.

```
mode ? [> ?.
A [> B <-
        call(A,S1,C1), call(B,S2,C2), arbitrate(S1,C1,S2,C2).

mode arbitrate(S1?,C1^,S2?,C2^).
arbitrate([success|S1],C1,S2,[stop|X]).
arbitrate(S1,[stop|X],[started|S2],C2).
arbitrate([Other|S1],C1,S2,C2) <-
        Other \== success, S2 \== [started|X]:
        arbitrate(S1,C1,S2,C2).
```

The first clause of *arbitrate/4* will detect if A has terminated successfully, and binds C2 to **[stop|X]**, thus preventing the evaluation of B. However, *arbitrate/4* may in its second clause detect when the evaluation of B starts (in a non-suspended state, if A has not yet terminated), and bind C1 to **[stop|X]**, aborting the evaluation of A.

7. Present state of the translator

A trial version of a source-to-source translator was designed, capable of converting a subset of LOTOS in to PARLOG. The implementation was constrained both by the incompleteness of the LOTOS to PARLOG mappings described in the section on Development, and by problems encountered in the construction of the translator itself (see below). The ADT part of the LOTOS language was not implemented, and there is no type-checking incorporated in the parser.

The translator was modularised, allowing flexibility in development, promoting ease of testing and facilitating software maintenance. All the software was written in PARLOG. The modules developed were:

(i) Tokeniser
(ii) Parser
(iii) Code Generator

The modules are executed in parallel, exploiting the stream-AND parallelism of PARLOG; a typical usage would be the call:

Example 6 .

```
mode translate(LotosFilename?, ParlogFilename?).
translate(LotosFilename, ParlogFilename) <-
     readfile(LotosFilename,Asciistream),
     tokeniser(Asciistream,Tokens),
     parser(Tokens,ParseTree),
     code-generator(ParseTree,ParlogCode),
     write-code(ParlogFilename,ParlogCode).
```

Note that while *tokeniser* passes the tokens in a stream to *parser*, the latter process incrementally produces a complex structure (channel)[4], the parse tree, thus permitting more concurrency than would a stream in its consumption by *code-generator*. A pictorial representation of the translation process is given in the figure below.

7.1. Reading a file to produce a stream of ascii characters.

The routine which reads a file and produces a stream of ASCII characters uses the PARLOG primitives which are implemented in "C". Sequential-AND operator are used in the code for **readfile** to ensure the correct sequence of file operations.

7.2. The Tokeniser

The **tokeniser** processes the stream of integers representing ASCII characters produced by **readfile**. In implementing this program the BNF for LOTOS has been adhered to, but all printable characters except for spaces and tabs are included in the output stream. The **tokeniser** predicate consumes a list of integers representing ASCII characters, and recursively replaces those groups of characters which represent LOTOS lexical tokens by the appropriate token. Detection of the empty list on the input stream determines the termination of the execution of **tokeniser**. Comments in LOTOS, which are delimited by "(*" and "*)" are not processed.

7.3. The Parser

---

[4] A *stream* (an incrementally constructed list) is a special form of a channel.

Figure 1 Translator program.

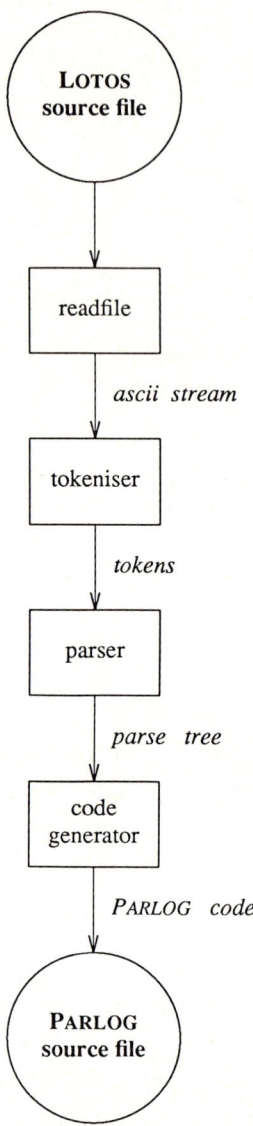

7.3.1. Overall design

The **parser** was implemented as a top-down recursive descent parser, using the parallel logic programming technique of difference-streams. A tuple (data-structure) is produced representing the parse-tree, whose general form is:

    `spec(specname(Specid),Params,Externaltypes,Definition,Rest)`

where Rest is a list of local definitions, the members of which are tuples of the form:

        `process(procname(Name),Params,Definition,Defns-rest)`

Each of the **process** tuples has its own local definition part, Defns-rest, which is itself a list of process tuples. The attributes of each tuple are at first left uninstantiated until ground later during the parsing. This technique has some similarities with "fixup" which is used when compiling: addresses of parameters can be left undefined until fixed during a subsequent pass.

7.3.2. Error checking

No error checking algorithms are incorporated in the parser which behaves like a standard predicate in PARLOG: when called it either succeeds and the parse-tree tuple is produced as output, or the call fails. The parser was not designed to include diagnostic abilities for the time being. As it was decided to exclude the ADT part of LOTOS from the implementation, type-checking is not performed by the parser.

7.3.3. Implementing the BNF

The sections from the LOTOS BNF which were implemented in the parser are:

```
6.2.1    Specification
6.2.2    Definition block
6.2.6    Process Definitions
6.2.7    Behaviour Expressions[5]
6.2.8    Value-expressions
6.2.9    Declarations
6.2.10   special-identifiers
```

Those sections not implemented at all were:

```
2.3   Data-type-definition
2.4   P-expressions.
```

Section 2.5 (sorts, operations and equations) was only implemented for *sort-list* and *simple-equation*.

7.3.4. Amendments to the BNF

The BNF contains one statement which is not LL1, and so presents difficulties for a straightforward implementation. The relevant section is 6.2.8:

```
value-expression =    [value-expression operation-identifier]
                      simple-expression
```

To facilitate writing the PARLOG code this was transformed into the following equivalent form:

```
value-expression = simple-expression <empty>
         | simple-expression operation-identifier value-expression
```

7.4. The Code Generator

The code generator was implemented as a recursive traverse of the parse-tree, creating a list structure suitable for input to the PARLOG library predicate **write_source**.

PARLOG predicates described above were used to map structures encountered in the parse tree on to PARLOG programs. Atomic events, value matching, value passing, value generation and the stop process are all translated successfully by the code generator. LOTOS expressions which can be translated are:

---

[5] Not sum-expressions or par-expressions.

(i)   Enable expressions (no value passing)
(ii) Parallel expressions
(iii) Hiding & gate selection expressions
(iv) Choice expressions (in the context of guarded expressions only)
(v)   Guarded expressions
(vi) Action-prefix expressions
(vii) Atomic expressions
(viii) Value expressions (a limited subset)

In addition, the block-structure of LOTOS as regards process declarations has been implemented in the translations. At present only self-recursion is translated correctly. No run-time support is included for variable references: outline methods to implement both this and correct referencing of process call are outlined later in this paper.

8. Using the lopar software

The software runs under Unix™ BSD 4.2+ and requires the PARLOG SPM system [Foster86]. Input to the translator is from a file containing a LOTOS specification. The translator will accept full LOTOS syntax, but only the dynamic part is converted from the parse tree into abstract code; the latter is then written out as PARLOG source code to file. The PARLOG code can then be compiled by the SPM compiler, producing a file containing PARLOG 'object' code acceptable to the SPM emulator.

In order to execute the PARLOG object code produced by the translator, it must be loaded into the SPM along with library routines needed, for example the code for the parallel operators and synchronisation routines. Also required is the LOTOS supervisor, whose function is equivalent to an observer of the execution of the specification. This supervisor enables the observations to be made available to the user, either as a trace on the console, or as output to file.

9. Improvements

Implementation of the ADT part of LOTOS would also enable improvements to be made in the language translator. Sort checking would then become possible. This would facilitate the inclusion of error checking facilities in the parser, allowing it to be used in a diagnostic mode to verify correct use of variables and expressions in a specification. Included in the diagnostic capabilities should be the ability of the parser to flag errors, to attempt to correct them and to carry on with the parsing without halting at the first error it encounters. A user friendly feature would be to return the user to the LOTOS source code under the control of a standard text editor at the point of the first non-recoverable error.

More work has to be done in the area of code generation. Translation of the choice operator needs to be included. The generator is lacking a full implementation of the scope rules and block structuring of LOTOS; some guidelines have been given in [Gilbert86] regarding the implementation of an environment stack both at translation time and at run time. This would be best implemented after the mapping of ACT-ONE into PARLOG has been achieved.

10. Comments on implementing LOTOS using PARLOG

LOTOS possesses the ability to specify communication systems using general methods which can be adapted to specific situations. It relies heavily on the concept of event-gates. The use of these as input parameters to process instantiations facilitates the construction of systems built out of communicating processes. Multiway synchronisation is a boon to specifiers, but is a very hard construct to implement; problems in this area are related to those of implementing constraints in logic programming [Lassez87, Choquet87]. It may well be that the construction of a LOTOS translator would be facilitated if only implementation-oriented styles of specification were acceptable as input, and the use of multi-way communication avoided.

The stream communication model employed by PARLOG requires the programmer to explicitly link processes which intercommunicate, linkage being achieved by the use of the logical variable. In order to achieve the flexibility inherent in LOTOS, a PARLOG implementation must create complex software entities which perform the redirection and synchronisation of message streams. These entities are implemented as PARLOG processes. They can cause the execution of the PARLOG code to be inefficient as the messages in the synchronisation streams are routed to the intended destination. The inefficiency is exacerbated by the complex operational semantics of some of the LOTOS operators when used in combination, notably the parallel and hiding operators.

11. Conclusions

The translator was implemented for a substantial subset of the mappings using PARLOG as the language to write all the necessary modules. It incorporates a tokeniser and parser which together conform to the BNF of LOTOS that was available at the time. Future changes to the BNF can easily be incorporated into the tokeniser and parser since they are written in PARLOG itself. Neither the tokeniser nor parser perform any kind of error checking, syntax or otherwise. The code generator does not implement ACT-ONE and thus does not perform translation-time type-checking. Moreover some of the LOTOS constructs which can be mapped into PARLOG are not incorporated in the code generator, notably the choice operator in any context other than guarded expressions. LOTOS's scope rules are incorporated in the code generator regarding process declarations, but recursive process instantiations are only supported for self-recursion. No provision is made for scope rules applied to the declaration of variables, as a run-time environment is not implemented: the LOTOS programmer is encouraged to declare explicitly as input all variables needed in any process.

The declarative nature of PARLOG facilitated the task of building the prototype translator, and modifications are relatively easy to perform. The system was used successfully to translate some simple LOTOS specifications, and given the complex nature of the task, we are satisfied that such a tool described here is useful in the development of system specifications using LOTOS.

Acknowledgements

This work was partly carried out while I was in receipt of an SERC grant, studying for the MSc in Computing, and also while I was funded by Alvey on "Implementation and Applications of PARLOG", Project number 043/098.

References

Bolognesi87.
    Tommaso Bolognesi and Ed Brinksma, "Introduction to the ISO Specification Language LOTOS," *Computer Networks and ISDN Systems*, vol. 14, no. 1, pp. 25-59, Elsevier Science Publishers, 1987.

Choquet87.
    Nicole Choquet, *Need for a Prolog handling constraints in a software engineering application,* CR-CGE, Laboratoires de Marcoussis, Marcoussis, France, 1987.

Clark86.
    Keith Clark and Steve Gregory, "PARLOG: Parallel programming in Logic," *ACM Transactions on Programming Languages and Systems*, vol. 8, no. 1, Jan 1986.

Ehrig83.
> H. Ehrig, W. Frey, and H. Hansen, "ACT ONE: An algebraic specification language with two levels of semantics," Bericht Nr 83-03, Techische Universitaet, Berlin, 1983.

Foster86.
> Ian Foster, Steve Gregory, Graem Ringwood, and Ken Satoh, "A Sequential Implementation of PARLOG," *3rd International Conference on Logic Programming, London. July 1986*, Dept of Computing, Imperial College, London. UK, March 1986.

Gilbert86.
> David Gilbert, "Implementing LOTOS in PARLOG," MSc Thesis, Department of Computing, Imperial College, London, UK, September 1986.

Gilbert87.
> David Gilbert, "PARLOG: a tutorial introduction.," *Proceedings of Parallel Processing and Supercomputing*, Begian Institute for Automatic Control, Antwerp, Belgium, November 19-20, 1987.

Gilbert87b.
> David Gilbert, "Executable LOTOS: Using PARLOG to implement an FDT," *Proceedings of IFIP Protocol Specification, Testing and Verification: VII, Zurich, Switzerland, 5-8 May 1987*, Elsevier Science, North-Holland, Amsterdam, Netherlands, 1987.

Gregory87.
> Steve Gregory, *Parallel Logic Programming in PARLOG: The Language and its Implementation,* Addison-Wesely, London, UK, 1987.

ISO87.
> ISO, *Revised Text of 2nd ISO / DP 8807 - LOTOS,* ISO, March 1987.

ISO/BSI86.
> ISO/BSI, "Working document DP 8807 LOTOS/86/1 FDT:278," IST/21/1/3 BSI 86/61840, April 1986.

Lassez87.
> Catherine Lassez, "Constraint Logic Programming," *BYTE*, pp. 171-176, BYTE, August 1987.

Milner80.
> Robin Milner, *A Calculus of Communicating Systems,* Lecture Notes in Computer Science, 92, Springer-Verlag, Berlin, 1980.

van Eijk88.
> Peter van Eijk, "Software tools for the specification language LOTOS," PhD thesis, Department of Informatics, University of Twente, Enschede, Netherlands, January 1988.

Transforming LOTOS Specifications With Lola :
The Parameterized Expansion. [a]

Juan Quemada, Santiago Pavón, Angel Fernández

Department of Telematics Engineering
Madrid University of Technology
ETSI Telecomunicacion, UPM
E-28040 MADRID SPAIN

LOTOS is a Formal Description Technique developed within ISO to specify services and protocols. Its use can be used also for the design of concurrent and distributed systems in general. This paper describes a tool for doing LOTOS to LOTOS transformations. It has applications in validation and in design by stepwise refinement. The transformations maintain the weak bisimulation congruence. The transformation include: expansion (transformation of parallelism into summation and prefix); parameterized expansion; internal action loop removal. Deadlock detection is possible with the result of this transformations.

1. INTRODUCTION.

LOTOS (1) is an FDT (Formal Description Technique) developed within ISO with the purpose of serving as an unambiguous language for describing service and protocol standards. Its underlying models are process algebras derived from CCS (2) and other calculi like Circal (3), CSP (4) for the description of behaviours and the abstract data type language ACT-ONE (5) for the description of data values. LOTOS specifications define the ordering in time of the events that a system may participate in. Time can not be represented in absolute terms. Only the relative ordering of events in time can be represented. These models make LOTOS very appropriate not only in protocol design. It is also very well suited for the design of concurrent systems in general.

The language represents systems from the observability point of view (2) and supports the concepts of abstraction and hiding allowing very modular systems descriptions at different levels of detail. Behaviours can be specified using two main methodologies: a constructive one based on phases and parts is well suited for the design of implementations and a constraint oriented one is well suited for more abstract requirement oriented specifications. The behavioural part is defined by means of an operational model, well suited for direct execution, while the data part, defined with an equational model, may require complex state of the art execution strategies. This may allow a rapid prototyping approach to software design with an adequate simulation tool.

Different types of relations among LOTOS specifications are available and provide a framework for determining semantical equivalences between the different levels of refinement in a top down or bottom up design. Observational equivalence (2), testing equivalence (8) and implementation relation (6) seem to be the most interesting ones. The observational equivalence is the strongest one (it is contained in all the others). The testing equivalence represents the black box approach, identifying two systems as equivalent if they present the same behaviour to an observer. The implementation relation defines how implementation can be derived from a given specification.

Transformations seem to be the only way to derive formally verified implementations. Direct verification of protocols against services or implementations against abstract protocol

---

[a] This work has been partly supported by INTELSA under the project "Desarrollo de un Entorno Experimental de Especificacion de Sistemas Concurrentes basado en LOTOS.

descriptions get into unmanageable state explosions. LOTOS to LOTOS transformations can play a significant role in LOTOS based engineering. Equational characterizations, expansion theorems and other mathematical transformations existing for the equivalences and relations mentioned may be automated and may serve as the first basis for a transformational approach to LOTOS. This tool represents a small step in this direction.

2. DESCRIPTION OF LOLA.

The LOLA (LOtos LAboratory) system is a transformational tool developed at the Department of "Ingeniería Telemática" of the Polytechnic University of Madrid for serving as an experimental environment for a transformational approach for LOTOS. An earlier version is described in (11). It has been designed in Pascal and supports different types of transformations on LOTOS specifications. It has been designed for easy upgrading. The current version runs on SUN systems.

The following transformations are described here: expansion of the specification; parameterized expansion; internal action loops removal. From the practical point of view the parameterized expansion is the most interesting one. The state explosion of the expansion (non parameterized) is greatly reduced in the parameterized expansion. Deadlocks can be made explicit on the output of the expansions. The main applications of these transformations are in validating specifications and in implementation derivation. The parameterized expansion of a specification can be seen as a way of producing an efficient implementation or also as a way of transforming constraint oriented specifications into monolithic ones.

The system is based on a recursive tree representation of standard LOTOS specifications in the computer memory, in which all the transformations are done. A pattern search and substitution language has been defined which allows the definition of rewrite rules for behaviours or data values. Other specific transformations directly coded in Pascal can also be added.

Equations in data types are treated as rewrite rules. Thus the tool does not process LOTOS, but an operational version of it where equations interpreted from right to left shall be a set of rewrite rules. These rewrite rules should be confluent and terminating for achieving proper operation.

Another limitation arises from the incompleteness of equational deduction with respect to inductive deduction in equational abstract data types. Transformations of data values or expressions of them and of its equality are done by rewriting. This means that the tool has some limitations with respect to value expressions handling. Equality of data values is provided but theorem proving is not complete. Induction may be needed for proving some theorems. And some may even be undecidable (12). Theorem proving is needed for guards and selection predicates evaluation in synchronization. Semiautomatic systems like REVE(10) may be used for generating confluent and terminating sets of rewriting rules out off sets of equations. It could also be used for inductive theorems demonstration through inductionless-induction.

In LOLA the semantic equality (=) has been made equal to an equality operator of name *equal*, which includes syntactic equality of ground terms after rewriting right and left sides, and for which additional equations can be provided. Thus, no complete semantical equality is supported in LOLA. Rewrite meaning has to be given to it through some rewrite rules.

For illustrating the transformations, a LOTOS specification of an alternating bit protocol will be used. It is represented below and includes only one direction in the information flow. Only a transmitter entity connected trough a semiduplex line to a receiver entity is represented. The result of the transformations of this example will be shown to illustrate them.

```
SPECIFICATION DataLink [ get, give ] : noexit

LIBRARY boolean ENDLIB

BEHAVIOUR
   HIDE   tout, send, receive  IN
      (  ( transmitter [ get, tout, send, receive ] (0)
         |||
             receiver [ give, send, receive ] (0)
         )
         |[ tout, send, receive ]|
             line [ tout, send, receive ]
      )

WHERE

   TYPE sequenceNumber IS boolean (* modulo two *)
      SORTS  SeqNum
      OPNS   0      :                   -> SeqNum
             inc    : SeqNum            -> SeqNum
             equal  : SeqNum, SeqNum -> bool
      EQNS FORALL x , y : SeqNum
           OFSORT SeqNum
              inc ( inc ( x ) ) = x ;
           OFSORT boolean
              equal ( x , x ) = true ;
              equal ( 0 , inc ( x ) ) = false ;
              equal ( inc ( x ) , 0 ) = false ;
              equal ( inc ( x ) , inc ( y ) ) = equal ( x , y )
   ENDTYPE

   TYPE BitString IS boolean
      SORTS    BitString
      OPNS     empty :                         -> BitString
               equal : BitString, BitString -> boolean
      EQNS OFSORT boolean FORALL x : BitString
              equal ( x , x ) = true
   ENDTYPE

   TYPE FrameType IS
      SORTS    FrameType
      OPNS     info, ack :                     -> FrameType
               equal     : FrameType, FrameType -> boolean
      EQNS OFSORT boolean FORALL x : FrameType
              equal ( x , x )      = true ;
              equal ( ack , info ) = false ;
              equal ( info , ack ) = false
   ENDTYPE

   PROCESS transmitter [ get, tout, send, receive ]
                       ( seq : SeqNum) : noexit :=
      get ?data:BitString
    ; sending [ tout, send, receive] ( seq, data)
   >> transmitter [ get, tout, send, receive ] (inc(seq))

   WHERE
      PROCESS sending [ tout, send, receive]
             ( seq:SeqNum, data:BitString ) : exit :=
         send !info !seq !data
```

```
                 ; (     receive !ack !inc(seq) !empty (* ack arrives *)
                      ; exit
                 []   tout
                      ; sending [ tout, send, receive ] ( seq, data)
                 )                  (* time out*)
        ENDPROC
   ENDPROC

   PROCESS receiver [ give, send, receive ]
                                     ( exp : SeqNum) : noexit :=
        receive !info ?rec:SeqNum ?data:BitString
     ; (     [ rec = exp ] ->
                 give !data
               ; send !ack !inc(rec) !empty
               ; receiver [ give, send, receive ] (inc(exp))
        []   [ inc(rec) = exp ] ->
                 send !ack !inc(rec) !empty
               ; receiver [ give, send, receive ] (exp))
   ENDPROC

   PROCESS line [ tout, send, receive ] : noexit :=
        send ?f:FrameType ?seq:SeqNum ? data:BitString
     ; (     receive !f !seq !data
               ; line [ tout, send, receive ]
        []   i
               ; tout
               ; line [ tout, send, receive ]
        )
   ENDPROC
ENDSPEC
```

3. DESCRIPTION OF THE TRANSFORMATIONS.

The transformations included in LOLA are a small part of all the conceivable ones. They are derived either directly either from the definition or from the basic theorems of weak bisimulation. The transformations are: expansion of the specification; parameterized expansion; internal action loop removal.

All the transformations transform the value expressions into theirs normal forms before doing anything on them. Equality is treated as equality of normal forms, with the abovementioned restrictions, for which additional equations may be given. In the following, for all the transformations, the problems caused by it are not mentioned. For the proof of some theorems, induction may be needed and this can not be automated. The transformations produced by the tool are still correct, but are not optimized in the following sense. Some guards and some selection predicates which are equivalent to true or false have not been removed (true case) or substituted by a stop (false case) because rewriting has not been enough for determining it.

3.1. Expansion.

Expanding a specification means removing parallelism, enabling, and disabling; substituting them for summation and action prefix. This is done by the application of the so called expansion theorems (1), (2). This transformation generates a new specification in a subset of LOTOS which includes only the following operators : actions, action prefix, alternative, choice statements, guards, process definition and instantiation. The transformed specification is strong bisimulation equivalent with the original. Some extension of the expansion theorems has been necessary for dealing with full LOTOS. This extensions affect the guard and choice statement. There exist in LOTOS specifications unresolvable guards which may depend on values supplied by the environment. This implies that not all the guards can be removed during the expansion.

The generation of the expansion stops when a *stop* is found, an *exit* statement is found or a behaviour is found which is equal to a previous one, for each branch of the expansion. When a duplicated behaviour is found the first one is transformed into a process instantiation-definition pair, and the duplicated one into a process instantiation one. The result of the expansion has a tree like form in the way of the charts of (7). For the termination of the expansion only finite sorts of data values and bounded parallel or disabling compositions are allowed. As a general rule, any behaviour expression that produces infinite transitions from a state will diverge.

The expansion of the alternating bit would produce the following specification.

```
specification datalink [ get, give ] : noexit

behaviour
   ProDup0 [ get , give ]

where

process ProDup0 [ get , give ] : noexit :=
   get ? data_6: bitstring ;
   ProDup6 [ get , give ] ( data_6 )
endproc

process ProDup1 [ get , give ] ( data_61: bitstring ) : noexit :=
   ( i ;
      i ;
      ProDup0 [ get , give ]
   [] i ;
      i ;
      ProDup2 [ get , give ] ( data_61 )
   )
endproc

process ProDup2 [ get , give ] ( data_62: bitstring ) : noexit :=
   i ;
   ( i ;
      i ;
      ProDup1 [ get , give ] ( data_62 )
   [] i ;
      i ;
      ProDup2 [ get , give ] ( data_62 )
   )
endproc

process ProDup3 [ get , give ] ( data_63: bitstring ) : noexit :=
   i ;
   ( i ;
      give ! data_63 ;
      i ;
      ProDup1 [ get , give ] ( data_63 )
   [] i ;
      i ;
      ProDup3 [ get , give ] ( data_63 )
   )
endproc
```

```
process ProDup4 [ get , give ] ( data_64: bitstring ) : noexit :=
   (  i ;
      i ;
      get ? data_21: bitstring ;
      ProDup3 [ get , give ] ( data_21 )
   [] i ;
      i ;
      ProDup5 [ get , give ] ( data_64 )
   )
endproc

process ProDup5 [ get , give ] ( data_65: bitstring ) : noexit :=
   i ;
   (  i ;
      i ;
      ProDup4 [ get , give ] ( data_65 )
   [] i ;
      i ;
      ProDup5 [ get , give ] ( data_65 )
   )
endproc

process ProDup6 [ get , give ] ( data_66: bitstring ) : noexit :=
   i ;
   (  i ;
      give ! data_66 ;
      i ;
      ProDup4 [ get , give ] ( data_66 )
   [] i ;
      i ;
      ProDup6 [ get , give ] ( data_66 )
   )
endproc

endspec
```

3.2. Parameterized Expansion.

The parameterized expansion is a variation of the previous expansion. It has only two differences with the previous one. The treatment of the finalization of the expansion and of the guards and selection predicates.

In this case the expansion is stopped when a stop, an exit or a parameterized behaviour of an existing one is found. By parameterized behaviour of an existing one we mean a behaviour which is exactly equal to the previous one except for some value expressions, which will be applications of the value expressions of the first one.

The only ways for the data values to affect the expansion is through guards, synchronization and selection predicates, thus the parameterized expansion must keep all the possible actions of every parameterization. Guards, synchronization and selection predicates shall be treated now congruently with this and they must be rewritten to a normal form but without doing any substitution of variables for values such that they are still valid for every possible instantiation. The values are used only for generating the actual parameters of the process instantiations.

This expansion stops much quicker and the state explosion problems appearing in the previous one depend only on the basic behaviour and not on the product of the states of the basic behaviour with the states of the (number of different) data values. The parameterized expanded form of a specification is somehow equivalent to an extended automaton.

The conditions for the parameterized expansion to terminate are different. Infinite sorts are allowed now but with respect to dynamic creation of processes the conditions are more restrictive. No form of dynamic creation of processes is allowed. In the previous one dynamic creation is allowed if finite but not here. As a general rule, any behaviour expression that produces infinite transitions (from the syntactical point of view) from a particular state will diverge.

The parameterized expansion of the alternating bit protocol is presented below. It shows clearly the differences with the previous one. The non parameterized stopped when the sequence number is exactly the same. Thus the protocol did two cycles (sending frames with 0 and sending frames with inc(0)) before it stops. In the parameterized one it only does one cycle. This is independent of the number of different values of the sequence numbers, it would had happened also for the natural numbers for example. In real protocols the number of cycles before one reaches exactly the same one with big sequence numbers and considering windows and so one, can be quite high. The number of states to be explored can be reduced by many orders of magnitude.

```
specification datalink [ get, give ] : noexit
behaviour
    ProDup0 [ get, give ] ( 0 , 0 )

where
process ProDup0 [ get, give ]
                ( nv_5, nv_6: seqnum ) :
                noexit :=
    get ? data_6: bitstring ;
    ProDup1 [ get, give ] ( nv_5, data_6, nv_6 )
endproc

process ProDup1 [ get, give ]
                ( nv_7: seqnum, data_31: bitstring, nv_8: seqnum ) :
                noexit :=
    i ;
    (  i ;
       (  [ nv_7 = nv_8 ] ->
             give ! data_31 ;
             i ;
             ProDup2 [ get, give ] ( nv_7, inc(nv_8), data_31 )
       [] [ inc(nv_7) = nv_8 ] ->
             i ;
             ProDup2 [ get, give ] ( nv_7, nv_8, data_31 )
       )
    [] i ;
       i ;
       ProDup1 [ get, give ] ( nv_7, data_31, nv_8 )
    )
endproc

process ProDup2 [ get, give ]
                ( nv_9, nv_10: seqnum, data_32: bitstring ) :
                noexit :=
    (  i ;
       i ;
       ProDup0 [ get, give ] ( inc(nv_9), nv_10 )
    [] i ;
       i ;
       ProDup1 [ get, give ] ( nv_9, data_32, nv_10 )
    )
endproc
```

endspec

3.3. Deadlock Detection on Expanded Specifications.

Deadlock detection can be done in any of the expanded forms. In fact they have been already calculated during the expansion. They have only to be made explicit. There will be visible deadlocks (actions leading to lonely stops which means that there are not outgoing transitions from those states) and invisible potential ones (in all the guards and selection predicates which may make a state equivalent to a lonely stop). The potentially invisible deadlock detection can suffer from the limitations of rewriting, because guards and selection predicates can be potential deadlocks not detected by rewriting the value expressions.

The example presented here has no deadlocks. It has many livelocks (closed i loops). This is deduced from the fact that it has no lonely stops, and some guard is always enabled allowing a way out from any state. Other properties as unproductive loops, recoverability, ... can be easily studied on the expanded form.

3.4. Closed Internal Action Loop Removal.

Any of the expanded forms obtained by the first two transformations, has a tree like form. The initial state is the root and the second process instantiation of the same process occurring in the path from the root to the leaves can be seen as recursion or jumps, which occur only in some leaves, to parts of the fundamental behaviour which is the tree.

By closed internal action loops it is meant a process definition which has a path in the tree which starts at a definition and ends which a call to the same definition that is composed only of internal ("i") actions, action prefix, alternative and process definitions or instantiations. Such loops represent divergent behaviour and are potentially dangerous behaviours. They can be removed according to weak bisimulation. The transformation consists in the elimination of all the internal action of the loop. This transformation applies also reductions like: a; i; B $\Rightarrow$ a; B and stop [] B $\Rightarrow$ B.

The application of this transformation to the first expanded form (non parameterized) of the alternating bit would produce the following output:

```
specification datalink [ get, give ] : noexit
behaviour
    beh1_ [ get, give ]
where
process beh1_ [ get, give ] : noexit :=
    get  ? data_1: bitstring ;
    give ! data_1 ;
    get  ? data_10: bitstring ;
    give ! data_10 ;
    beh1_ [ get, give ]
endproc
endspec
```

4. CONCLUSIONS AND FURTHER WORK.

The three transformations described can play an interesting role in protocol design. The final version of the tool including the parameterized expansion has been just finished and there is no extensive experience of their use. Until now only small examples have been passed through the tool and getting experience of its use in real systems design is one of the most important topics. Its utility has to be assessed in real developments.

The parameterized expansion has the highest interest because the reduced state space exploration. It can have applications in testing, deadlock detection and implementation derivation. The parameterized expansion is just a way of presenting the behaviour with all its possible events explicited. Testing in LOTOS consists in specifying a test process in LOTOS and making it synchronize with the specification to be tested and thus the result of the expansions are the results of the test.

Usually protocol implementations in operating systems, kernels and/or imperative languages are state machines which can be quiet large but efficient in actual Von Neumann type processors. The result of parameterized expansion is just a state machine in a very similar form to the extended automatons of state descriptions of protocols. In fact the expansion process is just a precalculation of all the synchronizations possible for some specification, removing the overhead of having to calculate it during runtime. Existing compilers or kernels supporting LOTOS type of synchronization show that this calculation requires many operations.

The transformations described here represent a first step in LOTOS to LOTOS transformations. The basic framework for introducing new transformations exist in LOLA and it is easy to do. Identification of useful transformations to be included is one of the most important lines for future developments.

APPENDIX A. THE DEFINITION OF THE PARAMETERIZED EXPANSION.

The parameterized expansion is obtained by generalizing the expansion theorems (LOTOS annex B) to include all the possible behaviours modifications that data values may produce through guards in LOTOS. Only the parallel composition is shown although expansions for the rest of the operators also exist.

The expansion is defined for behaviours containing only sumexpresions (*choice* $x_1 : t_1, \ldots, x_n : t_n$ [] B), choice expression ($B1$ [] $B2$), action prefix ($a; B$), guarded expression ([e]-> B) and action denotations with value offering ($g \ !v_1 \ !v_2 \ldots !v_n$). This formulation is general because other LOTOS constructs can be expressed in term of these ones like, value acceptance, selection predicates, ... LOLA uses a more efficient version of it in which specific rules exist for every LOTOS construct, which does not introduce any new idea but is much longer.

With respect to the data part it shall be stated that this algorithm works only under the assumption of the absence of any kind of overloading neither in variables nor operations during the whole expansion, which implies renaming of variables from time to time. The expansion has been defined here with full generality for equations in guards. LOLA is based on rewriting and uses a more operational way of composing guards.

At last it shall be mentioned that some preprocessing of LOTOS behaviours is needed to prepare behaviours to be expanded.

The main preprocessing is:

- choice v [] (choice v' [] B) $\Rightarrow$ choice $v.v'$ [] B
- [e]->([e']-> B) $\Rightarrow$ [$e.e'$]-> B
- [e]->(choice v [] B) $\Rightarrow$ choice v [] ([e]-> B)
- choice v [] ($B1$ [] $B2$) $\Rightarrow$ (choice v [] $B1$) [] (choice v [] $B2$)
- [e]->($B1$ [] $B2$) $\Rightarrow$ ([e]-> $B1$) [] ([e]-> $B2$)

Where the operation "." stands for concatenations of equations or of choice expressions (for example $(x = y) \cdot (suc(x) + y = x) \equiv (x = y, suc(x) + y = x)$ and (*choice* $x : t_1[] \cdot$ *choice* $y : t_2 \equiv$ *choice* $x : t_1, y : t2[]$)) and the symbol $\Rightarrow$ stands for transform into. Sequences of equations are accepted in guards, although this is sintacticly not correct, semanticly it does not introduce any problems. It can be represented in LOTOS as guarded expressions of guarded expressions.

The generalized expansion is: Let $B_1 = \sum_i CH_i \; G_i \; a_i; B_i$, $B_2 = \sum_j CH_j \; G_j \; a_j; B_j$, and $a_i = g \; !v_1 \ldots !v_n$, $a_j = g' \; !v'_1 \ldots !v'_n$; then

$$B_1 \; |[A]| \; B_2 =$$
$$\sum_i CH_i \; G_i \; a_i; (B_i \; |[A]| \; B_2) \quad \forall \; i \; | \; \text{gate}(a_i) \notin A$$
$$[] \quad \sum_j CH_j \; G_j \; a_j; (B_1 \; |[A]| \; B_j) \quad \forall \; j \; | \; \text{gate}(a_j) \notin A$$
$$[] \quad \sum_{i,j} CH_{i,j} \; G_{i,j} \; a_j; (B_i \; |[A]| \; B'_j) \quad \forall \; i,j \; | \; \text{gate}(a_i) = \text{gate}(a_j)$$
$$\land \; \text{gate}(a_i) \in A$$

where $CH_{i,j} = CH_i.CH_j$, $G_{i,j} = G_i.G_j.E$, $E = (v_1 = v'_1, \ldots, v_n = v'_n)$ and $B'_j = B_j[v_1/v'_1, \ldots, v_n/v'_n]$ being CH_i, CH_j choice expressions, G_i, G_j guarded expressions and B_i, B_j behaviours expression.

BIBLIOGRAPHY

1. ISO, "Revised DP8807: A Formal Description Technique Based on the Temporal Ordering of Observational Behaviour", July 1986.

2. R. Milner, "A Calculus of Communicating Systems", Springer, 1980.

3. G. Milne, "CIRCAL and the representation of Communicationi, Concurrency, and Time", TOPLAS (ACM), vol. 7, no 2, April 1985.

4. C.A.R. Hoare, "Communicating Sequential Processes", Prentice Hall, 1985.

5. H. Ehrig, W. Fey, H. Hansen, "ACT ONE: An Algebraic Language with two Levels of Semantics", Bericht-Nr. 83-03, Tech. Universitat Berlin.

6. E. Brinksma, G. Scollo, C. Steenbergen, "LOTOS Specifications, Their Implementation and Their Tests" Sixth International Workshop on Protocol Specification, Testing and Verification, Montreal, 9-13 June 1986.

7. R. Milner, "A Complete Inference System for a Class of Regular Behaviours", Journal of Computer and Systems Sciences, Vol. 28, No. 3, June 1984.

8. Nicola, R. de and M.C.B. Hennessy, "Testing Equivalences for Processes", Theoretical Computer Science, vol. 34, no. 1,2, pp. 83-133, Nov 1984.

9. R. Milner, "Calculi for Synchrony and Asynchrony", Theoretical Computer Science, 25(1983), pp 267-310, North-Holland.

10. R.Foorgard. "Reve-A Program for Generating and Analyzing Term Rewriting Systems" MIT/LCS/TR-343, September 1984.

11. J. Quemada, A. Fernández, J. Mañas. "LOLA: Design and Verification of Protocols Using LOTOS". IBERICOM. North Holland, 1987.

12. Gödel Kurt. "Uber Formal Unentscheidbare Satze der *Principia Mathematica* und Verwandter Systeme, I" Monatshefte fur Mathematik und Physik, 38 (1931) pp 173..198.

SDT "The SDL Design Tool"

Michael Atlevi

Telelogic Europe SA
33, Bld de la Cambre
1050 Brussels
Belgium

1. INTRODUCTION

It is widely accepted that the key to success for software development is through a thorough system design. This requires a suitable formal language. Such a language offers a well defined set of concepts, and makes it possible to use powerful computer based tools to create, maintain, analyse and simulate system descriptions.

There are several specification languages around the world, comparable to SDL. Why choose SDL? The most important reason is that SDL is an International Standard. Being an established standard means that SDL will have a long lifetime and that it will evolve in a controlled manner. Another reason is that SDL is both powerful and user friendly, powerful in the sense of its expressive capabilities and user friendly in the sense of its graphical representation. A third reason is that SDL is supported by powerful computer based tools.

SDT is a computer based tool that supports the CCITT specification and description language SDL, as defined in Recommendations Z.100.

SDT has been developed and is marketed by Telelogic AB. It is available to any organization on a commercial basis.

2. OVERALL DESCRIPTION

SDT is a set of tools rather than a single tool. SDT has been designed in a modular fashion, giving the user a more flexible and powerful use of SDL. Most of the modules are optional, and can be used independently of each other.

The **Graphical Editor** (SGE) is used to create and edit SDL system specifications and descriptions in the graphical notation of SDL. The editor performs various syntactical checks. This implies that, when a new symbol is added to an existing diagram, the editor accepts only those symbols that are correct according to the syntax rules of SDL.

The **Analyser** and **Converter** (SAC) performs two functions. The Analyser performs syntactical and semantical analysis of the SDL descriptions. It provides error reports and warnings in appropriate cases. The Converter translates between SDL's graphical representation (Gr) and its program-like representation (Pr), and vice versa, provided that the information is syntactically correct. In both cases the layout of the result is generated in accordance with built-in rules.

The **Report Generator** (SRG) prepares and prints documents based on the SDL descriptions. It also compiles and prints a variety of reports.

The **Maintenance** is used to move information from one Information Base to another Information Base, within the same environment or to a different environment.

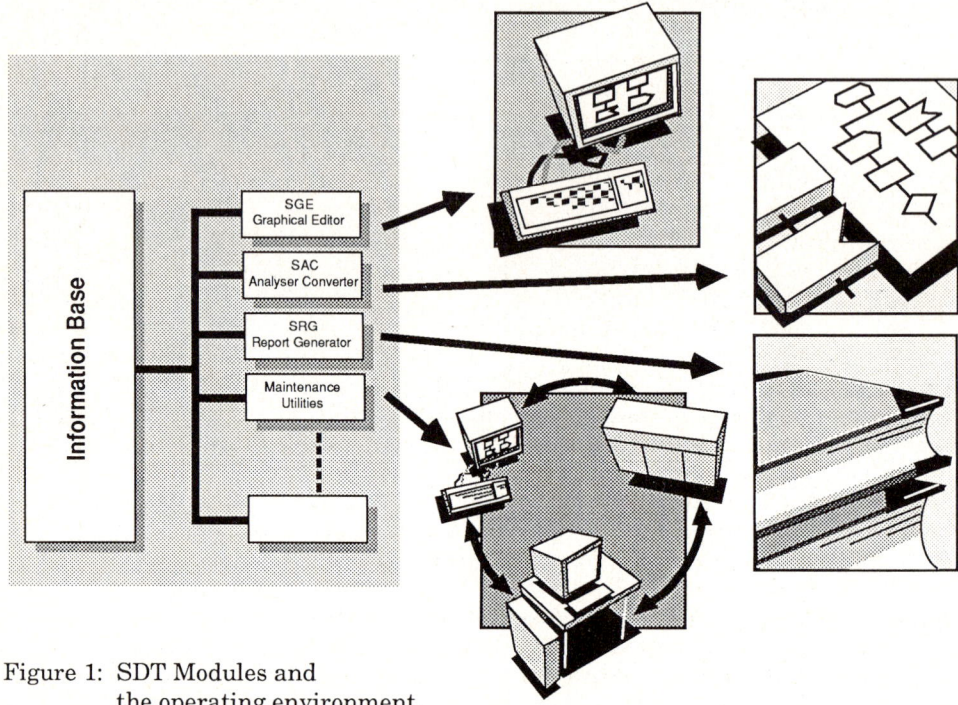

Figure 1: SDT Modules and the operating environment.

3. THE GRAPHICAL EDITOR

The Graphical Editor module in SDT is a window based editor for creation and maintenance of system descriptions in SDL's graphical representation. The Graphical Editor consists of three different types of editor, one for textual information, one for block diagrams and one for process graphs.

The SDL information in the Information Base, as seen from the Graphical Editor, is packed in *frames*. The frames constitute a hierarchical structure, following the syntax rules of SDL. They serve at the same time as menus or directories for accessing the desired piece of SDL information. The contents of a frame are SDL definitions or names of subordinate frames.

The layout of the display surface is organized in a working area which is surrounded by three menu areas and a dialogue area. In the working area the information is contained in windows. The windows are in separate planes, and can overlap each other. Only one window is active at any time, and this window is placed in front of all the other windows. The contents of a window is one *frame*.

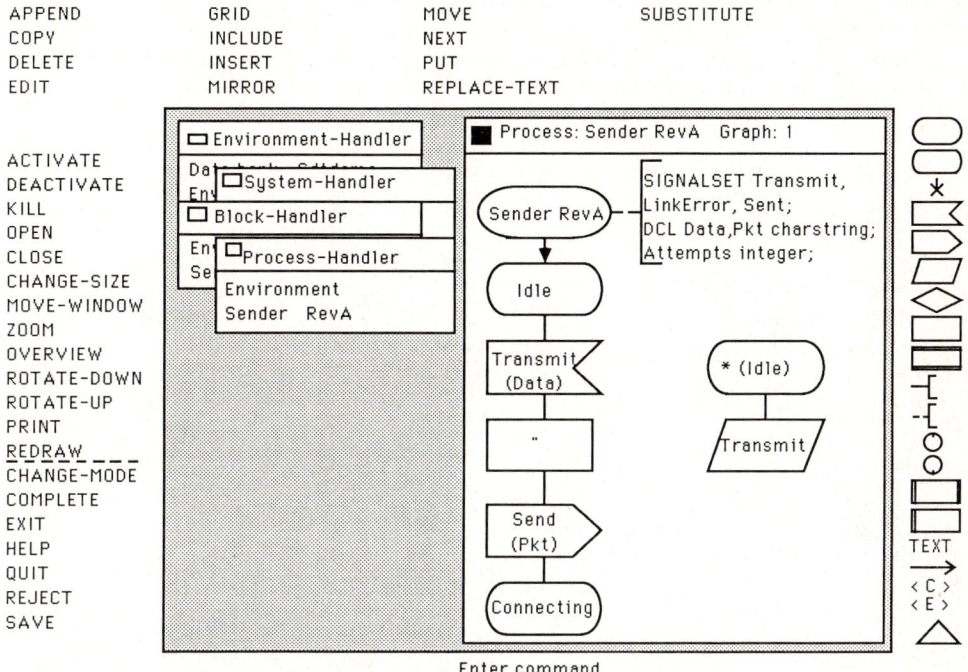

Figure 2: The layout of the display surface

4. THE ANALYSER & CONVERTER

The Converter module in SDT translates between SDL's graphical representation (Gr) and SDL's program-like representation (Pr) provided that the information is syntactically correct. It can also be used as a pretty printer in either graphical- or program-like representation. The layout of the result is generated according to built-in rules.

The Analyser is equivalent to a compiler except that no code is generated. Example of errors that the Analyser will detect are:

- Flow started with illegal symbol,
- State can't be reached, or option is not reachable,
- Illegal loop in flow,
- Transition following decision
- etc.

The Analyser and the Converter which are integrated can use either the graphical representation or the program-like representation as input and then, depending on which facility that has been chosen, use different paths as shown in figure 3, to reach its result.

The GrPr Converter performs the first conversion from the graphical representation to the program-like representation. The result of this function is a consecutive text that conforms to the program-like representation, with the exception, that it might not be syntactically correct since the graphical representation that was used for input may be incorrect.

The Pr Scanner and Parser use only the program-like representation as input. This function reads through the program-like representation and marks information such as keywords, identifiers, operators, etc. The syntax is then checked for correctness and an abstract syntax tree is built. If no errors were found during the syntactical analysis, the tree is passed either to the Unparser or the Semantical checker.

The Unparser converts the abstract syntax tree either into a textfile for the program-like representation or into the Information Base for the graphical representation.

The Semantical checker analyses the abstract syntax tree for semantical errors. Example of errors that may be found are :
- state can't be reached
- transition following decision or option is not reachable

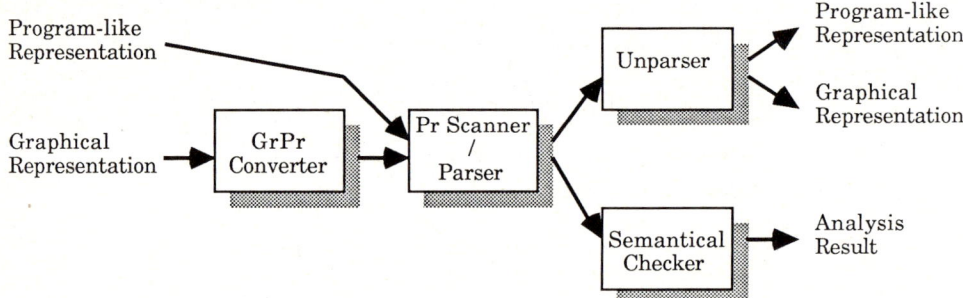

Figure 3: Logical flow of Analyser and Converter

5. THE REPORT GENERATOR

The Report Generator module in SDT is dedicated to handle SDL information in the format supplied by the Information Base. Implicit in the SDL concept is the wish to standardize. The SDT Report Generator is constructed to achieve this end. This explains some of the behaviour of the Report Generator which is different to traditional report generators.

The main facility of the Report Generator is the ordering of a report. This facility uses a table constructed according to the SDL hierarchy. That is, there are levels for; system, channel, block, process, procedure and macro. For each one of these, several documents can be generated, namely:

1. Connector references
2. Signal definitions
3. Data definitions
4. Parameter definitions
5. Signal-State
6. Nextstate
7. Transmitter information
8. Blocktree
9. Graph

Observe that all documents are not relevant to all SDL units, e.g. there is no Nextstate document for System.

As shown in figure 4, a wildcard may be used to order a certain set of documents for example all blocks within the specified system.

<UNIT>	<NAME>	<REV>	1	2	3	4	5	6	7	8	9
SYSTEM	S1	Rev1		X	X						X
BLOCK	*	*		X	X						X
PROCESS	P1	Rev1	X		X	X					X

Figure 4: Configuration of a table for ordering a report

6. FUTURE PLANS

Our policy of being in the forefront of development finds its strength in the future plans for SDT. These plans are divided into three parallel activities, namely :

- Functionalities
- Improvments
- Extensions

Concerning functionality developments, three different types of tools are to be included in SDT, these being:

- Program Generators
- Simulator
- Complexity Analyser

The **Program Generator** will transform an SDL system description to programs in some programming language. In the immediate future our plans are to include a SDL - Ada Program Generator and a SDL - C Program Generator in SDT.

The **Simulator** will simulate an SDL system by interpreting its description stored in the Information Base. The simulation will be performed interactively, i.e. the user can follow and control the course of the simulation.

The **Complexity Analyser** will calculate a complexity measure of an SDL system description in the Information Base. This measure can be used to predict resources needed to implement and maintain the system. It can also be used to indicate the need for a restructuring of the system in order to reduce its overall complexity.

Concerning improvments development, two inputs are very important, the user requirements and the SDL standard activities.

The user requirements development is a continuous process to improve SDT. Responding to new user requirements, SDT will provide a new user interface allowing the treatment of all system information in a unified fashion.

The SDL standard activities are very important, and at this very moment a new version of the SDL recommendations is being prepared, SDL 88. A redesign of SDT will be made to support SDL 88.

Concerning extensions development, we have just recently released a Graphical Editor on a Personal Computer.

LOTTE - A LOTOS Tool Environment

Wilfried H. P. van Hulzen

Department of Applied Computer Science
PTT - Dr. Neher laboratories
Leidschendam, The Netherlands

Abstract

This paper gives a brief description of a prototype LOTOS tool environment developed at the Dr. Neher laboratories of the Netherlands PTT. The intentions in the development of this environment were to integrate existing LOTOS tools, and to gather experience in the development and use of a specification environment for future developments. The paper gives a short description of the development process and an impression of the environment at the moment, sampling a few of the functions provided. Experiences in using the environment and a few of the resulting ideas for the future end the paper.

1 INTRODUCTION

The LOTOS Tool Environment 'LOTTE', developed at the Dr. Neher laboratories, provides a prototype environment for the integration of LOTOS tools. The intentions in the development of this environment were to gather experience in the development and use of a specification environment, integrating existing tools. It aims at giving easy and uniform access to existing and future tools.

The environment has been used successfully in several smaller projects and one larger project [4]. It appeared that specification-in-the-many and specification-in-the-large impose specific requirements on an environment, which are missing in LOTTE.

2 DEVELOPMENT OF LOTTE

At first, gathering experience, speed in the development and adaptability of the environment were considered more important than performance. To accommodate for this, the first versions of LOTTE, running on a UNIX^{TM} type system (VAX^{TM}/ULTRIX-32^{TM}, SUN^{TM}, were written as shell scripts (UNIX command files), using UNIX features where possible. In later stages of the development two of the shell scripts, considered to be major bottlenecks for the performance, were rewritten to C programs, improving the performance considerably.

3 GENERAL DESCRIPTION OF LOTTE

LOTTE constitutes a framework in which tools can be added when they become available. Each added tool will be accessible via an additional command in LOTTE, which is also added in the menu. This makes it quite easy for users to know which tools are available and get help on how to use them. LOTTE already gives access to several tools for handling and analysis of LOTOS specifications.

LOTTE uses build-in knowledge of the kind of the tools to provide a level of integration. For instance, once a specification name is given all commands in LOTTE dealing with specifications use that name until another name is given. It also checks conditions for the execution of tools. This is elaborated in a later section.

All documentation is on-line available in UNIX fashion. It is accessible via the command 'man', which gives access to the manuals for both LOTTE and UNIX. Further, a help command lists all LOTTE commands with a short description on terminal.

4 DESCRIPTION OF INTEGRATED TOOLS

At present the main functions in LOTTE are:

- a syntax and static semantics checker,
- an interactive report generator for gate sort lists analysis,
- an interactive single step simulator.

For certain commands successful completion can depend on successful completion of other commands. In the LOTTE environment it is possible to define these dependencies. LOTTE will then enforce them unless it is explicitly asked to ignore them. It is then up to the user to ensure that execution of these tools is possible. Examples in LOTTE are the report generator and the simulator, for which the specification should not contain syntactical or static semantical errors.

A derived mechanism is used to suppress repetition of actions. For instance, a user can ask for a check on static semantics. If, however, the specification has not been modified since a previous check, the results of this check are still valid. LOTTE detects this and will give these results instead of doing the check again.

4.1 Syntax and Static Semantical Analysis

For syntax and static semantical analysis LOTTE contains a multiple pass checker invoked by the **sss** command in LOTTE. The environment notifies the user of the result of the analysis, and tags the specification accordingly. This tag is inspected by other commands to determine the status of the specification.

4.2 Interactive Gate Sort List Report Generator

This tool, invoked by the **gsr** command in LOTTE, enables the user to detect gate sort list errors in an early stage (before simulation). Reports that can be asked for are:

- the lists of sorts offered at a gate of a process,
- the lists of sorts offered at a gate in a parallel expression,
- the lists of sorts if two processes communicate on indicated gates.

For parallel behaviour expressions, the tool can give a report of the use of gates in both behaviour expressions. Offers for which communication is possible are distinguished from offers for which communication is not possible. The user then can easily detect errors like missing or superfluous sorts, or transposing sorts. (gsr has not yet been updated for the latest version of LOTOS.)

4.3 Interactive Simulator

The simulator incorporated in LOTTE, called *hippo*, is a product of the SEDOS project under the EC supported ESPRIT program. This single step simulator is based on the theory developed in [1]. It it a recent addition to LOTTE, demonstrating its extendibility. The simulator is invoked by the command **hippo**.

When hippo has digested a specification, it asks which process in the specification should be simulated. For this *hippo* provides an extensive list of commands, including a help command for detailed information.

Apart from the analysis of the dynamic properties of a specification, it is possible to check the abstract data types with their equations using hippo. (The equations are interpreted as rewrite rules.) It offers the possibility to define synonyms and evaluate expressions using the operations defined in the abstract data types.

The full LOTOS language [2] is supported, with two restrictions:

- the equations in the abstract data types are interpreted as rewrite rules.
- the process definitions in the specification must be guardedly well-defined (no recursion of processes without first participating in an event).

4.4 Miscellaneous

Some minor functions present in LOTTE are:

- UNIX derived functions such as the editor **edit**, the change directory command **cd**, the list files command **ls**;
- Functions to show the status of a specification such as **order** and **show**.
- Functions to help in the development cycle (edit, check, correct, edit). The main tool in this category is **recover**.

The command **order** in LOTTE will list all files related to a specification which are relevant for the user in the order in which they are created. It enables the user to determine the recent history or check the status of a specification.

The command **show** will invoke the editor on the latest result file created. This can be the result of an analysis of the specification, a report created by **gsr**, or the specification itself.

The **recover** command eases correction of errors found in analysis of a specification. It creates a new version of the specification using the specification source information in the analysis result file. This enables the user to correct errors in the listing file (containing the error messages). **Recover** then creates a corrected version of the specification.

Finally, to give the user access to all UNIX commands, LOTTE provides a shell escape facility in UNIX style.

5 EXPERIENCES AND FUTURE DEVELOPMENTS

Although extensions to LOTTE are still for further study, several ideas already exist, some of which emerged during the development of larger specifications [4].

The monolithic aspect of LOTOS specifications poses major problems in the development of larger specifications, especially if this is done by a project team. Means to handle these specifications by a team should be developed (probably borrowing from software development techniques and environments).

The environment must deal with this problem. It should provide facilities for version control and piecewise editing and analysis. It could even handle the division of a specification in logical parts (e.g. processes, data types) using the tree structure of LOTOS specifications. Some data base structure to store specifications piecewise using an internal representation (instead of simple ASCII), maintaining versions and description of parts of the specification should be studied as one of the alternatives. The description of parts could include additional information for these parts such as an indication whether it is correct LOTOS, an object description (used and defined names, functionality information), results of tool preparation functions. Thus analysis of unchanged parts (mostly more than the changed parts) can be avoided.

The usage of an internal representation could also be beneficial for the integration of the tools in the environment, improving their overall performance. Currently all tools start from the ASCII file containing the specification. This results in functions being present and performed more than necessary (lexical scan, syntactical and semantical analysis), wasting time (in development and execution of tools) and space. Also, when a second (graphical) syntax for LOTOS is introduced, a shared internal representation for both external representations will be very useful.

Another point of discussion is ACT ONE, the abstract data type part of LOTOS. There is an urgent need to specify structures, to hide operators, and perform actualisation and renaming in a more user-friendly way. Also the extension of the standard library with (amongst others) integer, characters and strings of characters, all with suitable syntax is badly needed. The possibility of inclusion of processes in the library should also be considered.

References

[1] P. van Eijk, *Software tools for the specification language LOTOS*, Ph.D Thesis, Enschede, January 1988.

[2] ISO DIS 8807, *Information Processing Systems - Open Systems Interconnection - LOTOS - A Formal Description Technique Based on Temporal Ordering of Observational Behaviour*, ISO, July 1987.

[3] *Guidelines on the application of SDL, LOTOS and Estelle*, CCITT/ISO, to be published by the end of 1988

[4] P.A.J. Tilanus, Y. Yang, *Experience with LOTOS and environment LOTTE on an ISDN protocol*, Proc. of 'Specification and Verification of Concurrent Systems', BCS-FACS Workshop, Stirling, July 1988.

SPIDER - Service and Protocol Interactive Development Environment

Stuart G. Johnston
Hewlett-Packard Laboratories
Filton Road
Stoke Gifford
Bristol BS12 6QZ.

Abstract

The use of Formal Description Techniques in protocol development is intended to make protocol specifications unambiguous, and allow properties to be proved about these specifications. However, due to the size and complexity of many protocols, it is often infeasible to reason about formal descriptions by hand. This paper describes the first phase of a system intended to help protocol engineers use FDTs, which consists of a graphical simulator, with a textual and graphical interface for LOTOS, and GLOTOS, respectively.

1 Introduction

There are several motivations for using Formal Description Techniques (FDTs) to describe communication protocols [6]. However, due to the size and complexity of many protocols, in addition to the complexity of FDTs, it is often infeasible to reason about formal descriptions by hand. Therefore, a mechanised assistant or toolset is useful, to aid writing and manipulating formal descriptions.

SPIDER (Service and Protocol Interactive Development EnviRonment) is such a system. At present this consists of a graphical simulator for LOTOS [2], supporting both textual and graphical LOTOS.

2 Structure of the System

The core of the system is the *Labelled Transition System* (LTS). This is the semantic foundation of the FDT LOTOS. Several other useful languages (e.g. CCS [5], CSP [4]), can also be described in terms of LTSs. A LTS is similar to a finite state machine, which has explicit states, and actions which cause transitions between states.

A state may have more than one action associated with it, in which case the environment determines which state the system should evolve into. If more than one branch has the same action, then the resulting transition is *non-deterministic* (i.e. the environment has no control over which branch will be chosen).

Formally, a labelled transition system is a quadruple $LTS =< S, A, T, s_0 >$, where S is a set of states, A is a set of actions, T is a set of transitions of the form $s -a \rightarrow s'$, where

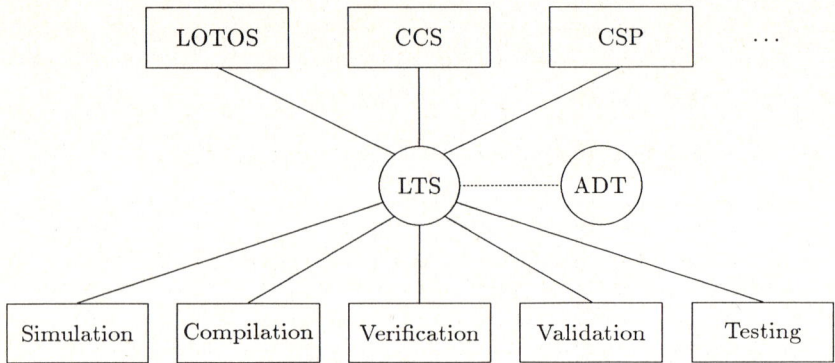

Figure 1: Overall structure of the SPIDER system

$s, s' \in S$, and $a \in A$, and $s_0 \in S$ is the start state. At any time the system will be in state $s \in S$, and will evolve into a new state s' if the action a occurs, and $s-a\rightarrow s' \in T$.

SPIDER is designed to be a toolset which provides a protocol engineer with support for performing several functions on a formal description. Figure 1 shows the overall structure of the toolset. The upper part of the diagram consists of FDT interfaces to the LTS system, whilst the lower part shows some of the functions to be provided to the user. These functions will work directly with the LTS defined by the FDT interface. In addition to the LTS system, Abstract Data Type (ADT) support is also provided, to allow languages which incorporate ADTs, such as LOTOS, to be supported by the toolset.

The first phase of SPIDER, which is described here, consists of the LOTOS front end, and the LTS simulator.

2.1 The LOTOS Front End

2.1.1 Input of a LOTOS Specification

Two interfaces for LOTOS are currently available—textual LOTOS and graphical LOTOS (GLOTOS) [1]. The textual LOTOS interface takes the form of a standard text file parser, which builds a parse tree corresponding to the specification, whilst the GLOTOS interface uses a special GLOTOS editor. The latter is a graphical editor, which allows GLOTOS specifications to be created and modified. The output from the editor is textual LOTOS, which can then be parsed (automatically, if desired) by the textual interface.

2.1.2 Static Semantics Checking

The static semantics of LOTOS serves two purposes—checking that a specification is semantically correct, and resolving scoping information of names (referred to as *the flattening mapping* in [2]). The static semantics checks are performed on the LOTOS parse tree, and so only syntactically correct LOTOS can be checked.

If the specification is semantically sound, then each process instantiation is linked to the corresponding process definition, to give a *canonical behaviour specification*, and a data presentation derived, which is a *canonical algebraic specification*. These are then used to perform the dynamic semantics of the specification.

2.1.3 Dynamic Process Semantics

In [2] the dynamic process semantics of LOTOS are defined in terms of LTSs. *Expansion theorems* map the LOTOS operators into LTSs, and so creating a LTS from a LOTOS description is a matter of applying these expansion theorems to the LOTOS description. Expansion can be performed in two manners—*lazy expansion* and *eager expansion*.

Lazy expansion only converts the FDT description into a LTS as the LTS is needed. For example, in the case of a simulator, only the set of possible next actions are needed at each step in the simulation. Therefore, only that part of the formal description necessary to provide this has to be expanded. When an action is chosen, the transition will result in another expression from the FDT, which is then expanded. This process can continue indefinitely if necessary, and so recursive processes, used in FDTs to describe repetitive behaviour, can easily be dealt with.

Eager expansion creates a complete LTS from the formal description. As most of the work is done in this stage, using the LTS (e.g. simulating it) should be simple and efficient. However, potentially infinite systems are more difficult to deal with.

2.1.4 Dynamic Data Type Semantics

As LOTOS has the notion of abstract data types (in the form of ACT ONE), support for this must be provided. The use of data types allows actions of a LTS to be enhanced with values. When an event occurs, these values are communicated between processes.

The dynamic semantics of ACT ONE is based on reducing a data term, or value, to a canonical form, from which further reduction is not possible. For example, in the case of library type `boolean` provided in LOTOS, the term `(not(true) and true)` would be reduced to `false`.

A *term-rewriting engine* is used to perform this manipulation of terms. An existing ADT system, Axis [3], is currently used to perform term rewriting. The canonical algebraic specification, obtained from the static semantics checking of the LOTOS specification, is passed to the Axis system, to create the types defined within the LOTOS specification. Whenever an ACT ONE term is subsequently encountered, such as terms within event offers, or premises in a guard, etc., this is also passed to the Axis system, which then performs the necessary rewriting, and returns the canonical form of the term.

3 Simulation of LTSs

Simulation of a protocol allows the designer to incrementally test the design, and debug the result, and so support rapid prototyping. It should be possible to observe the internal workings of the system, as well as interacting with the protocol as normal.

The LTS simulator is basically a tool for animating and interacting with LTSs. Lazy expansion is used to create the LTS from the FDT specification, as the structure of the specification can be used to create a graphical representation of the simulation, as it occurs.

During simulation, the user is effectively acting as the environment, to resolve choices within the derived LTS. Two modes of simulation are possible—interactive and purely

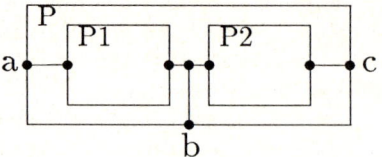

Figure 2: Graphical representation of processes

observational.

In the former, the user of the system experiments with the specification, in a step-wise manner, and observes the results before continuing. This allows the testing of particular special cases which may arise, e.g. the filling of a buffer to capacity. At each step of the simulation, the possible actions are presented to the user in the form of a menu. One choice is then selected, which causes the system to evolve into the next state, which is obtained using lazy expansion recursively.

The other mode of operation allows the behaviour to be pre-defined, and so the same test can be performed repeatedly without user intervention. A list of choices is defined by the user, and this is then used to guide the simulation.

An ADT expression can also be associated with an action, if desired. The user should specify the term when selecting the action. If the term is valid in that context, according to conditions imposed by the FDT specification, then the simulation will proceed. If the term is invalid, then it must be re-specified. An example of an invalid term in LOTOS would be boolean value `true`, or integer value 0, when simulating `g?x:int [x > 3]`....

In the case where the specification only presents a single data value, for example `g!3`, then the user need not supply a value.

Non-determinism can be handled in two manners. The user can choose to have non-deterministic choice presented in the same way as a deterministic one, i.e. the non-deterministic choices will appear in the menu. Alternatively, the choice between non-deterministic branches can be made randomly by the system.

The output from the simulation is displayed graphically, using a representation first proposed by Milner for CCS [5]. This draws each process as a labelled box, with associated gates drawn on the perimeter. If that process is defined in terms of two parallel processes, then it is drawn with two recursive processes, with lines of communication connecting the boxes. Figure 2 shows the graphical representation of the LOTOS process:

process P[a,b,c]:**noexit** :=
    P1[a,b] |[b]| P2[b,c]
endproc

Creation and death of processes is reflected in the graphical representation by drawing and erasing boxes, respectively. If a process evolves into a new one, then the name of the process on the display will change to reflect this.

4 Conclusions

Presented here is the first stage of a protocol engineers workbench, a graphical interactive simulator. Currently available are two LOTOS interfaces, with full syntax and static semantics checking, and implementation of the dynamic semantics. The simulator should aid the development of protocols, by allowing specifications to be rapidly tested and debugged. It also has uses in education of potential FDT users, as the results of a specification can be observed immediately.

SPIDER is a step towards increasing the acceptance of FDTs, as it will make their use more manageable, and will increase both the quality and maintainability of formal specifications. The modular design of the system, with several front end FDT interfaces possible, allows new and different languages to be experimented with, as well as simplifying the task of supporting new versions of existing standards.

References

[1] *Graphical LOTOS*. ISO/IEC JTC 1/SC 21/WG 1 N 565, December 1987.

[2] *LOTOS*. ISO DIS 88, July 1987.

[3] Derek Coleman et al. *The Axis Specification Language*. Technical Memo HPL-ISC-TM-88-020, Hewlett-Packard Labs., Bristol, July 1988.

[4] C.A.R. Hoare. *Communicating Sequential Processes*. *Series in Computer Science*, Prentice-Hall, 1985.

[5] Robin Milner. *A Calculus for Communicating Systems*. *LNCS*, Springer-Verlag, 1980.

[6] Harry Rudin. Protocol engineering: a critical assesment. In *Protocol Specification, Testing and Verification: VIII*, 1988.

A LISP Based LOTOS Environment

Günter Karjoth

IBM Research Division
Zurich Research Laboratory
8803 Rüschlikon, Switzerland

In this paper we describe an experimental tool system oriented to support formal description techniques based on process algebras. Although our system does not accept the full LOTOS language, it tackles some of the major problems in realizing effective LOTOS tools. Our tool set embodies a simulator to aid interactive analysis of formal descriptions and a transformer that provides automatic translation of regular processes into an equivalent state machine.

1. Introduction

This paper describes an experimental tool system for formal description techniques based on process algebras, in particular for LOTOS. Its objective is to study the potential of tools that support the user in the construction and analysis of LOTOS specifications, in the implementation of the specifications, and their later testing.

The kernel of our tool system is the language LL which can be regarded as an internal representation of LOTOS [1] in the form of LISP S-expressions. All dynamic LOTOS operators have a direct representation in LL. Contrary to [1], the description and manipulation of data structures and value expressions are defined in LISP; this avoided an implementation of a rewrite system for the evaluation of algebraically specified Abstract Data Types [2]. LISP is also the implementation language of the system.

The LL language and its interpreter are the principal items of the tool system. Therefore, the main interest has focused on the development of techniques to implement efficient simulation strategies for

- multiway synchronization,
- interactions with value-generation,
- branching over possibly infinite domains.

The capability to handle efficiently large-scale specifications and to explore thousands of their states are also of major concern because the performance of a simulator exhibits its usability for real specifications.

2. The Language
2.1. Data Types

The representation of values, value expressions, and data structures in LL is derived from the functional programming language LISP. To model the style of algebraically specified Abstract Data Types, a simple type system has been implemented.

Data types are explicitly declared and have as an optional parameter a list of constants which will be used by the simulator for sort checking and value generation:

(type t (c_1 c_2 ...))

The definition of a function is done with the operation

(fnc f E)

where E may be any LISP lambda expression suitable to perform the intended operation. Last, there is an operation that allows reference to be made to particular constants by name:

(const c E)

This notation for user-defined shorthands simplify input and make a display more intelligible to the human reader.

2.2. Processes

The process part of LL resembles a "low-level" representation of the process part of LOTOS, i.e. all simplifications that can be made by (literal) substitution have been performed. The correspondence between the 'basic' LOTOS operators and the LL operators is given in the following table:

operation	$LOTOS$	LL
Internal action	i	(tau)
Action	g!E?x : t	(g ! E ? x t)
Action with selection predicate	g!E?x : $t[P]$	(g ! E ? x t ?? P)
Inaction	stop	(stop)
Successful termination	exit(E_1,..., E_n)	(exit E_1 ... E_n)
Action-prefix	a;B	(seq a B)
Choice	B_1 [] B_2	(choice B_1 B_2)
Parallel	B_1 |[S]| B_2	(par S B_1 B_2)
Hiding	hide S in B	(hide S B)
Guarding	[P] → B	(if P B)
Instantiation	$b(E_1,...,E_n)$	(b E_1 ... E_n)
Generalized choice	choice x : t [] B	(CHOICE (x t) B)
Enabling	B_1 ≫ accept $x_1,...,x_n$ in B_2	(SEQ B_1 (x_1 ... x_n) B_2)
Disabling	B_1 [> B_2	(DIS B_1 B_2)
Relabeling		(replace U B)

In LL, process definitions are not parameterized with their formal gates. Instead, the auxiliary relabeling operator is used. The operation

(process b (x_1 t_1 ...) B_b),

where b is an identifier and B_b is a behavior expression, declares b to be a process. A shorthand for gate relabelings is

(let n (g_1 g_1' ... g_n g_n'))

which can be used in the relabeling operation.

3. The Simulator

The central tool in our system is the simulator. A simulator has many applications in the design process and shares much of its functionality with other tools [3]. To analyze the behavior of a specification, our simulator allows stepwise exercising of all the interactions to check whether these interactions conform to the expectations of the designer. Further, the simulator assists in the generation of test cases and provides a mechanism to check the actual behavior of an implementation against its specification.

3.1. Single-step execution

The simulator executes a process by developing its communication tree. User and simulator interactively navigate along one of many possible paths. At each step the user is presented with a list of possible events (the acceptance set) from which he can select the one to take place next:

```
State 1:
<1> g TCONreq ¢₂ provider {(GT ¢₂ 0)}
<2> i(k) 100
<3> h ¢₁
Select event <1 ... 3>:
```

The notation $¢_2$ in the example means that on gate g a value must be determined as the second parameter of this interaction. The values that may be bound to this parameter are restricted by a selection predicate excluding all values equal to or less than 0. Also for gate h a value has to be determined. The second event is an internal action at the hidden gate k having one parameter with value 100.

Based on the chosen event the resulting successor behavior is computed. If an action requires a value from the environment, the user is asked for it.

```
Give value for parameter ¢₂ of sort Nat:
```

It can be any LISP term compatible with the requested 'type'.

If there is a preceding state with at least one unexplored action the user is offered a backup command. This command leads the simulation to the latest state for which an alternative unexplored path exists. Backup does not offer an event again once it has occurred. Therefore all states of terminating behavior can be visited going depth-first.

The simulator properly treats nondeterminism caused by internal events and/or multiple events of the same kind. On demand the simulator provides the user with unique descriptions of the "origin" of possible events. At any time the behavior expression which forms the current state can be displayed. Further, the simulator records all information necessary to create the finite state model of the course of exploration.

If the user is not interested in selecting explicitly each next event, he/she can give control to the simulator to develop the next n steps. The depth of searching can be restricted by assigning a limit to the global variable $DEPTH$.

3.2. Exhaustive state exploration

The main objective of exhaustive exploration of the state space is to detect potential loops. In order to recognize loops, the simulator computes a normal form of the current state's behavior expression. This expression is used to check whether another state exists with the same normal form. Although no unique normal form exists for LOTOS expressions a sufficiently high number of matches is achieved. Expression comparison is done using a specialized form of hashing.

3.2.1. Input Expansion

Every read action that accepts values from a non-singleton domain leads to alternative behaviors depending on the given input. The automatic exploration of the state space requires that values be provided that normally would be established in interactions with the environment of the specified system. Input events have to be expanded to an equivalent set of output events having all possible parameter instances. Therefore, the read action is replaced in the acceptance set by a set of write actions offering all possible values from that domain. For this purpose the simulator uses the set of constants provided in the corresponding type declaration.

3.2.2. Domain Mapping

Process specifications containing value expressions tend to have infinitely many states. A technique to reduce the number of states has been implemented for properties where the individuality of a specific data type is of no concern (e.g. the actual message in the alternating bit protocol). If an injective function is provided by the user that maps the individual elements of an unbounded domain onto elements of a finite set, this mapped data will be used in state comparison.

3.3. Trace checking

The simulator may also be used as an (off-line) analyzer for traces of a protocol implementation under test. Connected with a trace file, the simulator can proceed as long as the current action read from the file does not cause a deadlock situation, i.e. is a member of the acceptance set of the current state. It may however happen that the specification allows some internal actions to occur before the next action actually observed during the execution of the implementation under test takes place. Therefore, the simulator will start to explore all branches leading to stable states, i.e. states where no internal action is possible. If the simulator reaches a state in which the current logged action is possible, trace checking is carried on from that state.

4. The Transformer

This tool provides automatic translation of regular processes into an observation-equivalent state machine. The translation deals separately with the control and data parts of processes. The regular process skeleton will be mapped onto a finite state machine whereas the data domain will be mapped onto a set of global variables manipulated by functions associated with the transitions of the finite state machine. The parallelism within processes is compiled into nondeterministic interleaving of the atomic actions, thereby resolving multiway synchronization.

Two different translation algorithms have been implemented. In the first one, based on simulation, the process is unfolded. The comparison of behavior expressions is essential for this algorithm. The second procedure is based on a chart construction algorithm as described in [4]. The state machine is an intermediate representation from which implementations in different target languages can be produced. Currently, Estelle-like statements are generated.

There are routines to preprocess behavior expressions such that the update of variables within the generated state machines is reduced. The granularity of events (to treat an input and several outputs as a single event) can be controlled by introducing "constraints" in the form of simple additional parallel processes.

5. Miscellaneous

Since the syntax of LL is a LISP-like prefix notation, many support tools normally found in LISP environments, such as structure editor, pretty printer, and debugger, are used in conjunction with the simulator. So far, the need for a specialized editor to handle the source of formal descriptions has been regarded to be rather small. The command **make-listing** produces a nice documentation per process, listing alphabetically all defined type, function and process declarations. Each process declaration also contains the label set of the defined process. The **script** command causes recording of the interactive terminal input/output for later analysis. The **silent** command is used to suppress verbose output when doing automatic state space exploration.

There are functions to perform checks on the static semantics that help detect, for instance, unguarded processes. A common source of errors in specifications is the mistyping of gate names. Thus, commands have been included to help the user determine the actual structure and connectivity of the given specification.

Further, there is a set of commands to enable the user to expand LL terms and to rearrange behavior definitions. This is a first step in the direction towards a general expression manipulation environment.

6. Future Work

The current version of our LOTOS environment is a first feasibility prototype covering just the central functions. The two important components which are yet to be included are an ADT interpreter and a front end for the LOTOS language syntax.

Currently a LOTOS specification must be translated manually into LL. The process specification is expanded and the definitions of all operations on data are rewritten in LISP. Except for non-constructively defined operators, this is straightforward. At the beginning this was very convenient because the application of the LISP EVAL function to evaluate expressions directly led to an easy implementation. But the theory of ADTs is an integral part of LOTOS. The ability to extend, combine, parameterize or rename data specifications contributes significantly to the elegance of the language. Thus a front end may translate the data part into a flat representation which can then be interpreted directly by conditional term rewriting.

The textual user interface is not sufficiently powerful to handle large real specifications. A high-resolution display with a window system will be used to support structuring and abstraction properly.

References

[1] ISO - Information Processing Systems - Open Systems Interconnection. *LOTOS - A Formal Description Technique Based on the Temporal Ordering of Observational Behaviour.* DIS 8807, 1987.

[2] H. Ehrig and B. Mahr. *Fundamentals of Algebraic Specification I: Equations and Initial Semantics. Monographs on Theoretical Computer Science*, Springer-Verlag, Berlin, Heidelberg, New York, 1985.

[3] P. van Eijk. *Software Tools for the Specification Language LOTOS.* PhD thesis, University of Twente, Dept. of Informatics, Enschede, The Netherlands, 1988.

[4] G. Karjoth. Implementing process algebra specifications by state machines. In *Protocol Specification, Testing and Verification VIII*, North-Holland, 1988. to be published.

From LOTOS to C

J.A. Mañas
T. de Miguel

Dpt. Ingeniería Telemática
E.T.S.I. Telecomunicación
Univ. Politécnica de Madrid
E-28040 Madrid, España

`jmanas@dit.upm.es`
`tmiguel@dit.upm.es`

LOTOS is a very high level language, too high level to allow direct implementation, although a development system would be very appreciated, and would greatly help to the acceptance of the language as a practical specification technique. Our system permits the implementer to refine a very abstract specification until it becomes a running piece of code. The output are portable C programs. This paper focuses on the functionality and features of the LOTOS compiler currently under development at Madrid.

1. INTRODUCTION.

Although there may be different definitions of the concept of implementation, our understanding is that implementing means deriving a real or physical system, able to interact with its environment. More concretely, we are mainly interested on getting programs that run on computers and behave according to a LOTOS specification.

Implementation may mean prototyping in many practical situations. It is a mean of providing a working module that is limited to demonstrating the functionality of the specification. The purpose of such a prototype is to ascertain that the functional requirements reflect and solve the user needs, and that the functional requirements can be implemented, that is, no impossible functions are required. Sometimes the prototype is much enough for what is needed, and no further implementation is required, but if time or space are critical, manual implementation may be required to tune the system.

Thus, a practical compiling tool must be able to produce fast prototypes, and must foresee the need to be part of a bigger system, or even to rely on hand coded submodules. It is expected that an application will use modules generated by this compiler and other modules provided by the user. The generated module may be "called" from other modules and the other way round, and collaborate with them in a flexible manner.

Due to the semantic gap between specification and implementation, the users of the tools are expected to provide information to the compiler covering implementation decisions. This extra information shall be integrated in the compiler input in order to keep a consistent specification of the implementation. After providing this extra information, the process will run automatically.

Output code shall be source code in a standard programming language in order to permit readability and portability. Readability is required both for checking the correct generation of code (a very important item for experimental prototypes that require extensive and careful debugging), and for allowing hand tuning to meet efficiency requirements after module profiling. Portability is required for obvious reasons of usefulness in general, and in particular because it is extremely frequent that a protocol will run between different computers.

Language C was chosen as the target language for being readable, portable, widely available, close to machine details, efficient, widely experienced as target language, and has a big pool of tools that can be used without licensing problems.

2. DESIGN PROCESS.

Compiling means merging a specification of behaviour with implementation decisions in order to produce a module able to fit a real application that runs on some computer.

A mechanism of annotations has been devised that permits the integration of both kinds of information into the same file, thus simplifying maintenance. Annotations are a special class of LOTOS comments that are interpreted by the compiler. The main ideas for annotations design are as follows

1. They do not modify the transition system that is specified in LOTOS. Such modifications shall be done by editing the source specification itself. A support tool for assessing some kind of observational equivalence would be advisable.

2. They have some recognizable effect on the interface of the implemented system, that is, they perform some observable action associated to state transitions specified in LOTOS.

3. Environment state may be accessed and allowed to delay possible synchronizations until a certain state is reached, e.g. waiting for 5 seconds or waiting until a peripheral warms up.

Many of the annotations are in fact program fragments that are included in the output of the compiler. Those fragments are executed when the state machine makes the transition to which they are associated. If there are several fragments associated to a transition, then they are executed in parallel (or in a random order, over which the user has no control).

On a properly annotated specification, the different parts of the compiler work unattended. There is a neat difference between the behaviour and the data part. In fact, the LOTOS compiler is the result of the close cooperation of a behaviour compiler *lbc*, and a data compiler *ldc*. Surely the first steps, syntax and semantics, are shared. The front end terminates providing a collection of processes on one hand, and a single data type on the other one.

3. BEHAVIOUR COMPILER.

Leaving out the data types, a LOTOS specification can be seen as a collection of behaviour units, *processes*, that interact. Each behaviour unit can be modelled as a finite automaton that synchronizes with the rest. In terms of C language, the LOTOS compiler generates reentrant code, organized as one C function per LOTOS process. These pieces of code behave as processes in conventional O.S., that is, relay on *system calls* to interactuate. The Run Time Support organizes the cooperation between units. The kind of information held in the Kernel is quite similar to the standard frames used in O.S., obviously adapted to the very sophisticated synchronization mechanism of LOTOS: *n-way symmetrical rendez-vous*.

Without annotations, the output of *lbc* is an automaton that moves according to the LOTOS specification, but isn't able to interactuate with the environment. The following annotations are available

1. Output actions

    · Associated to *action denotations* there may be specified actions to be performed. The automaton will perform it upon successful synchronization. For example, send !m (*| C *send message m* |*); REST

The body of the action is plain C code.

2. **Delays**

    The offer of an action may be delayed by a specified number of seconds. For example,

    (*| delay 5 |*) timeout !recv; REST

    where the `timeout` action is not offered till 5 seconds are over. Of course, in the meanwhile another action may disable the delayed one, for instance by means of a choice [] operator, thus giving up any opportunity for any timeout to happen.

3. **Synchronize with the world**

    The offer of an action may be delayed till a user provided predicate becomes true.

    (*| wait isdata() |*) read ?d: data; REST

    Where an active wait is carried on by repeatedly checking the predicate. As previously, a "choice" action may overtake the wait.

4. **Provide defaults for value negotiation**

    LOTOS permits synchronization between gates with a collection of requirements. For example,

    g ?m: int [P1(m)]; M |[g]| g ?n: int [P2(n)]; N

    The compiler permits to associate to the offer *default values* that are checked to fulfill the predicates. If no defaults were provided, no action would be carried on, since ad-hoc heuristics would be needed to generate values. Better let the implementer to state the heuristics directly.

    Defaults may be provided either as a list of values to try, and/or as a user function that is iteratively called to provide a collection of values, till someone succeeds.

We are currently evaluating the opportunity of an effective *cut off* annotation, something that actually prunes the synchronization tree upon user provided data. This effect can be achieved by means of tricky *waits* or *delays*, but the situation happens so often that an explicit annotation seems adequate.

4. DATA COMPILER.

The data part of LOTOS is much more complex to implement. First, there are plenty of constructions to combine types, and derive new types, and cope with scope of declarations. One of the very first steps in compiling is removing all this user oriented machinery. The process is known as *flattening* and the output is having just one, *canonical*, type for the whole specification.

Second, users must be aware that they are specifying algebraically. That means that standard equational reasoning must be applied to derive conclusions about actual data. That, strictly speaking, implies using theorem proving techniques, what sounds far unreasonable for actual implementations. The approach we use is to require the implementer to certify that the canonical type may be understood as a liable rewrite system. There are plenty of tools in the research community to check that fact, and even to help the implementer in modifying the original specification till the type may be securely implemented as a rewrite system. It is our personal experience, that 90% of the specifications are directly executable as rewrite systems, but it is advisable to check it.

Third, the rewrite system itself must be produced. The data part compiler provides a coded rewrite engine for the concrete data. For efficiency reasons, it is not a generic rewrite engine working on some data base, but a specific rewrite engine optimized for the user type. It is enriched with memory management features, and a drawing function to help debugging.

The default behaviour of the compiler may be easily overtaken in order to introduce user coded data types. This situation is rather usual since there are many types directly implemented by the hardware (as booleans or integers) where the compiled versions would be highly inefficient. In general, it is usually the case that libraries of data types are used despite its algebraic specification in LOTOS. For those situations, a collection of annotations is provided.

1. **name**.

    The implementation of LOTOS ADTs is based on unique identifiers. Those are numbers generated by the semantics analyzer. This is required to cope with overloading. C functions names are chosen after those unique identifiers, thus getting rather obscure codings (e.g. g12). That's necessary, but makes the code extremely unconvenient for humans. The first approach to tackle with this problem is to keep user identifiers. There are two limits to this. (1) there may be overloaded identifiers in LOTOS, but C doesn't support overloaded names on functions. (2) there may be valid LOTOS identifiers (e.g. +) that are not valid C identifiers. The solution to both problems was to add an annotation to those identifiers that may cause trobles.

    ```
    opns
      + (*| name plus |*): nats, nats -> nats
    ```

2. **extern**.

    In order to improve the system efficiency, it is often the case that the basic types of C may be used (e.g. integers), or that efficient implementations may be directly coded in C (e.g. for sets). It is desirable that these "optimizations" interface smoothly with the code generated by *ldc*. There is an annotation for it, extern. Either sorts and/or operations may be annotated as extern, with the obvious implications (i.e. operations on external sorts must be external too).

3. **equal**.

    For external sorts, *ldc* must be instructed about the *equal* function, since data representation is up to the user. Code will be generated to refer to the function provided by the user to check equality of terms of that sort.

4. **free**.

    For external sorts, *ldc* must be instructed about how to free memory allocated for terms of this sort, since data representation is up to the user. Code will be generated to refer to the function provided by the user to free terms that involve subterms of this sort.

5. **draw**.

    For debugging, there is an obvious need to be able to print the terms in a user friendly format. That's pretty easy for *ldc* data types (i.e. a classical tree traversal algorithm), but for user provided representations, the user must provide its printing function too. Of course, *ldc* keeps track of LOTOS and/or name annotated identifiers.

We are currently evaluating the opportunity to introduce an *exception* mechanism associated to operations. The exception would be raised if a user provided predicate on input arguments fails. It would be a mechanism of coping with partial functions, that are a very usual case, despite the fact that LOTOS doesn't support them. Obviously, this kind of annotations would severely affect the algebraic interpretation of the data types, but seems to be quite useful in actual practice.

5. MODULE INTEGRATION.

The LOTOS compiler provides two pieces of code. (1) A collection of C functions to implement the behaviour part, named APP.lbc; and (2) a collection of C functions to implement the data, named APP.ldc. These modules are to be loaded alltogether with the Kernel and the modules provided by the user, APP.ub for the user behaviour, and APP.ud for the user provided data implementations. The following picture shows the combination of modules.

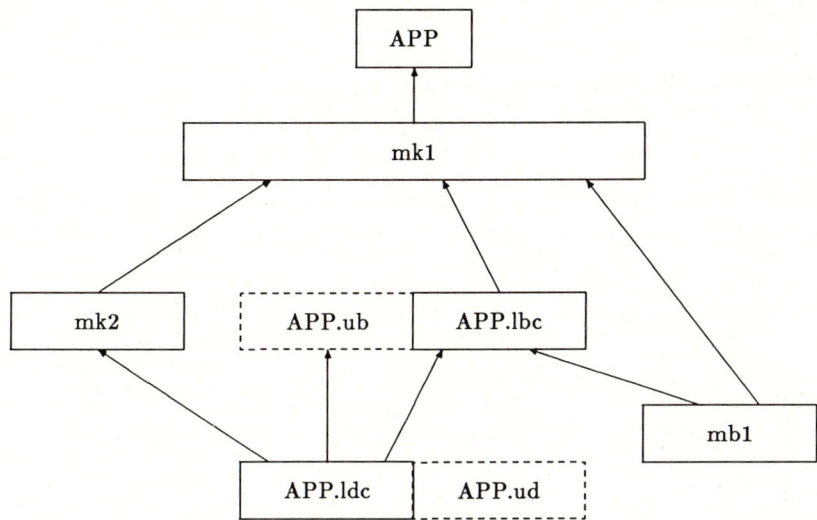

There are basically two mechanism to interactuate with other modules. Either the embedded scheduler of the Kernel is used, or an external scheduler steers the generated code. In the first, and most usual case, external modules are called upon internal decisions. In the second case, the code is required to execute in a slave mode, upon external request. In this second case, the compiled module "executes" one step and returns control to the calling module. A "step" is defined as one action synchronization or nothing to do but *waits* and/or *delays*.

6. STATUS.

There is currently a prototype compiler running on Sun-3 machines with BSD 4.2 UNIX. It is been used in Madrid to develop non trivial implementations of protocols. It cannot be so far regarded as a production tool, but under experimentation and debugging. The collection of annotations required keeps growing, as the need arises, but its rate is coming down. That means that the current offer is quite enough for actual protocols. Compiling time is not trivial, but reasonable. Execution time is quite acceptable, but for critical timeouts. Space requirements are too big, and further work is being carried on to decrease it. Certainly, there is plenty of self-test code embedded in the output, code that could be removed when we become more confident with its behaviour.

To give some figures, people at the department are currently developing a medium size protocol that is able to transfer data in a connection mode, with a data segmentation feature. The data types are coded in ASN.1. The protocol is more or less equivalent to a class 0 transport protocol. The LOTOS specification is 1000 lines long, were only signatures are provided for the data types, since the whole implementation is external. User written code (behaviour + data) is about 7000 lines. The time required by the compiler to process the LOTOS specification is 30 seconds, where 40 seconds must be added to run the C compiler and load together the pieces. The generated module uses 500K. It must be noted that a big portion of the code is not actually used (it should be organized as a library of data types rather than a huge collection of types and operations). If only actually used data were loaded, the size would come down to some 350K. A hand coded implementation is been developed at the same time by a parallel team. This second team shares the data types, but has recoded in plain C the LOTOS specification. The resulting module has a lower size, 370K. These data are not definite, since the product is currently under development. We plan to carefully evaluate both implementations when both of them are running, after clipping out redundant code and so.

8.   BIBLIOGRAPHY.

1. ISO IS 8807, *Information Processing Systems, Open System Interconnection,* LOTOS, *A Formal Description Technique Based on the Temporal Ordering of Observational Behavior.* ISO, July, 1988.

2. D.E. Knuth and P.B. Bendix. *Simple Word Problems in Universal Algebras.* Computational Problems in Abstract Algebra, J. Leech (ed.), Pergamon Press, 1969.

3. P. Lescanne. *Computer Experiments with the REVE term Rewriting System Generator.* 10th POPL Conf. Austin, Texas, 1983.

4. J.A. Mañas. Dining Philosophers: a Constrained Oriented Specification. SEDOS/C3/WP/40/M, E.T.S.I. Telecomunicación, Madrid, July, 1987.

5. J.A. Mañas. *A Tutorial on* ADT *semantics for* LOTOS *users. Part I: Fundamental Concepts. Part II: Operations on Types.* Dpt. Telemática, May, 1988.

6. J.A. Mañas, T. de Miguel and H. van Thienen. The Implementation of a Specification Language for OSI Systems. Int. Zurich Seminar on Digital Communications. March 1988, pp. 103-107.

7. J.A. Mañas and T. Robles. *The experience of Compiling an* ADT *language.* Submitted to CIL'89, Barcelona, March 1989.

8. J. de Meer. *Tutorial on* LOTOS *Data Types.* Hahn-Meitner-Institut Berlin GmbH. March 1986. Vol. 92, Lecture Notes in Computer Science, Springer Verlag, 1980.

EWS : AN INTEGRATED WORKSTATION FOR THE DESIGN AND THE AUTOMATIC GENERATION OF DISTRIBUTED SOFTWARE
ESTELLE SEDOS DEMONSTRATOR, Esprit Project 1265

Jean Michel AYACHE*, Jean DUFAU*, Michel HUYBRECHTS** and Eric MATTERA**

* VERILOG, Toulouse, France
** EXPERT SOFTWARE SYSTEMS, Ghent, Belgium
*** MARBEN, Paris, France

1. INTRODUCTION

The ESTELLE Workstation (EWS) is an integrated ESTELLE environment for the design of distributed software. EWS has been designed to support all classical software development phases such as editing, compilation and interactive debugging and provides also an approach towards automatic implementation of ESTELLE specifications [1].

EWS has been developed within **SEDOS ESTELLE DEMONSTRATOR** Esprit project 1265 by a consortium of three partners :

– **VERILOG** (prime contractor) Toulouse, France
– **EXPERT SOFTWARE SYSTEMS** Ghent, Belgium
– **MARBEN** Paris, France.

This development has been conducted in cooperation with several other partners of the project acting as counsel and evaluating EWS through a set of various applications.

These partners are **LAAS** (Toulouse, France), **CNET** (Lannion and Paris, France), **ETSIT** (Madrid, Spain), **ENTEL** (Madrid, Spain) and **BULL/DAS** (Louveciennes, France).

The objectives of the SEDOS ESTELLE DEMONSTRATOR project are :

  – to produce a basic set of **prototype tools** able to fit with an industrial software development context and able to increase efficiency and productivity of the development especially :

    . in the design phase : a **syntax oriented editor** allows an easy and efficient ESTELLE description with flexible syntactic handling of text changes, restructuring and on line syntactic checks ;
    . in the formalizing phase : a **semantic checker** analyses the semantic properties of a protocol description ;
    . in the validation phase : a **debugging oriented simulator** gives all facilities to experiment and debug the ESTELLE specification with a set of various simulation strategies ;
    . in the implementation phase : a **code generator** produces an early version of the aimed software in a classical programming language and an **implementation motor** allows the produced software to be integrated and to run within the target processor ;

  – to propose an open environment whose architecture is designed to integrate prototype tools from any origin through an **intermediate form** of the ESTELLE source (common data structure of all components of the environment) ;

  – to verify the **interest of ESTELLE** for existing industrial protocols taken in important application fields where there is a need for distributed architectures ; this phase of the project leads to the definition of evaluation criteria on the suitability and efficiency of ESTELLE and to the development of application examples selected for their complexity, their generality (in the application domain) and their importance [2] ;

  – to produce a set of **validated and usable protocols** selected in four important application fields :

    1. Computer Networks : ISO – TRANSPORT, SESSION, ACSE, ROSE, FTAM ;
    2. Industrial Systems : A flexible assembly cell, a power plant control system ;
    3. Telecommunications : protocols of layer 2 and 3 of the future paneuropean radiocellular network, a double call service in the ISDN framework ;
    4. Space communications : three layer 2 protocols COP0, COP1, COP2 from the CCSDS (Consultative Committee for Space Data Systems) ;

The following sections are dedicated to EWS description : general architecture of EWS (section 2), the editor (section 3), the translator (section 4), the code generator (section 5), the implementation motor (section 6) and the simulator (section 7).

2. GENERAL ARCHITECTURE OF EWS

EWS is comprised of five interconnected components whose functional relationships are the following (see figure 1) :

1. the **syntax oriented editor** constitutes the entry point of the software production line ; it is able to take into account an existing ASCII file or to support the user from the very first line ; the editor produces a syntax error free ESTELLE source on a ASCII file ;

2. the **translator** is in charge of computing an ESTELLE specification into an **Intermediate Form** file after semantics checks ;

3. the **C Code Generator** is in charge of producing C representations of all data structures and operations of the ESTELLE specification starting from the Intermediate Form informations ; the produced C code is available on ASCII files and is consistent enough to be compiled using the **ESTELLE primitives library** ;

4. the **implementation kernel** uses the C generated code and provides ESTELLE runtime primitives library and extra features for communications with the host machine to run the ESTELLE specification ;

5. the **debugging oriented simulator** allows interactive experimentation of the ESTELLE specification ; all objects previously produced for a given specification are involved to provide the use of an attractive interactive debugger :

. the **C generated code** is the basis for the specification execution (after compilation and biding with the existing simulator object code),

. the **Intermediate Form** provides symbolic informations to the user,

. the **ESTELLE ASCII source** is used by a "read only" version of the editor whose manipulation is combined with simulation features.

All the components are integrated within an **interactive monitor** which is in charge of verifying the consistency of the intended manipulations.

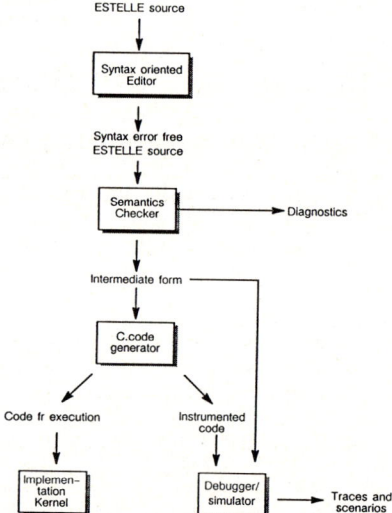

Figure 1 : General architecture of EWS

3. THE SYNTAX ORIENTED EDITOR

Syntax oriented editor is a very powerful editor for producing and maintaining ESTELLE source texts. It offers the advantages of an advanced screen oriented editor combined with the concept of syntax directed editing [3].

The EWS editor takes advantage of the available computer resources in using its knowledge of the programming language to support the programmer at every moment. The user can enter text in a linear manner, as with a normal full screen editor. However, optional menus, adapted to the syntactic context, assist the user during insertion. Furthermore, the editor will constantly check the validity of the entered tokens without any need of explicit call to the checking mechanism.

The editing manipulations are based on lexical units grouped into syntactical units which in their turn are grouped into larger syntactical units. Lexical units are the most elementary components of ESTELLE. Examples of lexical units are names, numbers, operators, keywords ... The only elements that can be inserted, edited, selected, deleted, replaced, moved ... are lexical units and syntactical units. Amending of names (character level) is also possible. Removing of structures are made safe by use of the clipboard concept.

Units selections are available through the use of a pointing device (mouse); manipulation activations are accessed by both mouse and keyboard ; moving through the text is accessed by pointing on the scroll bar.

Program texts are automatically formatted and can be displayed with different levels of detail according to viewing strategies. In the default configuration the full text is shown on the screen ; by command, the user can asked the editor to skip all comments, to show only the ESTELLE syntactical constructions, only the pascal constants, types and variables declarations, only the ESTELLE transitions ...

A view of the EWS editor screen is shown on Figure 2.

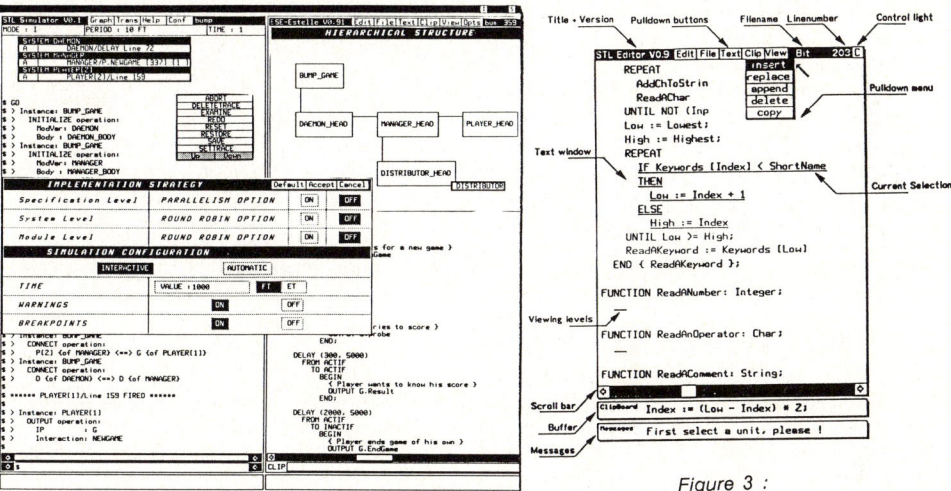

Figure 2 : EWS syntax oriented editor screen

Figure 3 : EWS debugging oriented simulator screen

The EWS editor combines the advantages of advanced text editors (full screen editor, use of a high-resolution display and use of mouse) and of syntactic directed editors (syntax error free editing, on-line help, automatic completing of the insertion when no non determinism is left, support of novice users).

As an advanced product, the EWS editor has been developed with the latest software technologies. In order to deliver a family of editors, it is constructed with the MIRA tool [4], offering flexibility in incorporating other languages. The internal data structure to represent the ESTELLE text is based on the abstract syntax tree concept. It involves a unique memory allocation scheme allowing both fast edition and efficient garbage collection.

4. THE TRANSLATOR

The **translator** [5] has three functions :

. as a **source analyser**, it delivers cross references on dedicated files,
. as a **Semantics Checker**, it delivers detailed diagnostics to the user,

. as a **Intermediate Form generator**, it translates the ASCII ESTELLE representation produced by the editor into a data structure suitable for further processings: this data structure (called the Intermediate Form of the ESTELLE specification [6]) is common for any other component of the production Iprocess; note that the Intermediate Form can be stored on a portable ASCII file.

The Intermediate Form is produced as a result of complete analysis (lexical, syntactical and semantical). Its contents preserves the semantic of the input specification (no loss of information) but its structure and access are more suitable for automatic processing. The Intermediate Form is the central point of EWS.

The entire translator is developed in portable C with the help of a compiler generation tool : SYNTAX [7].

5. THE C CODE GENERATOR

The purpose of the **code generator** is to translate an ESTELLE specification into a "C" program that can be executed according to ESTELLE semantics.

The same generated C programs can be monitored by both implementation and simulation motors : in that way, simulation can support a real validation of the code generated for implementation.

The C generated code is closely dependent of the organization chosen for implementation and simulation [8]. From both implementation and simulation motors, ESTELLE module instances are seen as independent "tasks" for which a specific context is generated. This context is comprised of :

. a set of data corresponding to the internal variables of the ESTELLE body,

. a set of data corresponding o the external variables and interaction points of ESTELLE module header,

. control data required by the motor to invoke the task evaluation or execution,

. a set of evaluation functions corresponding to all transition guards of the body,

. a set of execution functions corresponding to all transition statement parts of the body.

Note that the ESTELLE statements such as WHEN, OUTPUT, INIT ... are translated into a suitable sequence of calls to generic library C functions. All PASCAL parts of ESTELLE are translated into their corresponding C types or C control structures.

In case of simulation, extra instrumentation of the C code is processed in order to support debugging oriented features such as execution stop on breakpoints, read/write operations on internal variables of the ESTELLE module instances.

6. THE IMPLEMENTATION KERNEL

The **Implementation Kernel** forms the runtime library needed for the execution of generated C code in a real implementation environment. Primitives of this kernel enable implementation of an ESTELLE system (systemactivity or systemprocess) within a single task of the host operating system. This kernel provides C functions implementing all basic ESTELLE operations such as ATTACH, OUTPUT, FORONE ... [9].

The implementation motor is also comprised of an implementation motor which is in charge of handling scheduling between module instances. In addition, memory management routines are provided enabling manipulation of data buffers (assembling, fragmenting ...) without copying data. Moreover, primitives for communication with other tasks of the host operating system are provided, which enables to make the connection with the services provided on the implementation environment.

Implementation kernel has been designed to be as much as possible system independent. When migrating from one implementation operating system to another, only a few percentage of clearly located code has to be develop again (inter tasks communications and time clock management).

7. THE DEBUGGING ORIENTED SIMULATOR

The EWS **debugging oriented simulator** [10] allows an interactive execution of the ESTELLE specification.

Execution is possible to two major modes :

– full interactive mode i.e. each transition after each transition with opportunity for the user to select which transition has to be fired,

– automatic mode i.e. random selection of the transitions to fire during a simulation time denoted as simulation step and fully controlled by the user.

During execution of the transitions, traces to various specification objects can be made (variables, major state of module instances, contents of queues associated to interaction points) : any access to the specification objects is proposed on a symbolic mode (the user asks for objects with their ESTELLE identifier) while a set of Intermediate Form access functions ensure for consistency between ESTELLE symbolic objects and C real objects.

Execution can stop on breakpoints previously set by the user (inside transition statement parts or PASCAL procedures/functions).

Automatic backtracking on executed transitions can be performed as well as automatic replay. Executed transition sequences can be stored on files and replayed during further session.

All interactive features are fully supported by an advanced screen technology based on the use of pop-up menus, graphic displays, on-line commands interpretor. The EWS editor is used in a read only mode in order to support functions such as breakpoints selecting, automatic pointing on last fired transition, advanced pattern research.

A view of the simulator screen is shown on figure 3.

8. CONCLUSION

EWS has been developed under UNIX System V and is available on Appolo and Sun graphic workstations. All graphic and interactive features are supported by an integrated dedicated package which is in charge of the window management, the graphic displays and the input devices.

Next improvements of EWS will be related to separate compilation and separate code generation

With the concept of intermediate form, EWS constitutes an open environement on which additional tools such as verification tools, test sequences generator ... can be easily integrated to the existing toolset.

Sedos Estelle Demonstrator project is now standing its second phase in which EWS will be evaluated by partners. The main advances represented by the project are :

- the degree of integration of the tools to form a continuous production solution,
- their availability in a user-friendly environment,
- the degree of validation of the workstation through experimentation on significant number of applications,
- the illustration of the productivity increase in using ESTELLE formal description and using a dedicated workstation on actual examples.

Related documents

[1] : "Estelle - a formal description technique based on an extended state transition model", ISO DIS 9074 July 2, 1987.

[2] : "Example selection for ESTELLE Workstation evaluation", ESTELLE SEDOS Demonstrator, Esprit Project 1265.

[3] : "ESTELLE Syntax Oriented Editor : user's guide" , ESTELLE SEDOS Demonstrator, Esprit Project 1265.

[4] : "MIRA : A computer-aided software engineering tool, user's manual" EXPERT SOFTWARE SYSTEMS, Ghent, Belgium.

[5] : "Estelle Translator : Tutorial", ESTELLE SEDOS Demonstrator, Esprit Project 1265.

[6] : "Estelle Translator : The Intermediate Form", ESTELLE SEDOS Demonstrator, Esprit Project 1265.

[7] : "Syntax : manuel utilisateur" INRIA, France.

[8] : "Requirements for ESTELLE code generator", ESTELLE SEDOS Demonstrator, Esprit Project 1265.

[9] : "From ESTELLE formal semantics to ESTELLE Kernel implementation", ESTELLE SEDOS Demonstrator, Esprit Project 1265.

[10]: "Requirements for ESTELLE simulator", ESTELLE SEDOS Demonstrator, Esprit Project 1265.

An Object-Oriented Model For Estelle

Rachid Sijelmassi and Philip Gaudette

U. S. Department of Commerce
National Bureau of Standards
Institute for Computer Sciences and Technology
Gaithersburg, MD 20899, USA

Abstract. Estelle is a formal description technique for specifying communication protocols for Open Systems Interconnection (OSI). We present an object-oriented model for Estelle that is concrete enough to allow execution but abstract enough to remain concise and workable. A synchronization protocol captures the subtleties of parallelism in the semantics of Estelle and allows module instances to execute as if they were asynchronous. The remainder of the basic model defines objects that are very close to the entities defined by Estelle semantics. The model constitutes an unusually thorough specification of the output of a translator. It has been extended to allow appropriate observation and user control of the objects that simulate an Estelle formal description of a protocol. The combination of translation into the model and an implementation of the model provides a powerful tool for specifying, studying, and debugging distributed systems.

Keywords: OSI communication protocols, Formal description techniques, Estelle, Extended finite state machines, Object-oriented systems.

1. Introduction

Estelle is a formal description technique developed by the International Organization for Standardization (ISO) that has reached the status of Draft for International Standard [1]. Estelle has been designed to formally describe computer communication protocols for Open Systems Interconnection (OSI), although it is also appropriate for distributed systems in general.

We developed an object-oriented model for Estelle that provides a comprehensive treatment of the entities of Estelle syntax and semantics. Our model may interest users of Estelle as a source of insight into Estelle semantics, although this paper is not a tutorial. Implementors of Estelle tools should find the model instructive.

The Institute for Computer Sciences and Technology of the National Bureau of Standards supports the implementation and use of computer communication protocols for Open Systems Interconnection (OSI) developed by the International Organization for Standardization (ISO). In particular, the Formal Methods group is interested in specification techniques that allow the description of protocols with a precise formalism and in automated methods based on specifications to assist various protocol development tasks. Our model of Estelle and the various tools based on this model are part of that effort.

There are many ways to use a formal description in the process of validating, implementing, and evaluating a protocol, using automated tools. A validation tool can check for desirable properties of a protocol. A translation tool can generate interpretive code for a reference implementation or machine-oriented code as part of a protocol development environment. A test suite generator can produce a set of test cases that systematically exercise the protocol.

This work is a contribution of the National Bureau of Standards and is not subject to copyright.

Each of these potential tools is defined by a separate activation of a common representation of an Estelle Formal Description (EFD) that is the output of a translation. The explicit definition of this common representation constitutes our model of Estelle. The structure of the model must be powerful enough to represent all of the syntactic aspects of Estelle, although the model need not enforce syntactic constraints (since the translator can do so). This paper presents our model of Estelle and focuses on a single tool that is inherently useful and also demands a comprehensive treatment of Estelle semantics. This tool may be regarded as a simulation that is useful as a passive monitor or as a more active debugger.

Our model of Estelle is object-oriented [2]. Object-oriented languages are particularly suitable for defining programming and specification languages. Languages such as OBJ2 [3] are actually designed for that purpose. An object-oriented definition of a language represents the language constructs and concepts as classes of objects with a common structure and behavior. A program or a specification is defined by a set of objects of these classes. Their behavior is defined by their class membership and defines, in turn, the semantics of the program or specification. The ability to execute is the essential part of the behavior of the objects defined in the model. An EFD may therefore be activated simply by requesting the proper objects to execute. For the purpose of simulation, verification, or analysis, additional capabilities may be given to the classes of objects that constitute the model, providing the basis for an open-ended, yet integrated, set of tools dealing with separate aspects of Estelle specifications.

This paper describes a model of Estelle and some of the definitions of Estelle as motivation, but it is inadequate as an introduction to Estelle. Tutorial and detailed reference material may be found elsewhere [1][6][7][8]. Brief definitions of object-oriented concepts and terminology are given in this paper. Detailed information may be found in the ample literature on object-oriented systems, such as [2].

The next section describes the principles of a synchronization protocol that provides the proper global synchronization of module instances, even though the underlying behavior of the module instances is completely asynchronous. Section 3 outlines an object-oriented model that combines this protocol and the remainder of Estelle semantics. Section 4 describes a powerful tool for studying the behavior of Estelle specifications that results from integrating a syntax-directed editor with an object-oriented simulation environment.

2. The Synchronization Protocol

Systems are described in Estelle as hierarchies of communicating *module instances*. Module instances may be dynamically created and destroyed by certain other module instances. The behavior of each module instance is defined in terms of a state-transition model. Module instances communicate via interaction points, which are defined in terms of unbounded queues that allow exchange of *interactions* between module instances.

Synchronization in Estelle consists of constraints restricting the parallelism of transition executions in a hierarchy of module instances. In the formal definition of Estelle semantics [1], these constraints are expressed as global properties involving several module instances. Implementations of Estelle specifications using centralized schedulers may be directly derived from these rules [4][5], but this approach is inappropriate for distributed implementations. The problem can, however, be overcome by a synchronization protocol where every module instance behaves according to local synchronization rules.

The primary motive for defining a synchronization protocol is to define a model for Estelle that allows for arbitrary distributions of module instances of an activated EFD (i.e., module instances can be on different physical sites or systems). Therefore, the synchronization protocol is concerned only with the synchronization and communication aspects of Estelle semantics. This section describes a synchronization protocol that provides the behavior needed for this aspect of Estelle, even with the assumptions that no global information is available and that module instances run asynchronously.

The structure at any moment of an activated EFD may be described as a tree of module instances.

Initially, the tree contains a unique module instance, called the **specification** module. The tree's structure is dynamically modified as a result of the creation or destruction of child module instances by module instances already in the tree.

In Estelle, actions of module instances take place during execution of transitions. The execution context of a module instance is defined by a collection of variables and interaction points. Among these are exported variables and external interaction points of the module instance's children.

A transition of a module instance is said to be *enabled* under some conditions related to the current state of the module instance, to the values of the module instance's variables, to the values of the exported variables of its children, and to the interactions received by the module instance. Transitions have priorities attached to them. They may also be *delayed*. To be *fireable* an enabled transition must have the greatest priority among enabled transitions and, if delayed, must have been enabled for a specified period of time.

Module instances may execute only *offered* transitions, chosen from their fireable transitions. There are, however, other rules that govern the parallelism in an EFD, preventing in some cases the execution of an offered transition. The rules governing the creation of children, the parallelism of transitions, and the progress of time must be handled by the synchronization protocol. Two categories of transitions are distinguished for that purpose: initial and non-initial transitions.

The degree of parallelism for initial transitions is effectively nil. Initial transitions are executed by child module instances when they are created. The parent module instance is suspended while the child is executing its initial transition. The child's behavior is very limited until initialization is complete.

The degree of parallelism of non-initial transitions in an EFD tree is completely defined by the attributes of the module instances of the tree. Module instances may be unattributed or may have one of the attributes: **systemprocess, systemactivity, process,** or **activity**. Module instances with a systemprocess or a systemactivity attribute are called *subsystems*.

Distribution of attributes over a tree is partially dictated by syntactic nesting rules, in such a way that the following rules hold.
- The root of the tree is either an unattributed module instance or a subsystem.
- Unattributed modules may have only other unattributed modules or subsystems as children (immediate descendents).
- Attributed module instances may have only processes or activities as descendents (at any level of nesting).
- Systemactivities and activities may not have processes as descendents.

Unattributed module instances are inactive, meaning that all their transitions are initial. Therefore, executions of non-initial transitions take place only in subsystem subtrees. The part of an EFD tree composed of unattributed module instances and subsystems becomes static once the root of the EFD ends its initialization.

The behavior of any subsystem subtree may be decomposed into execution cycles characterized by the following rules.
- A module instance may not execute its offered transition if any of its ancestors has an offered transition.
- One transition, at most, may be executed in a systemactivity's or an activity's subtree.
- All transitions that may be executed according to the rules above must be executed and completed before a new execution cycle starts.

Estelle gives a loose interpretation of the concept of time. The only constraint is that timers of delayed transitions of module instances within a subsystem are uniformly updated between two consecutive execution cycles [9]. Subsystems are therefore not synchronized with each other.

The external results of transitions must also be handled by the synchronization protocol. A module instance may have exported variables that are accessible to its parent. Conversely, the module instance may access its children's exported variables. Mutual exclusion of a parent and a child prevent them from concurrently assigning values to such variables. Value changes resulting from the execution of a transition of a parent or a child do not affect the other before the end of an execution cycle.

Interactions are initiated as a result of **output** statements applied to interaction points. Such interactions are, however, discarded if the interaction point through which they are sent is not properly linked to another interaction point. Two interaction points may be linked by a chain of *attachments* followed by a *connection* followed by a second chain of attachments. Both chains of attachments may be empty. Interactions sent at either extremity of the communication link are received and enqueued at the other, and are ultimately processed by a transition. The interaction points of a module instance may be linked by the module instance itself, or by its parent, with some restrictions. The communication link between two interaction points may be destroyed by disconnecting the two connected interaction points of the link. It may be retracted by detaching two of the attached interaction points. Attachment and detachment of interaction points cause transfers of interactions from the old extremity of a link to the new extremity.

Interactions sent by a module instance may be destined to module instances anywhere in the tree. Interactions destined to an internal interaction point of the module instance may be immediately delivered to their destination, whereas interactions destined to other module instances must not be delivered before the end of the transition execution. Interactions that remain in the same subsystem must be received at the beginning of the next execution cycle. Interactions sent to module instances in another subsystem may be received at the beginning of any future execution cycle of that subsystem.

The last external effect of executing transitions concerns the destruction of children. When a module instance MI releases a child, all the child's external interaction points attached by MI are implicitly detached before the child and its descendents are destroyed.

The rules and constraints presented so far may be enforced by an appropriate synchronization protocol based only on message exchanges between parents and children. The different aspects of the protocol are outlined in the remainder of this section. The complete definition of an earlier version of the protocol may be found in another report [10].

2.1. Initialization

When a module instance is created in an EFD tree, it selects and executes an initial transition. When that execution ends, if the module instance is not the root of the EFD tree, it sends an *end_of_initialization* indication to its parent.

At the end of its initial transition execution, an unattributed module instance that is the root of an EFD tree sends an *exec_request* to all of its children. An unattributed module instance that receives an *exec_request* from its parent forwards it to its children.

When a subsystem ends its initialization, it waits for an *exec_request* from its parent (if it is not the specification). Thus, all subsystems of an EFD start their first execution cycle after the root of the EFD ends its initialization.

2.2. Selection of transitions

Selection of non-initial transitions to be executed within a subsystem is based on authorizations to execute that are granted to module instances. The management of these authorizations in a subsystem subtree obeys the following rules.
 - The subsystem is authorized to execute at the beginning of every execution cycle. A subsystem subtree execution cycle ends when all transitions selected for execution end. If the subsystem executes a transition, it is the only module instance authorized to execute. If one or more children are authorized to execute, each will indicate *end_of_execution* when done.
 - A module instance that is authorized to execute and that has fireable transitions will select and execute one of them.
 - A module instance that is authorized to execute and that has no fireable transitions sends an *exec_request* to one or to all of its children, authorizing them to execute. Systemprocesses and

processes send an *exec_request* to every child. Systemactivities and activities send an *exec_request* to a child that has, or whose descendents have, fireable transitions (see below).

- A process or activity that was authorized to execute sends an *end_of_execution* indication to its parent when it ends the execution of a transition or when it receives an *end_of_execution* indication from every child authorized to execute.
- In order to determine if any child has fireable transitions, a systemactivity or an activity sends an *offer_request* to all its children and collects their responses (either positive or negative). An activity that receives an *offer_request* from its parent answers positively either if it has fireable transitions or if at least one of its children answers positively to one of its *offer_requests*.

To evaluate their set of fireable transitions, module instances have to update their delayed transition timers at every execution cycle, whether they are authorized to execute during that cycle or not. Estelle requires that time progresses monotonically in discrete steps, independently between subsystems but uniformly within every subsystem subtree. Therefore, at the beginning of every execution cycle, a subsystem determines a positive value, Δt, to be the time elapsed since the last execution cycle.

The increment of elapsed time is communicated to all module instances in a subsystem according to the following rules.
- A module instance MI sends *update_requests* with Δt to every child if any one of the following conditions is satisfied: MI is authorized to execute and has fireable transitions, MI is asked to offer and has fireable transitions, or MI receives an *update_request* from its parent.
- A process or systemprocess authorized to execute without fireable transitions communicates Δt to its children as a parameter of the *exec_requests* it sends them.
- Under similar conditions, an activity or systemactivity sends Δt as a parameter of *offer_requests* to its children.

2.3. External results of transitions

The Estelle statements that may influence other modules are those that assign values to exported variables, that connect, disconnect, attach, and detach interaction points, that output interactions, and that initialize and release children. The next few paragraphs describe the synchronization operations related to these statements.

Every parent module instance has a copy of the exported variables of its children. When a module instance executes a transition, it acts upon these local copies. These copies are updated with values received as parameters of *end_of_initialization* and *end_of_execution* received from a child. Conversely, a child's exported variables are updated at the beginning of every execution cycle, using values carried by the *exec_request*, the *offer_request*, or the *update_request* it receives from its parent.

The construction of Estelle communication links is such that they match the tree structure of EFDs. Therefore, interactions from a module instance to another module instance may be relayed by module instances on the tree path linking them. A module instance MI keeps track of all of its children's external interaction points as well as the links established by MI between these interaction points and either MI's interaction points or other children's interaction points. That information enables MI to decide whether a received or locally produced interaction must be kept in one of its interaction point queues, forwarded to its parent, or forwarded to a child. Interactions to be relayed to the parent may be temporarily stored in a queue called *Ascending_Int*; interactions destined to a child C are stored in a queue called *C.Descending_Int*. When a module instance appends an interaction to either one of these queues or to one of its interaction point queues, the action is referred to as *dispatching*.

To connect or disconnect two interaction points, MI updates the local information it keeps concerning their links. These interaction points may be internal interaction points of MI or external interaction points of its children.

To attach an external interaction point Ip1 to an external interaction point Ip2 of a child C (**attach Ip1 to C.Ip2**), MI updates the information concerning Ip1 and C.Ip2, extracts from the queue of Ip1 interactions to be relayed to C.Ip2 and enqueues them in C.Descending_Int.

To output an interaction Int on an interaction point Ip (**output Ip.Int**), MI dispatches Int according to the possible links established by MI between Ip and some other interaction point.

When a module instance MI detaches an external interaction point Ip1 (**detach Ip1**) previously attached to an interaction point C.Ip2, two cases must be considered. If the attachment was made during the current transition execution, MI extracts from C.Descending_Int and appends to Ip1's queue the interactions previously destined for C.Ip2. Otherwise, MI sends a *detach_request* to C, waits for a *detach_response* from C, and appends the received interactions to Ip1's queue. When a module instance MI2 receives a *detach_request* from its parent, the interaction point Ip2 concerned may or may not be attached. If Ip2 is attached to a child's interaction point C2.Ip3 (the only possible attachment), then MI2 sends a *detach_request* to C2, waits for its response, and sends a *detach_response* to its parent with the interactions received from C2 as parameters. If Ip2 is not attached, MI2 extracts from Ip2's queue the interactions to be sent back as parameters of a *detach_response* to its parent. Interactions are extracted from Ip2's queue based on parameters of *detach_request* primitives and on information carried by the interactions themselves.

To initialize a new child C with a specific body B (**init C with B**), MI creates C, waits for its *end_of_initialization* indication, and updates the local copies of C's exported variables with the received parameters.

To release a child C (**release C**), MI sends a *release_request* to C, waits for a *release_response* from C and dispatches the interactions received as parameters. When a module instance receives a *release_request* from its parent, it sends a *release_request* to all of its children, waits for their responses, dispatches the interactions received as parameters of these responses, extracts interactions from its own external interaction points queues, and appends them to *Ascending_Int*. The resulting contents of *Ascending_Int* queue are sent as parameters of its *release_response* to its parent.

Interactions temporarily stored by attributed module instances and destined to module instances not in their subtree are relayed along ascending paths of the tree as parameters of *end_of_execution* indications. At the beginning of every cycle, interactions temporarily stored by an attributed module instance MI and destined to a descendent are forwarded to the appropriate child C as parameters of the first synchronization message sent by MI to C (*exec_request*, *offer_request*, or *update_request*).

Once they are initialized, unattributed module instance only serve as interaction relays enabling communication between subsystems. At the end of every execution cycle, a subsystem sends the contents of its *Ascending_Int* queue as a parameter of an *ascending_indication* to its parent. When it receives a *descending_request*, it dispatches the received interactions. An unattributed module instance that receives a *descending_request* or an *ascending_indication* dispatches the received interactions and sends *ascending_indications* and *descending_requests* to its parent and children. However, these messages are only sent to module instances for which there are interactions to be forwarded.

In summary, the synchronization protocol dictates the following behavior. Separate subsystems run asynchronously and in parallel once they end their initialization. Unattributed module instances act as interaction relays between them. In every subsystem, an execution cycle starts with descending synchronization messages that convey remaining results of the previous execution cycle and authorizations to execute (to some extent). When executions end, ascending results are transmitted up to the module instances to which they are destined or to the module instances that are responsible for relaying them down the tree. Other messages resulting from execution of init, detach, or release statements may be interleaved with those implied by this general scheme.

3. Object-oriented definition of Estelle

The synchronization protocol presented in section 2 is the first and most difficult step toward an object-oriented definition of Estelle semantics. It allows a view of a module instance as an object that may be activated by sending it messages. That object may in turn send messages to other objects. In order to obtain a full description of Estelle semantics, this approach must be completed with the identification and behavioral description of all of the particular kinds of objects defined by Estelle. After a necessarily brief introduction to object-oriented concepts and terminology, this section presents the general structure of our object-oriented model for Estelle.

In object-oriented systems, the object is the basic concept. An *object* has a private memory that consists of references to other objects. It also has a behavior defined by a set of *messages* that it will answer and *methods* for processing each message it receives. The only way to use an object is to send it messages, and the response to a message is itself an object. Objects may also answer messages that induce changes in their private memory.

Objects with the same behavior are *instances* of the same *class*. To define a class, one has to define the internal structure of its instances, the list of messages they answer, and the actions taken when they receive these messages. Typically, the method for a message is defined in terms of messages sent to other objects. A class is itself an object that must answer messages to create new instances of the class. Hierarchical relationships may be defined between classes. When a class, SC, is defined to be a subclass of a class C, instances of SC can answer all messages answered by instances of C, although methods for these messages need not be the same.

Some classes of our model of Estelle are illustrated later in this section using conventions derived from Smalltalk [2]. Categories of related messages are introduced by a comment in italics. Each message is shown as a message template followed by a comment in quotes that describes the effect of the message. Message templates without parameters consist of a single word, the name of the message. Message templates with parameters consist of a series of words ending in colons alternating with formal parameter names. The words ending in colons, concatenated, uniquely identify the message. Formal parameters are not typed. However, in the methods associated with a message they may be expected to answer certain messages.

To define a model in an object-oriented manner, one has to define the hierarchy of classes, the class behavior, and the behavior of instances. A particular system that may be represented in the model comprises a collection of instances of those classes. The advantage of such an approach is a one-to-one correspondence between the classes of a model and the different kinds of components of the systems being modeled. New functions may be introduced by adding new messages. The model may also be extended with new classes of related objects. These extensions may use parts of the original behavior of objects, but must not alter the functions already described. These qualities are particularly helpful for our goal of a cohesive set of tools.

All of the objects defined in an EFD, as well as objects needed for the EFD activation, are represented as instances of three categories of classes: definition classes, declaration classes, and activation-actor classes. The structure of an object and its relationships to other objects are directly derived from the Estelle definition and semantics of the corresponding concept. Messages to classes allow the creation of specific definitions, declarations, or activation actors. Messages answered by the created instances define the behaviors of the equivalent Estelle concepts.

Definition instances capture necessary information about various entities defined in an EFD that are self-contained and remain unchanged during activation (e.g., types, functions, transitions). Messages answered by definition classes allow the creation of new definitions. The messages answered by these instances define the semantics attributed to the corresponding definitions. For example, ordinal types define ordinal operations and their relationships to each other; record types define the possible components of a value.

Declarations instances are similar, but also give rise to active objects during activation (e.g., variable declarations, interaction point declarations). A declaration instance, which corresponds to a particular declaration statement of an EFD, is the result of a creation message answered by some declaration class. Instances of declaration classes can answer activation messages. Different declaration classes define different kinds of declarations. For example, a variable declaration (an instance of class *VariableDeclaration*) may be activated simply by the message *activate*, whereas a value-parameter declaration (an instance of class *InParameter*) may not be activated without a value. The answer to an activation message is an instance of an appropriate activation-actor class.

Activation-actor instances describe objects created during activations of EFDs (e.g., typed memory spaces, interaction points, module instances). Instances of activation-actor classes refer to related definition objects during interpretation. For example, a typed memory space defining a set uses messages sent to its type to answer set operation messages; a module instance uses messages to its module body to determine enabled transitions.

To illustrate the three categories of classes of the model and their relationships to each other, consider an Estelle type definition of the form $T = V1..V2$, and the variable declaration $X:T$. T is naturally represented as an instance of the definition class *SubrangeType*. Subrange types are ordinal types and *SubrangeType* is therefore defined as a subclass of *OrdinalType*. A subrange type is defined by a host type, a lower bound, and an upper bound. This is represented by the following definition.

    SubrangeType *subclass of* OrdinalType
        instance variables: H_type, L_bound, U_bound,

In order to create specific subrange types (such as T), *SubrangeType* class must answer a creation message of the form

    class message
       subrangeOf: O_type from: L_v to: U_v

where O_type, L_v, and U_v are the arguments representing the host type, the lower bound, and the upper bound of the created type. If V1 and V2 are ordered values of a type Ht, the class *SubrangeType* can answer the message *subrangeOf: Ht from: V1 to: V2* with an object representing the type T.

As a type, T must enable the creation of typed memory spaces representing values of T. As an ordinal type, it must define, among other things, the successor of any value of type T. These two operations may be achieved by the instance messages

    instance messages
      instantiate
        "answer an uninitialized value"
      succ: v
        "answer the successor of v, or an error"

The variable declaration $V:T$ is represented as an instance of the class *VariableDeclaration*. A variable declaration is defined by a name and a type. It answers mainly activation messages, creating instances of the activation-actor class *Variable*. A partial definition of the two classes could take the form

    Variable *subclass of* Object
        instance variables: name, typedValue

    class messages
      name: aName typedVal: aTypedVal
        "answer a new variable whose name is aName and whose typed value is aTypedVal"

    VariableDeclaration *subclass of* Object
        instance variables: name, type

    class messages
      name: aName type: aType
        "answer a new declaration associating aName with aType"
    instance messages
      activate
        "answers a variable whose name is the instance variable *name* and whose typed value is obtained from the instance variable *type*"

The messages answered by these classes and their instances, including the constraints and descriptions of their comments, reflect the semantic behaviors of the Estelle objects modeled. The methods for these messages constitute an implementation of the underlying behavior, but other methods may be substituted without changing the fundamental model. In addition, the methods may reveal semantic relationships between different objects that are not shown elsewhere. An example is the following method for the message *succ* answered by subrange types.

```
succ: V
  ((L_bound ≤ V) and: (U_bound > V))
    ifTrue: [↑ H_type succ: V]
    ifFalse: [↑ error]
```

L_bound, V, and U_bound may be considered as values of the ordinal host type of the subrange type. This host type defines an order among its values. The boolean objects O1 = (L_bound ≤ V), and O2 = (U_bound > V) are therefore defined, and so is (O1 and: O2). If the result is *true*, the answer of the subrange type ST which receives the message is the successor of V, determined by the host type of ST. Otherwise, it is an error.

This example also shows incremental capabilities of the model that are due to its object-oriented style. The base type of a subrange type may be an instance of any class, as long as the instances of that class define an order among their values and answer properly the message *ord: V*. An early version of the model might not include, for instance, enumerated types. When enumerated types are integrated later on, subranges of them will automatically become available as long as their implementation meets the above conditions.

The information contained in an EFD may be completely represented in the model as a collection of instances of definition and declaration classes. Class creation messages provide an interface for translation of Estelle sources into instances of the model. This interface may be extended with instance information messages that allow, for example, type checking. Additional classes (the activation actors) and additional message interfaces for definition and declaration objects represent an interpretation of Estelle semantics. The semantic interpretation should be strict, in the sense that all syntactic and semantic rules of the formal definition of Estelle must be enforced either by the translator or by the semantic interpretation. Furthermore, the semantic interpretation should allow (i.e., implement) all behavior that is allowed by the formal definition of Estelle for any EFD.

However, it is possible to extend the behavior of the model without violating the strictness of the semantic interpretation. Such extensions may simply allow observation of the behavior of Estelle objects or may allow user control of decisions that are not fully determined by the semantics of Estelle. This kind of extension can provide the basis for a simulation environment with a sophisticated user interface, as presented in the next section.

With our the synchronization protocol, module instances may act independently of other objects according to local information that is frequently updated, so local and synchronization behaviors of module instances may be defined in the same terms. However, synchronization messages sent by a module instance to another module instance cannot be directly interpreted as messages in all object-oriented systems. In particular, in many object-oriented systems (including Smalltalk) a message is comparable to a procedure call, and the sender of a message is suspended until the method for the message terminates. In such an environment, synchronization messages will obstruct asynchronous behavior of independent module instances.

Full independence of module instances can be implemented, even in such an environment, by associating a service queue and a message handler with every module instance. Synchronization messages sent by a module instance A to a module instance B are enqueued by A in the service queue of B, allowing A to proceed. The message handler of B reports to B the messages received in the service queue. The message to enqueue synchronization messages and the message to report them to a module instance are object-oriented messages.

4. Extensions to the model for simulation

This model of Estelle has been implemented in Smalltalk [2] as a set of classes. A translator has also been implemented to create the necessary objects for a particular EFD. Furthermore, the model has been extended, for the purpose of simulation, in three ways that are not considered in the formal definition of Estelle semantics — the module instances created by an EFD may be distributed across a number of sites in a simulation of a distributed environment, module instances and other important

Estelle objects may be observed as selectively or as comprehensively as desired, and behaviors that are not fully determined by Estelle semantics may be controlled explicitly by the user if desired.

Our software combines the translator, the model, and the extensions into a powerful tool for studying protocols. Thorough simulations, with simple screen animation and behavior tracing, allow the user to understand very well the behavior of a protocol. Control functions allow the user to search for specification errors by controlling time and non-determinism and by leading an EFD simulation into any situation permitted by Estelle semantics. The tool is known as WISE, for Workstation for Integrated Study of specifications in Estelle. The principal capabilities of the tool are presented in this section.

4.1. Translator

The translator consists of a syntax-directed editor created using the Cornell Synthesizer Generator [11][12]. The Cornell software is based on two levels of attribute grammars. The heart of the matter is an abstract syntax that describes a family of structures called *terms* that are constructed from smaller terms. The abstract syntax categories correspond very closely to the nonterminal symbols of the defining grammar for Estelle in [1]. Attributes attached to the terms carry context-sensitive information and enforce constraints.

An EFD is represented at all times by a consistently-attributed term tree. This structure can be edited in several ways, including replacement of one term by another term with a related structure, term transformation requested by command, or parsing of a textual fragment of an EFD into an appropriate term.

By design, the terms described by the abstract syntax resemble the objects of the classes in the basic model. Thus, it is straightforward to traverse the entire term for an EFD and to produce the necessary instantiation messages. These messages can be then interpreted by an executing Smalltalk model as initialization code to create an instance of the model. Then the simulation can begin.

Furthermore, the same process can be applied to smaller terms. In this case, a revision to a part of the EFD is translated into a related sequence of revision messages intended for an executing simulation. As these revisions are processed, some objects will become obsolete and subject to garbage collection. The simulation may then continue executing, with modified objects. This power of editing with immediate execution is, of course, risky but nevertheless useful for debugging. This capability has not been implemented, although the Smalltalk environment would not prevent it.

4.2. Distributed environment simulation

New classes enable the definition and simulation of distributed environments. A distributed environment is composed of instances of a class named *Site*. Each site has an independent clock, a message router, and a message handler to communicate with other sites. A parent and a child on the same site communicate directly, whereas module instances assigned to different sites use site message routers and handlers to communicate.

Prior to the activation of an EFD, the user creates the sites of a distributed environment. Every site has its own library, resulting from the translation of an EFD source and containing the model's representation of that EFD. When a user selects a site and requests the activation of an EFD, the **specification** module instance is activated and assigned to the chosen site. The user is thereafter asked for the site of every module instance created by the execution of an **init** statement. A module instance may be assigned to any site, regardless of the location of its ancestors.

The user interface of every site, called a site *observer*, is a window (*see Figure 1*) made up of three subwindows: a subwindow A that shows the value of the site clock, a subwindow B that contains the item *E.F.D* and the list of module instances assigned to the site, and a subwindow C that displays information related to the item selected in B. The figure shows two sites of a distributed environment and a request to the user to choose a site for a new module instance. The user may select the *E.F.D* item to show the source code of the activated EFD or (as in the figure) the name of a module instance on the site to show general information about that module instance.

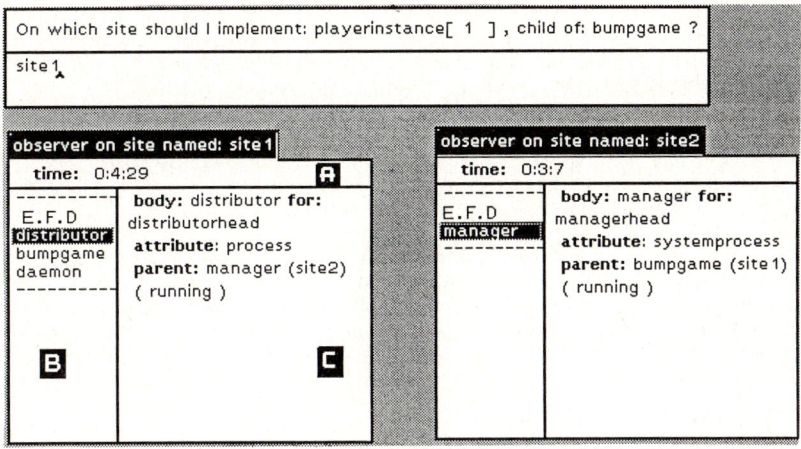

Figure 1. Implementation environment

A menu associated with every site observer appears when the user presses the appropriate button of the mouse *(see Figure 2.a)*. The clock of a site may be slowed down, accelerated, or interrupted to simulate slower machines or momentary loss of access to a site. Site failures may be simulated by selecting the *abort* item, which leads to the destruction of a site. A second menu, *(see Figure 2.b)* enables the user to open an observer on a module instance selected in the subwindow B of a site observer.

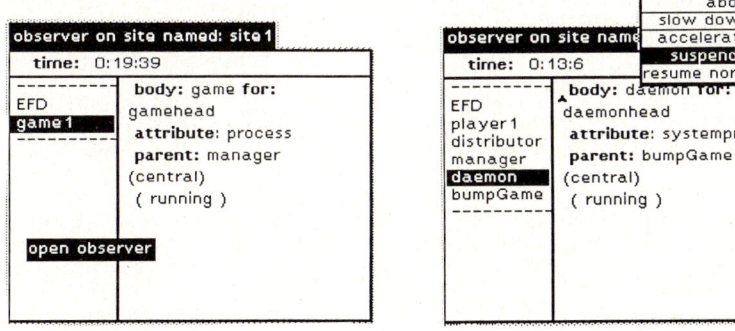

Figure 2.a. Site observer   Figure 2.b. Menu

4.3. Module instance interface

Similarly, module instance user interfaces are realized by *observers* and menus. However, it is not necessary to have an observer for every module instance, unlike sites. Module instance interfaces provide the user with different levels of functions, ranging from passive observation to a situation where the user acts as the body of a module instance.

4.3.1. Observation

Module instance observers *(see Figure 3.a)* are also divided into subwindows. Subwindow A displays the current major state and synchronization state of the observed module instance, along with its system status (running or interrupted). Subwindow B lists the elements of the context of the module instance: interaction points, variables, children, transitions currently delayed, module body, and module header. When an item of this list is selected, the corresponding information appears in subwindow C. Interaction points display their type, links, and queue contents. Variables display their type and value. A selected child displays its type (module header), its site, its interaction points, and its exported variables. Delayed transitions display their source code and the values of their timers.

The execution of a module instance may be traced using the *trace* item of the menu of subwindow B. When this item is selected, the contents of the trace are displayed in subwindow C *(see Figure 3.b)*. The trace is selective. Tracing may be enabled using a menu for various categories of events. The trace file may also be edited.

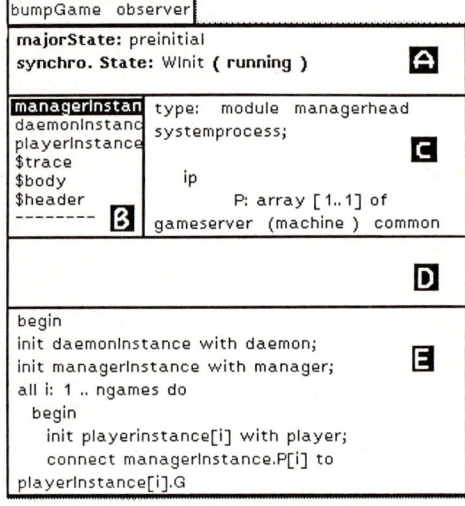
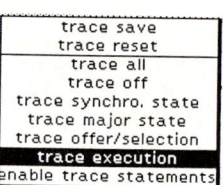

Figure 3.a. Module instance observer   Figure 3.b. Trace menu

Subwindow D is used by the observed module instance for warning and information messages to the user. When not used for other purposes, as described later, subwindow E displays the last transitions executed by the module instance. The number of displayed transitions is set by the user.

4.3.2. Speed Control and Debugging

A menu allows the user to modify the behavior of module instances *(see Figure 4)*. The user may slow down, accelerate, or interrupt the progress of a module instance, either to facilitate the observation or to cause some delayed transitions to become fireable. Speed control does not violate Estelle semantics, which do not specify the duration of operations. The user is allowed to define break points. Break point statements are comments interpreted by the translator. When a break point is reached, a message appears in the subwindow D, and the subwindow E is subdivided in four parts *(see Figure 5)*. A subwindow displays the stack, allowing the user to follow the chain of calls and retrieve the context

An Object-Oriented Model for Estelle 103

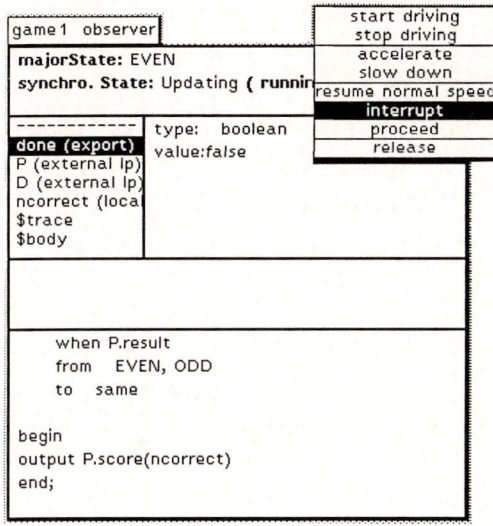

Figure 4. Module instance debugging

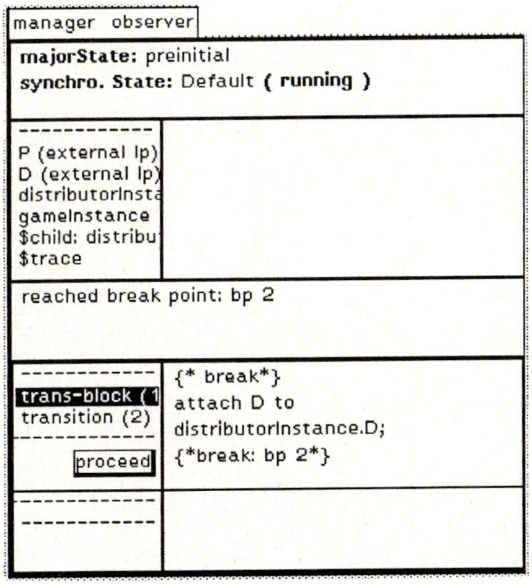

Figure 5. Break points

of actions that led to the break point. Other subwindows display the text and the local variables of the selected action. When a local variable is selected, its type and value are displayed in the last subwindow. A menu allows the user to proceed after inspecting the context. The same process is used when an error is detected, except that the erroneous module instance is aborted.

4.3.3. Driven Module Instance

The user may drive a module instance by resolving nondeterministic choices required by that module instance. Choices may occur during offered transition selections or child selections (for activities and systemactivities). To enter this mode, the user selects the *start driving* item of the menu *(refer back to Figure 4)*. Each time the module instance reaches a situation requiring a nondeterministic choice, the subwindow E of its observer is subdivided in two subwindows displaying the list of items to choose from and the text for the current selection *(see Figure 6)*. In the automatic mode, arbitrary choices are made by the simulation without user intervention.

Users may also control external bodies. In Estelle, a module body may be defined as *external*, meaning that it is provided elsewhere. Estelle semantics do not define a meaning for a specification that contains external bodies. An extension to our model allows a user to keep external bodies and simulate them. This extension may be used, for instance, to simulate the service of a lower layer when defining a communication protocol of the OSI model. Alternatively, of course, the EFD may be modified so that no external bodies remain.

The context of a module instance with an external body consists of external interaction points and exported variables (defined by the module header). Such a module instance always has two fireable transitions. A *null-transition* defines a transition with no effect. A *user-driven-transition* is interactively defined, if selected for execution. One transition is chosen to be offered in the usual nondeterministic way (randomly or by the user).

When a user-driven-transition is executed, the user is allowed to receive an input interaction through an external interaction point, assign values to exported variables, and build and output interactions through external interaction points. Note that these are the only actions with an external effect that may be taken by any module instance. After the user interactively *(see Figure 7)* completes a temporary definition of the external effects of a transition, the defined transition will be executed.

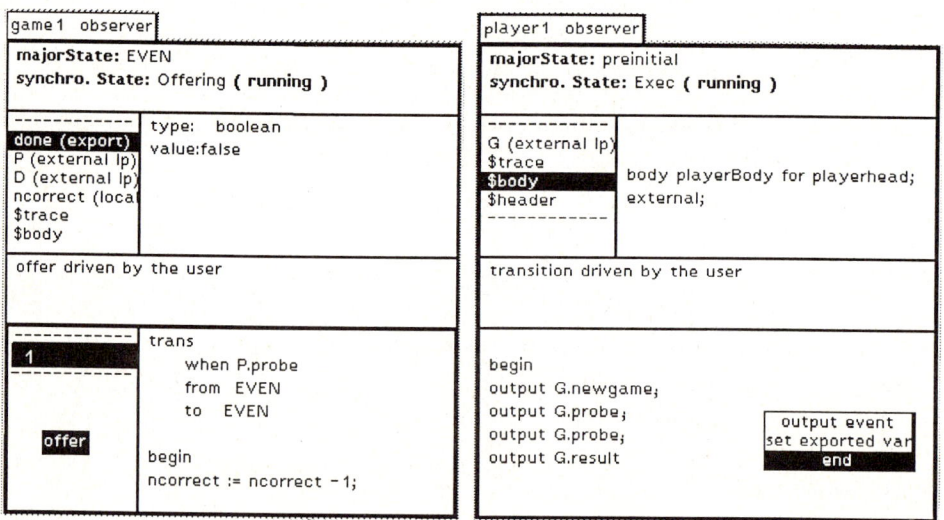

Figure 6. User driven module instance   Figure 7. External bodies

5. Conclusion

This model of Estelle is relevant to users of Estelle and to implementors of Estelle tools. It provides a comprehensive treatment of the entities of Estelle semantics that is concise and workable enough for human study, suitable for machine execution in an appropriate environment, and also suitable as a high-level specification for more efficient implementations. These qualities arise from the use of object-oriented methods.

The synchronization protocol demonstrates that the Estelle semantics of parallelism can be realized in a fully distributed environment with a modest number of local rules.

The object-oriented model provides a sound basis for a cohesive set of tools. The model was easily extended to handle distribution, observation, and control, which are sometimes troublesome issues. It should be possible to extend it in other ways for very different activations, such as validation of desirable properties of an EFD.

In combination with a syntax-directed editor for Estelle, the simulation provides a powerful tool for developing specifications of distributed systems, studying their behavior in simulation, and debugging protocols for communication within these systems.

References

[1] International Organization for Standardization (ISO). *Estelle: a Formal Description Technique based on an extended state transition model.* DIS 9074, July 1987.

[2] Goldberg, A.; Robson, D. *Smalltalk-80, The language and its Implementation.* Addison-Wesley, USA, July 1985.

[3] Futatsugi, K. et al. "Principles of OBJ2". *Proc. ACM Conf. on Principles of Programming Languages, 1984.*

[4] *User Guide for the NBS prototype compiler for Estelle.* National Bureau of Standards, Rep. ICST/SNA - 87/13, USA, October 1987.

[5] Ansart, J.P. et al. "Software tools for Estelle". *Protocol Specification, Testing and Verification VI, IFIP,* North-Holland, 1987.

[6] Linn, R.J. "A tutorial on the features and facilities of Estelle". National Bureau of Standards, USA, September 1986.

[7] Budkowski, S. et al. "Estelle, un langage de specification des systemes distribues". *Proc. 3ieme congres de nouvelles architectures pour les communications,* Paris, France, October 1986.

[8] Dembinski, P. "Estelle semantics". SEDOS Rep. 054, Paris, France, June 1986.

[9] Dembinski, P.; Budkowski, S. "Defining delays in a time independent model for Estelle". Rep. FDT 7581, Agence De l'Informatique, Paris, France, 1985.

[10] Sijelmassi, R.; Favreau, J.P. "An asynchronous model for Estelle and its applications". National Bureau of Standards, Rep. ICST/APM - 87/1, USA, January 1987.

[11] Demers, A.; Reps, T.; Teitelbaum, T. "The Cornell Program Synthesizer: A Syntax-Directed Programming Environment". *Communications of the ACM,* Sept. 1981, vol 24.

[12] Reps, T.; Teitelbaum, T. *The Synthesizer Generator Reference Manual.* Dept. of Computer Science, Cornell Univ., USA, 1987.

Specification of Object-Oriented Systems in LOTOS

Thomas Mayr
Technische Universität Wien
Institut für Angewandte Informatik
Argentinierstr. 8
A-1040 Wien, Austria
(mayr@slowhp.uucp)

Abstract

Object oriented system design is gaining acceptance in the field of distributed systems. There is a need to formally specify such systems. This paper examines how this can be done in LOTOS. An important concept of object orientation is subtyping because it supports the extendibility and reusability of specifications. The paper presents how subtyping can be integrated into LOTOS and how it affects the ACT-ONE part of LOTOS. A syntactic extension to make subtyping explicit in LOTOS is suggested.

Introduction

The concept of object orientation has become widely known by object oriented programming languages like Simula [Birtwistle73], Smalltalk [Goldberg80], and C++ [Stroustrup86]. In the object model, a system is regarded as a collection of communicating objects. The objects of the "real world" are modeled as objects in the language. This programming methodology supports the understandability of the system and encourages modular design and software reuse [Cox86].

In recent years object orientation has gained importance as a design methodology for distributed systems. For example most of the new developments in the field of distributed operating systems are based on an object model [TanRen85].

Another important example is the development of standards for distributed applications. Within the ISO [ISO88] the WG 7 for work on "Open Distributed Processing" currently develops a reference model for distributed applications. This reference model is based on the object model. Major contributions to this work are made by the ANSA project [ANSA87] and the ECMA.

As a consequence there is a strong need to formally specify object oriented systems. In this paper I present a way how object oriented systems can be specified in LOTOS [BolBri88].

The paper first explains the basic concepts of the object model and shows how these concepts can be expressed in LOTOS and ACT-ONE. In the second part of the paper the concept of subtyping is introduced. Subtyping is an important concept of object oriented system design since it supports the extendibility and reusability of specifications. It is shown how this concept can be integrated into LOTOS.

The Object Model: Basic Concepts

The elementary unit of structure in an object model is the object. The concept of an object is based on the idea of an abstract data type. Like an abstract data type an object offers a set of operations to the environment. The behavior of an object can be fully specified by describing the operations which are offered by the object. An object can be accessed only by invoking one of its operations.

An operation is the smallest unit of activity that has some meaning for the environment of the object. An object may offer its operations to the environment at one or more interfaces. Each interface provides a different set of operations.

A distributed system is modelled as a community of independent objects. Communication between objects is realized by operation invocations.

An operation invocation could be written in a programming language like notation as follows:

   x := [O <- Op-Name (Par-1, ..., Par-n)]

The operation identified by Op-Name with parameter values Par-1, ..., Par-n is invoked in object O. The result of the operation is assigned to variable x.

This is an operation which returns a result. There are also operations without response when information is transferred in only one direction.

An object type is a behavior specification that may be used to generate objects with a specific behavior. All objects of the same type have the same behavior specification.

Specification of Objects in LOTOS

The behavior of an object can be specified in terms of the operations it offers to the environment. Note that the behavior specification specifies the operations offered by an object as well as the set of allowed operation invocation sequences.

The behavior of an object can be specified in LOTOS as a recursive process of functionality noexit. An object type can be expressed as a process definition.

Let's for example specify the behavior of an object "printer" which models the real physical device printer.

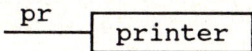

A printer P offers the following operations at the interface pr:

    [P <- begin (orig-id)]
    [P <- print (orig-id, line)]
    [P <- end (orig-id)]

As several objects may have simultaneous access to the interface pr, the different originator objects have to be differentiated by their orig-id, otherwise the printer would mix the output lines of the originator objects. Furthermore, the printer may sometimes become inactive when it runs out of paper.

The behavior of the printer can be specified as follows:

type Pr_op is
  sorts pr_op
  opns begin, print, end: -> pr_op
endtype

(* specification of sorts state and line has been omitted *)

process printer [pr] (s:state) : noexit :=

  (* operation begin *)
  pr!begin?id:orig_id; printer1 [pr] (id, s)
  where
  process printer1 [pr] (id:orig_id, s:state) : noexit :=
    (* operation print *)
    [s==ready] -> pr!print!id?l:line; printer1[pr] (id, s)
    []
    (* operation end *)
    pr!end!id; printer[pr] (s)
    []
    [s==paper_out] -> i; printer1[pr] (id, ready)
    []
    [s==ready] -> i; printer1[pr] (id, paper_out)
  endproc
endproc

An object of type "printer" offers only those operations which are allowed in a certain state.

This example shows that an object interface is best modelled as a gate in LOTOS. An object may have several interfaces, each interface realizes the connection to one or more objects with a compatible interface.

For example, a printer object might have also an interface m at which it offers some accounting information to a manager object:

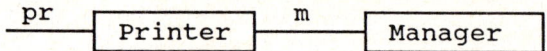

In our example all operation invocations are expressed as multi-part interactions. Though it is sometimes useful to differentiate between actively invoking an operation and passively receiving an operation invocation, this distinction is not made when specifying objects in LOTOS.

In general, an operation may consist of more than one interaction. As an operation is the smallest meaningful activity of an object, it is the designer who decides what is an operation. The notion of an operation is useful for the designer to decrease the complexity of objects. A typical example for an operation which consists of more than one interaction is a question followed some time later by a response:

calling object: called object:

    g!question!....;   g!question?....;
                                     h!consult!...?...;
    g!response?....;   g!response!....;

The delayed response could be caused by the fact that the called object itself has to consult another object before being able to respond.

So far we have only considered single objects which provide a certain behavior at their interfaces. In order to model an object system, all objects have to run in parallel and their interfaces have to be connected. This can be expressed in LOTOS with the parallel composition operator.

Let's consider a simple system consisting of two objects O1 [g1,g] and O2 [g2,g]. The fact that the two objects are composed into a system of two objects with their two interfaces g connected can be expressed in LOTOS as:

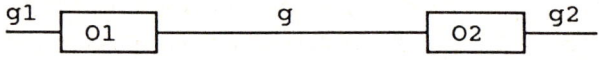

hide [g] in (O1[g1,g] |[g]| O2[g2,g])

In general, several objects may share an interface as it is the case in the printer example:

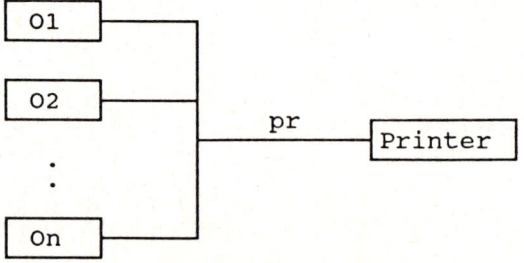

```
hide [pr] in     (( O1[pr] ||| O2[pr] ||| ... ||| On[pr] )
                 |[pr]|
                 Printer[pr] )
```

It is always possible to compose objects in a way that only two objects, the calling object and the called object, can participate in an interaction. Note that in the above specification an interaction at interface pr may take place only between the printer object and one of the originator objects. The originator objects O1, ..., On cannot interact among themselves over interface pr.

The number of objects in a system need not be static. Objects may terminate after some time and new objects may be created dynamically. An object has terminated when its behavior is equivalent to stop. Note that stop models object termination more properly than exit. Exit is used in the sequential composition of processes to transfer control from one process to another. There is no such transfer of control when an object terminates. Object creation is achieved simply by instantiation of the process which defines the object behavior.

Some objects allow certain operations to be executed concurrently. This can be expressed in LOTOS by using the operator ||| in the behavior specification of the object. Strictly speaking, the operator ||| realizes interleaving as opposed to true concurrency. By using the operator || the behavior of an object can be specified in the constraint oriented style [BolBri88].

The role of ACT-ONE

Since objects are based on the idea of an abstract data type (ADT) it seems straightforward to use the ACT-ONE part of LOTOS to model objects. However, the notion of an ADT in ACT-ONE differs from the notion of a type in the object model.

In the object paradigma an object is an ADT in the sense that it is completely specified by the operations it offers to the environment. The internal state of an object is hidden. In ACT-ONE the notion of an ADT is realized in the functional programming tradition where the operations are functions which are inherently stateless. An ADT in ACT-ONE defines value domains (sorts) and a set of functions (operations) ranging over these value domains.

A single object may be specified to a certain extent in the algebraic style of ACT-ONE. The behavior of the object will be described by modelling events as operations and by stating which sequences of operations lead to identical states ([JoMo85]). This approach raises some severe problems concerning partial operations (only total operations can be expressed in the initial algebra semantics of ACT-ONE) and concurrency (there is no explicit concurrency). These problems do not occur when objects are modelled as LOTOS processes.

It seems therefore reasonable to differentiate between the dynamic aspect of a system which models objects that persist and evolve in time and the static aspect of a system which models value domains and functions over these value domains. In [GoMe87] these two aspects are called the **object level** and the **functional level** of a system. In LOTOS the object level is best modelled with processes while the functional level can be modelled with ADTs in ACT-ONE.

The Concept of Subtyping

Besides data abstraction, another important concept of object oriented system design is subtyping. Subtyping allows for the hierarchical classification of object types by deriving a new object type from an existing type.

Essentially, an object type T' is a subtype of T (written T' <= T), if T' offers all the operations of T and the behavior of these operations is as in T.

T' inherits the behavior of T and can be regarded as an extension of T. This means that all operation invocation sequences that are allowed for T are also allowed for T'.

The subtype relation should be a partial order, i. e. the following laws of inequalities should be satisfied:

a) Reflexivity: T <= T
b) Transitivity: if T" <= T' and T' <= T then T" <= T
c) Antisymmetry: if T' <= T and T <= T' then T = T'

A formal definition of subtyping in LOTOS is given later in this paper. Some object oriented programming languages like C++, POOL [America87], and Trellis/Owl [Halbert87] support the concept of subtyping. However, subtyping in these languages is based solely on the syntax at the external interface of an object. This means that the subtype offers operations with the same name and compatible parameter types but the semantics of these operations may be different. What is needed is some form of behavioral subtyping to express the fact that the subtype inherits the behavior of the supertype.

Subtyping has two major advantages. The first advantage is that it supports the extendibility of a system. We could for example extend our system consisting of a printer object and several originator objects with a management object that communicates with the printer object over a separate interface m. For this purpose, we have to change the behavior of the printer object and add the new management object to the system.

The problem is how to make sure that the change of the printer object does not affect the communication with the originator objects. By requiring that the extended printer object is a subtype of the original object it is guaranteed that the additional operations for interface m do not affect the behavior at interface pr.

Subtyping allows for limiting the effect of change to the objects involved in the change. This is very important for the specification of complex systems because such systems usually have a long life time and therefore have to be adapted frequently to changing requirements during their life time. Subtyping for the purpose of system extension is also useful for the initial design of a system because one can use subtyping to move from a partial specification to a more complete specification.

The second advantage of subtyping is its support of the reuse of existing specifications. The idea behind the reuse of specifications is to have a library of general object types which are useful in many contexts. Unfortunately, these types are often too general to be useful in a specific context.

Subtyping solves this problem because one can define a subtype which inherits the operations of the library type but provides also some additional operations that are required for the specific context. For example, if we need a type which behaves like "printer" but has to provide the additional operation "line_feed", we just have to define a subtype of "printer" with the additional operation "line_feed".

Subtyping in LOTOS

As the LOTOS specification of an object type is a behavior expression we need a subtype relation for behavior expressions.

Though I have presented the concept of subtyping for operations, a more general approach is to consider subtyping w.r.t. interactions. Remember that an operation may consist of one or more interactions, and it is the designer who decides what is an operation. One can always regard a single interaction between two objects as an operation.

The subtype relation we are looking for is the relation ext (for extension) which has been defined in [BriScoStee87].

Definition:

The behavior expression P' is an extension of the behavior expression P (written P' ext P), if:

1) What is explicitly allowed according to P, is also allowed by P'
   (but more may be allowed);

2) What P' refuses to do after any sequence of interactions which is allowed according to P, can also be refused by P.

The first constraint states that P' offers at least those interaction sequences which are offered by P. The second constraint requires that P' may deadlock w.r.t. sequences that are accepted by P only if P may deadlock in the same situation.

The relation ext allows us to formally define the subtype relation for object types. A formal definition of the relation ext can be found in [BriScoStee87].

Definition:

Let P specify the object type T and P' specify type T', then:

$T' <= T$ iff P' ext P.

Let's consider some examples for subtypes (extensions) in LOTOS. For the moment, we do not deal with ACT-ONE types and gates. In this simplified model the events a1, a2, b1, ... in the following examples correspond to operations without parameters.

P1 := a1;a2;P1
 []
 b1;b2;P1

P2 := a1;a2;P2
 []
 b1;b2;P2
 []
 c1;c2;P2
 []
 c1;c3;P2

It is obvious that P2 is a subtype of P1 because the two constraints for the subtype relation are fulfilled. P2 has been constructed from P1 by adding two choice branches.

Process P3 is not a subtype of P1 because constraint 1 is not fulfilled. P3 does not accept an interaction sequence of the form <b1,b2,P1> but P1 does.

P3 := a1;a2;P3
 []
 b1;b3;P3

Process P4 is not a subtype of P1 because constraint 2 is not fulfilled. P4 may not accept an interaction sequence of the form <b1,b2,P1> while such a sequence is always accepted by P1.

P4 := a1;a2;P4
 []
 b1;b2;P4
 []
 b1;b3;P4

Similar to process P2, P4 has been constructed by adding a choice branch to P1. However, as opposed to P2, this has caused a nondeterministic choice for the operation b1 of P1. As a consequence, P4 is not a subtype of P1.

In order to reduce the burden of description it is important to be able to construct a subtype by adding some behavior to an existing type. A possible method to derive a subtype from an existing type will be briefly discussed later in this paper.

We have now defined a subtype relation for objects specified in LOTOS. According to [BriScoStee88] this subtype relation is a partial order, i.e. it is reflexive, transitive, and antisymmetric. Antisymmetry is satisfied in the following form:

P' <= P and P <= P' implies P' $=_{te}$ P.

The relation $=_{te}$ is the testing equivalence, i. e. P and P' cannot be distinguished by testing. For an observer the behavior of P cannot be distinguished from the behavior of P' and it is therefore justified to identify P with P'.

Furthermore, it is obvious that the subtype relation is a congruence w.r.t. the parallel composition. Since all objects in a LOTOS specification are composed with the parallel composition operator, this implies the following: if an object system is changed by replacing one or more objects by a subtype of them, then the overall behavior of the changed system is a subtype of the overall behavior of the original system. This means that the new system offers at least the behavior of the old system.

Possible Tools and Extensions for LOTOS to support Subtyping

In order to make the subtype relation in LOTOS explicit and to reduce the burden of description we need a syntactic extension to LOTOS which can be transformed by a precompiler to standard LOTOS.

For example, a subtype "enhanced_printer" of the type "printer" could be defined in a rather tentative syntax as follows:

process enhanced_printer is printer [pr] (s:state)

  where
  enhanced_printer1 is printer1[pr] (id:source_id, s:state)
    with
     [s==ready] -> pr!line_feed!id;enhanced_printer1[pr] (id,s)
endproc

The precompiler would have to expand this expression to:

process enhanced_printer [pr] (s:state) : noexit :=

  (* operation begin *)
  pr!begin?id:orig_id; enhanced_printer1 [pr] (id, s)

  where
  process enhanced_printer1 [pr] (id:orig_id, s:state) : noexit :=
    (* operation print *)
    [s==ready] -> pr!print!id?l:line; enhanced_printer1[pr] (id, s)
    []
    (* operation end *)
    pr!end!id; enhanced_printer[pr] (s)
    []
    [s==paper_out] -> i; enhanced_printer1[pr] (id, ready)
    []
    [s==ready] -> i; enhanced_printer1[pr] (id, paper_out)
    []
    [s==ready] -> pr!line_feed!id;enhanced_printer1[pr] (id,s)
  endproc
endproc

Because such a construction method does not ensure the subtype relation, the precompiler has to check whether the enhanced printer is really a subtype of printer. A first approach to solve this problem is to allow in the subtype only such choice branches which do not cause nondeterminism with a choice in the original type (see process P4 above). This topic requires some further study.

Extending ADTs

Building a subtype usually requires an extension of the ADTs in a specification. ACT-ONE allows to define new ADTs by extending and combining existing ADTs.

For example, the above specification of "enhanced_printer" requires the following extension of the ADT Pr_op:

```
type Enhanced_Pr_op is
   extending Pr_op
   opns line_feed: -> pr_op
endtype
```

This extension enriches the functionality of the ADT Pr_op without doing any harm to the old operations defined in Pr_op. When extending ADTs in order to provide the functionality needed by a new LOTOS subtype it is important to make sure that the semantics of the old operations are not affected. This is guaranteed if the extension defines new sorts and/or new operations which are not referred to in the old specification. It is not allowed to identify distinct data elements of the old ADT. In other words, the extension has to be consistent [EhMa85]. Note that in the above extension the keyword _extending_ ensures the consistency of the extension. This keyword is a syntactic feature of the algebraic specification language OBJ2 [GoMe87] and is not present in ACT-ONE.

The following example is an extension which is not consistent because it identifies "begin" with "end".

```
type Enhanced_Pr_op is Pr_op
   opns line_feed: -> pr_op
   eqns begin = end
endtype
```

Since all names are global in ACT-ONE, "begin" and "end" will be equaled in the whole specification and this may fundamentally change the semantics of the overall system. To restrict the use of ADTs to consistent extensions allows for incrementally extending the functionality of existing ADTs without compromising the semantics of old operations.

To summarize, one may change a LOTOS specification by replacing a LOTOS type by its subtype and by consistently extending ADTs.

The notion of Subtyping for ADTs

We have defined a subtype relation for LOTOS processes such that the subtype exhibits also the behavior of the supertype. If for example "enhanced_printer <= printer" then an "enhanced_printer" is also a "printer". The subtype relation thus specifies a hierarchical classification of objects. A similar inclusion relation to specify a hierarchical classification can be defined for sorts because there is a similarity between an object type and a sort insofar as both are notions for classification. An object type classifies objects and a sort classifies data elements.

A hierarchical classification of sorts can be specified with a subsort relation. To state for example that the sort "nat" (for natural numbers) is a subsort of sort "int" (for integer) we write "nat $\leq$ int". This means that a natural number is also an integer.

The formal basis for the notion of subsorts is an order-sorted algebra ([GoMe87], [Wegner87]) which is a many-sorted algebra with an ordering relation $\leq$ on its sorts. The subsort relation is interpreted as a subset relation and overloaded operations have to agree when restricted to the same subsorts.

The following example "number" from [Poigne84] is a specification of the sorts "nat" and "int":

<u>type</u> number <u>is</u>
  <u>sorts</u> nat $\leq$ int
  <u>opns</u> 0: -> nat
        succ, _-1: nat -> nat
        succ, pred: int -> int
        _+_: nat, nat -> nat
        _+_: int, int -> int
  <u>eqns</u>
        forall x, y: int, n:nat

        ofsort int
        pred(succ(x)) = x
        succ(pred(x)) = x
        pred(x) + y = pred(x+y)
        succ(x) + y = succ(x+y)
        0 + x = x

        ofsort nat
        0 -1 = 0
        succ(n) - 1 = n
<u>endtype</u>

Note that due to the subsort relation "nat $\leq$ int" all equations of sort "int" are also equations of sort "nat". ACT-ONE does not support the notion of subsorts. OBJ2 is an example of a language that permits the definition of subsorts.

The explicit definition of subsort relations in ADTs is not essential for object oriented LOTOS specifications. However, with subsorts the concept of hierarchical classification, which is characteristic for object oriented design, can be also applied to value domains.

Conclusion

LOTOS is well suited for specifying object oriented systems. The behavior of an object can be specified as a LOTOS process and gates are used to model the interfaces of an object. A system of communicating objects can be specified as a parallel composition of the respective processes.

Subtyping is a powerful concept to support the extendibility and reusability of specifications. It is possible to integrate this concept into LOTOS and to formally define the subtype relation. In order to make subtyping explicit in LOTOS, some syntactic extensions to LOTOS are suggested. These extensions could be resolved by a precompiler for LOTOS. The notion of subsorts which is similar to the notion of subtyping in LOTOS can be defined for ADTs. ACT-ONE however does not support subsorts.

Acknowledgements:

I would like to thank Helmut Kerner, Helmut Rainel, and the referees for their helpful comments.

References:

[America87]   P. America, "Inheritance and Subtyping in a Parallel Object-Oriented Language", ECOOP 87: European Conference on Object-Oriented Programming, AFCET 1987

[ANSA87]   A. Herbert, J. Monk (editors), "The ANSA Reference Manual", Release 00.03, Advanced Networked Systems Architecture, June 1987

[Birtwistle73]   G. Birtwistle et al., "SIMULA BEGIN", Studentlitteratur, Lund, Sweden 1973

[BolBri88]   T. Bolognesi, E. Brinksma, "Introduction to the ISO Specification Language LOTOS", North Holland, Computer Networks and ISDN Systems 14 (1987)

[BriScoStee87]   E. Brinksma, G. Scollo, C. Steenbergen, "LOTOS Specifications, their Implementations and their Tests", Protocol Specification, Testing, and Verification, VI; North Holland 1987

[Cox86]   B. Cox, "Object-Oriented Programming: An Evolutionary Approach", Addison-Wesley 1986

[EhMa85]   H. Ehrig, B. Mahr, "Fundamentals of Algebraic Specification 1", Springer Verlag 1985

[Goldberg83]   A. Goldberg et al., "Smalltalk-80: The Language and its Implementation", Addison-Wesley 1983

[GoMe87]   J. Goguen, J. Meseguer, "Unifying Functional, Object-Oriented and Relational Programming with Logical Semantics", Research Directions in Object-Oriented Programming (editors: B. Shriver, P. Wegner), MIT Press 1987

[Halbert87]   D. Halbert, P. O'Brien, "Using Types and Inheritance in Object-Oriented Languages", ECOOP 87: European Conference on Object-Oriented Programming, AFCET 1987

[ISO88]   ISO/TC97/SC21/WG7 N2510, "Working Document on Topic 4 - System Modelling - March 1988 Version"

[JoMo85]   M. Joseph, A. Moitra, "Algebraic Specification Of A Communication Scheduler", TAPSOFT 85, LNCS 185, Springer Verlag 1985

[Poigne84]   A. Poigne, "Another Look at Parameterization using Algebras with Subsorts", LNCS 176, Springer Verlag 1984

[Stroustrup86] B. Stroustrup, "The C++ Programming Language", Addison-Wesley 1986

[TanRen85]   A. Tanenbaum, R. Van Renesse, "Distributed Operating Systems", Computing Surveys, Vol. 17, No 4, December 1985

[Wegner87]   P. Wegner, "The Object-Oriented Classification Paradigm", Research Directions in Object-Oriented Programming (editors: B. Shriver, P. Wegner), MIT Press 1987

An Object-Oriented Model For ASN.1

Philip Gaudette, Steve Trus, and Sarah Collins

U. S. Department of Commerce
National Bureau of Standards
Institute for Computer Sciences and Technology
Gaithersburg, MD 20899, USA

Abstract. ASN.1 is a data definition language associated with the OSI Presentation Layer. Our model of ASN.1 provides an object-oriented definition of types and values, the most basic concepts of ASN.1. The model is both a target for syntax-directed translation and an input to several tools for working with ASN.1. One tool allows evaluation of an abstract syntax in ASN.1 by providing a collection of transformations of values. Some difficult problems of ASN.1 tools, such as macros, are also discussed.

Keywords: Abstract Syntax Notation One (ASN.1), OSI communication protocols, protocol specification, Presentation Layer, Object-oriented.

1. Introduction

Abstract Syntax Notation One (ASN.1) is like *War and Peace*, more often mentioned than read. But it can't be ignored because a vital part of application layer protocols for Open Systems Interconnection (OSI) [1] is specified in ASN.1. Protocol entities at the application layer exchange complex data objects; presentation layer entities convert these machine-dependent structures into octet strings for transfer by the lower layers. To specify the interface, the structure of all possible application data objects and a machine-independent means for encoding those objects must be defined. For OSI application protocols, those definitions are written in ASN.1.

This paper is not a tutorial on ASN.1 (some tutorial material is available [2]). Instead, it describes a model of ASN.1, a basic framework of objects and their relationships capable of carrying the full information content of a valid ASN.1 source text and capable of using that information in practical computations. We assume some familiarity with the ASN.1 standards [3] [4] and some experience with the notation.

The model itself merits attention as an abstraction of the concepts of ASN.1. With techniques from object-oriented programming and syntax-directed translation, the model becomes a design for a set of ASN.1 tools. Those who are developing standards with ASN.1 components or applying the standards, especially for prototypes, may find that the tools are useful. Those who are developing other tools based on ASN.1 should find the model instructive.

The Institute for Computer Sciences and Technology of the National Bureau of Standards supports the implementation and use of computer communication protocols for Open Systems Interconnection (OSI) developed by the International Organization for Standardization (ISO).

This work is a contribution of the National Bureau of Standards and is not subject to copyright.

In particular, the Formal Methods group is interested in specification techniques that allow the description of protocols with a precise formalism, and in automated methods based on specifications to assist various protocol development tasks. Thus, we have developed software that is flexible enough for several different tasks rather than efficient enough for production use.

Section 2 describes the basic design for a cohesive set of tools, which is based on syntax-directed translation and object-oriented activation of the translator output. Section 3 describes the subject of types in ASN.1, along with the model of types used in our tools. Section 4 similarly describes the model of values. Section 5 combines the model with specific operations in several related activations, each a tool for processing ASN.1 values. Section 6 discusses some difficult issues that arise in an attempted general treatment of ASN.1 but that aren't necessary to a basic understanding.

Most of the system described is implemented (exceptions are noted), using well-known tools and techniques [5] [6] in a Unix environment. Object-oriented programming is used as a design method, but the implementation consists of traditional source code in the input languages of yacc, lex, and C. All software is in the public domain, and will be available for distribution costs from the National Technical Information Service of the U. S. Department of Commerce. Contact the authors for details. The software is not supported at all.

2. Cohesive Set of Tools

The goal of our ASN tools project is an open-ended set of tools for working with ASN.1 source texts, based on a common foundation for cohesiveness and reusability. This goal suggests a design that divides the problem into translation and activation phases. The output of translation, which is also the input for activation, constitutes the common foundation.

Translation converts an ASN.1 source text, an *abstract syntax*, into an intermediate representation that captures relevant information in a form suitable for various computational tasks. (This meaning of the term abstract syntax should not be confused with its usage in the literature on compilers and translators.) Except for minor variations, the same intermediate representation and translator should serve for many different purposes.

Activation adds appropriate behavior to the translator output by providing procedures that use the intermediate representation as input, in effect as interpretive code. For example, an encoder/decoder activation, described later, implements the most common use of ASN.1. The exact nature of activation depends, of course, on the kind of software tool that is desired, and different activations may require very different procedures. To ensure generality, activations should not be constrained, except by the definition of ASN.1 itself.

The detailed specification of this intermediate representation constitutes a *model* of ASN.1. Various models of ASN.1 are possible in principle, but our goals dictate a single model that is comprehensive enough for an assortment of activations and close to the definition of ASN.1 for the sake of correctness. Our model is object-oriented [7] [8] in that the design itself and some of the notation used in design documents are object-oriented. However, the implementation of the model, translator, and activations uses more conventional techniques, mostly because we did not have an object-oriented programming environment available for this project. The same design method, used in a closely related project [9] but with an object-oriented implementation as well, was even more successful.

Unix is a trademark of AT&T.

In the model, entities defined by an abstract syntax are identified with *objects* of the object-oriented design. Each kind of entity that may appear in an abstract syntax gives rise to a *class* of objects in the model. A class is defined by the structure of memory to be reserved for objects of that class, by the procedures associated with those objects, and by creation procedures applied to the class itself to create new objects.

An object is an *instance* of a class, the result of invoking a creation procedure. It has a private memory, structurally identical to other objects of the same class but with its own distinct contents. Typically, the memory contains references to other objects or to machine-oriented objects such as integers that are available in the host computer. An object can respond to *messages* by invoking its procedures, defined with the class. Most object-oriented systems use some additional concepts, but these basic ones are sufficient for our purposes.

A *model instance* comprises a collection of objects, each an instance of one of the classes of the model. The object memories contain references to other objects of this model instance (or machine-oriented objects), giving the model instance an intricate internal structure.

The result of translation of a valid abstract syntax is a model instance. Naturally, the structure of the model instance closely resembles the structural relationships of the entities of the abstract syntax. Some parts of the abstract syntax, such as comments and typographic details, are deemed to be irrelevant to the desired activations. All other information in the abstract syntax must be captured by the objects themselves, by links among objects, or by machine-oriented data stored in the objects.

The model constitutes a detailed specification of the output of the translator; the translation of any valid abstract syntax must be an instance of the model. For the sake of simplicity or regularity, however, the model may be too permissive, allowing instances that do not correspond to a valid abstract syntax. The translator provides the necessary enforcement in these cases. In combination with the tools of syntax-directed translation [5], the model is an excellent framework for semantic analysis and generation of interpretive code.

Moreover, the model provides a cohesive foundation for a set of activations. A model instance is activated by sending a message to a selected object to request some appropriate behavior. The object responds by invoking its procedures, which typically involve further messages to object references stored by the primary object to request more detailed behavior. The net effect of all of the messages can be a very complex computation that, nevertheless, retains the cohesiveness of the underlying model.

With these concepts in hand, our model of ASN.1 can be described in terms of its classes. Activations can be described as procedures applicable to these classes, along with combinations of the procedures into useful tools.

3. Model of Types

The heart of ASN.1 is a notation for complex types. To work with a source text in ASN.1, our software first converts all of the type definitions of a set of modules into an internal representation of types — the objects described below. These objects can then be used to process values of the defined types, which is the important activity for protocol implementations.

An abstract syntax written in ASN.1 consists primarily of a collection of *type* definitions, each of which assigns a *type reference* name to a type denotation of some kind. Such a reference name can be used to indicate the denoted type, perhaps as part of the denotation of a more complex type. These type definitions, along with some other definitions, are packaged in a distinct name space as an ASN.1 *module*. A complete abstract syntax may consist of several modules.

A type denotation specifies the structure of a collection of *values*, the values of that type. Valid ranges, constraints between parts of complex values, and semantic interpretations of values are not specified, except in certain constructs and even then as a minor role.

The model provides *ModuleDefn* (module definition) objects, one for each ASN.1 module in an abstract syntax. A ModuleDefn object stores, among other things, a dictionary of type definitions. *Dictionaries* simply store a collection of associations between a name and an object, with procedures for adding a name-object association or for returning the object, if any, associated with a name. The type dictionary associates type references with the objects that model type denotations. The behavior of module objects is limited, mainly just allowing access to various defined objects. The collection of modules in an input is grouped as a dictionary in the *Input* object. A single object of this class, globally known, provides an entry point into the model instance that is shared by translation and activation processes. Its behavior, too, is limited to providing access.

ASN.1 provides about 20 *primitive types* that can be used as given or included as parts of more complex types. Some of the primitive types are BOOLEAN, INTEGER, BIT STRING, and various character string types. All primitive types are based on familiar data structures, although the type denotations include some features that can lead to rather elaborate types and values.

It also provides five main *constructor types* that denote the construction of a more complex type from one or more other types (not necessarily primitive). For example, the constructor
SEQUENCE { <element type list> }
denotes a sequence of values of each of the element types.

These type denotations, along with references to defined types, are modelled with appropriate subclasses of the *TypeDesc* (type descriptor) class, which is an abstraction of the common requirements of all type descriptors. Exhibit 1 shows the subclasses of TypeDesc and the corresponding ASN.1 types.

Objects of any subclass of TypeDesc may need to store a name, a default value, a list of tags, and a list of coercion calls. Names are used for a TypeDesc that is being assigned to a type reference, and also for named elements of structured types. A default value, or an OPTIONAL indication, may also appear for elements of SET and SEQUENCE types. Tags and coercion calls are discussed below.

There are specific subclasses for the major categories of ASN.1 types. For example, a *SequenceTypeDesc* models a structured type that is built up from a collection of elements or alternatives by storing a dictionary of TypeDesc parts. Their procedures iteratively process values of the appropriate parts in a manner that differs slightly among the three classes. Named and optional elements require some complications as well.

Several type denotations provide a kind of indirection, including references to defined types. For example, a *DefinedTypeDesc* object consists of necessary information associated with the type reference itself along with a link to a TypeDesc object for the type to which the type name referred. Behavior consists mainly of calling corresponding procedures using the link type.

References to primitive types are handled in the same way. With the indirection mechanism in hand, little additional information is needed to model each of the primitive types. *PrimitiveType* objects containing the extra details, basically the universal tag for each primitive type, are created during initialization of the translator. A reference to a primitive type results in the creation of a *PredefinedTypeDesc* object that is linked to some PrimitiveType object.

ASN.1 provides a *tag* feature that attaches extra information to some type denotations for use in encoding. Every type denotation has a tag of some sort, although the tags for built-in primitive and constructor types (the UNIVERSAL tags) are specified by the ASN.1 standard and do not appear in the abstract syntax itself. Tags are modelled as Tag objects containing the necessary fields. TypeDesc objects include a list of tags. Although it is rarely seen, a type denotation may have several explicit tags in ASN.1. If the universal tags are counted (as in this model), many type denotations have multiple tags. Thus, a list of tags is needed, rather than a single tag. The tag objects are used by encoding and decoding procedures applied to values, using TypeDesc objects to access the tags.

4. Model of Values

The standard for ASN.1 is concerned with several aspects of values, although not what they are or how they are used. Nevertheless, a concept of values and operations on values is implied by the standard. Our model for values includes an internal representation for values that is suitable for a variety of operations, along with transformations of internal values to and from other useful representations.

The standard describes one external form — value notations derived from type notations. For a complex type denotation constructed from the type notations provided in the standard, the corresponding value denotations constitute a small language — a notation for all values of the complex type. Such a value is called a "value in the defined notation" in the standard, but we use the more manageable phrase *print value*. In the standard and elsewhere, explanations of types often include examples of values to illustrate the types; these examples are print values.

The standard (in particular [3]) also includes Basic Encoding Rules, a collection of rules for

TypeDesc subclass	ASN.1 type
RepeatingTypeDesc	
SetOfTypeDesc	SET OF ...
SequenceOfTypeDesc	SEQUENCE OF ...
StructuredTypeDesc	
ChoiceTypeDesc	CHOICE { ... }
SetTypeDesc	SET { ... }
SequenceTypeDesc	SEQUENCE { ... }
IndirectTypeDesc	
SelectionTypeDesc	alternative < ChoiceTypeRef
DefinedTypeDesc	TypeReference
ExternalTypeDesc	ModuleRef . TypeRef
PredefinedTypeDesc	any primitive type

Exhibit 1. TypeDesc subclasses.

each kind of type notation that specifies an encoding in strings of octets for all value fragments of that type. Thus, a complex type denotation leads to a complex encoding scheme capable of representing any value of that type in a standard way. For well-designed types, the encoded octet strings can easily be decoded by a mechanism using knowledge of the encoding rules and the type. Following the usage of the OSI Presentation Layer, a value represented in this external form is a *transfer value*. The ASN.1 and Presentation standards specifically contemplate the future possibility of defining different sets of encoding rules, perhaps for purposes such as encryption or efficient transfer of specialized values, but only the Basic Encoding Rules are currently in use.

The Presentation Layer standard [10] [11] is largely concerned with processing transfer values. The form of values at the interface between the Presentation and Application layers is "a local matter". This interface can be implemented in several ways, but for our purposes it is appropriate to follow the OSI Reference Model as closely as possible. Consequently, we define a *local value* as a value of some type represented in data structures in any form that is appropriate for an application entity.

We also define *coercion* as a bidirectional mapping between local values in an application entity's data structures and values in the internal representation of our model. Our software provides a fairly general means to specify coercion, using non-standard extension to ASN.1. Function calls known as *coercion calls* may be embedded in type definitions to define the mapping of individual parts of a value, while the value structure determines the overall control flow of the mapping.

This design has an interesting property relevant to practical implementations as well as to research tools. An application entity can be allowed to represent its data in a manner most appropriate for its processing needs. The application data structures must be capable of representing the full range of expected values, and it must be possible to perform coercion in both directions, but no other constraints are necessary. Print values, transfer values, and internal representations of values are likely to be inappropriate for application layer implementations.

The model's internal representation of values allows very general operations on values, at the cost of memory space. Each fragment of a value is represented as a *ValueDesc* (value descriptor) object of some kind. Subclasses of ValueDesc define the objects that are created for parts of values, while the ValueDesc class itself defines the common behavior of all value parts.

Each ValueDesc object is linked to a corresponding TypeDesc object in a properly formed value. Typically, the value object contains specific value data while the type object contains generic information that is necessary for processing any value of that type.

Furthermore, the structure of value objects is complete in the following sense. In a complete value structure, if any two value objects are directly linked, then their corresponding type objects are also directly linked. It is quite feasible to omit some value objects that serve only as placeholders in a complete structure, because the missing links can be inferred from the remaining parts of the type and value structures. However, the requirement that value structures be complete simplifies operations on values.

Any ValueDesc object will be linked to a TypeDesc object, and each subclass of ValueDesc is constrained to link to certain subclasses of TypeDesc. The proper construction of these links is the essence of type checking in this model. Exhibit 2 enumerates the subclasses of ValueDesc and their relationship to TypeDesc subclasses.

ValueDesc subclass	Corresponding TypeDesc
ConstructorValueDesc	SetTypeDesc SequenceTypeDesc SetOfTypeDesc SequenceOfTypeDesc
TerminalValueDesc	PredefinedTypeDesc
IndirectValueDesc	
SelectionValueDesc	ChoiceTypeDesc
DefTypeValueDesc	DefinedTypeDesc
DefinedValueDesc	any TypeDesc
ExternalValueDesc	any TypeDesc
NamedConstValueDesc	PredefinedTypeDesc

Exhibit 2. ValueDesc subclasses.

A ValueDesc object contains several fields, most importantly a link to its type. A name field is used during parsing and type checking of print values, which often include named values or constants. Length and encoding fields provide temporary storage during the encoding of values. These objects must respond to messages requesting any of the transformations discussed in the next section. These procedures are not implemented as part of the ValueDesc class, however, because each subclass must implement them in its own way.

A *ConstructorValueDesc*, used for some constructor types, including SEQUENCE, must store a dictionary of value parts. A typical procedure consists of recursive calls to each part, with processing order and other constraints among parts determined by the type corresponding to the ConstructorValueDesc.

TerminalValueDesc objects store a lexical token appropriate for some primitive type. The type corresponding to a TerminalValueDesc is a PredefinedTypeDesc that links to a PrimitiveType and also carries information (such as tags) associated with the reference to the primitive type rather than with the primitive type itself. Procedures for these objects are based on tables of acceptable matches between primitive types and lexical tokens.

DefTypeValueDesc may be inserted in the value structure to ensure completeness by providing a level of indirection in the value structure that corresponds to indirection in the corresponding type structure. These objects typically result from some kind of type checking process rather than from parsing of a print value. That sort of indirection differs, of course, from references to defined values, which are captured as *DefinedValueDesc* and *ExternalValueDesc* objects. With values, references to named constants may also occur. Although syntactically similar to value references, named constants require somewhat different procedures and are represented by *NamedConstValueDesc* objects.

5. Free Value Activation

Our model can be activated in several ways. The main one described in this section leads to a useful tool for studying the collection of values defined by an abstract syntax. In the ASN.1 standard, values appear in modules but only for value definitions and default values. The standard does not explicitly describe any role for a value by itself, outside of any module definition, although such values are important in practice. We call them *free values* here, so the general tool for working with them is a free value activation.

The tool accepts standard module definitions as input, except that macros aren't implemented and coercion calls may be specified as an extension to ASN.1. Between module definitions, the tool accepts non-standard *free value commands*, or requests to perform transformations on values. The free values may use the type and value definitions previously encountered within modules.

Values may be transformed between the internal representation (ValueDesc structures) and any of four external representations. In keeping with the encode and decode transformations, a transformation to an external form is named with an "en" prefix and a transformation from an external form is named with a "de" prefix. Print values, transfer values, and local values have been mentioned already. In addition, the tool includes a means to store an internal structure on a file, as a *filed value*, for later retrieval. Exhibit 3 shows the representations and transformations.

For the "en" transformations, an existing value structure is traversed recursively to create some external representation of that value, using information contained in the corresponding types. For the "de" transformations, the value structure is constructed during a recursive traversal of the type structure, using information from an external value representation as well as type information.

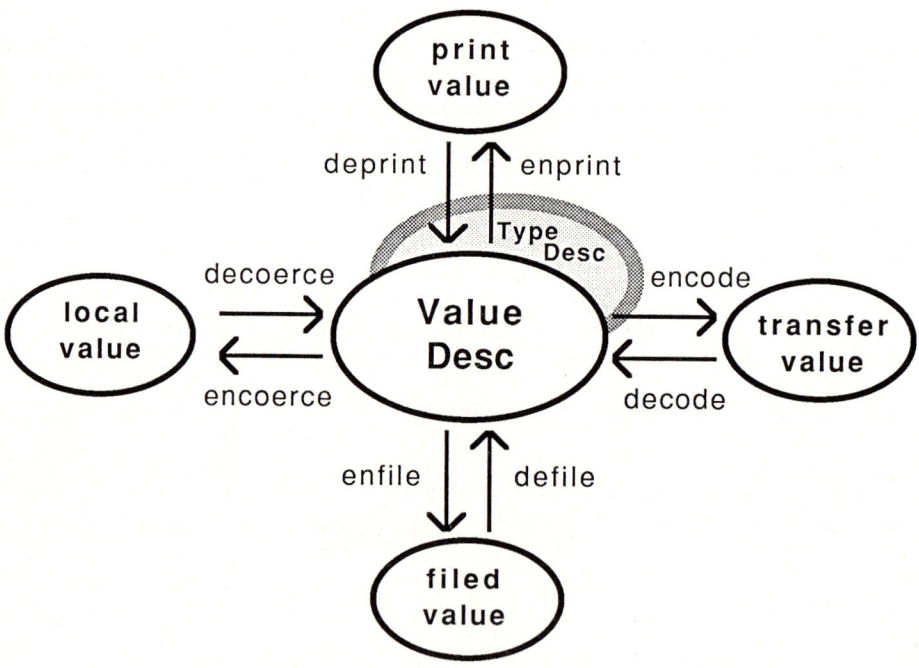

Exhibit 3. Free value activation.

Print values may be parsed and checked against their type (the deprint transformation), using basically the same grammar for values that is needed within module definitions. Conversely, a ValueDesc structure can be enprinted in the defined notation.

The encode transformation builds an encoded octet string (assuming Basic Encoding Rules) by traversing an existing value structure and referring to the corresponding types. It traverses the value structure twice. The first pass builds encoded fragments from the bottom up and determines the length of the encoding of all subtrees. (The encoding length of a subtree depends on the lengths of subordinates.) The second pass simply outputs the fragments from the top down.

The decode transformation builds a value structure from an encoded octet string (assuming Basic Encoding Rules) based on an existing type structure. It is responsible for building ValueDesc objects, storing pieces of the octet string in them, linking them to their corresponding types, and verifying the internal structure of the octet string in the process.

The encoerce transformation traverses an existing value structure. At each node, the corresponding type may include some encoercion calls. The implementation of a coercion call will often use the current value node as one of its arguments. The net effect of all of the encoercion calls for a value structure must be a complete data structure containing a local value. The encoerce transformation provides a control structure (largely dictated by the value structure being traversed) while the encoercion calls provide piecemeal mappings of value nodes into parts of the local value representation.

The decoerce transformation builds a value structure by traversing an existing type structure and using a local value to fill in parts of ValueDesc objects and to make decisions about the structure of the new value. Decisions are required to select alternatives of a CHOICE, to determine if an OPTIONAL element should be omitted, and to mark the end of a repeating type. The decoerce transformation builds much of the value structure by making decoercion calls when such decisions are needed. Other decoercion calls provide local data required for the terminal value descriptors.

Storing and retrieving filed values is actually an extension of a more general facility of this implementation. All objects can be filed, including type and module objects as well as values. With this facility, it is possible to take a snapshot of the internal memory of the system in the midst of translation, restore the memory from a snapshot, and continue translation with additional input. Moreover, a snapshot can be created by one program and used by another program that shares certain basic functions. Snapshots are used to store initial data for primitive types, to transfer a collection of type definitions from a translator to a different sort of activation, and to store filed values.

The free value activation provides all of these transformations in the guise of a simple command language. It is suitable for studying an abstract syntax, testing a system of coercion calls, and performing other evaluation tasks. Some of the same transformations can also be organized into a different activation that can be embedded in a larger system with a specific practical purpose. Once embedded, the transformations may be difficult to test, so we recommend a thorough evaluation with the free value activation.

For example, another group at NBS developed a test system for a protocol implementation that used a test suite represented as ASN.1 values. The abstract syntax defined a small test language with parameters defined in a separate module. Some of the parameters of a test were standard values from the underlying protocols, also defined in ASN.1, and some of these values were quite complex. A test case was denoted as a print value from the combined abstract syntax. A test case was processed in two steps. Its print value was first parsed and checked by the deprint transformation and the resulting internal value was saved (by defile). Later, in a separate process, these values were retrieved (by enfile) and decoerced into local values suitable for use by the rest of the test system. This division of effort, which was convenient for the test system implementors, is illustrated by the two dark arrows in Exhibit 4.

In another group, the transformations were reorganized into a prototype encoder and decoder for a protocol implementation. In this activation, shown in Exhibit 5, a local value may be decoerced and encoded into an octet string, or an octet string may be decoded and encoerced into a local value. This design for an encoder-decoder, particularly the notion of local values, may be useful for protocol implementors, but our software is more suitable for prototypes because it uses memory space extravagantly for the sake of generality.

6. Advanced Issues

The model and free value activation described above are sufficient for an interesting software tool. However, several topics from a comprehensive treatment of ASN.1 tools have been deferred to this section.

Forward References

Forward references are valid and routine in ASN.1. For example, an element of a SEQUENCE may consist of a type reference whose definition appears later in the same source text. Furthermore, circular references are also valid, so it may not be possible to rearrange the type definitions of a module to eliminate forward references.

Multi-pass translation methods are often used for such problems. This solution was

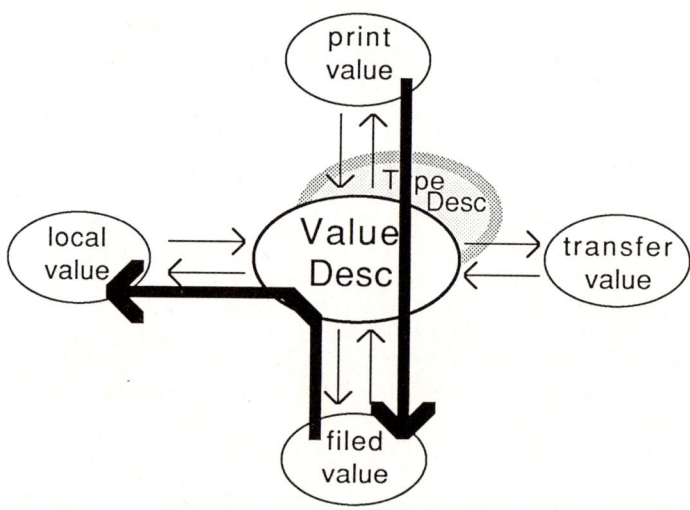

Exhibit 4. Test system activation.

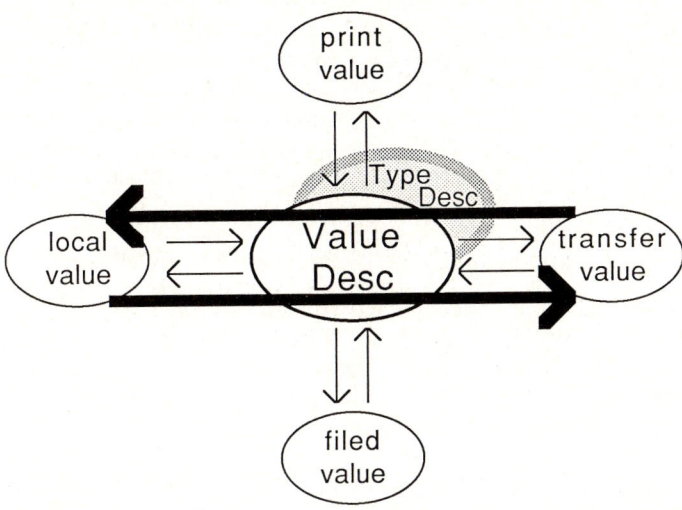

Exhibit 5. Encoder-decoder activation.

undesirable for our project because we are interested in incremental processing of an abstract syntax, with at least partial results before the complete input has been processed. Instead, our translator maintains a dictionary of objects that contain unknown references within each ModuleDefn object. When the end of a module has been reached, it attempts to resolve each of these unknowns, successfully in the case of a forward reference. The object with the unknown reference contains all necessary context information to complete the model instance. Any unresolved references for types indicate an error.

This simple scheme works fine for types within a module. External references to definitions in unknown modules can be handled by repeatedly resolving outstanding unknowns in all modules of an abstract syntax at the end of each module that is encountered. Current software doesn't handle references to unknown modules.

Unknown value references also present difficulties because, syntactically, value references and uses of named constants are identical. However, all such references within a module can be resolved in one of two ways: by normal resolution of a forward reference to a subsequent value definition, or by type checking that results in the detection of a named constant usage. Thus, it is reasonable to attempt to resolve value references, to refrain from indicating errors for unresolved value references, and then to check the types of all values encountered in a module (value definitions or default values). Type checking may result in many errors, including unknown value references. This procedure assumes that value definitions take precedence over named constants if identical names are used. Unfortunately, the ASN.1 standard is unclear on this point.

Finally, forward references to macro definitions are very hard, because the macro definition actually changes the input language that must be parsed. A separate pass to collect macro definitions may be the best solution.

Validation

An abstract syntax may be considered a formal description of a collection of values that serves as a specification used in implementing encoders and decoders for those values. The abstract syntax can also be regarded as a formal object in its own right, one which can be inspected to determine whether it has certain properties that may be required by constraints in the ASN.1 standard or may simply be desirable for well-behaved protocols. Some such properties can be validated automatically for ASN.1. Our tool provides only basic kinds of validation.

A number of obvious syntactic checks apply to ASN.1 modules: syntax and spelling, references to names that are never defined, multiple definitions of names within a context, distinct values for named constants, distinct numbers within a tag class, and appropriate use of tag classes. Syntactically valid values can be written (and parsed) without conforming to the appropriate type. Therefore, type checking is necessary for values that appear in modules and for print values that occur as free values.

Some tag rules ensure that transfer values are decodable. For example, the alternatives of a CHOICE should have distinct tags (from any mixture of tag classes, including the unwritten universal tags). If these rules are violated, ambiguous transfer values can result. It is also possible to determine whether transfer values can be decoded without regard to their type definition (because use of IMPLICIT has not obscured any essential universal tags), but this property doesn't seem very important in practice.

Ambiguities in the notation for print values arise frequently, but with less severe consequences than transfer value ambiguities. Type definitions that omit names for elements of SET, SEQUENCE, or CHOICE types are legal but may lead to print values that cannot be parsed. They may also lead to print values that can be parsed in principle, but only with elaborate lookahead techniques. Furthermore, names of element types, defined values, and named constants can be duplicated (although not within a particular category) in ways that lead to print value ambiguities.

Macros

ASN.1 macros provide a textual means for extending the notation of ASN.1, but they are quite different from text substitution macros found in some programming languages. Macros in ASN.1 are fairly difficult to process mechanically, so they have been omitted from most implementations of ASN.1 tools, including this one. This section describes the general problem and some limited facilities provided with our tool.

A macro definition provides distinctive type and value notation, and uses of a macro define new types or values using the extended notation. Thus, definition of a macro constitutes an extension of ASN.1 itself, while use of a macro is similar to ordinary type and value definitions except for the notation used.

A macro definition consists of two small (sometimes trivial) grammars of production rules, one for TYPE NOTATION and one for VALUE NOTATION. The syntax items of production rules may include type and value constructs from basic ASN.1, as well as literal strings and other notational devices. A macro use denoting a type consists of a sentence that can be produced from the TYPE NOTATION rules. A macro use denoting a value consists of a VALUE NOTATION sentence; in general, it may depend on the corresponding type.

The net effect of macro definition and use is a collection of ordinary types and values, albeit denoted in extraordinary ways. The resulting types and values may possess properties indicated by the special notation of their macros that are correlated with each other in a manner that is peculiar to macros. The use of a macro creates some types and values, and also expresses the constraints and relations among the newly created parts. The semantic correlations require a somewhat sophisticated reading of the abstract syntax, however, and may not be suitable in the general case for automatic processing. Even a general syntactic handling of macros is difficult. Each macro definition must lead, effectively, to a special parser for the newly defined notation. The full translator must be able to switch repeatedly among the macro parsers and the ordinary ASN.1 parser.

Macros can be eliminated by hand from an ASN.1 text, since the ultimate result must be ordinary types and values. The semantic correlations may be lost in the process and require handling in some other way. Some of the correlations can be preserved syntactically, however, as in the following example.

In a common technique, macro uses define a number of related entities, such as protocol operations or possible values for some field of protocol control information. Each use of the macro defines a distinct entity with a value reference name, an identifying code (often an INTEGER), an ordinary ASN.1 type that serves as an argument for certain uses of the entity being defined, and perhaps other arguments for other uses. In some other module, a protocol data unit (PDU) is defined as an ordinary type with, among other parts, an integer field for the identifying code and an argument field of type ANY.

The PDU may be used with a defined entity by filling in the identifying code and an argument of the appropriate type, as specified in the macro use that defined the entity. In effect, the identifying code and the argument type are correlated. Furthermore, the argument field of the PDU isn't really type ANY, but rather a choice among all of the argument types found in all of the uses of this particular macro.

It isn't difficult to identify these correlations and to rearrange the arguments of all uses of a macro into one or more CHOICE types, which can then be substituted for the ANY types of PDUs. However, this process will often lead to decoding ambiguities because the alternatives of the new CHOICE types might not have distinct tags. The ambiguities can be resolved because of the semantic correlations. The identifying code in the PDU, or some other external source, contains the information necessary to determine which alternative should be decoded, in lieu of a distinct tag.

Our tool provides a simple but non-standard mechanism, called pseudo-tags, for resolving ambiguities using such information. Each pseudo-tag is indexed by a small natural number and contains a tag number (easily implemented as integer arrays). A particular pseudo-tag contains the information necessary to distinguish a particular alternative.

For encoding, pseudo-tags are ignored. Their only role is in the decoding process. Before or during the decoding of a transfer value, each pseudo-tag may be set to a specific tag number. The value of that pseudo-tag may then be used, as if it appeared in the transfer value, to select the proper alternative of a CHOICE. In this way, pseudo-tags can play the role of distinct tags without introducing non-conformant transfer values.

7. Conclusions

Our object-oriented model of ASN.1 proved to be effective as a clear and simple foundation for several activations and as a target for syntax-directed translation. After some more activations have been developed, it should meet its objective of providing the basis for a cohesive set of tools.

In particular, the concepts of local value and coercion seem to be broadly applicable to ASN.1 users, including implementors of encoder-decoders for protocols. Although our internal representation of values may be too general for practical use, it can be readily adapted for better efficiency.

The free value activation has also been useful. As a means to evaluate an abstract syntax, it provides several features not always found in ASN.1 parsers. Our users wanted better validation capabilities, however. As a value processor, it has been very handy for parsing print values, building and inspecting transfer values, and preparing filed values for other activations.

Automatic or semi-automatic processing of ASN.1 macros is not easy. Further research, leading to a model like this one but capable of handling macros, is desirable.

References

[1] IEEE. "Special Issue on Open Systems Interconnection". *Proceedings of the IEEE*, vol. 71, no. 12, December 1983.

[2] Chappell, D. "A Tutorial on Abstract Syntax Notation One (ASN.1)". Omnicom Information Service 25, December 1986. Omnicom, Inc., Vienna VA.

[3] International Organization for Standardization Committee ISO/TC97/SC21. *Information Processing — Open Systems Interconnection — Specification of Abstract Syntax Notation One (ASN.1)*. ISO International Standard 8824, 1987.

[4] ISO/TC97/SC21. *Information Processing — Open Systems Interconnection — Specification of Basic Encoding Rules for ASN.1*. ISO International Standard 8825, 1987.

[5] Schreiner, A.T.; Friedman, H.G., Jr. *Introduction to Compiler Construction with Unix*. Prentice-Hall, Englewood Cliffs NJ, 1985.

[6] Aho, A.V.; Ullman, J.D. *Principles of Compiler Design*, Addison-Wesley, Reading MA, 1979.

[7] Goldberg, A.; Robson, D. *Smalltalk-80, The Language and its Implementation*. Addison-Wesley, Reading MA, 1983.

[8] Schmucker, K. *Object-Oriented Programming for the Macintosh*. Hayden, Hasbrouck Heights NJ, 1986.

[9] Sijelmassi, R.; Gaudette, P. "An Object-Oriented Model for Estelle". in this volume.

[10] ISO/TC97/SC21. *Information Processing — Open Systems Interconnection — Connection Oriented Presentation Service Definition*. ISO Draft International Standard 8822, 1986.

[11] ISO/TC97/SC21. *Information Processing — Open Systems Interconnection — Connection Oriented Presentation Protocol Definition*. ISO Draft International Standard 8823, 1986.

Modelling OSI in SDL

Ferenc Belina, Telelogic, Malmö
Dieter Hogrefe, University of Hamburg, Hamburg
Sebastiano Trigila, Fondazione Ugo Bordoni, Rome

This paper discusses how to model OSI in SDL, especially concerning the relation between different layers, and the concepts of service and protocol. It is shown that the OSI architectural concepts can be described in SDL in a straightforward manner, giving a precise meaning to these concepts.

1 Introduction

1.1 Explanation of OSI concepts

The OSI concepts used in this paper are defined in [1] and [2]. In this section an explanation is given of the key concepts, in order to make the paper more self-contained.

The conceptual model of a *layer service* uses the concepts *service provider*, *user* and *service primitive*. The service provider for a given layer is an abstract machine offering a communication facility to users in the next higher layer. The service is accessed by the users at *service access points* by means of service primitives, see fig 1.1. A service primitive can be used for connection management (connection, disconnection, resetting, etc), or be a data object (normal data or expedited data). There are only four kinds of service primitives:
- request (from user to provider)
- indication (from provider to user)
- response (from user to provider)
- confirmation (from provider to user)

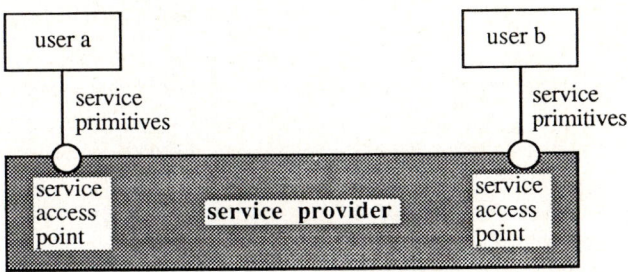

Figure 1.1 Model of layer service

A *service specification* is a way to characterize the behaviour of the service provider, both locally, stating legal sequences of service primitives transferred at one service access point, and end-to-end, stating correct relationship between service primitives transferred at different service access points. A service specification does not deal with the internal structure of the service provider; any internal structure given when specifying the service is just an abstract model for describing the externally observable behaviour of the service provider.

Except for the highest layer, the users of a layer service are *protocol entities* of the next higher layer, which cooperate in order to enhance the features of the layer service, thus providing a service of the next higher layer. The cooperation is carried out in accordance with a predefined set of behaviour rules and message formats, which constitute a *protocol*. According to this view, protocol entities of (N)-layer and the (N-1)-service provider provide together an implementation of the (N)-service provider (see fig 1.2).

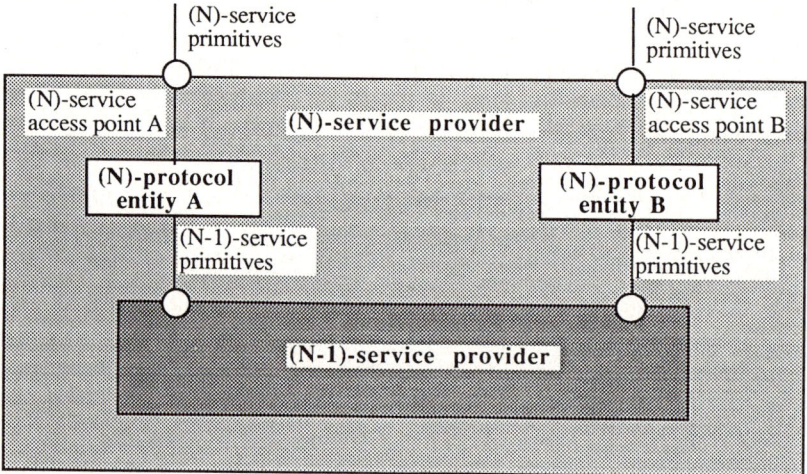

Figure 1.2 Implementation of the (N)-service provider

The implementation of the (N)-service provider shown in figure 1.2 may of course be much more complicated. For example there may be (N)-relay protocol entities which are not connected to any protocol entity of the (N+1)-layer. In this paper we do not consider such cases for the sake of brevity.

Protocol entities communicate by exchange of *protocol data units*. These are transferred as parameters of service primitives of the underlying layer. The sending protocol entity encodes protocol data units into service primitives, the receiving protocol entity decodes protocol data units from the received service primitives. A protocol is based on the properties of the underlying service provider. The underlying service provider may for example lose, corrupt or misorder messages, in which case the protocol should contain mechanisms of error detection and correction, resynchronization, retransmission etc, in order to provide a reliable and usually more powerful service to the next higher layer.

1.2 OSI architectural concepts in SDL

The OSI architectural concepts can be modelled in SDL in a number of alternative ways, mainly depending on what aspect should be emphasized. First a basic approach is described, then other approaches are outlined as variants of the basic approach. SDL is defined in [3], and a tutorial information can be found in [4].

In the examples the graphical syntax of SDL is used as far as possible. Note, however, that for practical reason some information that is required by the syntax rules may be omitted, or represented by a series of dots (...), which is, of course, not part of the syntax.

2 Basic approach

2.1 Service specification

A service specification for layer N can be modelled in a straightforward manner as a block *Nservice* containing two processes *NserviceA* and *NserviceB*, see figure 2.1.

In figure 2.1 the users of this service are in the environment of the system and can be considered as processes, capable of communicating with the system on terms of this system. Note that the representation of the users and the area filling in figure 2.1 is not part of the syntax, these are included only to aid understanding.

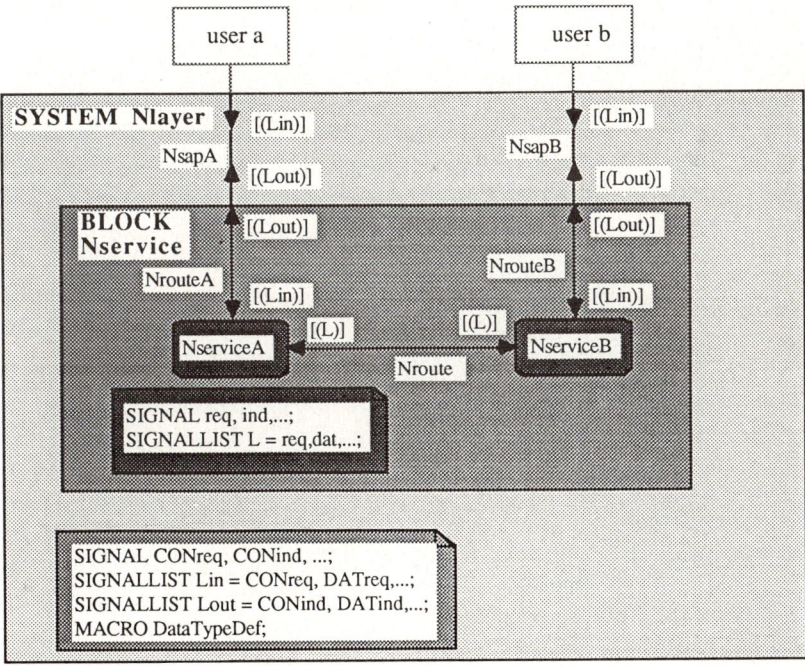

Figure 2.1 (N)-service specification, represented in SDL

A service access point is represented by a channel (*NsapA*, or *NsapB*), conveying signals, which represent service primitives. A signal may carry values of the types given in the signal description. The data type descriptions (other than for predefined data) are contained in the remote *macro* description *DataTypeDef*, which is omitted here as irrelevant for the purpose of the present discussion.

Of course, in the most general case there may be more than two processes involved in the service specification. An example can be found in [5]. We will here consider only two processes, one for each service access point, for the sake of brevity. The following discussion applies, however, also to the case where there are more processes for a service access point.

The figure shows some examples of signal definitions. As suggested by some signal names, a connection oriented service is assumed. In the case of a connectionless service, a great deal simplications can be made. However, this case will not be treated further, for the sake of brevity.

Both local and end-to-end aspects of a service specification are dealt with here. Local behaviour is expressed independently by the processes *NserviceA* and *NserviceB*. These processes communicate with each other by signals (*req,ind,...*), which are internal to the block and are conveyed on the signal route *Nroute*. End-to-end behaviour is expressed by the mapping (performed by each process) between service primitives and internal signals on *Nroute*. The processes *NserviceA* and *NserviceB* are mirror images of each other. The reason for having two of them, instead of only one, is to faithfully model a possible collition situation in the service provider.

Non-deterministic behaviour is an inherent feature of the service provider, because it may refuse connection attempts and may disrupt established connections on its own initiative. How this can be modelled in SDL, see [5] and [6].

Please note that the description of the block *Nservice* contains only *reference* to the processes *NserviceA* and *NserviceB*; these processes are described by *remote descriptions*, placed outside the block description, and not shown here, because they would force the reader to pay attention to features necessarily specific of a given service.

2.2 *Service implementation*

The service implementation corresponding to figure 1.2 is modelled by adding a block substructure to the block *Nservice*, see figure 2.2.

In the *system diagram* (the upper part) of figure 2.2, a block substructure reference (a block symbol containing the name *Nservice implementation* of the block substructure) has been introduced. The description of the block substructure is given in a remote *block substructure diagram* containing three blocks: *NentityA*, *NentityB* and *N_1service*. The first two blocks represent (N)-protocol entities, while the block *N_1service* represents the (N-1)-service provider. The description of *N_1service* is analogous to the description of *Nservice*, and is not shown in this figure (being a remote description).

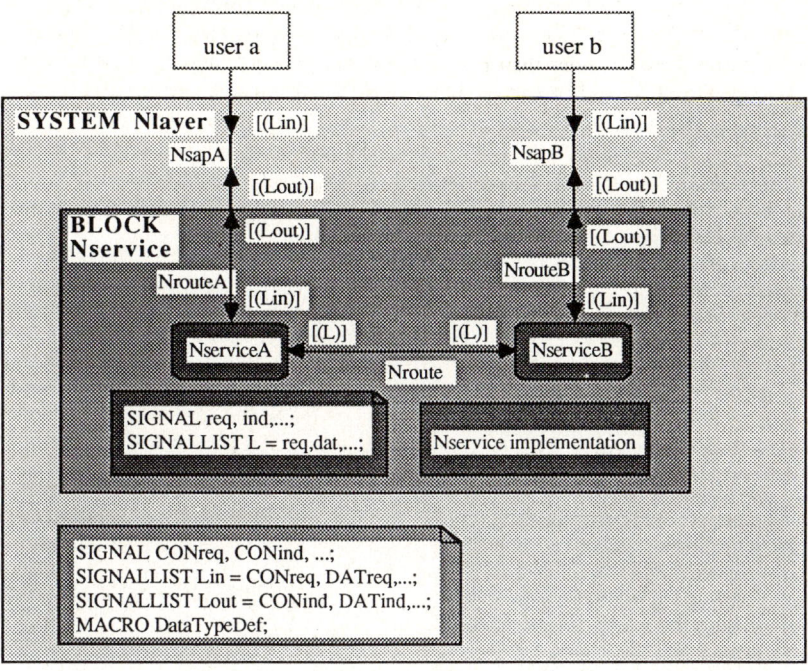
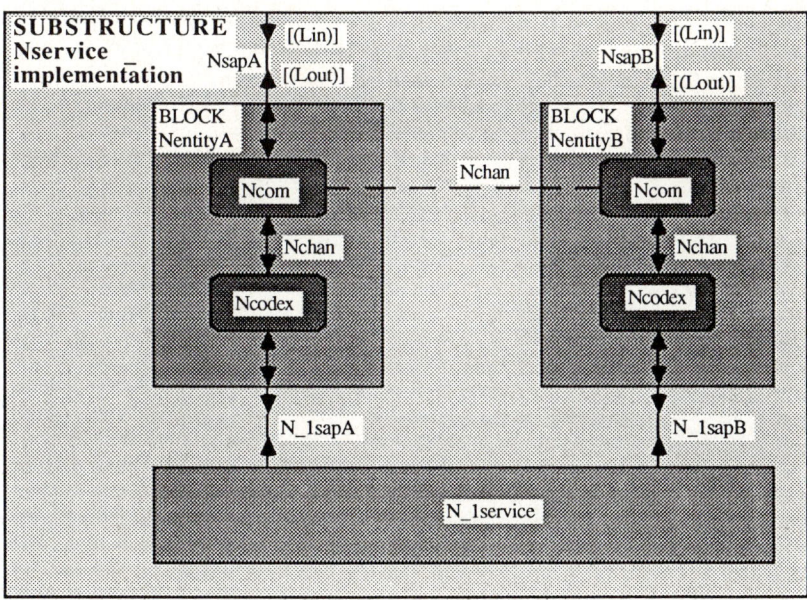

Figure 2.2
(N)-service specification and implementation, represented in SDL

A protocol entity block contains one or more processes, depending on the characteristics of the protocol. In this case two processes have been chosen, *Ncom* and *Ncodex*. Process *Ncom* handles the sending and reception of protocol data units, while process *Ncodex* takes care of the transmission of protocol data units using the underlying service. Conceptually, the processes *Ncom* communicate directly via an implicit channel *Nchan* (conveying protocol data units), but in reality they communicate indirectly via processes *Ncodex* and the underlying service provider.

3 Alternative approach using channel substructure

This approach is obtained from the basic approach in figure 2.2 by grouping the processes differently, introducing the real channel *Nchan* and using channel substructure, see figure 3.1. The channel *Nchan* conveys protocol data units, indicated by the signal list *Npdu*. This approach emphasizes the protocol view and the horizontal orientation of OSI.

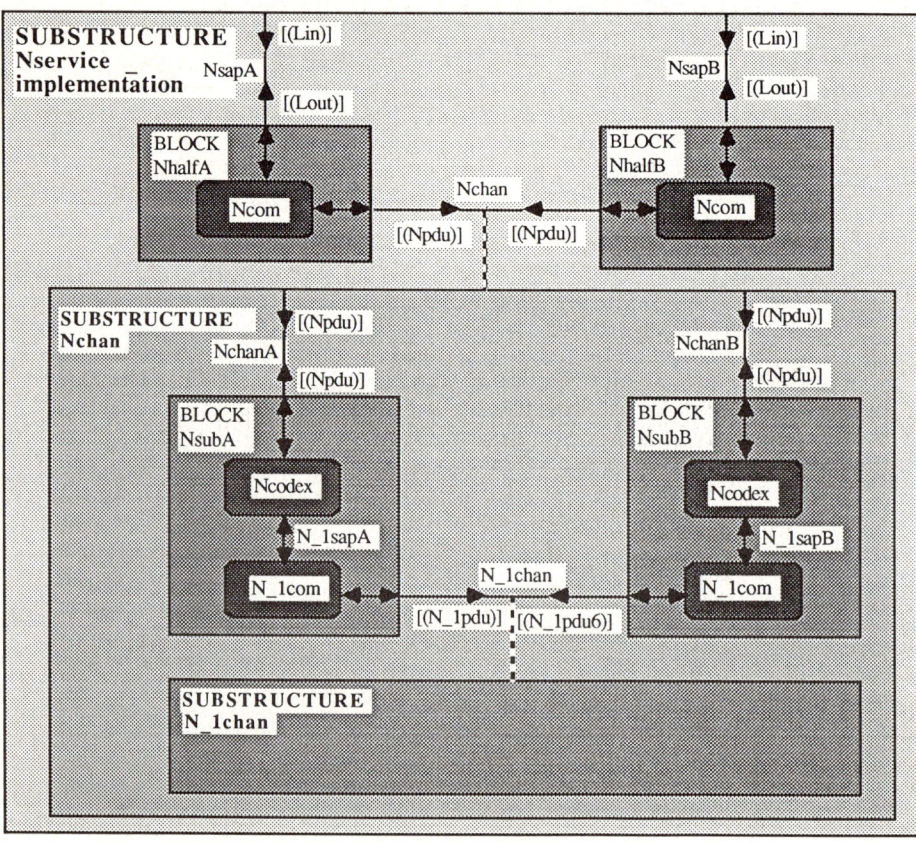

Figure 3.1 The protocol view of OSI

Note that in this approach the blocks within a channel substructure do not represent protocol entities, and overlap two adjacent layers. The service primitives are hidden in these blocks, and are conveyed on the signal routes N_1sapA, N_1sapB, N_2sapA, N_2sapB ect. However, the chosen highest (N)-layer must be treated separately, as indicated in the figure. Note also that the system diagram (upper part of figure 2.2) is not affected by this approach.

4 Symmetrical OSI architecture

When the OSI architecture is symmetrical, that is when entities of the two sides of the OSI architecture are mirror images of each other, the descriptions of these entities are identical except for the entity name. The common description can be given only once by using a macro, see figure 4.1. In this figure only the block diagram of the block *Nservice* in figure 2.1 is shown.

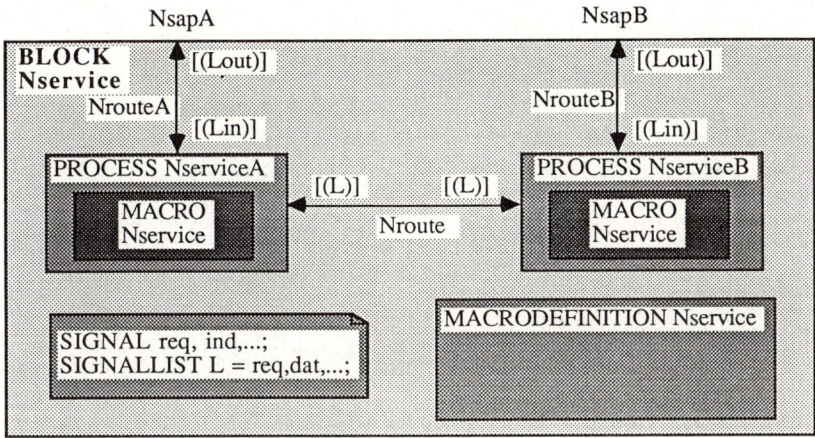

Figure 4.1
Using macro to represent a symmetrical OSI architecture

An alternative approach is to represent only one side, see figure 4.2, which is a modification of the system diagram in figure 2.1. The channel *NsapB* has been replaced by the channel *Nchannel*, conveying the internal signals L. These signals are now on the system level, and their descriptions have been moved accordingly. Note that this approach cannot be used in combination with channel substructuring (shown in figure 3.1).

5 Conclusions

The OSI reference model is widely used within both ISO and CCITT for the specification of services and protocols. This reference model has been defined in a natural language. SDL and other formal description techniques are used more and more extensively for the same application area. This paper shows how the OSI reference model itself can be formally described in SDL, in addition to the description of individual services and protocols.

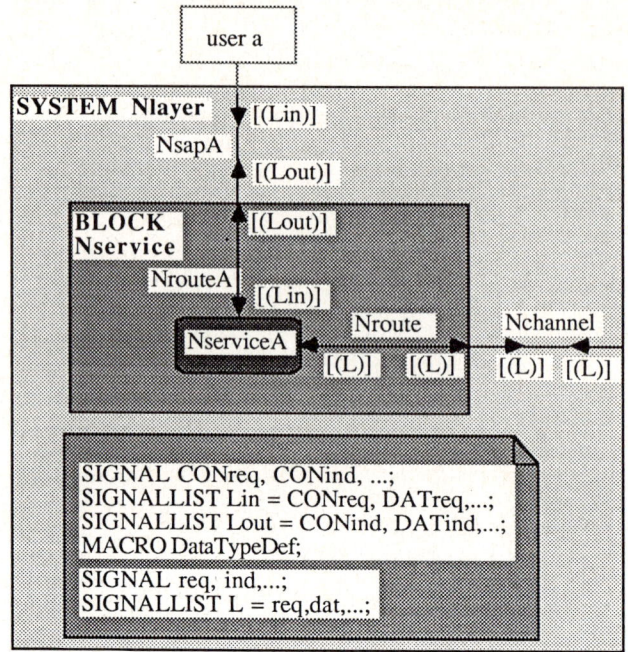

Figure 4.2
Representing only one side of a symmetrical OSI architecture

References

[1]   ISO TC97: *Basic Reference Model*, International Standard, ISO/IS 7498, 1984.
[2]   ISO TC97/SC21: *OSI Service Conventions*, Technical Report ISO/TR 8509, 1987.
[3]   CCITT Recommendation Z.100: *Specification and Description Language SDL*,
      COM X - R 15, 1987.
      Annexes A-F to Z.100, COM X - R16, R25-29,R 42.
      (These will be published in the Blue Book, Volume VI.20-24, ITU General Secretariat - Sales Section, Place des Nations, CH-1211 Geneva 20)
[4]   Belina F, Hogrefe D: *Introduction to SDL*, this volume.
[5]   Hogrefe D: *Protocol and service specification with SDL: the X.25 case study* (University of Hamburg report N° FBI-HH-B-134/88, Hamburg, 1988).
[6]   CCITT/ISO Manual: *Guidelines for the application of Estelle, LOTOS and SDL*, 1988.

GRAPHICAL VIEWS OF PROCESS-ORIENTATED SPECIFICATIONS

DW Bustard, AC Winstanley*, MT Norris, RA Orr & S Patel[†]

*Department Of Computer Science	[†]Software Engineering Division
The Queen's University of Belfast	British Telecom Research Laboratories
Belfast, BT7 1NN	Martlesham Heath, Ipswich, IP5 7RE
Northern Ireland	England

Process-oriented specifications are used to define the intended behaviour of concurrent systems. The main aim of this paper is to consider how graphics might be used to clarify the relationships among the various definitions which constitute such specifications and so make their meaning more apparent. The paper looks specifically at graphical representations for specifications expressed in the process-oriented language LOTOS but the general approach taken is relevant to other languages of this type including CCS and CSP. The various graphical representations that are discussed are intended to be particularly suitable for interactive observation at a computer terminal or workstation.

1. INTRODUCTION

A process-oriented specification (or indeed any system) is composed of distinct components which are related in various ways. The underlying assumption in this paper is that the meaning of such specifications can be more readily perceived if it is possible to view selectively particular relationships among the components of the specification. Moreover, it is assumed that many of these relationships are best presented in a graphical form. Nowadays, graphical images are often constructed interactively on a computer terminal or workstation and so it is further assumed that graphical representations of a specification would also be developed and viewed in this way. The paper deals specifically with graphical representations of the relationships present in LOTOS (Language Of Temporal Ordering Specification) [1] specifications but a similar approach can be taken to the development of suitable representations for other similar languages such as CCS (Calculus of Communicating Systems) [2] or CSP (Communicating Sequential Processes) [3].

LOTOS is a general-purpose process-oriented specification language. Its concurrency features are based on CCS and CSP. In addition, it includes an algebraic data typing facility based on ACT ONE [4].

LOTOS has been widely used by the OSI (Open System Interconnection) community for the specification of protocols and services [e.g. 5-7]. A draft international standard for the language was issued by ISO in July 1987 [1] and a full international standard is expected to follow shortly. A CCITT/ISO Working Group is currently considering graphical representations for LOTOS, with the objective of promoting the use of the language. The graphical representations are known as GLOTOS (Graphical LOTOS). This work is at an early stage of development and the ideas expressed in this paper are, in effect, a contribution to that effort.

The first section of the paper identifies the main objectives and requirements affecting the design of graphical representations for LOTOS specifications and the second section presents and assesses proposals for graphical representations based on these criteria. The proposals have undoubtedly been influenced by other work on graphical interfaces as, for example, in [8-11] but are not derived directly from any one source.

2. GRAPHICAL LOTOS: OBJECTIVES AND REQUIREMENTS

The graphical LOTOS Working Group has produced a document [8] identifying the objectives and potential requirements of GLOTOS, together with a number of proposals for its form. The single objective stated in [8] is to "promote the use of LOTOS". One interpretation of this objective is that GLOTOS is aimed at potential users of the language who prefer to deal with specifications expressed in a graphical rather than a textual form. Another interpretation, and the one preferred here, is that GLOTOS is intended to benefit *all* LOTOS users, including those already experienced in the use of the textual notation. From this viewpoint, graphics is seen as a means of illuminating those aspects of LOTOS text which might otherwise be difficult to perceive. More specifically, given that any specification is made up of a number of *definitions* that are related in various ways, graphics can serve to clarify the relationships involved. These relationships include the *nesting* of definitions, the *derivation* of definitions and the *interaction* of definitions.

The requirements identified in [8] need to be observed when deciding on possible graphical representations for such relationships:

(a) *Role of graphical representations*: There are two perceived roles for graphical LOTOS representations: one is as *building bricks* in the construction of a specification and the other is as *views* extracted from the textual description (for documentation and analysis purposes). It is desirable that both roles be supported with the same notation.

(b) *Relationship with LOTOS*: The most significant constraints on GLOTOS are that there should be a two-way mapping between GLOTOS and LOTOS, and that GLOTOS should carry the same semantics as LOTOS. These limitations emphasise that GLOTOS is intended to be an interpretation of LOTOS and not a new language as such.

(c) *Automated support*: With modern computing facilities, it seems reasonable to assume that any graphical images will be produced electronically and so might be quite elaborate. Nevertheless, as simplicity and portability are implicit objectives in any design work, it seems prudent to restrict the graphics involved to line drawings, unless what results fails to convey the required information adequately. This then allows for the possibility of hand-drawing.

The next section discusses possible graphical representations for various relationships among definitions in LOTOS specifications, taking account of the constraints (a) - (c) given above. The discussion is illustrated using a LOTOS description of the well-known children's game of pass-the-parcel. The rules of the game, expressed in natural language, are as follows:

"Children seated in a circle pass a present, wrapped in several layers of paper, from one to another as music is played. The music stops from time to time. When this occurs the child with the parcel removes its outermost wrapper. If the present is uncovered the game terminates; otherwise the music is restarted and the parcel is circulated once again. The game is begun by an adult who passes the parcel to one of the children. The parcel is then circulated in a clockwise direction. If two children have a hand on the parcel when the music stops the child receiving the parcel is assumed to have possession. The game may be interrupted at any time by an adult calling the children to tea."

A full version of the LOTOS description of the game is supplied in an appendix. It is intended that the discussion that follows be comprehensible without the need to study the specification in detail.

3. GRAPHICAL VIEWS OF LOTOS SPECIFICATIONS: A PROPOSAL

3.1 Specification Environment

In general, a LOTOS specification is made up of:
- a hierarchy of process and data type definitions, describing the intended system behaviour
- a set of environment parameters identifying
  - data *types* in the specification taken from a data type library
  - possible interactions, or *events*, involving the system specified and its environment
  - named *values* that are supplied by the environment.

Thus a *total* LOTOS specification has an environment-defined component in addition to that supplied by the specification writer. This relationship is suggested in Figure 1.

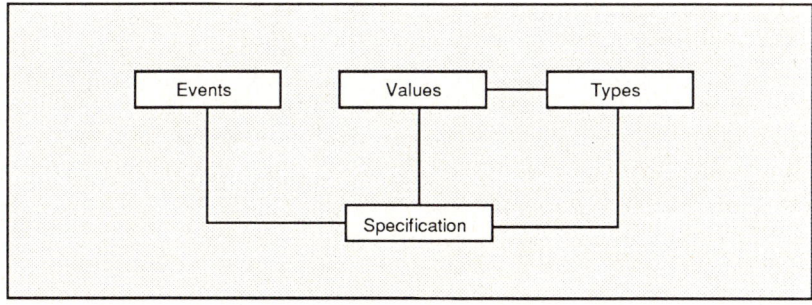

Figure 1: General Specification Diagram

In Figure 1 a rectangular box denotes each distinct component of a specification and connecting lines indicate the relationships that are present. In this case the main specification description refers to environment events, values and type definitions, where some of the values are of a type defined in the library. Strictly speaking all those types defined within a specification at its topmost level are *visible* in the environment but the "types" referred to in Figure 1 identify only those types defined in the library. It is intended that all library types should be available for study and not just those used within the specification.

In some specifications there may be no external events present, or no environment values supplied, or the values may be of a type defined within the main specification. The top-level diagram would then be adjusted accordingly. One possibility is that the parts that are not relevant are shown *faded* to permit a common top-level structure. For example, Figure 2 shows the top-level diagram for the pass-the-parcel specification, for which there are no external events.

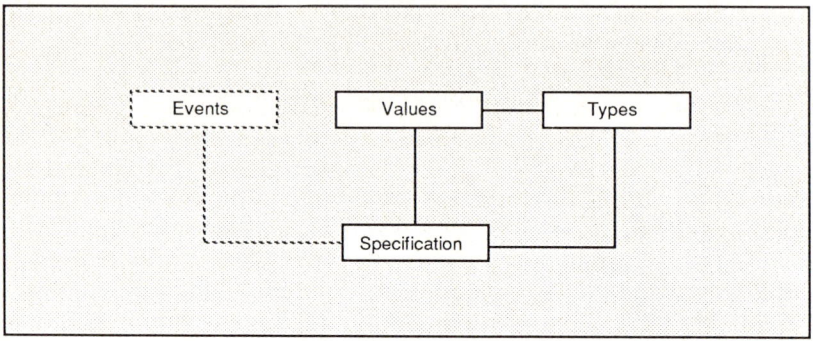

Figure 2: Pass-the-parcel Specification Diagram

In addition to the absence of external events, it is immediately apparent from Figure 2 that there are environment values which are of a type defined in the library and that there are library types used within the specification. The purpose of the diagram is to convey this limited amount of information quickly and clearly. The intention is that other details should be found *elsewhere*. In particular, if the diagram is viewed interactively then it should be possible to select any component of it for further investigation. Selecting the *Values* box, for example, might reveal a list of the names of environment data values and their corresponding types.

It is felt that, in general, it is undesirable to include such information directly in a diagram as this inevitably obscures the structure of the diagram and often requires that it be of a larger dimension than would otherwise be possible. Moreover, no matter how much information is added to any diagram some further explanation is usually required. Most diagrams, for example, require a supplementary summary of their structure and purpose. Given that a diagram cannot be expected to provide *all* of the information needed by *all* possible observers, it seems reasonable to design a range of diagrams (*views*) that convey information on particular aspects of each specification. This approach has been taken in designing the graphical representations that appear throughout this paper.

3.2 Specification Hierarchy

LOTOS specifications contain process definitions that are nested in a hierarchical fashion - much like procedures in a block-structured programming language. Types may also be defined within this hierarchy. In any particular specification the structure involved may not be obvious from a cursory study of the text, especially for large specifications and so it is useful to summarise this structure in some way. Using a graphical notation, the structure might be presented in a *tree* form, with the main specification block at its root. For example, consider Figure 3, which gives a nesting diagram for the pass-the-parcel specification.

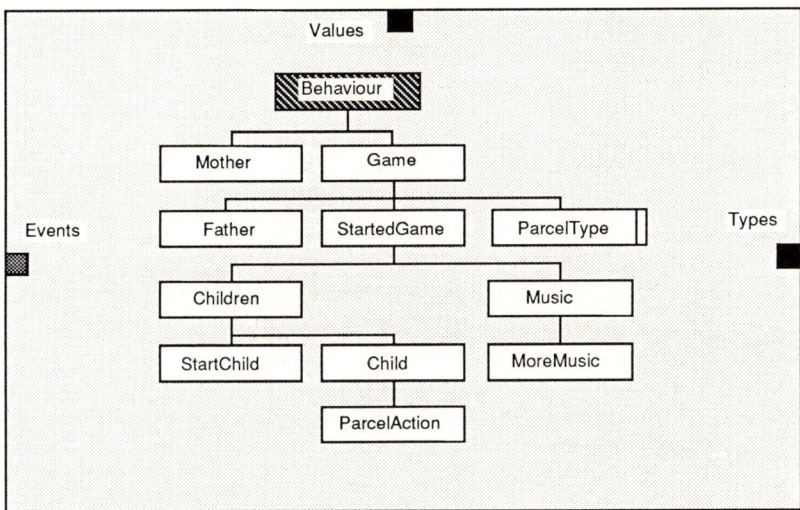

Figure 3: Pass-the-parcel Nesting Diagram

The LOTOS pass-the-parcel description contains ten process definitions and one type definition - that of the parcel. Process and type definitions are both represented by named boxes. Data type boxes are distinguished visually from those of processes by a line on their right hand side. Small boxes, on the edge of the diagram, are used to denote events, values and types available at this level. The specification and each of its local process definitions has a *behaviour expression* which is denoted by the shaded box at the top of Figure 3.

At the topmost level are two processes *Mother* and *Game* (mother stops the game when tea is ready). *Game* is shown to contain two sub-processes: *Father* and *StartedGame*, together with the data type *ParcelType*. *StartedGame*, which describes the behaviour of the game after the father has passed the parcel to the first child, contains two nested process definitions: *Music* which describes the starting and stopping of the music and *Children* which describes the children passing the parcel. The *Children* process has two local processes: *Child* describing the behaviour of a child and *StartChild* which is responsible for instantiating an appropriate number of *Child* process instances and connecting them in a circle, using event gates. The processes *MoreMusic* and *ParcelAction* describe details of their respective enclosing process definitions: *Music* and *Child*.

A diagram is a good way to summarise the nesting structure of the definitions in a specification but there are other useful alternatives. Figure 4, for example, shows the information contained in Figure 3 as a suitably indented list of process and type definitions. For some observers this may indeed be the preferred form so if the presentation is handled by a computer system it might be desirable to support both types of representation.

```
SPECIFICATION PassTheParcel
  PROCESS Mother
  PROCESS Game
    TYPE ParcelType
    PROCESS Father
    PROCESS StartedGame
      PROCESS Music
        PROCESS MoreMusic
      PROCESS Children
        PROCESS Child
          PROCESS ParcelAction
        PROCESS StartChild
```

Figure 4: Textual Summary of Specification Nesting

Figure 4 has the advantage that it occupies less space than Figure 3. When a diagram exceeds the printed page, or a VDU screen, then some adjustment to the presentation is required. There are three main options: one is to compress the diagram, another is to expand the size of the presentation medium and a third to spread the information over several diagrams. The third approach seems preferable for LOTOS specifications since they have a hierarchical structure, making it natural to have separate diagrams for relatively self-contained parts of that structure. For example, in the pass-the-parcel specification, the static structure of *StartedGame* might be given separately from the rest of the specification as implied in Figures 5. The *StartedGame* box has been given a thicker edge to indicate visually that its sub-structure may be found elsewhere.

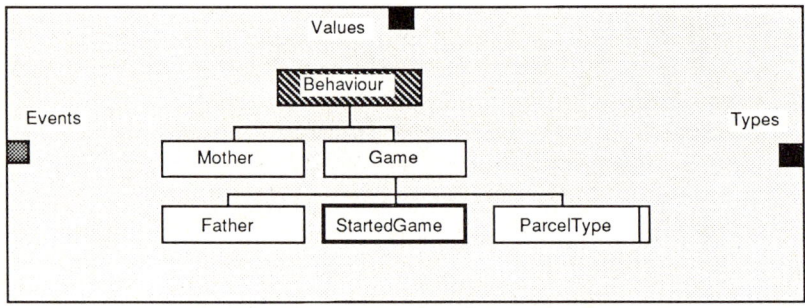

Figure 5: Nesting Diagram: with suppression

Figure 6 shows how the corresponding nesting diagram for *StartedGame* might be given.

Note that :
- the connector for events is now solid as the *StartGame* process has an event parameter (that corresponding to the passing of the parcel)
- the connector for types is also shown solid as it refers to all types that are within the scope of the *StartedGame* process.

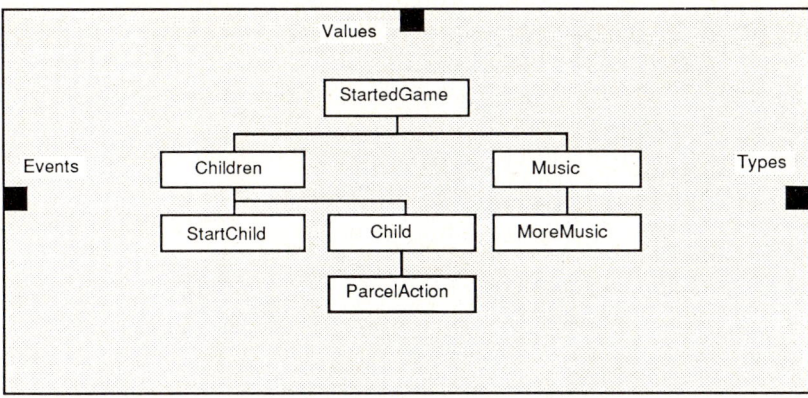

Figure 6: *StartedGame* Nesting Diagram

3.3 Definition Derivations

The behaviour of one process is frequently described in terms of the behaviour of other processes – often in a recursive fashion. This relationship can be represented by a *graph,* with processes at its nodes and arcs connecting each process to any process named in its *behaviour expression*. Figure 7, for example, shows a process derivation graph for the pass-the-parcel specification, indicating the dependency among the process definitions involved.

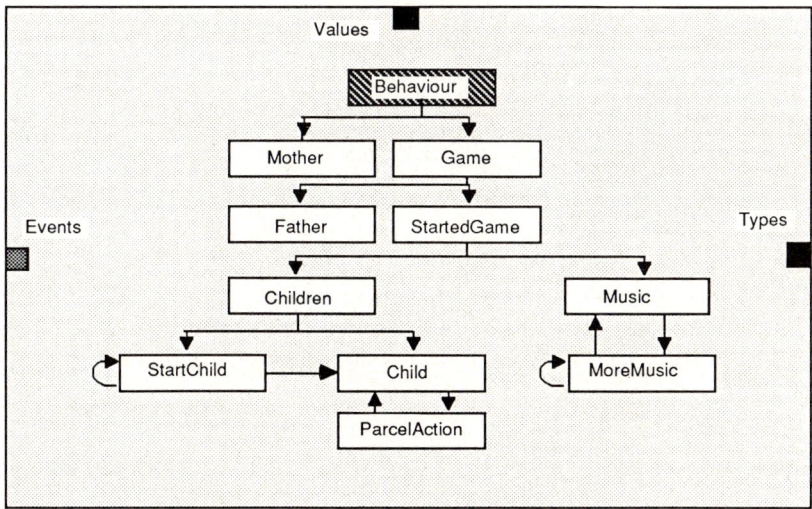

Figure 7: Pass-the-parcel Process Derivation Diagram

In Figure 7, an arc connects each process node to any process referenced directly within the behaviour expression of its definition. Some processes (e.g. *MoreMusic*) include recursive references to themselves (to describe iterative behaviour) which is denoted by self-referential arcs.

Note that:
- The arcs in the nesting and derivation diagrams are similar for the pass-the-parcel example. In principle, there need not be any obvious relationship between the two diagrams but such a relationship is likely if the developer of a specification makes an attempt to localise definitions as much as possible.
- Large derivation diagrams can be presented in a hierarchical fashion, using the same approach described for nesting diagrams.

Many data types are constructed from other (simpler) data types. Data types do not have recursive definitions so a *tree* might be used to represent the derivation dependency for any particular type – the type itself being at the root of the tree. Usually those types defined in a specification will be based on other types defined in the library. Thus it is appropriate to give a type derivation diagram in a form that shows all the types that are involved, as illustrated in Figure 8 for *ParcelType*. *ParcelType* is derived from the standard data types *Boolean* and *NaturalNumber*, where *NaturalNumber* is itself based on *BasicNaturalNumber* and *Boolean*.

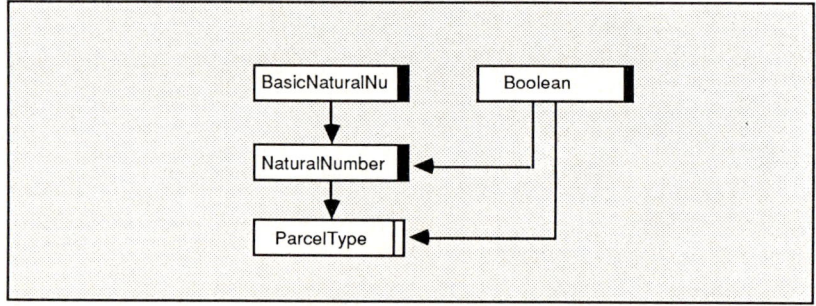

Figure 8: *ParcelType* Type Derivation Diagram

Note that:
- in the diagram, library types are distinguished visually from those defined within the specification;
- LOTOS also has a facility for defining *formal* data types, from which actual data types can be derived, so it is desirable to distinguish formal and actual types visually (not illustrated);
- boxes in this diagram and elsewhere are of fixed size so when names exceed the space available they are truncated as, for example, in the case of *BasicNaturalNumber* in Figure 8.

3.4 Definition Interactions

Under this heading might be included the use of types and values by processes, and the interaction among processes via *event gates*. Unfortunately, however, much of this information is *dynamic* and, in general, can only be determined by interpreting or *animating* a specification.

One interaction that can be deduced statically is that between process and type definitions. Processes manipulate data values using operations defined on the types of those values. This usage can be reflected in a *graph* whose arcs connect process nodes to data type nodes appropriately. Figure 9 shows a Process-Type interaction diagram for the pass-the-parcel example. The layout of this diagram is based on the Nesting diagram in Figure 3.

As might be expected the *Father* and *ParcelAction* (local to *Child*) processes perform operations on values of *ParcelType*. In addition the *Children* and *StartChild* processes, and the top level behaviour component of the specification operate on natural numbers and *Child* operates on Booleans, where the corresponding data types are defined in the library.

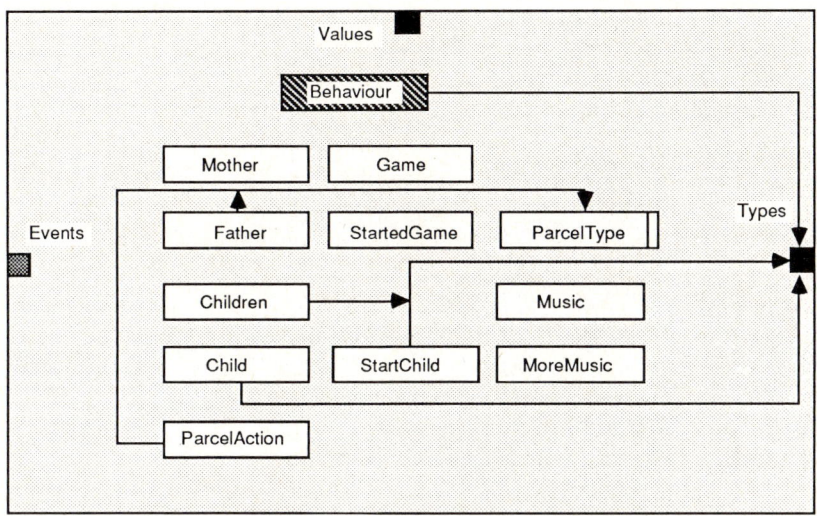

Figure 9: Pass-the-parcel Process-Type Interaction

3.5 Behaviour Expressions

Behaviour expressions for processes vary in form and complexity. In some cases a behaviour expression will simply identify the sequence of events in which the process can participate. In other cases the behaviour of a process may be defined in terms of the concurrent interaction of two or more process instances. Most commonly a behaviour expression will contain process instances *and* events (*gates*) combined in various ways. The ISO/CCITT GLOTOS working document [8] presents a number of different proposals for the representation of behaviour expressions. What is described here takes a simpler approach. In essence, the simplifying technique is to hide some of the LOTOS language details under the assumption that this detail, if required, can be found at other levels - usually by interactive examination of the diagrams. Consider Figure 10, for example, which shows a possible pictorial representation of the behaviour expression for the *Father* process in the pass-the-parcel example.

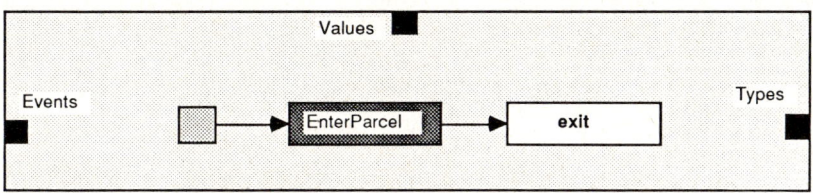

Figure 10: *Father* Process Behaviour Diagram

Here the *Father* process is described by the single event *EnterParcel* which represents the passing of the parcel to a child in the ring of children. The *EnterParcel* event is represented by a patterned rectangle, the exit from the process corresponds to the standard *action denotation* **exit** defined in LOTOS, and finally the patterned box identifies the entry point to the process. Details of the parcel (data value) that is associated with the *EnterParcel* event are not shown in this diagram but might be obtained by "selecting" the *EnterParcel* rectangle.

As a second example of the representation of behaviour Figure 11 shows a possible representation for the *ParcelAction* process.

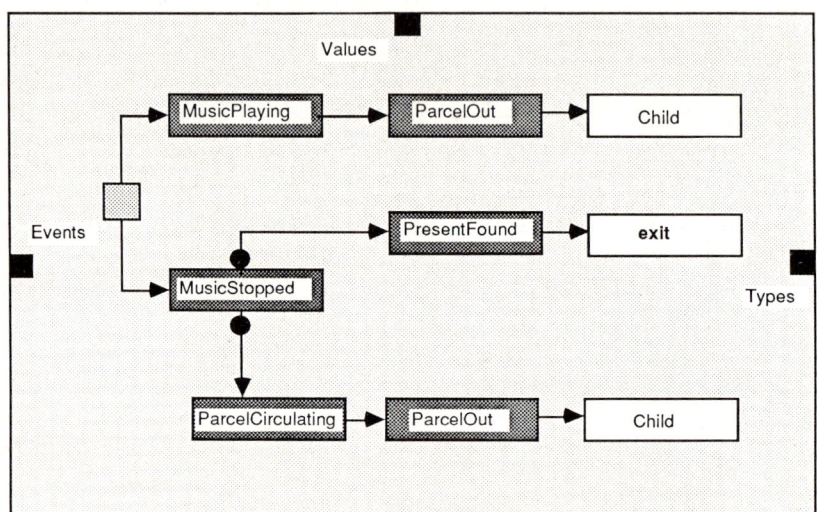

Figure 11: *ParcelAction* Process Behaviour Diagram

The additional points to note here are that:
- Process instances of Child (denoting a return to the initial child state - expecting a parcel) are represented by a plain rectangle.
- Where two or more arrows emerge from an event node in this graph it indicates that a *choice* of following event is offered. If there are preconditions (guards) on the events concerned these are denoted by dark circles on the incoming lines. For example, the event following *MusicStopped* is either *ParcelCirculating* or *PresentFound*, depending on whether or not wrappers remain on the parcel.

Figure 12 illustrates the case where a behaviour expression contains process instances that are intended to run concurrently. This is the behaviour description for the *StartedGame* process. Here two processes *Children* and *Music* are combined with a symbol |•| which is suggestive of the LOTOS operator |[...]| and indicates that the two processes run concurrently, synchronising on at least one event. Similar symbols can be used to denote other LOTOS operators.

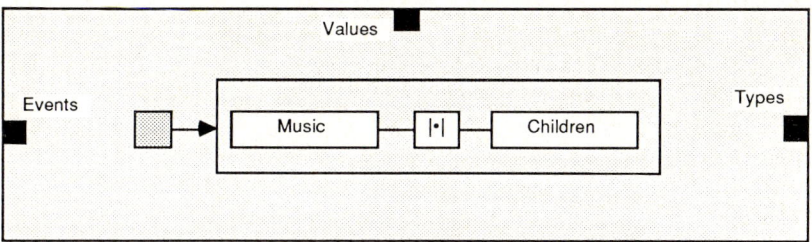

Figure 12: *StartedGame* Process Behaviour Diagram

This example concludes the discussion of possible graphical views of LOTOS specifications.

4. Conclusion

This paper has presented an approach to the graphical representation of relationships among the definitions which constitute a LOTOS specification. The graphics used is deliberately simple, and the diagrams are deliberately spare in an effort to present the relationships involved in as clear a form as possible. These diagrams are in essence an *overview* of the relationships that they describe and so prepare the observer for more complicated detail existing at some logically lower level. That detail might be the text of the specification in LOTOS, documentation in natural language or perhaps other graphical images, as appropriate.

The suitability of this approach to the graphical representation of LOTOS specifications will inevitably depend on its method of use. The underlying assumption is that the graphical images are constructed and maintained by a computer system. In addition, it is likely to be most beneficial in cases where the observer of the specification has the ability to browse interactively among the various views of the specification. Another assumption is that LOTOS specifications will be defined hierarchically. The language certainly encourages this approach but it is also possible to construct flat specifications. Those who choose to take the latter approach may find that a large number of definitions then exist at the same level, thereby making their presentation difficult without the support of relatively sophisticated graphical facilities.

A demonstration system, incorporating the ideas expressed in this paper, is currently under development. The approach has been applied to a number of examples, including a Remote Operations Service Element (ROSE) [12].

ACKNOWLEDGEMENTS

The authors of this paper would like to thank the Director of the British Telecom Research Laboratories for permission to publish this paper.

Thanks are also extended to the reviewers of an earlier draft of this paper for their helpful comments.

REFERENCES

[1] ISO, 'Information processing systems - Open systems interconnection - LOTOS - A Formal Technique Based on the Temporal Ordering of Observational Behaviour', ISO DIS 8807, July 1987

[2] MILNER, R., 'A Calculus of Communicating Systems' in Lecture Notes in Computer Science (Springer-Verlag, 1980)

[3] HOARE, C.A.R., 'Communicating Sequential Processes' (Prentice Hall International, 1985)

[4] ERHIG, H. and MAHR, B., 'Fundamentals of Algebraic Specification 1', (Springer-Verlag, 1985)

[5] CARCHIOLO, V., *et al.*, 'A LOTOS Specification of the PROWAY Highway Service', IEEE Transactions on Computers, Vol. C-35, No. 11, November 1986

[6] ISO: 'Formal Specification in LOTOS of a Transport Protocol', ISO/TC 97/SC 21/WG1 454, June 1987

[7] TURNER, K.J., 'A Practical Formal Description Technique for OSI', Proceedings International Open Systems '87, London, March 1987

[8] ISO, 'Working draft answer to Q48.4 - Graphical representation of LOTOS', ISO/IEC JTC 1/SC 21/WG1, N2552, April 1988

[9] CCITT, 'Functional Specification and Description Language (SDL)', Recommendations Z100-104, VIIIth Plenary assembly, Malaga-Torremolinos, 1984

[10] REISIG, W., 'Petri Nets: an introduction', (Springer-Verlag, 1982)

[11] KILGOUR, A.C. and EARNSHAW, R.A. (eds), 'Graphics Tools for Software Engineering: Visual Programming & Program Visualisation', (British Computer Society, London, March 1988)

[12] FREESTONE, D. and AUJLA, S., 'Specifying ROSE in LOTOS', this volume

APPENDIX: Pass-the-parcel Specification in LOTOS

specification PassTheParcel (ParcelSize: Nat, Players: Nat): **exit**

  library NaturalNumber, Boolean **endlib**

  behaviour
    [Players le succ(0)] -> (**exit**)
    []
    [Players gt succ(0)] -> (Game(ParcelSize, Players) [> Mother)
    where
    process Mother: **exit**:=
      i ; **exit**
    endproc (* Mother *)

    process Game (ParcelSize: Nat, Players: Nat): **exit** :=
      hide EnterParcel **in**
      Father [EnterParcel] (ParcelSize) |[EnterParcel]| StartedGame [EnterParcel] (Players)
    where

      type ParcelType **is** NaturalNumber, Boolean
        opns (* operations *)
          NewParcel: Nat   -> Nat
          WrappersRemain: Nat -> Bool
          Unwrap: Nat   -> Nat
        eqns (* equations *)
          ofsort Bool **forall** n: Nat
            WrappersRemain (n) = (n ne 0);
          ofsort Nat **forall** n: Nat
            Unwrap (Succ(n)) = n;
            Unwrap (0) = 0;
            NewParcel (n) = n;
      endtype (* ParcelType *)

      process Father [EnterParcel] (ParcelSize: Nat) : **exit** :=
        EnterParcel! NewParcel (ParcelSize); **exit**
      endproc (* Father *)

      process StartedGame [EnterParcel] (Players: Nat): **exit** :=
        hide MusicPlaying, MusicStopped, ParcelCirculating, PresentFound **in**
          (Music [MusicPlaying, MusicStopped, ParcelCirculating, PresentFound]
            |[MusicPlaying, MusicStopped, ParcelCirculating, PresentFound]|
          Children[EnterParcel, MusicPlaying, MusicStopped, PresentFound, ParcelCirculating]
            (Players))
      where

      process Music [MusicPlaying, MusicStopped, ParcelCirculating, PresentFound]: **exit**:=
        MusicPlaying; MoreMusic [MusicPlaying, MusicStopped, ParcelCirculating, PresentFound]
        where
        process MoreMusic [MusicPlaying, MusicStopped, ParcelCirculating, PresentFound]: **exit**:=
          (MusicPlaying;
           MoreMusic [MusicPlaying, MusicStopped, ParcelCirculating, PresentFound])
          []
          (MusicStopped;
          ((ParcelCirculating;
            Music [MusicPlaying, MusicStopped, ParcelCirculating, PresentFound])
            []
          (PresentFound; **exit**)))
        endproc (* MoreMusic *)
      endproc (* Music *)

```
process Children [EnterParcel, MusicPlaying, MusicStopped,
              PresentFound, ParcelCirculating] (Players: Nat): exit :=
    hide FirstLink, NextLink in
    (Child[EnterParcel, FirstLink, NextLink, MusicPlaying, MusicStopped, PresentFound,
           ParcelCirculating] (true)
     |[FirstLink, NextLink]|
     StartChild [EnterParcel, FirstLink, NextLink, MusicPlaying, MusicStopped, PresentFound,
           ParcelCirculating] (succ (succ(0)), Players))
where

    process Child [EnterParcel, Parcelin, ParcelOut, MusicPlaying, MusicStopped,
                 PresentFound, ParcelCirculating] (ParcelFromFather: Bool): exit :=
      [ParcelFromFather] -> (* first child accepts parcel from Father *)
        (EnterParcel ? TheParcel: Nat;
          ParcelAction [EnterParcel, Parcelin, ParcelOut, MusicPlaying, MusicStopped,
              PresentFound, ParcelCirculating] (TheParcel))
    []
      [not (ParcelFromFather)] ->
        (Parcelin ? TheParcel: Nat;
          ParcelAction [EnterParcel, Parcelin, ParcelOut, MusicPlaying, MusicStopped,
              PresentFound, ParcelCirculating] (TheParcel))
    where
      process ParcelAction [EnterParcel, Parcelin, ParcelOut, MusicPlaying, MusicStopped,
                 PresentFound, ParcelCirculating] (TheParcel: Nat): exit :=
        ( MusicPlaying;
          ParcelOut ! TheParcel;
          Child [EnterParcel, Parcelin, ParcelOut, MusicPlaying, MusicStopped,
                 PresentFound, ParcelCirculating] (false))
      []
        ( MusicStopped;
          ( let UnwrappedParcel: Nat = Unwrap (TheParcel) in
            ( [Not (WrappersRemain (UnwrappedParcel))] ->
              (PresentFound; exit)
            []
              [WrappersRemain (UnwrappedParcel)] ->
                ( ParcelCirculating; ParcelOut ! UnwrappedParcel;
                  Child [EnterParcel, Parcelin, ParcelOut, MusicPlaying, MusicStopped,
                    PresentFound, ParcelCirculating] (false))
            ) (* selection on WrappersRemain or not WrappersRemain *)
          ) (* scope of UnwrappedParcel *)
        ) (* MusicStopped selection *)
      endproc (* ParcelAction *)
    endproc (* Child *)

    process StartChild [EnterParcel, FirstLink, PreviousLink, MusicPlaying, MusicStopped,
                 PresentFound, ParcelCirculating] (Identity: Nat, Players: Nat): exit :=
      [Identity eq Players] -> (* last child *)
        (Child [EnterParcel, PreviousLink, FirstLink, MusicPlaying, MusicStopped,
            PresentFound, ParcelCirculating] (false))
    []
      [Identity lt Players] -> (* child other than the first or last instantiated *)
        (hide NextLink in
          Child [EnterParcel, PreviousLink, NextLink, MusicPlaying, MusicStopped,
              PresentFound, ParcelCirculating] (false)
          |[NextLink]|
          StartChild [EnterParcel, FirstLink, NextLink, MusicPlaying, MusicStopped,
              PresentFound, ParcelCirculating] (succ (Identity), Players))
    endproc (* StartChild *)
  endproc (* Children *)
 endproc (* StartGame *)
 endproc (* Game *)
endspec (* PassTheParcel *)
```

NONDETERMINISM AND SDL

Dieter Hogrefe, University of Hamburg
Amardeo Sarma, Research Institute of the Deutsche Bundespost

With the new CCITT Blue-Book Recommendation, the specification language SDL has reached a stable state. Its use is widely spread in the field of telecommunication. However, one feature SDL still lacks is the capability to specify nondeterminism. In this paper, this is shown to be a very important attribute, especially for service specifications. The case for nondeterminism in SDL is argued and it shown how this may be incorporated into the existing SDL with a minimum of change.

1. Nondeterminism in specifications

Formal specification languages like SDL are designed to specify the behaviour of systems unambiguously. So far, specifications written in SDL deal mainly with the behaviour of data communication protocols and services and telecommunication switching systems.

A specification is a high level description and explains how a system should react in any situation. When using SDL, these situations are denoted by states and the reaction of the system in any state is given by a transition ending in a new state. These state transitions are initiated by input signals. An implementation is considered correct with respect to the specification if it shows the specified behaviour. The behaviour of the system here refers to all possible reactions to all possible signals.

A formal specification usually defines an abstract machine. If in every state the reaction resulting from a certain stimulus from the environment is uniquely defined, the abstract machine is said to be deterministic. Many specifications of telecommunication switching systems using formal specification languages are deterministic. Also, most telecommunication protocols can be described this way /4, 8/.

However, in some cases, a specifier may not wish to or perhaps cannot specifiy unique reactions in certain situations. It may be intended to hide details of the specification not relevant or of no interest at a particular level of abstraction. In a state-oriented model, this means that, starting at a specific state, there is more than one possible transition resulting from a specific stimulus from the environment. This behaviour is said to be nondeterministic. The selection of an actual transition is made inside the system and is beyond the control of the observer. There is nothing mysterious about this kind of specification: it arises from the deliberate decision to ignore the factors which influence the selection. Nondeterminism allows a greater degree of freedom within specifications because it allows the specification of a class of reactions to stimuli, thereby permitting a greater degree of abstraction.

Unfortunately, CCITT has so far refrained from introducing nondeterminism into SDL, mainly because users have not demanded this feature in their practical work. However, it should be noted that many users and also the CCITT itself use "informal text" to hide details. This is an indirect indication of the need for nondeterminism as one form of abstraction.

Examples of the nondeterministic specification style within telecommunications can be found in OSI-service specifications /4,5,6/. A service usually allows a number of different protocols to provide the service. The significance of the service concept has been argued in /12/. For example, a data-link service may be provided either by a protocol using an alternating bit for error correction and retransmission or by one using a sliding window. There may be differences in the performance of the protocols, but the functional service provided to the users will be the same. An example of a service specification is given in the next section.

2 Example of a nondeterministic specification

This section gives an example of a nondeterministic specification which will serve as a basis for the explanation of the concepts and notations introduced in the following chapters. The example, taken from /13/, is a very simple connection-oriented data-link service which allows to build up and terminate a connection as well as to transmit data via a connection that has been set up successfully. In this section, the example is introduced using time-sequence diagrams. Later, in Chapter 4, this example will be specified formally using SDL with the newly introduced constructs for nondeterminism. For reasons of brevity, the service is an asymmetric one, which may not be very useful in a real OSI environment but is sufficient to explain the concepts of this paper. With a few extensions, it may be completed to become a symmetrical service.

The service INRESservice offers two service access points to its users, called USAPini and USAPres in the following.

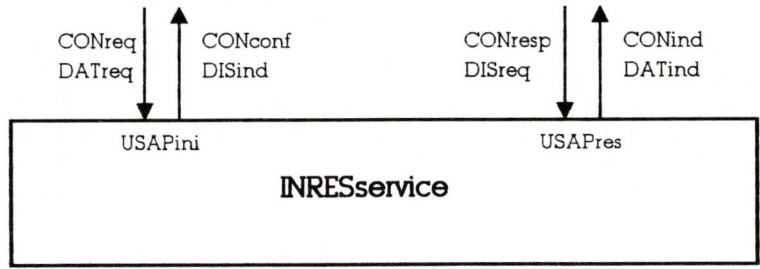

Fig. 2.1 Overview of the service provider

INRES is the abreviation of INitiator and RESponder. The service allows a user to initiate a connection at the service access point USAPini. A user at the service access point USAPres may respond to this connection attempt by accepting or rejecting the request.

The service may be accessed by the users at the service access point **USAPini** with the service primitives
       CONreq, CONconf, DISind and DATreq(d),

and at the service access point **USAPres** with the service primitives
       CONind, CONresp, DISreq and DATind(d).

The primitives **DATreq** and **DATind** are used for data transmission and therefore have a parameter **d** carrying user data. The sequence of service primitives of a successful connection establishment is shown in Fig. 2.2 by means of a time-sequence diagram. For the semantics of the time-sequence diagrams used here, see /7/.

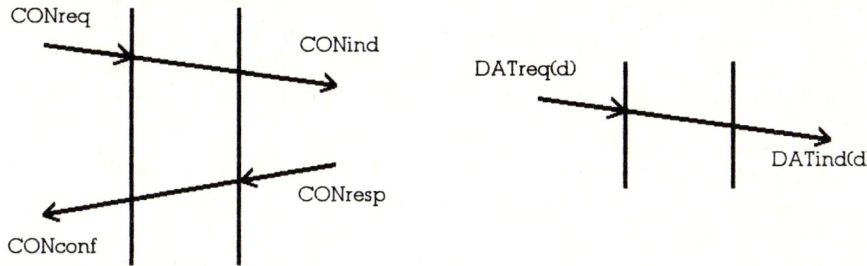

Fig. 2.2 Successful connection establishment

Fig. 2.3 Successful data transmission

After successful connection establishment, the initiating user may issue any number of DATreq(d) primitives, which will under normal circumstances, be conveyed to the responding user as DATind(d) (Fig. 2.3). Of course, the resonding user may reject the connection attempt. This is shown in Fig. 2.4. The responding user may also terminate the connection at any time with a DISreq.

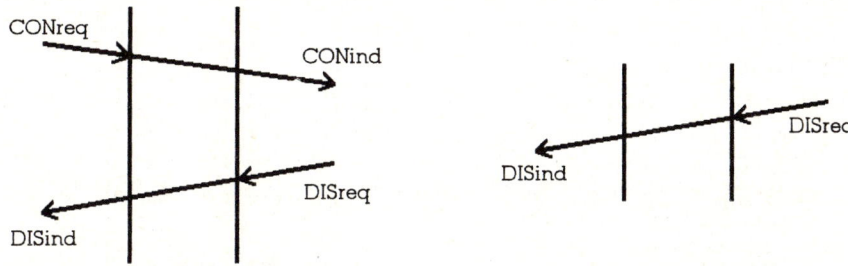

Fig. 2.4 User rejected connection attempt

Fig. 2.5 User termination of a connection

In general, services are unreliable, implying that the service provider may reject a connection attempt (Fig. 2.6) or a request for data transmission (Fig. 2.7).

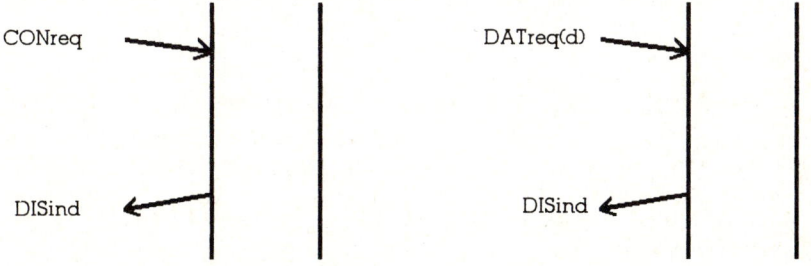

Fig. 2.6 Provider rejected connection attempt

Fig. 2.7 Provider rejected data transmission

The behaviour shown in Fig. 2.2 and Fig. 2.6 already indicates the nondeterministic nature of the service provider, because the behaviour of the service following the receipt of the CONreq primitive is unknown. Two different initial reactions are possible and correct. Since the decision between the two alternatives is beyond control of the service user, the provider cannot be specified in a deterministic fashion. The provider may also terminate the connection on receiving a request for data transmission, which is another nondeterministic feature. Besides, the user that issues a CONreq and subsequently receives a DISind cannot determine whether it is the service or the responding user that has rejected the service.

This is only an at most semi-formal description of the service provider and cannot be regarded as complete. Usually, when describing a service informally, one does not think of the whole range of possible behaviour. Most often, many types of behaviour will only occur to a specifier when trying to specifiy the service formally. Most semi-formal service descriptions are incomplete in this way, e.g. /9/. This shows the importance of a more rigorous specification of services.

3 Nondeterminism in current SDL Specifications

Despite the original intention to confine SDL to model deterministic finite-state machines communicating asynchronously via infinite buffers, nondeterministic elements have crept into the SDL definition. These are:

Nondeterministic delays on channels

Whenever a process communicates with another in the same block, the signals are placed without delay into the input buffer of the receiving process whether or not a signal route has been specified. This is new in the Blue Book - the delay queue conceived in the Red-Book recommendations for communication between processes of different process type has been eliminated. When a process communicates with another process in a different block, the signals must be directed via one or more channels. These channels have a nondeterministic delay, which means that the time taken between the output of a signal from one process and it being deposited into the buffer of the receiving process is unknown. When different signals take a route via the same channels, their order is preserved in spite of their nondeterministic delay. If signals take routes via different channels, their order at the receiving process cannot be determined. An implementation may or may not resolve this nondeterminism.

Consider Fig. 3.1, which shows a system containing two blocks B1 and B2, both containg exactly one process. BLOCK B1 contains the "main" process, which answers to request "Query" from the environment by making a nondeterministic choice between "Ans_1" and "Ans_2" and sending the chosen signal back to the environment.

PROCESS P1 in BLOCK B1 sends "Req_1" and "Req_2" to PROCESS P2 via different channels C1 and C2 on receiving "Query" from the environment. Since the delays on the channels are nondeterministic, which of the two signals is received first by PROCESS P2 is unknown. In case it is "Req_1", "Conf_1" is sent to PROCESS P1, in case it is "Req_2", "Conf_2" is sent. PROCESS P1 waits for the response from PROCESS P2 and sends "Ans_1" to the environment if it receives "Conf_1" from PROCESS P2 and "Ans_2" if it receives "Conf_2". PROCESS P2 has an intermediate state to consume the second signal from PROCESS P1. This system clearly shows a nondeterminitic behaviour. However, an implementation of this service will usually be deterministic.

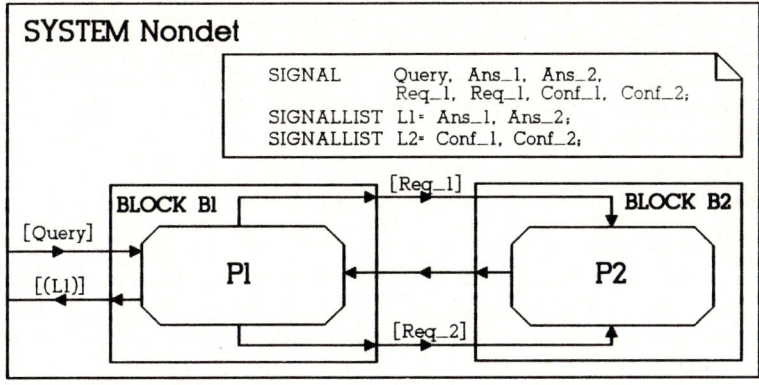
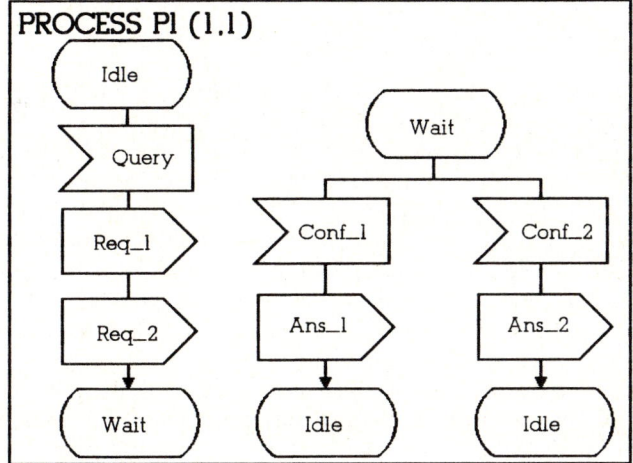
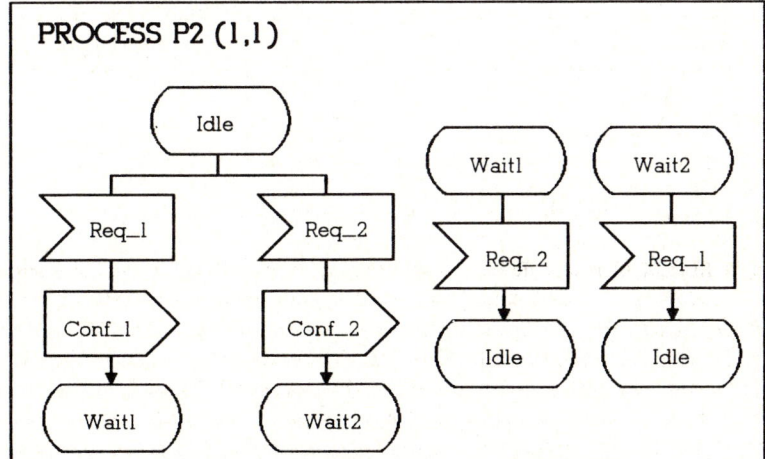

Fig. 3.1 Example of nondeterminism

Nondeterminism through parallel operation

A very general property of parallel systems can also lead to nondeterminism. Since how "fast" or "slow" a process is does not form part of the specification, it is impossible, in general, to ascertain which of two parallel processes replies first in response to signals from a third process.

Nondeterministic evaluation of enabling conditions

The enabling condition in SDL is a shorthand notation. This can be converted to the basic form of SDL using decisions and the expansion into a number of states. However, this combination can lead to a nondeterministic behaviour if we have multiple enabling conditions and these include IMPORT and SENDER. This is because the transformation into basic SDL requires that the enabling conditions are evaluated in decisions in a nondeterministic order before one of the states created by the expansion is entered. There are 2^N expanded states if there are N enabling conditions /3/. If the decisions corresponding to the enabling conditions have mutual side-effects, the state reached cannot be determined.

Fig. 3.2 gives an example of this kind of nondeterminitic behaviour using SENDER and IMPORT. If SENDER, which is the process identifier (PId) of the process the last signal was received from, is evaluated in one enabling condition (SENDER = PARENT) and an IMPORT is used in another (a = (IMPORT(b,OFFSPRING)), the result of the first enabling condition depends on which process the last explicit input was received from only if it is evaluated before the second enabling condition. Otherwise, assuming there are no further IMPORT statements in the remaining enabling conditions, SENDER has the same value as OFFSPRING, in which case the first enabling condition is evaluated to be false.

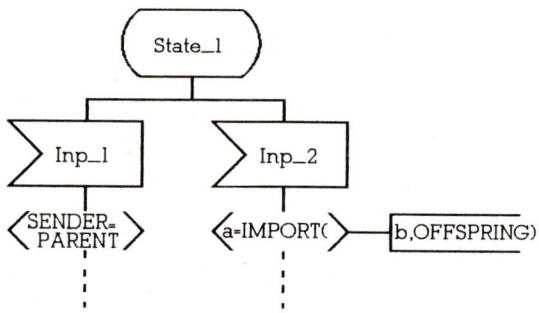

Fig. 3.2 Nondeterminism with the enabling condition

The OPTION facility

It is sometimes argued that the OPTION facility in SDL allows modelling some kind of nondeterminism explicitly during specification. However, OPTION is a static construct and cannot be described as "real" nondeterminism. OPTION allows the description of alternatives which have to be resolved by making a final choice of one of the types of behaviour specified. An implemented system no longer has the choice of exhibiting the alternative kinds of behaviour. The options are removed when the system is implemented. Furthermore, the choices have to be expressed explicitly and cannot be left open.

Informal Text

This is one example of using nondeterminism without calling it by name. Within CCITT, "informal text" is widely used in the SDL diagrams for service and protocol specifications to abstract from bothersome details. Whereas the tasks with informal text have no formal meaning (we pretend they are not there), decisions with informal text cannot be interpreted formally. In the Formal Definition of the dynamic semantics (Z.100, Annex F.3), an informal function returns a boolean value for each branch with informal text. We believe it is reasonable to assign a nondeterministic decision for most practical uses of decisions with informal text.

4 Nondeterminism as an extension to SDL

Athough there is implicit nondeterminism in SDL specifications, it is currently not possible to specify nondeterministic behaviour explicitly. It has been agreed upon to avoid making significant changes to the language SDL in future, especially changes that invalidate existing specifications. Therefore, the suggestions made here do not introduce any new symbols or constructs, but rather extend the meaning of existing constructs to include nondeterminism.

There are essentially two different kinds of nondeterministic behaviour that are frequently used in state-oriented specifications. These are:

- nondeterministic choice, which results in more than one transition being possible from a certain point,
- spontaneous transition, where a state transition occurs without any input.

A nondeterministic choice allows the system to behave in any of the specified ways. Any implementation which behaves in one of the specified ways is a correct implementation. During the course of implementing the system, some of the nondeterministic features may be removed leading to a deterministic behaviour where nondeterminism was specified. A different implementation might make a different choice when removing nondeterministic features and therefore exhibit a different behaviour but still be correct with respect to the specification.

The interpretation of a spontaneous transition is that the system may perform a state transition for no observable reason. It is only the result of the transition that can be observed. Any implementation that yields the same result, no matter how it is obtained, is a correct implementation. In our service example, the behaviour of the service provider is such that it may at any time send a disconnection indication to the service user which initiated the connection attempt. Further information on the formal link between specification and implementation is given in /11/.

In the specification language *LOTOS*, the nondeterministic choice is modelled by the occurence of the same interaction within a choice operator. In the following examples, a, b, c and d are event names:

$$(a;b;\textbf{stop} \:[]\: a;c;\textbf{stop})$$

The spontaneous transition is modelled in *LOTOS* with the internal event i which causes the so-called silent transition:

$$(a;b;\textbf{stop} \:[]\: i;c;d;\textbf{stop})$$

In *Estelle*, the mechanism is quite similar. In the following, the nondeterministic choice is modelled by two transitions which can be activated by the same input ip.a in the same state STATE_1:

from STATE_1 to STATE_2 **when** ip.a **begin** (transition1) **end**
from STATE_1 to STATE_3 **when** ip.a **begin** (transition2) **end**

The spontaneous transition is modelled in *Estelle* with a transition with no input:

from STATE_4 to STATE_5 **begin** (transition2) **end**

The spontaneous transition may be selected at any time when the corresponding *Estelle* module is in the state STATE_4.

Nondeterministic choice

For this purpose, we introduce a new language construct called NDECISION, which is the empty DECISION symbol in SDL/GR.

The NDECISION symbol has two or more transitions leading from it (Fig. 4.1 shows an example). The choice of the transition following the symbol is nondeterministic. Both the symbol and the branching arms are empty, i.e., they have no attached notation or text, not even "informal text". Except for this restriction, the NDECISION symbol follows the same syntax rules as the DECISION symbol. The interpretation of the NDECISION is that a concrete implementation may convert the NDECISION into a DECISION with possibly additional variables. The NDECISION may even model arbitary actions and interactions, eventually leading to two exit points. On the other hand, the choice may be random or depend on some factor beyond the control of the implementation.

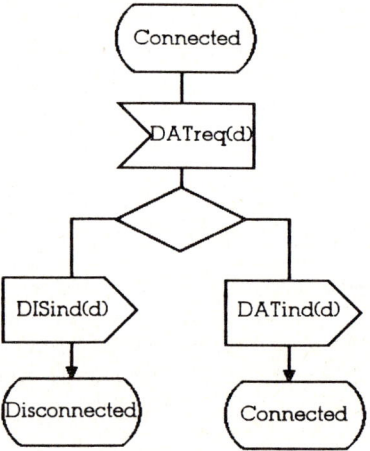

Fig. 4.1 Nondeterministic choice using the NDECISION construct

Nondeterministic choice can also be modelled in SDL by allowing the same signal to appear more than once in the state diagram of the process. An example is shown in Fig. 4.2. This representation can always be converted to the form using the NDECISION construct.

In case an INPUT signal appears more than once in the set of inputs following a state, this is converted to a single input with the same signal followed by a nondeterministic decision. The number of branches the nondeterministic signal has is equal to the number of inputs with the mentioned signal.

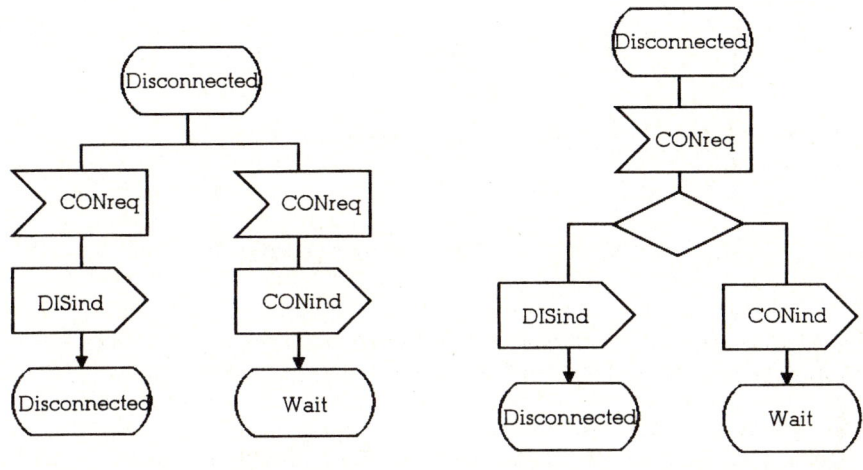

Fig. 4.2a   Multiple appearance of input signals

Fig. 4.2b   Transformed Form

Spontaneous transition

We propose to use the NINPUT construct, shown in the SDL/GR representation below, to model spontaneous transitions.

The NINPUT symbol leads to a possibly spontaneous transition similar to that following any other INPUT symbol. No signal is extracted from the buffer. The implication of using NINPUT is that any implementation that either omits the input, conceives a spontaneous transition or uses a concrete INPUT signal that must be added to the valid input set is a valid interpretation. A STATE followed by a NINPUT does not imply that this transition will eventually be chosen, given enough time. Just as a "normal" input may never be received, a NINPUT may never be chosen, although this is usually unlikely as in the case of a spontaneous transition. In our representation, we restrict NINPUT to abstracting from possible input signals or spontaneous transitions. It may not be used to abstract from other events such as the initiation of a transition resulting from a change in data values (as in the case of continuous signals). This restricts the possible interpretations of the NINPUT symbol. Just as in the case of INPUT, the

NINPUT symbol is only allowed to follow the STATE symbol. A possible application is shown in Fig. 4.3.

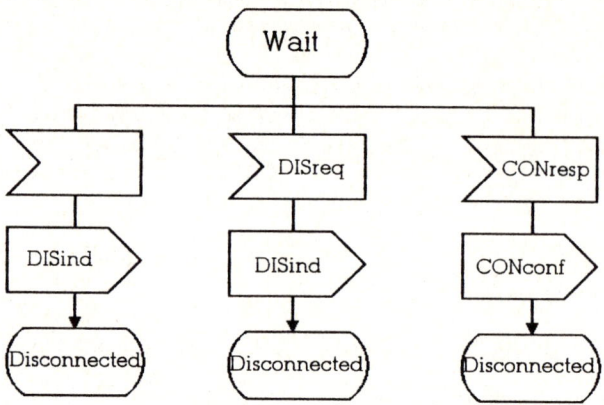

Fig. 4.3 Spontaneous transition using NINPUT

NINPUT and NDECISION have been used here to distinguish them from their current deterministic counterparts. Of course, the introduction of nondeterminism into SDL may well choose to extend the semantics of INPUT and DECISION instead.

5 Conclusion

SDL has been defined by CCITT to model extended **deterministic** finite state machines. The restriction to deterministic machines, however, reduces the expressive power of the language. In fact, nondeterminism is a useful if not indispensible tool in many application areas.

The paper has shown a possible introduction of nondeterminism into SDL and how it may enhance the expressive power of the specification. Some examples were shown to underline the need for nondeterminism and new constructs were discussed. Specifications using SDL (1988) remain valid despite these additions. We believe that the use of SDL in the protocol area has made it necessary to look at these and similar aspects. In our view, the introduction of nondeterminism will increase the acceptance and the use of SDL.

The examples show that the nondeterministic extension is applicable to OSI service specifications. Fig 4.1 to Fig. 4.3 together form the specification of the example given in Chapter 2. The extensions to the language do not invalidate existing specifications.

We propose that the introduction of nondeterminism should be one of the topics for the maintenance of SDL in the coming CCITT Study Period from 1989 to 1992.

References

/1/ ISO TC97/SC21: ESTELLE: A formal description technique based on an extended state transition model, Draft proposal ISO/DP 9074, September 1986.

/2/ ISO TC97/SC21: LOTOS: Language for the temporal ordering specification of observational behaviour, Draft proposal ISO/DP 8807, June 1986.

/3/ CCITT SG X: Recommendation Z.100: Specification and Description Language SDL, Contribution Com X-R15-E, 1987.

/4/ ISO TC97/SC21: Guidelines for the application of ESTELLE, LOTOS, and SDL, Document SC21/WG1/N451, June 1987.

/5/ ISO TC97: Basic Reference Model, International Standard, ISO/IS 7498, 1984.

/6/ ISO TC97/SC21: OSI Service Conventions, Technical report ISO/TR 8509, 1987.

/7/ Hogrefe, D.: OSI Service Specification with CCITT-SDL, ACM Comp. Comm. Review, 1988.

/8/ Hogrefe, D.: Protocol and Service Specification with SDL: a case study, report no. FBI-HH-B-134/88, Univerity of Hamburg, 1988.

/9/ ISO TC97: Network Service Definition, Draft International Standard, ISO/DIS 8348, 1986.

/10/ CCITT Recommendation X.250: Formal Description Techniques for Data Communication Protocols and Services, CCITT Red Book, 1984.

/11/ Brinksma, E., Scollo, G.: Formal notions of implementation and conformance in LOTOS, Memorandum INF-86-13, Twente University, 1986.

/12/ Vissers, C.A., Logrippo, L.: The importance of the service concept in the design of data communication protocols, Protocol Specification, Testing and Verification V, North Holland, 1985.

/13/ Hogrefe, D.: Estelle, LOTOS and SDL: Standard Spezifikationssprachen für verteilte Systeme, Springer-Verlag, Heidelberg, 1988.

THE BOYER-MOORE THEOREM-PROVER AND LOTOS

Sukhvinder S. AUJLA[*] and Matthew FLETCHER[†]

[*] Formal Methods Group
Research and Technology/Information Services Standards Division
British Telecom
St Vincent House
Ipswich, United Kingdom

[†] University College
University of Oxford
Oxford, United Kingdom

The Boyer-Moore theorem prover is a highly automated tool. When it is presented with a conjecture it attempts to construct a proof within its current theory, with no user interaction. With no former experience of automated theorem proving the authors investigated its possible application to the process algebra of the ISO Formal Description Technique LOTOS. The Boyer-Moore was used to prove the correctness of complicated transition predicates and the equivalence of LOTOS processes. This paper reports on that work and its results.

1. INTRODUCTION

Proving theorems is a fundamental aspect of many established branches of engineering, for example, calculating tolerances and stresses. However, the majority of software engineers perform no such proof of their designs. One reason for this omission is the use of languages in which rigorous proof cannot be performed. It is partly to overcome this weakness that rigorously defined languages, termed formal description techniques (FDTs), are being developed.

Computer based proof assistants and theorem provers have been, and still are being, developed. The former check each step of a manually performed proof, while the latter attempt to conduct the proof.

This paper describes our attempt at applying the Boyer-Moore (BM)[1,2] theorem prover to the FDT LOTOS (Language Of Temporal Ordering Specification)[3,4]. We use the BM to prove the correctness of a complicated transition predicate and the equivalence (observational congruence) of two LOTOS process definitions. ACT-ONE, the datatyping sub-language of LOTOS, was not included in our investigation.

The reasons for choosing the BM and LOTOS are twofold. First, we have experience of LOTOS which is presently a Draft International Standard of the International Standards Organisation (ISO). Second, the BM has a high reputation, was available and is highly automated. This paper assumes no knowledge of the BM.

A short introduction to the BM is given in section 2, and a longer introduction can be found in [5]. Our chosen representation for the LOTOS syntax is discussed in section 3 with the rule base in section 4. This is followed in section 5 by an introduction to the transition predicate and equivalence rule theories (with full listings in appendices A and B respectively). Section 6 discusses the various issues arising and finally, we present our conclusions in section 7.

2. INTRODUCTION TO THE BOYER-MOORE THEOREM PROVER

The BM is a highly automated theorem prover in the sense that no user interaction occurs during a proof attempt. Given a conjecture, the BM tries to prove it by applying in-built rules within the context of the current knowledge base (theory).

The BM has three types of proof mechanism: rewrite rules, elimination rules and induction schemas. Rewrite rules specify how expressions can be transformed to equivalent ones, elimination rules specify how certain terms can be eliminated and induction schemas specify how results can be proved by induction.

The BM applies transformations according to a set of heuristics. These are divided into seven categories [5], listed below. The BM starts at 1 moving down the list, moving back to 1 after a successful transformation. If it is unable to apply any of the heuristics, the proof has failed.

1. Simplify the formula by using type information and applying axioms, definitions and rewrite lemmas.
2. Convert to clause form (ie. conjunctive normal form) and try to prove each clause separately.
3. Eliminate destructors eg. replace the formula $P(x-1,x)$ by $P(y,y+1)$.
4. Use certain equalities and "throw them away".
5. Generalize the formula by introducing variables for terms that have "played their role".
6. Eliminate irrelevant terms.
7. Try induction.

These mechanisms are all applied within the context of the current theory. All theories are built upon the initial knowledge base called ground-zero, which consists of the logical connectives (and, or, not and implies), the natural numbers and lists.

The logical connectives are defined using the Lisp "if" function, which takes the form:

(if <condition> <body1> <body2>)

If <condition> is evaluated to be true then <body1> is evaluated, otherwise <body2> is evaluated. The definitions of the logical connectives used are:

    (and p q)   := (if p (if q TRUE FALSE) FALSE)
    (or p q)   := (if p TRUE (if q TRUE FALSE))
    (not p)   := (if p FALSE TRUE)
    (implies p q) := (if p (if q TRUE FALSE) TRUE)

The natural numbers and lists are defined in terms of the only data type provided by the BM, called a shell. It is used to construct inductively generated objects. A shell data type is characterised by:

    exactly one constructor of the type,
    exactly one base object from which the type is constructed,
    exactly one recogniser that recognises that type, and
    any number of destructors which return specific components from the type.

There must also be a well-founded relationship on the type. This is necessary for the application of induction. If the shell representation can be used then the BM's powerful induction principle can be applied. However, if shells are not used then this power is lost and only rewrite and elimination rules can be used.

The shell description of natural numbers is:

    constructor   : add1
    bottom object   : zero
    recogniser   : numberp
    destructor   : sub1

and the well-founded relation is lessp.

The shell description of lists is:

    constructor   : cons
    bottom object   : nil
    recogniser   : listp
    destructors   : car (returns first element) and cdr (returns list without first element)

and the well-founded relation states that the number of elements in the cdr of a list is less than the number of elements in the list.

A theory may contain any number of shell data types, provided each follows the rules. Shells cannot, however, be mixed.

3. REPRESENTATION OF LOTOS

Since LOTOS processes are inductively generated objects, the most obvious way of representing them seemed to be by using the BM's shell data type. However, shells allow only one constructor and only one bottom object; LOTOS has several constructors (eg [] and ||) and two bottom objects (exit and stop). Further, recursive processes would be impossible to define, since all objects must be built from the bottom object by the application of the constructor a finite number of times. Thus, for example, the recursive process P := a;P cannot be represented. For these reasons, we abandoned the idea of using shells. Eventually, we decided to use undefined functions. An undefined function is declared as follows:

(dcl ch (P Q))

where dcl is the keyword, ch is the mnemonic for choice, and P and Q are processes. Note that the idea of a process has not been added. The distinction between processes and events is left to the user.

3.1. Events and Processes

Specific events and processes are represented by literals, eg 'b. Thus the special events d and i and special processes stop and exit are represented by 'd, 'i, 'stop and 'exit respectively.

3.2. Functionality

The functionality of a terminating process is exit and is taken as the default (exit with parameters is excluded). For non-terminating process the functionality is noexit and is represented as (noexit P).

3.3. Constructors

Each LOTOS constructor is represented by a mnemonic with parameters, as follows:

Operator	LOTOS	Boyer-Moore
Action prefixing	a; P	(seq a P)
Enabling	P >> Q	(en P Q)
Deterministic choice	P [] Q	(ch P Q)
Non-deterministic choice	i;P [] i;Q	(ch (seq 'i P) (seq 'i Q))
Parallel Composition	P |[a,b]| Q	(par P (list 'a 'b) Q)
Disabling	P [> Q	(dis P Q)
Hiding	hide mid in P	(hide (list 'mid) P)

3.4. Recursion

Recursively defined processes cannot be represented analogously to their LOTOS representation. This is because the underlying LISP interpreter will not allow objects to be defined in terms of themselves – unless they are explicitly defined functions with a decreasing parameter on each recursive call.

The chosen representation of recursive processes (eg. P := a; P) is by the introduction of a repetition operator, rep, where (rep x) represents the event or process x repeated indefinitely. Thus process P in the example above would become (rep a). This is a reasonable model for tail recursion, which should be sufficient for specifications in practice.

4. CONSTRUCTING A THEORY IN THE BOYER-MOORE THEOREM PROVER

When axiomatising the LOTOS combinators, we encountered an unexpected problem. When we added axioms and rules, we found that the BM was unable to complete a proof which had previously been possible. The commentary below illustrates this by reference to the ch operator.

The convention used throughout this paper is to preceed user input with an arrow (->), output is in italics and comments are within the delimiters (* and *).

> -> (dcl ch (P Q))
> (* declares the function ch *)
> -> (add-axiom com-ch (rewrite) (equal (ch P Q) (ch Q P)))
> (* gives commutativity of ch *)
> -> (prove '(equal (ch P (ch Q R)) (ch P (ch R Q))))
> (* enters the conjecture *)

This conjecture simplifies, applying axiom com-ch to:

t.

proved

However, when the associativity axiom ass-ch is added, the BM fails to prove the same conjecture.

> -> (add-axiom ass-ch (rewrite) (equal (ch P (ch Q R)) (ch (ch P Q) R)))
> -> (prove '(equal (ch P (ch Q R)) (ch P (ch R Q))))

It rewrites:

	(ch P (ch Q R))	
as	(ch (ch P Q) R)	applying ass-ch,
then as	(ch R (ch P Q))	applying com-ch,
then as	(ch (ch R P) Q)	applying ass-ch,
then as	(ch Q (ch R P))	applying com-ch,
then as	(ch (ch Q R) P)	applying ass-ch,
then as	(ch P (ch Q R))	applying com-ch.

It has now returned to where it started and loops until the LISP stack crashes.

This feature is extremely undesirable. Normally in a formal system, adding new axioms can only increase the number of theorems, never lead to old theorems being unprovable. The explanation of the BM's failure lies in how it decides whether to rewrite an expression or not. The BM will only rewrite an expression if it becomes more alphabetically ordered, where singletons are given more alphabetic precedence than tuples. eg. It will rewrite (ch Q P) as (ch P Q) but not vice versa.

The reason BM uses alphabetical ordering is to avoid infinite loops. Unfortunately this approach also leads to infinite loops when they are avoidable, as above. To overcome the problem, the BM needs to be given more axioms and the task is to determine a minimal set of such axioms. Clearly, the fewer axioms which need to be added, the more useful the system will be.

As an experiment, to determine the axioms required, the twelve possible forms of the choice between three options were alphabetically ordered. Axioms were then added to rewrite the twelfth to the eleventh, the eleventh to the tenth, etc. The BM warned the user each time an axiom was added which it considered redundant. These axioms were immediately deleted. Thus, a minimal set of axioms was constructed.

The resulting axioms were as follows:

    (add–axiom ass1–ch (rewrite)   (equal (ch P (ch R Q)) (ch P (ch Q R))))

    (add–axiom ass2–ch (rewrite)   (equal (ch Q (ch P R)) (ch P (ch R Q))))

    (add–axiom ass3–ch (rewrite)   (equal (ch (ch P Q) R) (ch R (ch Q P))))

    (add–axiom ass4–ch (rewrite)   (equal (ch Q (ch P R)) (ch P (ch Q R))))

    (add–axiom com–ch (rewrite)   (equal (ch P Q) (ch Q P))

The same problem also occurred with the par operator.

5. ADDING RULES

The semantic basis of LOTOS process algebra is defined in section 7.5.3 of the Draft International Standard [3] using transition predicates.

A transition is an expression of the form:

    P –a–> Q

which is interpreted as: process P can engage in event a and subsequently behave like process Q.

A Transition Predicate is a rule of the form:

        Transition–1, (Transition–2 ... Transition–n)
        ―――――――――――――――――――――――――
        Transition–conclusion.

which is read as: if Transition–1, (Transition–2 ... Transition–n) can occur then Transition–conclusion can occur.

Anything that can be proved about LOTOS is provable using the Transition Predicates. All Equivalence rules are deducible from the Transition Predicates but as they state equivalence between processes, they provide a more useful method of reasoning about processes. The Equivalence Rules are used to rewrite and manipulate LOTOS expressions into equivalent ones. Thus it is possible to show two LOTOS processes to be equivalent by applying the rules and reducing them to the same LOTOS expression.

There are may different types of equivalence. In this paper we use Milner's observational congruence [6]. The rules used are taken from Appendix B of [3], where a guide to some types of equivalences can also be found.

5.1. The Transition Predicates

Transitions were represented in as (trans P a Q) and Transition Predicates as (implies (hypotheses) (conclusion)). A full list of Transition Predicates entered can be found in Appendix A. What follows is an example of a proof conducted within this system. It is an example of reasoning about a complex process. The LOTOS formulation of the conjecture is to prove:

$$\frac{P \ -a-> \ Q}{((P \ [] \ R) \ >> \ S) \ [> \ T \ -a-> \ (Q \ >> \ S) \ [> \ T}$$

This is entered into the BM and successfully proved. As before input is preceeded by an arrow (->), output is in italics and comments are surrounded by (* and *).

    -> (prove '(implies (trans P 'a Q)
              (trans (dis (en (ch P R) S) T) 'a (dis (en Q S) T))))

This simplifies, rewriting with tr-en1, tr-ch1, and tr-dis, and unfolding the definition of equal to:

t.

proved

NB The BM list lemmas or axioms used in reverse chronological order.

5.2. The Equivalence Rules

The Equivalence Rules from [3] were represented as (equal (expression-1) (expression-2)). Rules to describe properties of the LOTOS combinators were entered (for a full list see Appendix B). What follows is a proof conducted within this System, to show that one process is observationally equivalent to the parallel composition of two smaller ones. The definitions of processes simple_duplex_buffer and one_time_buffer are taken from [3].

    process simple_duplex_buffer[in_a,in_b,out_a,out_b]: **noexit** :=
        in_a; (in_b;   (out_a; out_b; **stop** []   out_b; out_a; **stop**)
               [] out_a; in_b; out_b; **stop**   )
    [] in_b; (in_a;   (out_b; out_a; **stop** []   out_a; out_b; **stop**)
               [] out_b; in_a; out_a; **stop**   )
    endproc

    process one_time_buffer[in_data,out_data]: **noexit** :=
        in_data;   out_data;   **stop**
    endproc

these are added into the BM, for example the one-time-buffer is:

    -> (defn one-time-buffer (in-data out-data)
           (noexit (seq in-data (seq out-data 'stop))))

The conjecture to be proven is that simple_duplex_buffer is equivalent to two instantiations of one_time_buffer in parallel (intuitively one one_time_buffer in each direction), ie

one_time_buffer[in_a,out_a] ||| one_time_buffer[in_b,out_b]

This conjecture is entered into the BM and it is proved correct.

```
-> (prove '(equal (simple-duplex-buffer in-a out-a in-b out-b)
           (par  (one-time-buffer in-a out-a)
                 nil
                 (one-time-buffer in-b out-b))))
```

This formula can be simplified, using the abbreviation one-time-buffer, to the new conjecture:

```
(equal (simple-duplex-buffer in-a out-a in-b out-b)
       (par  (noexit (seq in-a (seq out-a 'stop)))
             nil
             (noexit (seq in-b (seq out-b 'stop))))),
```

which simplifies, rewriting with com-ch, par-nox, seq-nox2, com-par, ch-nox, nox-nox, par-seq-nox, and par-nox-seq, and opening up simple-duplex-buffer, to:

t.

proved

6. DISCUSSION

We chose at the start of the project to ignore the ACT–ONE aspects of LOTOS. The reason was simply to reduce the size of the problem. Adding ACT–ONE would, most likely, not be trivial.

One of the tasks was the search for a workable representation of the LOTOS process algebra within the BM. Our attempt at using the BM's "shell" datatype failed because its mould was too restrictive. This meant that the inductive proof mechanisms of the BM could not be used.

The representation we finally used for the operators was the BM's "undeclared function". This provided a syntactic representation without any semantic definition. This was quite deliberate, since what we wanted to do was to add the semantics by constructing two separate theories: the transistion predicate theory and the equivalence rule theory. The former is the standard semantic definition of LOTOS given in [3] and the latter (given in Annex B of [3]) is derived from the trasnition predicate definitions.

When a conjecture is presented to the BM it attempts to prove it. After the attempt it states which axioms and lemmas it used and in which order. For a proof which succeeds the information is adequate to trace the proof path. However, for a proof which fails there is inadequate information. For example, it says what it has attempted but not why it chose that route. If the system is caught in an infinite loop then it is the LISP interpreter which gives an error message after its stack has overflown, and no details of the loop are given. The LISP trace function must be used to deduce further information.

To use the BM effectively one must at least have a good idea of how it works. For example, the order in which axioms are added and lemmas proved, may be important to a successful outcome. It is an unforgiving environment to work in.

The possibility of automatically translating LOTOS definitions into our representation is quite feasable for a subset of the process algebra. This was outside the scope of the project but could be the focus of future work.

7. CONCLUSIONS

LOTOS is a rigorously defined language and properties of specifications written using it are provable. This paper has demonstrated the use of the Boyer-Moore (BM) theorem prover to prove observational equivalence and a complicated transition.

A major difficulty was deciding how to represent LOTOS in the BM. Since induction is the BM theorem prover's most powerful proof mechanism and the shell data type provides the means for representing inductively generated objects, using shells in the representation appeared to be important. Unfortunately, they proved too restrictive for our purpose. A more expressive language would have been better.

The BM is completely automated; when the user enters a conjecture, no further interaction is permitted while an attempt is made to establish its truth. Since the proof is not an exhaustive search, if a wrong step is taken, a provable conjecture may not be proved. The responsibility for checking falls to the user.

This work proved useful for two main reasons. First, it demonstrated the care necessary when using a theorem prover. Second, it showed the importance of a sufficiently expressive language. Future work could usefully include the investigation of other theorem provers and their applicability to both the process algebra and the data typing of LOTOS. Systems which allowed the user to be involed in a proof attempt would seem appropriate.

ACKNOWLEDGEMENTS

Acknowledgement is made to the Director of Research and Technology of British Telecom for permission to publish this paper.

Support from colleagues, especially David Freestone, was greatly appreciated.

The work reported in this paper was performed under FORMAP, a collaborative project between British Telecommunications plc and the General Electric Company plc, within the UK Alvey programme (SE/051).

Matthew Fletcher was funded under the British Telecom student sponsorship scheme.

REFERENCES

[1] Boyer R S, Moore J S. "A Computational Logic", Academic Press, New York, 1979.

[2] Boyer R S, Moore J S. "Metafunctions: proving them correct and using them efficiently as new proof procedures" in The Correctness Problem in Computer Science eds Boyer R S, Moore J S. Academic Press, London, 1981.

[3] Information processing systems ISO/TC 97/SC 21 – "Open Systems Interconnection – LOTOS – A Formal Description Technique based on the Temporal Ordering of Observational Behaviour", ISO DIS 8807.

[4] Bolognesi T, Brinksma E, "Introduction to the ISO Specification Language", in Computer Networks And ISDN Systems, Vol 14, Number 1, Pages 25-59, 1987.

[5] Lindsay P A, Moore R C, Ritchie B, "Review of Existing Theorem Provers", Technical Report Series UCMS-87-8-2 Department of Computer Science, University of Manchester.

[6] Milner R, "A Calculus of Communicating Systems", Springer-Verlag LNCS 92.

APPENDIX A: THE TRANSITION PREDICATES SYSTEM

The Transition Predicates represented are a subset of those stated in [1]. In some cases they have been simplified, for instance, the Transition Predicates defining deterministic choice allow choice between an infinite number of processes. This has had to be modified to a choice between a finite (but unbounded) number of events.

A.1. Examples of Translation from Transition Predicates to the Boyer-Moore

(a)   a;P -a-> P

          (add-axiom tr-seq (rewrite) (trans (seq a P) a P))

(b)   P -a-> Q

          P [] R -a-> Q

          (add-axiom tr-ch1 (rewrite) (implies (trans P a Q) (trans (ch P R) a R)))

(e)   stop generates no inference rules

          (add-axiom tr-stop (rewrite) (not (trans 'stop a P)))

(f)   P -a-> Q   R -a-> S

         ---------------------------------- provided $a=g_i$ for some $i \in [1..n]$

         P $|[g_1,...,g_n]|$ R -a-> Q $|[g_1,...,g_n]|$ S

         (add-axiom tr-internal (rewrite)
                (implies (and (trans P a Q)(trans R a S))(is-el a lst))
                (trans (par P lst R) a (par Q lst S))))

A.2. The Transition Predicates System

(dcl trans (P a Q))

A.2.1 Choice

(dcl ch (P Q))
(add-axiom tr-ch1 (rewrite) (implies (trans P a Q) (trans (ch P R) a Q)))
(add-axiom tr-ch2 (rewrite) (implies (trans P a Q) (trans (ch R P) a Q)))

A.2.2. Action-Prefixing

(dcl seq (a P))
(add-axiom tr-seq (rewrite) (trans (seq a P) a P))

A.2.3. Enabling

(dcl en (P Q))

(add-axiom tr-en1 (rewrite) (implies (and (trans P a Q)(not (equal a 'd)))
                                     (trans (en P R) a (en Q R))))

(add-axiom tr-en2 (rewrite) (implies (trans P 'd Q)
                                     (trans (en P R) 'd R))))

A.2.4. Parallelism

(dcl par (P lst Q))

(add-axiom tr-par1 (rewrite) (implies (and (trans P a Q)(not (is-el a lst)))
                                      (trans (par P lst R) a (par Q lst R))))

(add-axiom tr-par2 (rewrite) (implies (and (trans P a Q)(not (is-el a lst)))
                                      (trans (par R lst P) a (par R lst Q))))

(add-axiom tr-par3 (rewrite) (implies (and (trans P a Q)(trans R a S)(is-el a lst))
                                      (trans (par P lst R) a (par Q lst S))))

A.2.5. Disabling

(dcl dis (P Q))

(add-axiom tr-dis (rewrite) (implies (and (trans P a Q)(not (equal a 'd)))
                                     (trans (dis P R) a (dis Q R))))

(add-axiom tr-dis2 (rewrite) (implies (and (trans P a Q)(not (equal a 'd)))
                                      (trans (dis P R) a Q)))

A.2.6. Hiding

(dcl hide (lst P))

(add-axiom tr-hide (rewrite) (implies (and (trans P a Q)(not (is-el a lst)))
                                      (trans (hide lst P) a (hide lst Q))))

(add-axiom tr-hide2 (rewrite) (implies (and (trans P a Q)(is-el a lst))
                                       (trans (hide lst P) 'i (hide lst Q))))

A.2.7. Miscellaneous

(defn is-el (x lst) (if (not (listp lst)) nil
                        (if (equal lst nil) nil
                            (if (equal (car lst) x) t
                                (is-el x (cdr lst))))))

This function is used in several Transition Predicates to test whether a gate is present in a list of gates. It is not a Transition Predicate itself.

(add-axiom tr-stop (rewrite)   (not (trans 'stop a P)))

(add-axiom tr-internal (rewrite) (implies (and (trans P 'i Q)(trans Q 'i R))
                                          (trans P 'i R)))

APPENDIX B: THE EQUIVALENCE RULES SYSTEM

The Equivalence Rules represented are a subset of those stated in [5].

B.1. Examples of Translation from LOTOS to the Boyer-Moore

(a) stop >> P = stop
     (add-axiom en-st (rewrite) (equal (en 'stop P) 'stop))
(b) P ı[...]ı Q = Q ı[...]ı P
     (add-axiom com-par (rewrite) (equal (par P lst Q) (par Q lst P)))

B.2. The Equivalence Rules System

B.2.1. Choice

(dcl ch (P Q))
(add-axiom ass1-ch (rewrite) (equal (ch P (ch R Q))(ch P (ch Q R))))
(add-axiom ass2-ch (rewrite) (equal (ch Q (ch P R))(ch P (ch R Q))))
(add-axiom ass3-ch (rewrite) (equal (ch (ch P Q) R)(ch R (ch Q P))))
(add-axiom ass4-ch (rewrite) (equal (ch Q (ch P R))(ch P (ch Q R))))
(add-axiom com-ch (rewrite) (equal (ch P Q)(ch Q P)))
(add-axiom ch-st (rewrite) (equal (ch 'stop P) P))
(add-axiom ax-ch (rewrite) (equal (ch P P) P))

B.2.2. Action-Prefixing

(dcl seq (a P))

B.2.3. Enabling

(dcl en (P Q))
(add-axiom ax1-en (rewrite) (equal (en (en P Q) R)(en P (en Q R))))
(add-axiom en-st (rewrite) (equal (en 'stop P) 'stop))

B.2.4. Recursion

(dcl rep (a))
(add-axiom ax-rep (rewrite) (equal (seq a (rep a))(rep a)))
(add-axiom rep-stop (rewrite) (equal (rep 'stop) 'stop))
(add-axiom rep-stop2 (rewrite) (equal (rep (seq a 'stop)) a)))

B.2.5. Parallelism

(dcl par (P lst Q))
(add-axiom com-par (rewrite) (equal (par P lst Q)(par Q lst P)))
(add-axiom ass1-par (rewrite)
      (equal (par P lst (par Q lst R))(par P lst (par R lst Q))))
(add-axiom ass2-par (rewrite)
      (equal (par Q lst (par P lst R))(par P lst (par R lst Q))))
(add-axiom ass3-par (rewrite)
      (equal (par (par P lst Q) lst R)(par R lst (par Q lst P))))
(add-axiom ass4-par (rewrite)
      (equal (par Q lst (par P lst R))(par P lst (par Q lst R))))

B.2.6. Disabling

(dcl dis (P Q))
(add-axiom ass-dis (rewrite) (equal (dis (dis P Q) R)(dis P (dis Q R))))
(add-axiom dis-st (rewrite) (equal (dis 'stop P) P))

B.2.7. Distributive Axioms

(add-axiom seq-rep (rewrite) (equal (seq a (rep (seq b a)))(rep (seq a b))))
(add-axiom par-seq (rewrite) (equal (par (seq a P) nil (seq b Q))
          (ch (seq a (par P nil (seq b Q)))
          (seq b (par (seq a P) nil Q)))))
(add-axiom en1 (rewrite)(equal (en (ch P Q) R)(ch (en P R)(en Q R))))

(defn is-el (x lst) (if (not (listp lst)) nil
      (if (equal lst nil) nil
      (if (equal (car lst) x) t
      (is-el x (cdr lst))))))

This function is used in several Equivalence Rules to test whether a gate is present in a list of gates. It is not an Equivalence Rules itself.

```
(add-axiom par-rew (rewrite) (implies (and (is-el a lst)(not (is-el b lst)))
                              (equal (par (seq a P) lst (seq b Q))
                                     (seq b (par (seq a P) lst Q)))))
(add-axiom par-lst (rewrite generalize) (implies (is-el a lst)
                              (equal (par (seq a P) lst (seq a Q))
                                     (seq a (par P lst Q)))))
```

B.2.8. Noexit

```
(dcl noexit (P))
(add-axiom par-nox (rewrite)         (equal (par 'stop nil (noexit P)) (noexit P)))
(add-axiom par-nox-seq (rewrite)
                 (equal (par (noexit (seq a P)) nil (noexit (seq b Q)))
                        (noexit (ch (seq a (par P nil (noexit (seq b Q))))
                                    (seq b (par (noexit (seq a P)) nil Q)))))) 
(add-axiom par-seq-nox (rewrite) (implies (is-el a lst)
                 (equal (par (seq a P) lst (noexit (seq a Q)))
                        (seq a (par P lst (noexit Q))))))
(add-axiom en-nox (rewrite) (equal (en (noexit P) Q) (noexit P)))
(add-axiom seq-nox2 (rewrite) (equal (seq a (noexit P)) (noexit (seq a P))))
(add-axiom nox-nox (rewrite)         (equal (noexit (noexit P)) (noexit P)))
(add-axiom ch-nox (rewrite)(equal (ch (noexit P)(noexit Q)) (noexit (ch P Q))))
(add-axiom par-nox2 (rewrite) (equal (par P lst (noexit Q)) (noexit (par P lst Q))))
(add-axiom nox-par (rewrite)         (equal (noexit (par 'stop lst P)) (noexit P)))
```

B.2.9. Hiding

```
(dcl hide (name body))
(add-axiom hide-ch (rewrite) (equal (hide n (ch P Q)) (ch (hide n P)(hide n Q))))
(add-axiom hide-en (rewrite)         (equal (hide n (en P Q)) (en (hide n P)(hide n Q))))
(add-axiom hide-seq2 (rewrite) (equal (hide n (seq n P) (hide n P)))
(add-axiom hide-seq3 (rewrite) (implies (not (equal n a))
                              (equal (hide n (seq a P))
                                     (seq a (hide n P)))))
```

Using Estelle for verification
An experience with the T.70 teletex transport protocol

Marc Phalippou, Roland Groz

CNET LAA/SLC/EVP, BP 40, F-22301 LANNION Cedex, FRANCE
e-mail: mcvax!inria!cnetlu!groz

Abstract: *Formal Description Techniques (FDT) for protocols are now backed by software tools. It is possible to perform automatic verification of reasonably large protocols. This paper reports an experience in using Estelle tools (Veda and Xesar). Estelle is a FDT standardized by ISO. The tools were applied to T.70 (CCITT transport protocol for telematic services).*
Errors and inconsistencies were found in the CCITT recommendations. This paper analyses the results, and discusses the use of FDTs and tools in that particular case.

Keywords: protocols, transport protocol, Estelle, verification, simulation, temporal logic.

1. INTRODUCTION

Formal Description Techniques (FDTs) were designed to represent protocols and services in a formal language. The primary purpose was to help avoiding ambiguities so frequent in the informal wording of standards. Formal languages make it possible to run automatic tools. In fact, tools are a necessary complement to the use of FDTs. Without verification tools, FDTs are of less use than informal description, because they are too restrictive and more difficult to read.

Tools have been developed in the last few years for the main standard FDTs: SDL, Estelle and Lotos. Functions provided by different tools cover

— syntactic processing of formal descriptions (with syntax-oriented or graphic editors, and compilers);

— verification or validation (static checks, dynamic analysis, simulation);

— performance evaluation (with markovian analysis or simulation);

— automatic implementation;

— test generation...

In CNET (Research Centre for French PTT), some work has been done on Estelle, and, more recently, on SDL [Cavalli 88]. We have had for a few years some experience with Estelle, with applications to telecom-related protocols (switching in [Dinsenmeyer 87], radiotelephone etc...), or other protocols (message-handling as described in CCITT series X.400 recommendations). Our main thrust has been on protocol verification.

The verification tools we use have now grown mature enough for a convenient use on realistic applications. In previous papers, we had already advocated the use of several complementary *techniques* [Groz 85] for the verification of protocols. The time was now ripe for comparing the use of *tools* based on different techniques. Preliminary work [Brossard 87] assessed the use of three tools on two (academic) distributed algorithms. The tools used were:

— Ogive [Pradin 79], which performs static and dynamic analysis on Petri-nets;

— Xesar [Fernandez 85], verifying temporal logic formulas on Estelle descriptions;

— Veda [Jard 88], our Estelle simulator.

We considered that the four examples proposed in [CCITT 88] provided a good benchmark for a comparison of the tools we use for Estelle descriptions. In this paper, we report our experience on the use of these tools on those examples. We used Veda on all four examples, Xesar on Stenning,

T.70 and Abracadabra, and Ogive on Stenning only. In fact, we concentrate in this paper on T.70 (the transport protocol defined by CCITT for telematic services).

- It is the most complex of the four examples; hence, the worst-case (most severe benchmark) for verification tools.
- It is a real protocol (and a standard).
- The problems it raises (in terms of modelling etc) cover those raised by the other examples.
- The service definition was available; whereas it is not quite clear what service the "bump game" is supposed to offer (except excitement for some people, but this is not an easily-formalized notion !).
- Stenning protocol verification (with Xesar in particular) had already been presented in other papers [Richier 87].

The remainder of this paper is divided as follows. Section 2 presents the tools applied to T.70 (Veda and Xesar); it also refers to other tools that we use in our approach. Section 3 discusses the use of Estelle for a specification such as T.70. Section 4 gives the results of the validation of T.70, and describes the errors that were found. Section 5 comments the features and shortcomings of the tools we used. Section 6 summarizes our experience on T.70.

Whereas we briefly present the tools used in section 2, we do not present Estelle. No particular knowledge of Estelle is necessary to read this paper. However, those interested in this language will find the definition in [ISO 87], and more readable descriptions in recent papers like [Budkowski 88] and [Courtiat 87b].

2. VERIFICATION ENVIRONMENT

2.1 Background

Our group in CNET is in charge of protocol verification methods. Since other groups in the french PTT participate to the definition or standardization of protocols (in CCITT in particular), there is a real need for protocol validation. Unfortunately, the tools available when we started (in 1982) were scarce, and could not take into account real-size protocols. In order to be able to cope with such protocols, we developed a non-exhaustive verification method based on simulation. This led to the development of Veda, which we describe in section 2.3. At the same time, we used proof techniques and Ogive, which we applied to restricted versions of the real protocols. We also started cooperation with the university of Grenoble, for the development of an "industrial" version (Xesar) of their prototype Cesar, which sounded promising.

We have based our protocol environment on Estelle. This environment now consists of

- **Vedaedit**, a graphical editor for Estelle, developed by Verilog, as a preprocessor to Veda. This editor can be used in the first stages of protocol design: definition and graphic design of the architecture (module headers, channel types and connections etc).
- **Estelle WorkStation (EWS)**, developed by Esprit Project P1265 (Sedos Estelle Demonstrator) [S.E.D. 88]. This includes a syntax-oriented editor, a compiler, a debugging-oriented simulator, and a code generator. As members of this project, we are currently evaluating EWS on two applications: pan-european mobile communication cellular system, and the design of an ISDN switch.
- **Xesar** for verification.
- **Veda**, as a verification-oriented simulator. A special version for performance evaluation is under development.

Not many verification tools have been developed around Estelle. Most tools dealing with Estelle are oriented towards specification aids (such as syntax editor, and interactive simulation), or code generation. This is the case for the EWS, or a similar workstation developed by Bull, or other tools developed in northern America (e.g. [Vuong 88]). In fact, although numerous verification tools exist for formal methods such as Petri nets or finite state machines, few have been integrated into software environment handling FDTs.

2.2 Xesar

Figure 1 illustrates the functions of Xesar. In fact, the user never has to get "inside" the Xesar box. From an external point of view, the only inputs to Xesar are:

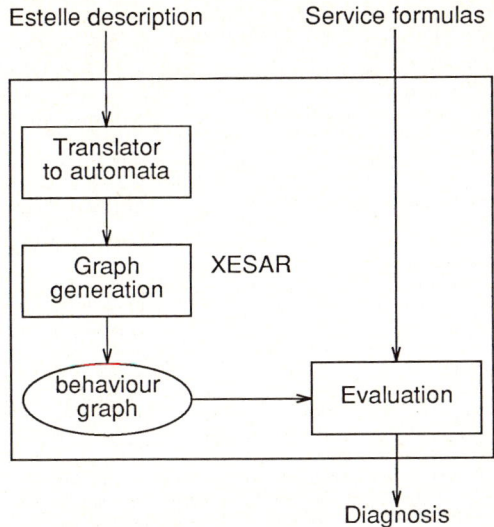

Figure 1. Structure of Xesar

— the protocol description (in Estelle/R);

— the service description (in LTAC logic formulas).

The diagnosis consists in detecting which formulas are falsified by the protocol behaviour. If an error is found, a complementary tool, **Cleo**, [Rasse 87] traces the behaviours that lead to the falsification of a formula.

Currently, Xesar limits the graph size to 65535 states. This is reasonably large. With such a tool, verification can be done with little modelling effort (since the protocol is described in raw algorithmic form in Estelle), for protocols that do not exhibit too much asynchrony. The only difficulties lie in the languages:

1. Estelle/R is a restricted and modified version of Estelle. It supports only static architectures (no trans part with "inits" in parent bodies). In our opinion, this is not too serious a restriction. In what is probably a large majority of protocol specifications, no explicit dynamism is needed. This is the case for T70, for which the CCITT text specifies only one entity: dynamic creation of entities is outside the scope of this protocol specification. Fully-fledged dynamism seems useful either for specifying OSI (dynamic) architectures, or for deriving efficient implementations. In the case of protocol *verification*, we only need to validate the intercourse between communicating entities, and there are at most two of them for T70 (and most peer-to-peer OSI protocols).

    As a matter of fact, "/R" does not stand for "restricted", but for "Rendez-vous". Xesar uses a rendez-vous semantics for outputs within transitions. This kind of rendez-vous is akin to the rendez-vous in the 1978 version of CSP [Hoare 78]. It is not the rendez-vous proposed in [Courtiat 87a], which is of the same nature as the one that exists in Lotos. Basically, the rendez-vous used is asymetric: the emitter is blocked (inside its transition, on its "output" statement) until the receiver is ready to input the message (i.e. fire a transition with a corresponding "when" clause). To represent the asynchronism of Estelle queues, explicit queues must be used in Xesar where necessary; alternatively, it must be ensured (with suitable delays for instance), that no deadlock stems from rendez-vous communications. This complicates the modelling of the protocol in Estelle.

2. The logic used by Xesar is LTAC, a conditional branching time temporal logic. The basic (monadic) operators are shown on figure 2. They represent the 4 combinations of universal and existential quantifications on nodes and paths of the behaviour tree. All operators can be conditioned by a formula. For instance, AL(f) can be conditioned by formula g. This is written AL[g](f). The meaning is: f must be true on all paths and all nodes starting from here (=now), as long as g holds. In effect, X[g](f) restricts the interpretation of operator X

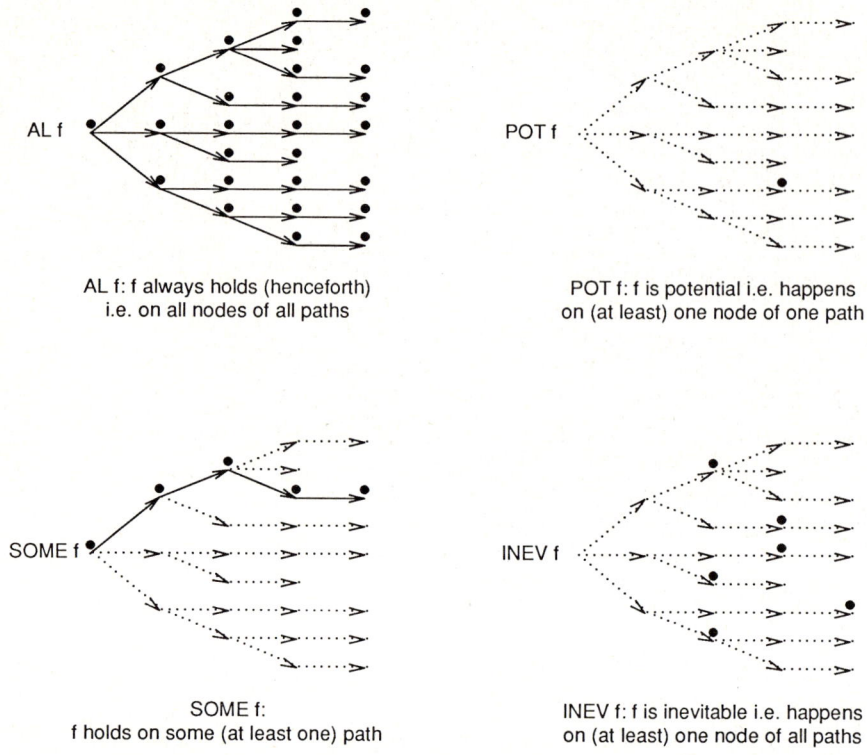

Figure 2. The four basic temporal operators of LTAC (branching-time) logic

to the connected subgraph from "now" where g holds.

These operators are rarely used directly. Most of the time, the service specification is written using macro-operators, which are combinations of the more basic ones. Examples of useful macro-operators include:

- FAIR(f) ≡ AL[not g](POT(g)). This means that, as long as g has not been reached, it is possible to reach it. In effect, it ensures that g is inevitably true at some point in any fair execution.

- NOT (f TO g) UNLESS h ≡ f => not POT[not h](g and not h). This formula means that it is not possible to reach a state satisfying g from a state sastisfying f without passing through a state satisfying h. This is very useful for specifying sequence of events in services.

As can be seen, the language for expressing service properties is a high-level one (temporal logic). The only drawback is that it is not so easy to master it, and translation from the usual informal service descriptions is not straightforward.

Xesar was developed by the Laboratoire de Genie informatique (Grenoble university) and Cap Sogeti Innovation, under a contract from CNET. For more details on the tool and its use for protocol verification, see [Fernandez 85] and [Richier 87].

2.3 Veda

Veda is a simulator of Estelle specifications. It is mainly oriented towards protocol (partial) verification using the classical technique of random simulation runs. Veda was developed by our group in CNET [Jard 88]. The advantage of being able to simulate any protocol description, with no size restriction, balances the fact that the verification is only partial: errors can be detected, but the absence of any error detection even for long simulations cannot guarantee protocol correctness, because the coverage is not exhaustive.

The verification method in Veda is based on an observer principle. The service to be verified is expressed in terms of a program that accesses the protocol internal states and events, and checks the soundness of the sequence of events observed. This program is run on-line, along with the program being simulated. Observers are described in a language that is almost the same as Estelle (with a few extensions to enable easy references to the objects observed). This approach is illustrated on figure 3.

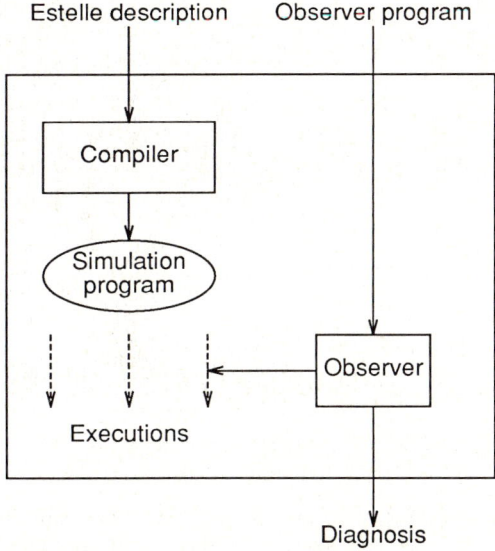

Figure 3. Verification of properties in Veda (using an observer)

There is no real limit on the size of protocols that can be validated using Veda. Protocols consisting of thousands of lines of Estelle, and an unbounded state space have been simulated.
Developments are under way to include performance evaluation in Veda, and facilities for orienting the simulation (towards some particular sequences of events or situations).

3. REMARKS ABOUT THE USE OF ESTELLE

3.1 Context definition

In this part we are making some comments that result from our situation as Estelle users. They are not supposed to constitute a general evaluation of the Estelle language: they only sum up the problems we had (and the solutions we found) when using Estelle for validation purposes with the tools that we described in the preceding section.
Our thesis is that validation specific constraints lead to Estelle descriptions of protocols that can differ significantly from specification oriented descriptions. We are going to analyse and justify these differences.
Our validation study deals with the four examples which have been selected by ISO/CCITT in order to illustrate the use of Formal Description Techniques. [CCITT 88] The remarks we made apply to all of them. Nevertheless in this paper most of our concrete examples make reference to the Transport Protocol (derived from T.70).

3.2 What we do not have to describe

The first step in the modelling of a system is to define what is relevant for our study and what can be safely omitted. It will be much easier to manipulate a short description with only significant features than a complete but too complex model.

This is a first major difference from what happens with a specification point of view. A characteristic of a specification is to be exhaustive; various aspects must be included, which represent different levels of abstraction in the protocol description. In the particular case of the transport protocol, we can distinguish at least three main aspects:

— the protocol mechanism, i.e. the algorithm used to establish a connection, transfer data and terminate the connection. This part of the specification is described in natural language in CCITT recommendations and summarized in the appendices in the form of state transitions diagrams and state tables. [CCITT 85b] [CCITT 88]

— resource management problems, for instance management of transport protocol entities, links between TSAP and TCEP, addressing problems, identification of transport connections, links with NSAP. This is partially described in some CCITT recommendations [CCITT 85a] and almost totally ignored in some others. [CCITT 85b] Some of these points can be considered as being implementation choices.

— precise data description, such as the description of TPDU formats given in [CCITT 88] (section 11.1.6). This is a very low level description since it deals with individual bits. It is described by figures in CCITT recommendations [CCITT 85b]. Hopefully, X.409 syntax will soon replace these descriptions.

In the T.70 validation study, we decided to focus on the protocol mechanism. It results from this choice that we can forget the two other aspects in our model; in effect, we consider only one transport entity between a sender and a receiver so that we do not care about management of different protocol entities and addressing problems. In a similar way, we are interested in the different information fields which are part of a TPDU but we do not care about what their bit structure will be in the real implementation. As a consequence, we have a short Estelle description, which is useful for the programmer, and a simple program structure (avoiding dynamic creation of module instances, for example, and complex Pascal data types), which is useful regarding our tools capacities.

In fact, the other aspects of the protocol specification should be validated in separate studies, since they are not situated at the same level of abstraction in a software development process based on progressive refinement of specifications.

3.3 What we have to describe

In a protocol specification, the environment is described by references to other specifications. We use "environment" to mean the service provided by the lower OSI layer, the service that has to be provided to the upper layer and the primitive functions which are used by the protocol in order to provide this service. In the examples of [CCITT 88], this environment is described in two ways:

— the other OSI layers which interact with the specified layer are modules with "external" bodies.

— the functions used by the specified protocol are functions declared as "primitives".

For the kind of validation that we want to perform (random and exhaustive simulations), we need a fully specified system. The environment (network, service ...) must be explicitly modelled. So "external" bodies have to be replaced by effective descriptions. We used for this CCITT service descriptions. [CCITT 85a], recommendations X.213 and X.214 (cf. next paragraph). These documents provide informal and even semi-formal descriptions (tables, state-transition graphs)/ so they must be translated first into formal descriptions. This translation is not too difficult since Estelle itself is based on a state-transition model.

The problem of primitive functions descriptions is more complex, because we must avoid over-specification. For example, the transport protocol described in [CCITT 88] uses the function MAP_TADDRESS for which the only specifications are the definition and value domains. Any Pascal description of such a function will constitute a particular choice, and this should be avoided. Other functions, like IS_VALID_TPDU, make calculations on the structure of data, which we chose not to represent in our model (in the preceding section we explain our reasons for that). So we will have some difficulties to code them ! Two different solutions can be adopted in order to handle these difficulties, depending on the role played by the function in the system:

— some functions handle parameters or data that are not directly linked to the protocol mechanism that we want to represent: for instance MAP_TADDRESS, mentioned above, since as we explained address management is not relevant for our study. These functions can be omitted and the related parameters will not be represented in our model. (They can be considered like transparent data for us)

— other functions are related with the algorithm: for example, depending on the value returned by IS_VALID_TPDU different actions will be performed by the protocol. In this case, we chose to avoid the description of the function and to represent the different possible actions by several possible transitions: the non-determinism of Estelle is used to simulate the different possible results of the function. In this way, we avoid over-specification. (In order to have a readable specification, it is very useful to write in a comment that the choice is the result of a "hidden" primitive function !)

3.4 Estelle and service descriptions

Note: by "service description" we mean the service provided by an OSI layer to the layer immediately above. We make reference to the network service defined in CCITT recommendation X.213 and to the transport service defined in CCITT recommendation X.214. In these texts, the "service" describes the full interface between two layers and in particular details the primitives used and all their possible sequences.

In a validation study, "service" description is used for two rather different purposes: modelling of the system and modelling of the requirements.

We already explained that the system to validate must be completely defined; both the protocol and the environment must be modelled. That indicates a "natural" way of structuring the Estelle specification in three modules: one for the layer being studied, and one for each adjacent layers. In the particular case of T.70 protocol, that means user, transport and network module.

In order to validate all the authorized behaviours of the transport protocol, the user and the network modules must have the most general possible features allowed by the relevant services. What we need is an automaton, which accepts every input allowed in the service definition and performs the corresponding output. Non-determinism is used to model the many possible answers of the environment to a particular solicitation: for instance, when the user of a transport protocol receives a Tcon_ind request, the possible answers are Tcon_resp or Tdis_req. Other features imply spontaneous actions from the environment, such as the initial request for a connection or a reset initialized by the network that model an error in a lower layer.

The service model that we used for network representation is the waiting list model defined in CCITT recommendation X.213. This work allowed to detect a deficiency in this model, as explained in the next part of this paper.

The second use of a "service" description is for the requirements of the system to validate: we would like to be able to check that the transport protocol, using the relevant network service, provides the appropriate transport service to the session layer. (This is the real validation phase.) In the VEDA approach, such a description of the service takes place in an observer (cf. section two). What we have to check is that all "observed" occurrences of primitives at the interface between transport service provider and transport service user are allowed by the service definition. Basically, the natural representation of the service in this case is an automaton seen as an acceptor for primitive sequences. For some verifications a finite automaton is powerful enough (authorized succession of primitives at one particular side of the connection), but not in the general case: in order to check that the number of data units delivered to the receiver user is compatible with what has been sent, a pushdown automaton is required. Both can be easily programmed in Estelle, using the Pascal facilities rather than specific Estelle facilities; but, for instance, counting possibilities are not provided by ordinary temporal logic formulas: in the comparison of the two techniques that we used for requirements representation, this is a powerful incentive in favour of observers, which are described in a programming language including Pascal facilities.

As a conclusion to service descriptions, we must insist on the fact that the two different needs for using service listed above imply different descriptions. For instance, the network service (X.213) had to be described in Estelle within the system. The transport service is described with an observer for Veda, hence in a variant of Estelle, and with LTAC formulas for Xesar.

This is a remaining difficulty in the tools currently available[1]. But it remains true that, whatever the tools, the transport service description used for verification of the transport protocol can hardly serve as a basis for simulating (e.g.) the session protocol.

3.5 From informal to formal descriptions

In conclusion, the main points that are relevant for validation purposes are:

— selecting what we want to validate, and as a consequence what we need to represent and what we do not need to represent.

— be careful to have an homogeneous description from an abstraction level point of view: at a high functional specification level data should rather be represented by Estelle modules than by bit strings.

— as a consequence of these two points, the translation from informal to formal is quite easy to perform. Little effort (a few days) was needed to produce the Estelle description of the T.70 system (about 500 lines for the protocol, 1000 for the whole system including the users and the network) and the observer modelling the service (about 200 lines of code, which can be compared to the 20-odd complex temporal logic formulas needed to describe the service for XESAR).

— in the negative part, we notice the necessity of two different modelling of the "service", and some kind of incompleteness of the service described: this point will be explained in the next section.

4. VALIDATION RESULTS

4.1 Precise objectives of the study

Once again, let us recall the definition of validation that we used: on the one hand we have a system (the protocol) described at a particular level of abstraction; on the other hand, a service which is an observable behaviour of the system at a higher level, i.e. taking into account only some particular interactions of the system with its environment. The purpose of the validation is to prove that all possible observable behaviours of the system are compatible with the requirements: the observed sequences must be a subset of the sequences allowed by the service specification.

Depending on which particular tool (VEDA or XESAR) we used, the results have different meanings: since XESAR builds the complete state graph of the system, the formulas we prove constitute general statements on the protocol studied. We can conclude: "the protocol has these properties". After a study with VEDA, we say: "in all the simulation cases that we have explored, the behaviour of the system was compatible with its requirements". Let us notice that in the case of errors one particular simulation sequence is enough to conclude to the incorrectness of the protocol.

It would be satisfying for the effective validation method to reflect this simple presentation: the protocol, the requirements and a tool for comparison. We will show that this objective is not completely reached yet. Some errors can be detected by a systematic comparison of the protocol and the requirements (this is detailed in a first paragraph), but other errors cannot be detected using this method, and we explain why in a second paragraph.

4.2 Comparing the system and the specification

This should be the only validation step. In reality, it is what we are able to conclude when all the problems which will be explained in the next section have been solved. We suppose here:

---

1. As a matter of fact, a direct translation from logic formulas into observers is considered for Veda, but this is not really a solution to the problem raised above:

    — First, because only linear temporal logic is relevant for simulations.

    — In any case, a language more powerful than that kind of logic must be used to express services that include counting properties.

— that we have correctly translated the informal system into an Estelle program: this applies to the protocol, the underlying service and the user.
— that we have correctly defined the requirements in a formal way, either into temporal logic formulas (XESAR) or into an Estelle-like observer (VEDA).

The work is then performed by the tool automatically (see section two for a description of the tools).

Let us give an example of what can be detected by both tools in the particular case of T.70. We detected a difference between the service provided by the T.70 transport protocol, using the facilities of the network service described in the X.213 recommendation, and the transport service described in X.214 recommendation. Figure 4 illustrates the inconsistency between protocol and service.

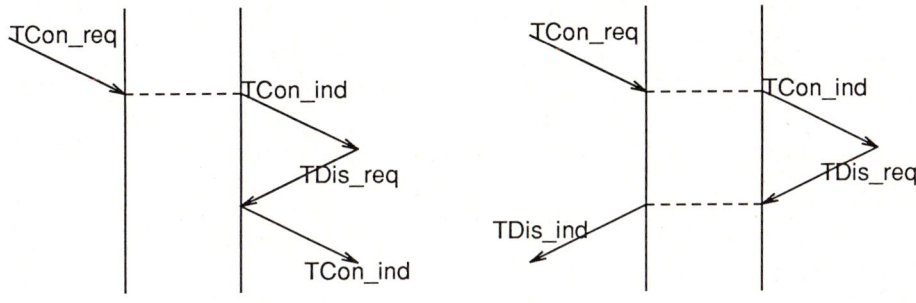

T.70 transport protocol   X.214 transport service

Figure 4. Behaviour difference between T.70 and X.214

NB. Henceforth we will follow the naming conventions of the T.70 recommendation.
We consider two transport protocol entities, named calling and called. During the connection establishment phase, the calling entity sends a TCR tpdu to the called entity. Provided that some conditions are satisfied, the called entity transmits a Tcon_ind to the user, which can answer with a Tdis_req if it does not want to establish a communication. The called entity sends a TCC tpdu to the calling entity. T.70 protocol allows the calling entity to try again to establish a connection by sending a new TCR. This will cause the delivery of another Tcon_ind to the user. If we examine the global succession of primitives allowed in the system by service description X.214, this is not correct: after a Tdis_req has been issued by one user, the transport connection attempt must be terminated with a Tdis_ind delivered to the other user.
This difference of behaviour was detected immediately with XESAR, and after a few simulations with VEDA. The tools also allowed to check the other requirements of conformance of the protocol with what was expected.

To illustrate the use of temporal logic, here is the service formula that was falsified by T.70.

NOT (after_user_2_tdis_req TO g10) UNLESS both_idle

where both_idle is a predicate that is defined to be true whenever both entities are in the idle state; and g10 is an auxiliary formula that expresses the fact that no other transport service primitive can be emitted:

both_idle == at(user[1].idle) and at(user[2].idle)
g10 == enable_user_2_tcon_resp or enable_user_2_tdt_req
   or enable_user_2_tdis_req or enable_transport_2_tcon_ind
   or enable_transport_2_tdt_ind or enable_transport_2_tdis_ind

Auxiliary formulas of the form enable_x_2_y express the fact that primitive y can be emitted by entity x. For instance:

enable_user_2_tdis_req == enable(user[2].tdis_req_1) or enable(user[2].tdis_req_2)

because tdis_req can be emitted in two situations, which correspond to the two transitions tdis_req_1 and tdis_req_2.

4.3 Errors directly detected by the tools

In this paragraph we analyse some validation aspects which do not result from a comparison between a system and its specification, but which are directly related to the analysis of the Estelle specification by means of the tools. Some of them are part of the normal debugging process of the Estelle description and their detection at this stage of validation seems justified. But some other should be detected by the normal process of comparison system/specification: unfortunately they do not, principally because we do not know how to express correctly some properties required (time constraints for instance). We will give three examples:

— some errors may have been introduced in the modelling of the system in a part where they are not expected, and consequently not specifically observed. In a first attempt to describe the network service with the waiting lists model given in X.213, an error occurred in the chaining of network primitives at one side of the network connection, because the model proposed in the CCITT recommendation does not represent correctly the disconnection process (see figure 5).

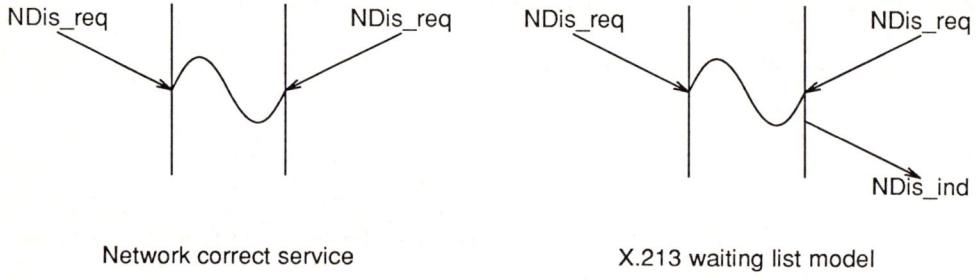

Figure 5. Error detected in the X.213 waiting list model

This caused the receiving transport entity to be blocked in a particular state due to a non-specified reception. But the calling side was still performing normal actions. At the transport/session interface, nothing bad could be detected. One side was performing normal connection attempts, and the other side was supposed to be disconnected. The problem has been detected with VEDA by tracing the exchanged messages at the network/transport interface (which is a way of observing at a lower level). At the higher observed level, more sophisticated specification description would have been necessary to detect the error (for instance fairness properties: an infinite sequence of connection attempts that fail).

— some errors result from some unspecified situations which have been "forgotten" in the protocol specification. The behaviour of our tools depends then on the default action which has been defined. With VEDA, in some cases, the tool detects the problem and sends a warning "unspecified reception". This allowed to detect a deficiency in the T.70 specification (which has been observed with XESAR too).
This is illustrated on figure 6.
NB. Notations in the following make reference to the T.70 recommendation and in particular the notations introduced in the appendices.
During the data transfer phase, if an invalid tpdu is received, the transport process (calling or called) sends a TBR tpdu, activates a timer and goes into the "0.3" state. It can remain in this state during some time. While the transport process is in this state, the user can still send Tdt_req since it has not been informed of the problem which has occurred at the lower layer. This event is not specified in the CCITT recommendation.

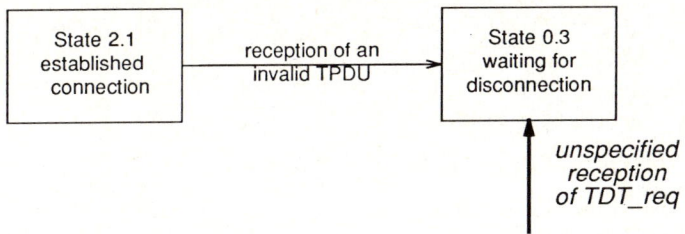

Figure 6. Unspecified reception in T.70 specification

This kind of error may not appear at service level because the behaviour of the system is not specified, and everything depends on the way the problem is handled by the validation tool. For instance, the message received unexpectedly may be simply ignored, without any consequence at service interface. We will then think to have validated the protocol while we would only have validated the behaviour of our validation tool ! Or it may cause a general blocking of the system, which will not be detected by the observer, since our description of the requirements by means of observable sequences does not include time constraints. (Notice that on the contrary it is very easy to detect this with XESAR using the predefined predicate "sink")

— other results that can be obtained with the tools include checking that all the transitions are used. XESAR is very suited for this kind of check. Of course the results are valid only if the environment is correctly modelled and produces all possible interactions with the system. This can show "useless" parts of the specification of the protocol, which are not always easy to detect manually at conception level. A consequence is to allow a simplification of the protocol.

This short list gives an idea of the problems that are not detected by the systematic method of comparing two behaviours. The difficulty lies in the non-systematic aspect of this part of validation. It is rather difficult to produce an exhaustive check-list that could be applied to all cases. Improvements should occur in modelling allowing to refine behaviours descriptions and including more and more things in the systematic way.

To conclude this overview of our validation study, we can make a reference to a similar work [Najm 87] based on a LOTOS specification of the class 0 transport protocol. Some of the modelling choices (selecting only significant aspects of the protocol for validation) are the same as we explained in the previous part. No errors were found in [Najm 87]. But this is probably because all the errors that we pointed out are due either to the T.70 protocol or to the waiting list network service model, and the LOTOS paper apparently deals only with X.224 class 0 transport protocol, which is slighty different.

4.4 Advantages of the mixed VEDA/XESAR approach

Let us sum up the contribution of the different tools to the above results:

— XESAR allowed to detect the unspecified reception in the T.70 protocol (this corresponds to a "sink" state in the behaviour graph). It detected also the behaviour difference between T.70 and X.214.

— VEDA detected these two errors, but the detection was less easy than with XESAR. In particular, the behaviour difference was first discovered with XESAR, and parameters had to be adjusted in a VEDA experiment in order to give to the wrong situation a greater probability to appear; then a careful study of the trace of the experiment allowed to understand the reasons of the observed phenomenon. On the contrary, the X.213 waiting list model error was detected only with VEDA, because the complexity of this model (if we refer to the number of states) prohibits its modelling with XESAR.

These examples illustrate the benefits of a mixed approach versus a single-technique approach. The exhaustive analysis of XESAR allows to detect some "rare" errors which may not appear in a VEDA simulation due to their low probability. Tuning simulation parameters turns out to be a difficult art. On the contrary, big state graphs can only be explored with a non-exhaustive tool. This is why neither of the two methods could have easily detected all the above listed errors.

Another advantage of the mixed approach is to allow a comparison of the results of both methods, which is important to check that the errors are not errors of modelling (for the service representation for instance, the two models are fully independent). Moreover, it is easier to understand the error causes by comparing two essentially different detections.

5. PROBLEMS LINKED TO THE USE OF OUR TOOLS

5.1 General remarks

In this section we describe the specific problems that we had when using the particular tools VEDA and XESAR.

The first point is that, at the time of writing, neither tool uses quite standard Estelle. VEDA uses a different syntax, derived from an earlier version (CCITT Recommendation X.250) of Estelle. It is being adapted to the new standard syntax but for our study the up-to-date version was not available. Anyway the full list of Estelle constructs will not be supported, especially dynamic creation of instances of modules, at least in a first step. XESAR uses a subset of Estelle, because the construction of the exhaustive state graph of the system prohibits the use of some features: only finite data types can be used (e.g. no dynamic structures), the dynamic creation of instances of modules is not supported ...

Our first approach consisted in translating the application examples listed in [CCITT 88] into a form acceptable for the tools. In the case of relatively small specifications (Stenning protocol for instance) this could easily be done. But for larger or more complex programs like the transport protocol, the translating effort was very important. Anyway it was useful in at least two ways: first we obtained a very large system that XESAR could not handle, and this fact convinced us that we did not need to be as exhaustive as the reference program for our particular purpose. Secondly, when trying to translate precisely the program, we discovered some "useless" transitions in it in an attempt to understand the purpose of each transition.

Our second approach was to start directly from the CCITT reference documents (this was in fact mandatory for the service descriptions for which we did not have formal specifications). Our conclusions is that the difficulty of this formalisation process depends greatly on each particular case. It was very easy to produce T.70 Estelle description; it would have been more difficult to produce a class 0 transport protocol directly from recommendation X.224. A general remark is that it seems more difficult to produce Estelle descriptions of services than descriptions of protocols.

In a completely different matter, we can notice that both tools offer few facilities to analyse the errors that have been detected. A great part of the time of the study is dedicated to understand what is the cause (in terms of the protocol) of the detected errors. Developments of the tools are being made to support more analysis facilities. However, whatever the aids, and whatever the verification technique used, the ultimate understanding of an error requires human interpretation.

5.2 Specific VEDA problems

We will focus on two main points:

— the first one lies in the mechanism of communication between instances of modules which exchange messages through unbounded queues, according to Estelle semantics. This causes some problems because it do not represent correctly the communication between adjacent OSI layers. This fact has been analysed in [Courtiat 87a]. In a few words, we can say that some service primitives can cross each other in the communication channel, creating unwanted situations. Such an event has occurred during a VEDA simulation, and an error was signalled by the observer which would have been incorrectly attributed to the protocol. The fact is that Estelle does not formalize exactly the OSI concept of a synchronized exchange of values between layers. In [Courtiat 87a] a different version of Estelle is proposed in order to solve this problem.

— the second one is linked to the technique of random simulation used in VEDA. When the structure of the specification to be validated includes a lot of non_determinism, with many possible transitions at each calculus step, some parts of the state graph will be hardly explored. It may be difficult to detect some errors which have a very low probability to appear during a random simulation. For example during the initialisation of a transport connection, T.70 protocol includes many decision steps where the connection may be refused. Since Estelle does not support a probabilistic choice between transitions, successful connections were very rare events. The difference between T.70 and X.214 behaviours, which we explained before, could be detected only after many simulations.

This kind of problem will be solved when a mechanism for guiding simulation is introduced in the tool. Some work is currently being done in this direction in our team in CNET.

5.3 Specific XESAR problems

We already outlined the limitations which result from the exhaustive aspect of a XESAR simulation: the supported language is a strict subset of Estelle, and this implies some constraints on the programming style. Moreover, the number of states grows in an exponential way and we reached the limits of our tools with the most complex studied examples, the abracadabra protocol and the transport protocol. With abracadabra, we obtained more than 25000 states: the tool needs about one megabyte of memory and 15 minutes of cpu time of a 68020 based machine to achieve its computation. In the T.70 case, the number of possible states was much higher, and we had to put limitations to what we represented in the model. The environment only could perform a strict subset of all the possible interactions, for example by introducing time constraints on its actions.

Another critical point lies in the rendez-vous mechanism introduced for communications through the channels. It causes some blocking problems which are not due to the protocol under study. The reason is that when a transition with an output is selected, this transition is "blocked" until the receiver module reaches an input statement corresponding to the blocked output: a collision can occur with two events like this, resulting in the blocking of the two modules. The best way to solve this problem would be to change the communication mechanism (for instance to a non-blocking synchronisation mechanism as was stated before). We used different techniques to cope with it: time constraints on the environment in order to avoid the collisions, or conditioned temporal logic formulas in order to avoid the part of the state graph related to these blockings.

Finally, a specific XESAR difficulty lies in the use of temporal logic for specifying the requirements. The expressive power of temporal logic formulas is not always sufficient to express all relevant properties of the system. Let us give an example related to the transport protocol: a global property of the system is that the number of data units send at one side of the connection is always greater than the number of data units received (the remaining units are still inside the system). This property is hardly expressible with XESAR's temporal logic formulas. It stems from the fact that this logic must be associated with (efficient) checking based on an exhaustive behaviour graph; therefore, computations on unbounded types (such as integers) cannot be included in this logic.

Moreover, as in the case of VEDA, we need two different representations for the "service", one inside the system in Estelle/R (to represent the underlying network for instance) and another one in temporal logic formulas for specifying the requirements. This fact can be considered as a difficulty: it would be very interesting if the network service used to describe the environment within the system could be expressed in temporal logic formulas too!

6. CONCLUSION

The validation study that we performed on the four examples selected by ISO/CCITT for the application of Formal Description Techniques was based on Estelle descriptions of protocols and on the two complementary tools VEDA and XESAR.

It allowed to point out the following items about the modelling of the system and its requirements:

— need for an Estelle description different from the one for specification purposes, in order to take into account only those aspects that are relevant for the particular validation objectives.

— need for a complete environment description, but taking care of avoiding over-specification or implementation choices.

— need for two different descriptions of the service, one within the system (protocol environment) and one outside (modelling of the requirements).

The main results that we obtained are:

— detection of a difference between the service provided by the T.70 protocol and the transport service described in X.214.

— detection of an unspecified reception in the T.70 protocol.

— detection of a deficiency in the network service model based on waiting lists presented in X.213.

It is interesting to point out that the whole study required relatively little effort: about two man-months for an unexperienced user of protocol specifications. It shows some of the benefits of formal descriptions of protocols and services, which allow to reduce the ambiguity of natural language and which can be manipulated by automatic tools. The tools we used, VEDA and XESAR, proved to be able to handle real size systems such as T.70 and its environment.

As a conclusion, our experiment shows that Estelle is well adapted both for describing validation-oriented specifications of real protocols, and for the study of these descriptions with powerful validation tools.

Acknowledgements

We are grateful to an anonymous referee for his helpful and detailed comments.

REFERENCES

[Brossard 87] J.Y. BROSSARD, "Comparaison d'outils de validation pour algorithmes distribues et protocoles", Note Technique Cnet LAA/SLC/263

[Budkowski 88] S. BUDKOWSKI, P. DEMBINSKI, "An introduction to Estelle: a specification language for distributed systems", to be published in Computer Networks and ISDN Systems.

[Cavalli 88] A.R. CAVALLI, E. PAUL, "Exhaustive analysis and simulation for distributed systems, both sides of the same coin", Congres Genie Logiciel IV, Paris, Octobre 1988

[CCITT 85a] CCITT Red Book. Volume VIII.5 Recommendations X.200 to X.250

[CCITT 85b] CCITT Red Book. Volume VII.3 Recommendation T.70

[CCITT 88] CCITT Study Group X - Reports R 29 and R 30 (January 1988) "Manual on application of SDL, Estelle and Lotos"

[Courtiat 87a] J.P. COURTIAT, "Contribution a la description formelle de protocoles", these de Docteur d'Etat, Toulouse, 1987

[Courtiat 87b] J.P. COURTIAT, P. DEMBINSKI, R. GROZ, C. JARD, "ESTELLE: un langage ISO pour les algorithmes distribues et les protocoles", Technique et Science Informatiques, vol.6, n.2, 1987 (french version);
"Estelle: An ISO language for distributed algorithms and protocols", Technology and Science of Informatics, vol 6, no 5, 1987, John Wiley & Sons Ltd (english version).

[Dinsenmeyer 87] I. DINSENMEYER, O. LOUVET, R. GROZ, "Utilisation de techniques de description formelle (TDF) pour la specification de logiciels de commutation", Annales des telecommunications, 42, no 7-8, 1987.

[Fernandez 85] J.C. FERNANDEZ, J.L. RICHIER, J. VOIRON, "Verification of protocol specifications using the CESAR system", Protocol Specification, Testing and Verification, V. North-Holland 1985

[Groz 85] R. GROZ, C. JARD, C. LASSUDRIE, "Attacking a Complex Distributed Algorithm from Different Sides: an Experience with Complementary Validation Tools", Computer Networks and ISDN Systems 10, 1985

[Hoare 78] C.A.R. HOARE, "Communicating Sequential Processes", Communications of the ACM, August 1978, p. 666-677.

[ISO 87] ISO/TC 97/SC 21, "Estelle: a formal description technique based on an extended state transition model", ISO DIS 9074, 1987

[Jard 88] C. JARD, R. GROZ, J.F. MONIN, "Development of VEDA: a prototyping tool for distributed algorithms", IEEE Transactions on Software Engineering, March 1988

[Najm 87]   E. NAJM, "A verification oriented specification in Lotos of the Transport Protocol", Protocol Specification, Testing and Verification VII, Zurich 1987

[Pradin 79] B. PRADIN, "Un outil graphique interactif pour la validation de systemes a evolution parallele decrits par reseaux de Petri (OGIVE)", These de Docteur-Ingenieur, Toulouse, 1979

[Richier 87] J.L. RICHIER, C. RODRIGUEZ, J. SIFAKIS, J. VOIRON, "Verification in XESAR of the sliding window protocol", Protocol Specification, Testing and Verification VII, Zurich 1987

[Rasse 87]   A. RASSE, "Cleo: logiciel d'explication et d'observation de programmes", rapport de DEA, Institut National Polytechnique de Grenoble.

[S.E.D. 88] SEDOS ESTELLE DEMONSTRATOR (Esprit Project 1265), "EWS - The Estelle Workstation", FORTE'88, North-Holland 1988.

[Vuong 88]   S.T. Vuong, R.I. Chan, W.Y.L. Chan, "An Estelle-C compiler for Automatic Protocol Implementation", Protocol Specification, Testing and Verification, VIII, North-Holland 1988.

SQUIGGLES: A TOOL FOR THE ANALYSIS OF LOTOS SPECIFICATIONS [1]

Tommaso Bolognesi
Maurizio Caneve

CNUCE - C.N.R.- Via S. Maria 36 - 56100 Pisa - ITALY
phone: +39-50-593230; fax: +39-50-576751
e-mail: BOLOG @ ICNUCEVM (bitnet); BOLOG @ CNUCE-VM (arpanet)

Some fundamental definitions and properties related to *strong*, *observational* and *testing-equivalences* are collected. It is shown that, in the context of LOTOS processes with finite-state representations, the verification problem associated with anyone of these three equivalences can be solved by properly applying an efficient algorithm recently proposed by Paige and Tarjan. Tool 'Squiggles' was implemented in order to experiment with the application of the illustrated analytical techniques to basic LOTOS specifications.

0. INTRODUCTION

Notions of behavioral equivalence play an important role in defining strategies and developing tools for the analysis of distributed and concurrent systems, such as computer network protocols. The role of behavioral equivalences becomes crucial whenever the semantics of the specification language adopted is based on such notions. This is the case for LOTOS, the Formal Description Technique being standardized by ISO [7, 4]. On the other hand, a lively discussion is still in progress on which equivalence is to be applied when: the differences within the spectrum of proposed equivalences are clear on theoretical grounds [6], but the practical criteria which should guide the LOTOS user in selecting a specific equivalence are still to be assessed.

Here we concentrate on three equivalences; however we will refrain from discussing their pros and cons as far as they refer to the intended meaning or use of a LOTOS specification. The main purposes of the paper are to collect some definitions and properties of *strong*, *weak* (or *observational*), and *testing-equivalences*, to study some algorithms for the verification of such equivalences, in the context of basic LOTOS processes (no data types), or of finite labelled transition systems, and to illustrate a tool which implements these algorithms.

The paper is organized as follows. After a review of the fundamental definitions and properties of strong, weak and testing equivalences, Section 1 introduces a problem called "relational coarsest partition": its solution is shown to be useful for verifying any one of the three equivalences between two finite labeled transition systems. In Section 2 we discuss verification algorithms, and show how an efficient algorithm by Paige and Tarjan for solving the *relational coarsest partition problem* is useful for verifying all three equivalences considered. Section 3 illustrates tool "Squiggles", and its application to a few LOTOS specifications. The merits and weaknesses of the tool are considered in Section 4, and some future developments of it are anticipated. Tool "Squiggles" presented here is a substantial enhancement of the "Double Squiggle" tool developed for project ESPRIT / SEDOS, first presented in [3].

---

[1] This work has been partially supported by the University of Twente, in the framework of ESPRIT Project SEDOS (Software Environment for the Design of Open Distributed Systems -ST410).

1. THEORETICAL BASIS

This section provides a collection of definitions and theoretical results on which verification algorithms are based. We show that weak equivalence verification can be transformed into an instance of a strong equivalence verification problem, which in turn can be formulated in terms of a "relational coarsest partition" problem. Analogously, we show that the testing equivalence verification problem can be transformed into a kind of string equivalence verification problem, which in turn can be formulated in terms of a "relational coarsest partition" problem. All equivalences are typically defined for processes that are represented as *labeled transition systems*.

Definition 1.1. (LTS.)
A *Labeled Transition System* (LTS) is a quadruple $<S, s_0, \Sigma, \Delta>$, where:
- S is a countable set of states;
- $s_0 \in S$ is the initial state;
- Σ is a countable set of actions (or labels)
- $\Delta \subseteq S \times \Sigma \times S$ is a relation called the transition relation.

We will use the notation $p \xrightarrow{\mu} p'$, $\mu \in \Sigma$, whenever $(p, \mu, p') \in \Delta$. The transition relation is naturally extended to the *transition sequence* relation, also denoted by the arrow symbol. For any sequence $s = \mu_1 \ldots \mu_n$ ($n \geq 0$) of actions and any pair of states p and p', we write:

$$p \xrightarrow{s} p'$$

if there exists a sequence of states $p_0, p_1, \ldots p_n$, with $n \geq 0$, such that $p = p_0$, $p_0 \xrightarrow{\mu_1} p_1, \ldots, p_{n-1} \xrightarrow{\mu_n} p_n$, $p_n = p'$.

Given state p of some LTS $<S, s_0, \Sigma, \Delta>$, we associate to it a set of action strings as follows:

$$\text{Strings}(p) = \{s \text{ in } \Sigma^* \mid \exists p' \text{ such that } p \xrightarrow{s} p'\}.$$

On this basis we may define the simplest notion of equivalence between LTS states, following the classical language equivalence of automata theory:

Definition 1.2 (String equivalence.)
Two states p and q of a LTS are *string equivalent* iff $\text{Strings}(p) = \text{Strings}(q)$. •

Finally, a *Finite Transition System* (FTS) is a LTS in which the sets S and Σ are both finite.

1.1. Strong and weak equivalences

For convenience, we recall here only the basic definitions of strong and weak (observational) equivalences. A detailed treatment of this topic is found in [10, 11]. These equivalences are stronger than string equivalence. That is, the partitions they yield over the universe of automata states are more refined than the partition induced by string equivalence.

In order to define strong equivalence, it is useful to first define the function F [11]. Let $<S, s_0, \Sigma, \Delta>$ be a transition system. Let $\text{Rel} = \{R \mid R \subseteq S \times S\}$ be the set of binary relations over set S. Function F : $\text{Rel} \to \text{Rel}$ is defined as follows.

Definition 1.1.1. (Function F.)
Let R be a binary relation over S. Then:

$F(R) = \{(p, q) \mid p, q \in S$ and for every $\mu \in \Sigma$

    (i) if $p \xrightarrow{\mu} p'$ then $(\exists q': q \xrightarrow{\mu} q'$ and $p' R q')$

    (ii) if $q \xrightarrow{\mu} q''$ then $(\exists p'': p \xrightarrow{\mu} p''$ and $p'' R q'')$ •

We are now ready to define strong equivalence, again with respect to transition system $<S, s_0, \Sigma, \Delta>$.

Definition 1.1.2. (Strong bisimulation, strong equivalence.)
(i)   A binary relation $R \subseteq S \times S$ is a *strong bisimulation* if $R \subseteq F(R)$.
(ii)   States p and q of a transition system are *strongly equivalent*, written $p \sim q$, if there exists a strong bisimulation R such that p R q. •

Definition 1.1.2.(ii) amounts to saying that $\sim$ is the *largest* strong bisimulation over S (this result derives from the monotonicity of function F with respect to set inclusion).

Usually we are interested in strong equivalence between *two* disjoint transition systems with initial states p and q, that is, systems with disjoint state spaces. This case is handled by defining the union of the two LTS's, in the usual way, and verifying $p \sim q$ in the new system.

From strong equivalence we can derive a weaker equivalence based on the idea of an *unobservable action*, denoted τ in CCS [10] and 'i' in LOTOS. In particular we can extend the transition relation Δ in order to essentially ignore the τ-actions that a transition system performs.

Definition 1.1.3. (double arrow '$\Rightarrow$'.)
Let $\Sigma_{obs} = \Sigma - \{\tau\}$ be the set of *observable actions*; let ε be the empty string; let s be a string of at most one observable action ($s \in \Sigma_{obs} \cup \{\varepsilon\}$) and let p and q be states. We define a 'double arrow' relation with elements of type $p = s \Rightarrow q$ as follows. We write $p = \varepsilon \Rightarrow q$ iff there exists a sequence of states $p_0, p_1, \ldots p_n$, with $n \geq 0$, such that:

$$p = p_0, p_0 \xrightarrow{\tau} p_1, \ldots, p_{n-1} \xrightarrow{\tau} p_n, p_n = q$$

Notice that it is always $p = \varepsilon \Rightarrow p$. We also write $p = \mu \Rightarrow q$, with $\mu \in \Sigma_{obs}$, iff

$$p = \varepsilon \Rightarrow p', \; p' \xrightarrow{\mu} p'', \; p'' = \varepsilon \Rightarrow q \quad •$$

Let $<S, s_0, \Sigma, \Delta>$ be a transition system. We define now a new function $G : Rel \to Rel$, similar to function F in Definition 1.1.1, to account for the presence of τ-actions.

Definition 1.1.4. (Function G.)
Let R be a binary relation over S. Then:

$G(R) = \{(p, q) \mid p, q \in S$ and for every $s \in \Sigma_{obs} \cup \{\varepsilon\}$

    (i) if $p = s \Rightarrow p'$ then $(\exists q': q = s \Rightarrow q'$ and $p' R q')$

    (ii) if $q = s \Rightarrow q''$ then $(\exists p'': p = s \Rightarrow p''$ and $p'' R q'')$ •

We are now ready to introduce a weaker notion of equivalence among transition system states, called *weak equivalence* (or *observational equivalence*).

Definition 1.1.5. (Weak bisimulation, weak equivalence.)
(i)   A binary relation $R \subseteq S \times S$ is a *weak bisimulation* if $R \subseteq G(R)$.
(ii)   States p and q of a transition system are *weakly equivalent*, written $p \approx q$, if there exists a weak bisimulation R such that p R q. •

On the basis of the definitions of strong and weak equivalences, it is easy to show that $\sim\ \subseteq\ \approx$.

Example.

The two FTS's in Figure 1.1.1 are weakly equivalent: the weak bisimulation sufficient to prove it is shown by the dotted segments in figure. Conversely, the reader may easily prove that the two FTS's are not strongly equivalent.

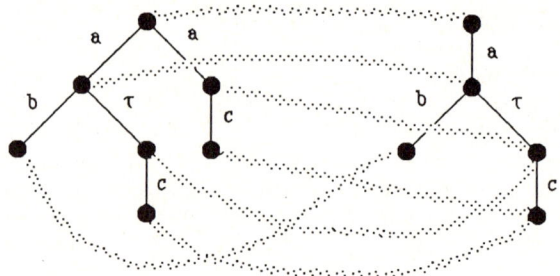

Figure 1.1.1 - A bisimulation

1.2. The relational coarsest partition problem

The *(mono-)relational coarsest partition* (RCP) problem is defined as follows.

Input:

A set S, an initial partition Π_{init} of S into disjoint blocks ($\Pi_{init} = \{A_1, A_2, ..., A_p\}$), and a binary relation T over S.

Output:

A partition Π_{fin} of S into disjoint blocks ($\Pi_{fin} = \{C_1, C_2, ..., C_q\}$), such that:

1) Π_{fin} is a *refinement* of Π_{init} (i.e. each C_j is a subset of some A_j).
2) For p, q in block C_i and any block C_j: $T(p) \cap C_j \neq \emptyset$ iff $T(q) \cap C_j \neq \emptyset$.
3) Π_{fin} is the *coarsest* partition (i.e. has the fewest blocks) that satisfies (1) and (2).

Given an element p of S, T(p) denotes the set $\{q \in S \mid (p, q) \in T\}$. Analogously, given a block B_i of some partition Π of S, we write $T(B_i)$ to denote the set $\{q \in S \mid \exists p \in B_i : (p, q) \in T\}$, and we write $T^{-1}(B_i)$ to denote the set $\{q \in S \mid \exists p \in B_i : (q, p) \in T\}$.

Condition (2) above can be rephrased by saying that the final partition must be *stable*, where *stability* is defined as follows. Given partition $\Pi = \{B_1, B_2, ..., B_n\}$, we say that Π is *stable with respect to B_i* if for any block B_j it is either $B_j \cap T^{-1}(B_i) = \emptyset$ or $B_j \cap T^{-1}(B_i) = B_j$. Notice that this amounts to saying that $T^{-1}(B_i)$ is the union of zero or more blocks of Π. Finally, we say that partition Π is *stable* iff it is stable with respect to all of its blocks.

The RCP problem can be generalized to the *multi-relational coarsest partition* problem (multi-RCP) by replacing the relation T of the RCP problem with an i-indexed family of relations T_i. Of course stability of the final partition must now simultaneously hold with respect to all of these relations.

1.3. Strong equivalence via coarsest partition

Given a FTS $K = \langle S, s_0, \Sigma, \Delta \rangle$, we may construct an instance of the multi-RCP problem as follows:

1) Set S of the multi-RCP problem is identified with the set S of states of K;
2) Π_{init} is the universal relation $S \times S$;
3) every relation T_i is obtained as the restriction $\Delta \mid_{\mu = \mu_i}$, that is,

$$T_i = \{(p, q) \in S \times S \mid (p, \mu_i, q) \in \Delta\}.$$

We recall that a binary relation over some set S is an equivalence iff it can be represented as a partition of S, so that we may allow using the terms "equivalence" and "partition" as synonyms. In particular, it will be convenient to think of a partition as a set of pairs (of states) rather than a set of blocks. Bearing this in mind, it can be proved that the solution Π_{fin} of the instance of the multi-RCP problem above *is* the strong equivalence relation over S of Definition 1.1.2.

Theorem 1.3.1. $\Pi_{fin} = \sim$ (for the proof see [3]).

1.4. Weak equivalence via strong equivalence

It is possible to prove or disprove the weak equivalence between states p and q of an LTS K by proving or disproving that they are strongly equivalent in an LTS K' derived from K. If $K = \langle S, s_0, \Sigma, \Delta \rangle$ then

$$K' = \langle S, s_0, \Sigma_{obs} \cup \{\varepsilon\}, \Delta' \rangle$$

where $\Sigma_{obs} = \Sigma - \{\tau\}$, ε is the empty string, and

$$\Delta' = \{(p, s, q) \mid p, q \in S, s \in \Sigma_{obs} \cup \{\varepsilon\}, p =s\Rightarrow q\}.$$

Theorem 1.4.1. $p \approx q$ in K iff $p \sim q$ in K' (for the proof see [3]).

The transformation from K to K' was first introduced in [8]. A wider discussion and bibliography on the topics discussed so far in Section 1 is contained in [5].

1.5. Testing-equivalence

We consider here a further useful equivalence for comparing LTS's. Indeed we will concentrate on *strongly convergent* FTS's, that is on those systems which cannot perform any infinite sequence of τ-actions. Before defining *testing-equivalence* we need a number of preliminary definitions. We will refer as usual to a generic LTS $K = \langle S, s_0, \Sigma, \Delta \rangle$, and let $\Sigma_{obs} = \Sigma - \{\tau\}$ denote the set of observable actions.

Definition 1.5.1 (Traces.)
The set *Traces(p)* of traces originating at state p is defined as follows: Traces(p) = {s in $\Sigma_{obs}{}^*$ | $\exists$ p' such that p =s$\Rightarrow$p'}. •

Definition 1.5.2 (Out.)
Given state p, the set of observable actions *Out(p)* is defined as follows:
Out(p) = {a in Σ_{obs} | p =a$\Rightarrow$p' for some p' in S}.

Definition 1.5.3 (Outs(P), MinOuts(P).)
Let $P = \{p_1, ..., p_n\}$ be a set of states. We define the following families of sets.

$$\text{Outs}(P) = \{\text{Out}(p_i) \mid p_i \in P\}$$

Furthermore, let MinOuts(P) be the largest subfamily of Outs(P) such that if $L_1, L_2 \in \text{Outs}(P)$ and $L_1 \subseteq L_2$ then $L_2 \notin \text{MinOuts}(P)$. •

Definition 1.5.4 (after.)
Let P be a set of states and $s \in \Sigma_{obs}{}^*$ be a string of observable actions. Then *P after s* is a set of states defined as follows:

$$P \text{ after } s = \{p' \text{ in } S \mid \exists \, p \text{ in } P \text{ such that } p = s \Rightarrow p'\}. \quad \bullet$$

Definition 1.5.5 (must.)
Let P be a set of states and L be a set of observable actions. We write:

$$P \text{ must } L \quad \text{iff:}$$
$$\quad \text{for any } p \text{ in } P$$
$$\quad L \cap \text{Out}(p) \neq \emptyset. \quad \bullet$$

Definition 1.5.6 (Must(P) and MinMust(P).)
Let P be a set of states and L be a set of observable actions. We define the following set:

$$\text{Must}(P) = \{L \subseteq \Sigma_{obs} \mid P \text{ must } L\}$$

Furthermore, let MinMust(P) be the largest subfamily of Must(P) such that if $L_1, L_2 \in \text{Must}(P)$ and $L_1 \subseteq L_2$ then $L_2 \notin \text{MinMust}(P)$. •

We are ready for the definition of testing equivalence between (states of) strongly convergent FTS's.

Definition 1.5.7 ($=_{te}$).
Let p and q be two states. We write $p =_{te} q$ iff:
$\quad$ for any s in $\Sigma_{obs}{}^*$:
$\quad\quad \text{Must}(\{p\} \text{ after } s) = \text{Must}(\{q\} \text{ after } s)$

It can be shown that $p =_{te} q$ implies $\text{Traces}(p) = \text{Traces}(q)$.

Example
With respect to the two FTS's in Figure 1.5.1 we may write:

$\quad$ p1 after ab = {p3, p4};
$\quad$ q1 after ab = {q4, q5};
$\quad$ Must (p1 after ab) = {{c, d}, {a,c,d}, {b, c, d}, {a, b, c, d}} = Must (q1 after ab);
$\quad$ MinMust (p1 after ab) = {{c, d}} = MinMust (q1 after ab).

By considering all traces, all reachable state sets and associated Must families for p1 and p2, one can conclude that $p1 =_{te} q1$. Note that p1 and q1 are not strongly nor weakly equivalent.

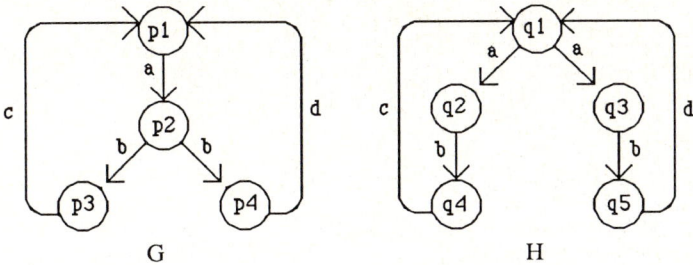

Figure 1.5.1. - Two testing equivalent FTS's.

Proposition 1.5.8.
Must(P) = Must(Q)   iff   MinMust(P) = MinMust(Q)   iff   MinOuts(P) = MinOuts(Q).
The proof is omitted for space reasons.

Corollary 1.5.9
From Definition 1.5.7 and Proposition 1.5.8 it follows immediately that

$p =_{te} q$ iff:
       for any s in $\Sigma_{obs}{}^*$:   MinOuts({p} after s)   =   MinOuts({q} after s)   •

The characterization of testing equivalence given in Corollary 1.5.9 is the one on which we have based the design of the algorithm for testing-equivalence verification presented in Section 2.

1.6. Testing-equivalence via extended string equivalence

It is possible to prove or disprove that two FTS's G and H are testing equivalent by proving or disproving that two derived *extended* FTS's G" and H" satisfy a version of string equivalence, which we call *extended string equivalence*, and denote by '≡'. Consider the FTS $G = <S, g_0, \Sigma, \Delta>$, where $\Sigma = \Sigma_{obs} \cup \{\tau\}$. First we derive from G the FTS G', with root g'_0 and transition labels in $\Sigma' = \Sigma_{obs} \cup \{\varepsilon\}$, as described in Section 1.4. Then we build the *extended* FTS G", with root $g_0"$ and transition labels in Σ_{obs}, which is the deterministic automaton which recognizes the same strings on Σ_{obs} recognized by G'. We call G" 'extended' because everyone of its nodes is labelled by a family of subsets of Σ_{obs}. A node X of G" is given label MO iff

       $\exists s \in \Sigma_{obs}{}^* : g_0" \xrightarrow{s} X$, and
       MinOuts ($\{g_0'\}$ after s) = MO.

Definition 1.6.1. (extended string equivalence: '≡'.)
Given two extended FTS's G" and H", with roots, respectively, $g_0"$ and $h_0"$, we write $g_0" \equiv h_0"$ iff

- Strings($g_0"$) = Strings($h_0"$), and
- whenever $g_0" \xrightarrow{s} g_1"$ and $h_0" \xrightarrow{s} h_1"$, for some $s \in \Sigma_{obs}{}^*$, the nodes $g_1"$ and $h_1"$ have the same MO-label. •

Theorem 1.6.2.
Given two FTS's G and H with roots g_0 and h_0, and their derived extended FTS's G" and H" with roots $g_0"$ and $h_0"$, it is: $G =_{te} H$ iff $G" \equiv H"$.   (The easy proof is omitted.)

2. ALGORITHMS

This section is meant to introduce the algorithms that we have implemented in order to achieve our analytical goals, and their interrelations. The central algorithm, useful for verifying all three equivalences considered, is due to Paige and Tarjan.

2.1. Paige and Tarjan's algorithm for strong equivalence

Paige and Tarjan have studied the (mono-)RCP problem introduced in Section 1.2, and given an algorithm to solve it in $O(m \log n)$ time, where m is the size of the relation T and n is the size of the set S [12]. Their algorithm, called PT-algorithm in the sequel, is based on the notion of *splitter*.

Definition 2.1.1. (Splitter.)
A block P of a partition Π is said to be a *splitter* in Π if $\Pi \neq \text{Split}(P, \Pi)$, where $\text{Split}(P, \Pi)$ is the partition obtained by substituting each block Q in Π such that $Q \cap T^{-1}(P) \neq \emptyset$ and $Q \cap T^{-1}(P) \neq Q$ by the blocks $Q_1 = Q \cap T^{-1}(P)$ and $Q_2 = Q - T^{-1}(P)$.

As observed by Paige and Tarjan, the simplest solution to the RCP problem is given by the following "naive" algorithm, which also makes use of splitters :

$\Pi := \Pi_{init}$;
$W := \Pi_{init}$; /* W is the set of all potential splitters */
while ($W \neq \emptyset$) do /* there is at least one splitter */
    remove a block P from W;
$\Pi := \text{Split}(P,\Pi)$;
    add to W all the new blocks added to Π;

Figure 2.1.1 - Naive algorithm

The naive algorithm runs in $O(mn)$ time, essentially because it uses all the possible splitters in Π. The improved complexity $O(m \log n)$ of the PT-algorithm is due to the fact that in the latter all potential splitters are used, while in the former once a block is split into two new potential splitters, only the smallest one is later used. This idea can be found also in a classic $O(n \log n)$ partitioning algorithm [1, p. 159] for deterministic automata.

We can now apply the PT-algorithm to solve the multi-RCP problem (defined in Section 1.2). This is done by the algorithm in Figure 2.1.2, where $PT(\Pi,T_i)$ is the solution of an instance of the RCP problem and T_i is the relevant relation.

$\Pi := \Pi_{init}$;
repeat
    for every T_i do $\Pi := PT(\Pi,T_i)$
until no changes are made on Π.

Figure 2.1.2 - Multi-PT algorithm

It can be proved that the complexity of the above algorithm is unchanged with respect to the PT-algorithm, namely it is $O(m \log n)$.

2.2. Closure algorithms for weak equivalence

As it appears from Section 1.4, the transformation of the weak equivalence verification problem into a strong equivalence verification problem requires the computation of the double arrow relation $=\mu\Rightarrow$, for $\mu \in \Sigma_{obs}$, on a given LTS $K = <S, s_0, \Sigma, \Delta>$. It is clear that the double arrow relation can be seen, thus computed, as the composition of two relations, as follows:

where
$$p =\mu\Rightarrow q \text{ if } p =\varepsilon\Rightarrow p' \text{ and } p' —\mu\Rightarrow q$$

$$p' —\mu\Rightarrow q \text{ if } p' —\mu\rightarrow p'' \text{ and } p'' =\varepsilon\Rightarrow q.$$

Notice that $=\varepsilon\Rightarrow$ is the transitive closure of relation $—\tau\rightarrow$; a classical $O(n^3)$ closure algorithm can be found in [1].

We now can compute $=\mu\Rightarrow$ via an "ε-driven transitive closure" algorithm described in [3], which uses $=\varepsilon\Rightarrow$ to compute first $—\mu\Rightarrow$ and then $=\mu\Rightarrow$. It is easy to show that the complexity of this algorithm is still $O(n^3)$.

2.3. State minimization preserving strong equivalence

Given two FTS's, say F1 and F2, the strong equivalence between (the roots of) F1 and F2 can be proved or disproved by running the multi-PT algorithm on the FTS obtained by taking the union of F1 and F2. Of course the same algorithm can be run on a unique FTS, say F, in order to minimize its states and obtain the smallest FTS strongly equivalent to F.

In spite of the similarity of our problem with the classical state minimization problem discussed in [1], it is important to point out that the latter addresses only *deterministic* finite state automata and is designed to preserve a different notion of equivalence, namely language equivalence.

2.4. From basic LOTOS specifications to finite transition systems

A basic LOTOS specification can be interpreted as a labelled transition system (LTS), via the axioms and inference rules of the language [7, 4]. On the other hand we have so far described verification algorithms in the context of *finite* transition systems (FTS's). It is thus important to devise algorithms for translating a basic LOTOS specification into a FTS, whenever this is possible. A most simple and direct approach to writing such a translator is to express directly in Prolog [15] the axioms and inference rules of the LOTOS operational semantics, and to use such program for generating the transition system via a breadth-first or depth-first strategy. Unfortunately we cannot guarantee that the construction of the transition system will always terminate; a discussion on sufficient conditions for being able to derive a FTS from a given basic LOTOS program is found in [5].

2.5. Larsen's inference system

In [9] Larsen proposes a decision procedure for verifying strong or weak equivalence between two LOTOS processes, or directly between two FTS's. The solution to this verification problem via the RCP problem consists of computing directly the relation '~' or '≈', that is, the *largest* bisimulation B_{max} over the set of FTS states, and then checking whether a given pair (p, q) belongs to B_{max}. Conversely, Larsen's decision procedure attempts the construction of a *minimal* bisimulation containing the given pair of LOTOS processes or FTS states. The procedure may involve backtracking, when the processes are non-deterministic, thus its time complexity is essentially exponential.

It must be observed that Larsen's decision procedure covers a wider class of problems than the multi-PT algorithm of Figure 2.1.2. If S_1 and S_2 are two basic LOTOS specifications which do not admit a representation in terms of FTS's, and they are equivalent, then Larsen's procedure never terminates. However, if they are not equivalent, the procedure *may* terminate, and report inequivalence.

2.6. FTS determinization and coarsest partition for testing-equivalence

A two-step strategy for proving that two FTS's G and H, with roots g_0 and h_0 are testing equivalent, i.e. that $g_0 =_{te} h_0$, is directly suggested by Theorem 1.6.2.

Step1.
Build the two extended deterministic FTS's G" and H" with roots g_0" and h_0", related to G and H as discussed in Section 1.6.
To do this, first we transform the FTS's G and H into FTS's G' and H' via the closure algorithms of Section 2.2. Then we transform G' and H' into G" and H" by applying a slight refinement of the classical "subset construction" algorithm (see [2], p. 93) for transforming a non-deterministic finite state automaton into a deterministic one which recognizes the same strings of observable actions. By this construction every state, say g" of G", represents a set $\{g_1', ..., g_n'\}$ of states of G'. The refinement of the algorithm simply consists in computing, for every newly created state g" of G", a MO-label MinOuts(g") (see Section 1.6), which is derived from the family of sets $\{Out(g_1'), ..., Out(g_n')\}$. H" is treated analogously.

Step 2
Prove or disprove that g_0" $\equiv$ h_0", i.e. that g_0" and h_0" are extended string equivalent.
This can be achieved by applying the multi-PT algorithm of Figure 2.2 to the FTS G" $\cup$ H", provided that the initial partition of the whole set of states is $\Pi_{init} = \Pi_{MO}$, where Π_{MO} is the partition where states are grouped according to their MO-labels. Then, if Π_{fin} is the final partition computed by the algorithm, we will conclude that :

$$g_0" \equiv h_0" \text{ (thus } g_0 =_{te} h_0) \quad \textit{iff} \quad g_0" \text{ and } h_0" \text{ are in the same class of } \Pi_{fin}.$$

The correctness of the conclusion above (thus, of the whole two-step approach) is guaranteed by the following theorem, where it is implicitly assumed that we deal with deterministic, extended FTS's G" and H".

Theorem 2.6.1
$g_0" \equiv h_0"$ *iff* $g_0"$ and $h_0"$ are in the same class of Π_{fin}.
The proof omitted for space reasons.

It is clear that the computational bottleneck of the two-step procedure above for testing equivalence is represented by the construction of G" and H", which may take exponential time. In fact, it has been proved that the verification of testing equivalence between FTS's is a PSPACE-complete problem [8], thus the existence of polynomial time algorithms for it is highly unlikely .

3. DEVELOPMENT AND APPLICATION OF TOOL 'SQUIGGLES'

The name 'Squiggles' has been chosen after the symbols '~' and '≈' of strong and weak (or observational) equivalence. The tool is formed of three components: a *Prolog* component and a *C language* component, for carrying out actual verification, and the user interface. This structure is the result of the following design choice: Prolog has been adopted since it allows for the rapid prototyping of the desired functions of the tool; when a satisfactory architecture is sketched in Prolog, then some components are identified as bottlenecks, and are replaced with efficient, C language implementations. The coexistence of executable, rapidly developed components, with efficiently implemented ones has proven useful for developing the tool in its current version. The same methodology can of course be applied for its future enhancements. For example, verification algorithms for new equivalences can be investigated in Prolog, thus augmenting the functions of the tool; and functions currently realized in Prolog which prove particularly inefficient (such as the translation of a LOTOS specification into a graph), can be implemented in C. These two efforts can be largely carried on concurrently.

3.1. Tool architecture and user interface

Squiggles has been implemented on a Sun 3/50 workstation, running Unix BSD4.2. It also uses *SunView 3.2* and *Quintus Prolog 2.2*. The SunView environment (Sun Visual/Integrated Environment for Workstations) is a system which allows one to develop interactive applications with user-friendly, graphics-based interfaces. Quintus Prolog is known to be the most efficient Prolog running on Sun workstations. The functional layers of Squiggles are summarized in Figure 3.1.1.

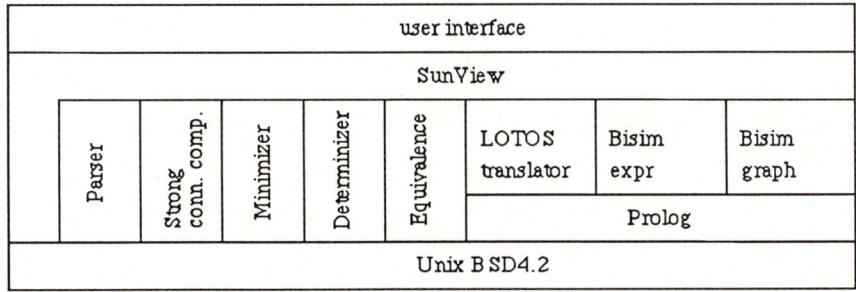

Figure 3.1.1 - Functional layers of Squiggles

During execution of Squiggles, three Unix processes run concurrently. The first process consists of the user interface, which communicates with the other two processes by using the appropriate Unix facility for exchanging messages. The second process consists of the Prolog environment and the three blocks (Prolog programs) directly on top of it in Figure 3.1.1. The third process consists of all the remaining blocks on top of the Unix layer. A block diagram of the tool is given in Figure 3.1.2; it includes all the modules of Figure 3.1.1 plus some other modules used by them.

The thin arrow in Figure 3.1.2 can be read as a 'uses' relation: for example, the LOTOS translator module uses the LOTOS semantics module. The thick arrow in Figure 3.1.2 identifies the input and output file types of the modules. The tool handles three file types, identified by the file name extensions '.lotos', '.plotos' and '.graph'. A file '.lotos' contains a basic LOTOS specification; a file '.plotos' contains the translation of a basic LOTOS specification into a Prolog term; a file '.graph' contains the symbolic representation of a FTS derived from some basic LOTOS specification. A file of type graph contains also a number of sections which can be produced and appended to it by some modules of the tool. For clarity the presence of such sections is denoted in Figure 1.3.2 by suffixes (namely '.c', '.c.e', and '.c.e.d') to the file extension.

A brief description of the blocks in Figure 3.1.2 is given below.

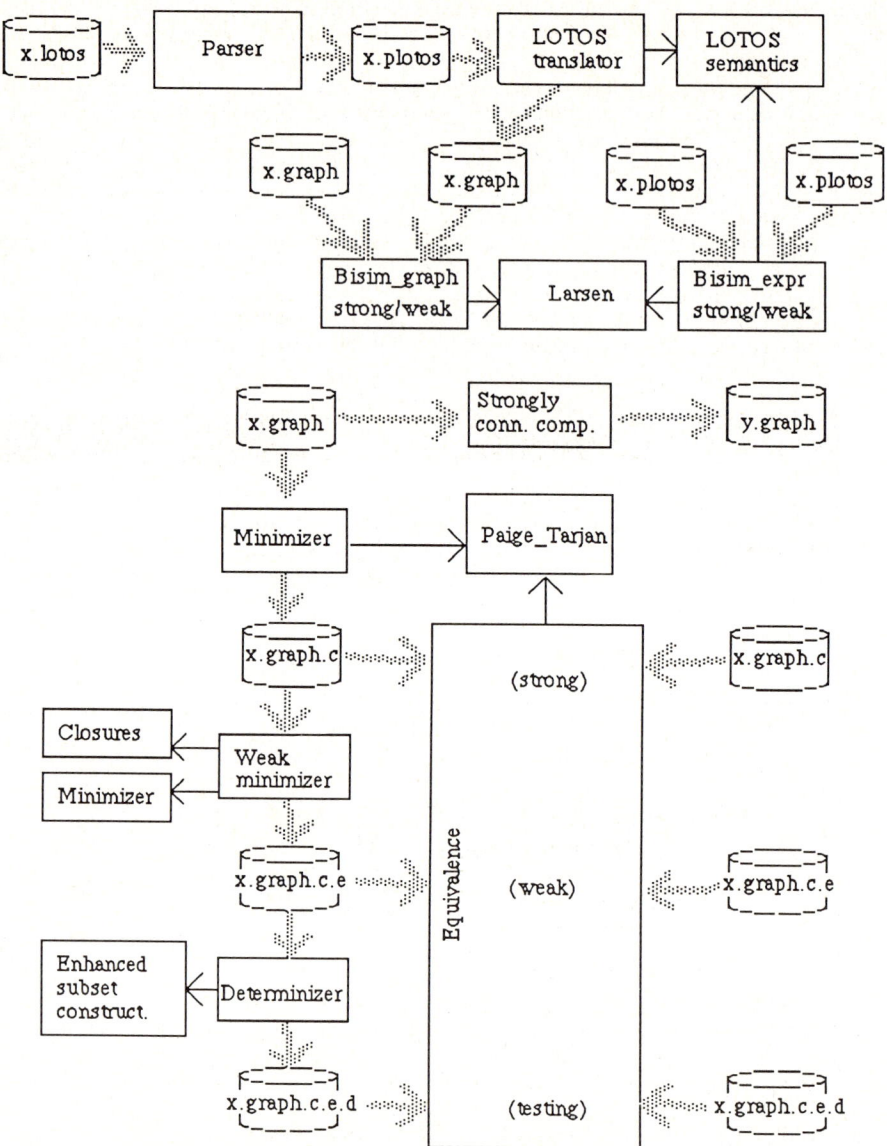

Figure 3.1.2 - Block structure and file types

- Block 'Parser' accept some file 'x.lotos' and produces a file 'x.plotos'.
- Block 'LOTOS translator' accepts some file 'x.plotos' and produces a file 'x.graph', by using a Prolog implementation of the operationale semantics of LOTOS.
- Blocks 'Bisim_expr' and 'Bisim_graph' verify the the strong/weak equivalence between, respectively, two plotos-files and two graph-files. Both blocks use block 'Larsen', which implements Larsen's decision procedure for equivalence verification (see Section 2.5).
- Block 'Strongly conn. comp.' accepts some file 'x.graph' and produces file 'y.graph' whose nodes are the *strongly connected components* of 'x.graph' (the algorithm for doing this was not discussed in Section 2; see, for instance, [14]).

- Block 'Minimizer' minimizes some file 'x.graph', via the multi-PT algorithm of Section 2.1, and produces another file 'x.graph.c' where the appended section '.c' contains a coded minimized FTS strongly equivalent to the initial graph.
- Block 'Weak minimizer' computes the closure (see Section 2.2) of the FTS contained in file 'x.graph.c' and produces file 'x.graph.c.e', where the appended section '.e' contains a coded and minimized version of such a closure.
- Block 'Determinizer' accepts file 'x.graph.c.e' and produces file 'x.graph.c.e.d', where the appended section '.d' contains a coded representation of the deterministic, extended FTS derived from the FTS contained in section '.e' (see Section 2.6).
- Block 'Equivalence' performs the strong / weak / testing equivalence verification between graph-files. All three verifications make use of the multi-PT algorithm (see Section 2.1).

The user interface of Squiggles consists of a multiple window which includes several sub-windows, as shown in Figure 3.1.4. We give now a short description of the sub-windows.

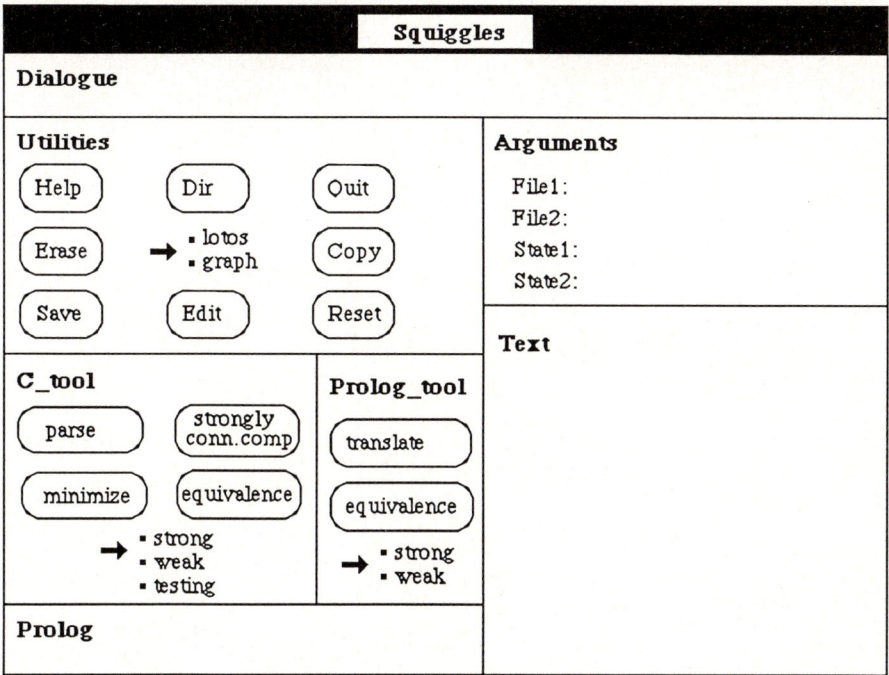

Figure 3.1.4. - User interface window

1) *Arguments* - It includes four fields, called File1, File2, State1, State2. These are used in various circumstances to indicate on which file(s) the relevant operation is to be performed. For convenience the files in the first two fields will be called File1 and File2 in the sequel. File1 and File2 should be written without their extensions (.lotos or .graph), since the extension indicated by the selector in the Utilities window is assumed. Fields State1 and State2 can be filled by the user with the two FTS states which should be tested for equivalence.

2) *Utilities* - It is a panel with eight buttons for performing general bookkeeping and file editing functions, and a selector, which is used to select between modes 'lotos' and 'graph'.

3) *Dialogue* - informs the user on the operations being executed and on their results.

4) *Text* - displays graph-files or lotos-files for editing, or the directories of such files.

5) *C_tool* - contains a button for parsing the lotos-file File1, a button for minimizing the graph-file File1, a button for determinizing graph-file File1 and building its associated extended FTS, a button for checking the equivalence between graph-files File1 and File2, a selector for choosing between strong, weak and testing equivalence or minimization (minimization preserving testing-equivalence is not implemented), and a button for finding the *strongly connected components* of graph-file File1.

6) *Prolog tool* - contains a button for translating (the plotos version of) a lotos-file File1 into a graph-file with the same name, a button for checking the equivalence between graph-files *or* lotos files File1 and File2, and a selector for choosing between strong or weak equivalence.

7) *Prolog* - is a window on Prolog, which should not strictly concern the end user of the tool.

3.2. Applications and performance

For testing the performance of the different components of Squiggles we have built a series of basic LOTOS specifications of increasing complexity. The starting element of the series is process max2, defined in Figure 3.2.1. The next element is max3, also defined in Figure 3.2.1.

```
           specification max3[in1,in2,in3,out]

           behaviour
                   max3[in1,in2,in3,out]
           where
                   process max3[in1,in2,in3,out] :=
                           hide  mid in
                                (max2[in1,in2,mid] |[mid]| max2[mid,in3,out])
                   endproc

                   process max2[a,b,c] :=
                           a;b;c;stop [] b;a;c;stop
                   endproc
           endspec
```

Figure 3.2.1 - A lotos specification

For convenience, we may express the way max3 is derived from max2 via the shorthand notation: max3 = max2 * max2. That is, we use the multiplication symbol to abbreviate the combination of the LOTOS *parallel composition* operator (such as '|[mid]|', which expresses synchronization gate 'mid') with the *hiding* operator (such as '*hide* mid *in* ...'), with hiding of the synchronization gates. As a consequence, the complete series of examples can be shortly described as follows:

```
        max2         max3 = max2 * max2       max5 = max3 * max3
                     max7 = max5 * max3       max9 = max5 * max5.
```

In Table 3.2.1, column 0 shows the performance of the Parser (from basic LOTOS to plotos), and column 1 that of the translator from basic LOTOS specifications to FTS's. Column 2 indicates the size of the derived FTS. In columns 3, 4 and 5 show the times for, respectively, FTS strong minimization, weak minimization and determinization. Columns 6 and 7 contain the times taken to verify, respectively, the strong and weak-equivalence of an FTS with itself: for each entry, the first line refers to the C tool (multi-PT algorithm), while the second line refers to the Prolog tool (Larsen's procedure). Column 8 contains the computation times for verifying the testing equivalence of an extended FTS with itself.

Table 3.2.1 (Times are expressed in seconds)

	0. Pars.	1. Trans.	2. |States|	3. ~-Min.	4. ≈-Min.	5. Determ.	6. ~	7. ≈	8. =te
max2	0	6	5	0	0	0	0 6	0 7	0
max3	0	7	11	0	0	0	1 10	1 20	1
max5	0	47	47	1	1	1	1 406	1 4353	1
max7	0	1872	191	6	6	3	9 -	6 -	9
max9	0	16872	767	45	52	29	68 -	49 -	80

The analysis of the experimental data clearly indicates that the bottleneck of the tool is the translation of LOTOS specifications into FTS's. For example, the translation of max9.lotos into max9.graph (with 767 states) took more than 4 hours, while the overall cost of verifying that max9.graph is weakly equivalent to itself (strong and weak minimization plus actual verification) took less than three minutes. It is not appropriate to directly compare the two figures for each entry of columns 6 and 7 with each other, since one figure refers to verification on FTS's and the other refers to verification on LOTOS specifications. However, even if we apply Larsen's procedure (in Prolog) directly to FTS's, we obtain performances which can hardly compete with those obtained by the C tool.

Incidentally, we remark that each one of the FTS's derived by the translate function for these examples is already minimum with respect to strong equivalence. For the specific list of examples chosen the input and output FTS's of the determinizer always have the same size, while in general one should expect a combinatorial state explosion.

It is clear that further experiments, with more significant LOTOS specifications, are needed for a more realistic evaluation of the functionalities and performances of the tool.

4. CONCLUSIONS

A number of definitions and properties of strong, weak and testing equivalences have been discussed, and some algorithms have been illustrated. Most of the results discussed in Sections 1 and 2 can be found in the open literature; however, having implemented them in a single tool, we found it useful to also collect them in a single paper. Essentially, the original parts of our work (besides the development of the tool), are the ones dealing with the verification of testing-equivalence: due to these achievements, we are now able to apply the Paige and Tarjan's algorithm for the verification of *all three* equivalences.

Tool Squiggles has been introduced. It verifies strong, weak and testing equivalences between basic LOTOS specifications or finite labelled transition systems, and generates the strongly connected components of a FTS. The idea of developing both a Prolog and a C language component of the tool has proven useful for two main reasons. Firstly, it allows a clear separation of the two concerns of rapid prototyping and of efficient performance. Secondly, in the case where the functions of the two components overlap (i.e. verification of strong and weak equivalence between FTS's), it allows for the "cross debugging" of implementations of different algorithms which perform the same task.

The analysis of the experimental data acquired so far indicates that the next function of the tool to be implemented in C should be the translation from basic LOTOS to FTS's. It must be observed, however, that handling symbolic expressions (such as LOTOS behaviour expressions) in C is not as simple as handling FTS's. Therefore the advantage of moving from Prolog to C in this case may not be as apparent as in the case of the actual verification function.

In spite of the widely recognized importance of equivalence notions in the context of formal descriptions of distributed systems, much work remains to be done in order to incorporate the algorithms illustrated above into a coherent methodology for effectively supporting the software production process based on LOTOS.

Acknowledgement. We express our gratitude to Scott Smolka, for many useful, long-distance discussions on some of the topics discussed in Sections 1 and 2, and to Piergiorgio Cremonese for discussions on the verification of testing equivalence.

REFERENCES

[1] A. V. Aho, J. E. Hopcroft, J. D. Ullman, *The design and analysis of computer algorithm*, Addison-Wesly Publishing Company, 1974.

[2] A. V. Aho, J. D. Ullman, *Principles of Compiler Design*, Addison-Wesley, 1979.

[3] P. Boehm et al., "Toward Practical Verification of Lotos Specifications", document ESPRIT / SEDOS / N. 121, University of Twente, October 1987.

[4] T. Bolognesi, E. Brinksma, "Introduction to the ISO Specification Language LOTOS", Computer Networks and ISDN Systems, Vol. 14, No 1, 1987.

[5] T. Bolognesi, S. A. Smolka, "Fundamental Results for the Verification of Observational Equivalence: a Survey", proceedings of the IFIP Seventh International Symposium on Protocol Specification, Testing, and Verification, H. Rudin and C. West (eds.), North-Holland, 1987.

[6] R. De Nicola, "Extensional Equivalences for Transition Systems", Acta Informatica, Vol. 24, pp. 211-237, 1987.

[7] ISO- Information Processing Systems- Open Systems Interconn.- "LOTOS- A Formal Description Technique Based on the Temporal Ordering of Observ. Behaviour", DIS 8807, 1987.

[8] P. C. Kanellakis, S. A. Smolka, "CCS Expressions, Finite State Processes, and Three Problems of Equivalence", Proceedings of the Second Annual ACM Symposium on Principles of Distributed Computing, pp. 228-240, Aug. 1983.

[9] K.G. Larsen, "Context-Dependent Bisimulation Between Processes", Department of Computer Science, University of Edinburgh, Technical Report No. CST-37-86, May 1986.

[10] R. Milner, *A Calculus of Communicating Systems*, Lecture Notes in Computer Science, Vol.92, Springer-Verlag, 1980.

[11] R. Milner, "Calculi for Synchrony and Asynchrony", Theor. Comp. Sci. 25, pp.267-310, 1983.

[12] R. Paige, R. E. Tarjan, "Three Partition Refinement Algorithms", SIAM J. COMPUT, Vol. 16, No 6, December 1987.

[13] R. Paige, R. E. Tarjan, R. Bonic, A Linear Time Solution to the Single Function Coarsest Partition Problem, Theoretical Computer Science, 40, pp. 67-84, 1985.

[14] E. M. Reingold, J. Nievergelt, N. Deo, *Combinatorial Algorithms: Theory and Practice*, Prentice Hall, 1977.

[15] L. Sterling, E. Shapiro, *The Art of Prolog; Advanced Programming Techniques*, The MIT Press, 1986.

TRANSFORMATION FROM LOTOS SPECS TO GALILEO© NETS

Saturnino Marchena† & Gonzalo Leon‡

†Alcatel Standard Electrica
Ramirez de Prado 5. 28045 Madrid, Spain.
‡ETSITM, Universidad Politecnica
Ciudad Universitaria s/n. 28040 Madrid, Spain.

This paper presents a combined approach to concurrent system specification using two different description techniques, LOTOS formal specification language and Galileo specification and design language. LOTOS is a standard specification language but it has lack of analysis methodology. The experience of using Galileo as a design method is quite satisfactory for analyzing the system properties. The central issue of this paper is to define a formal transformation from a LOTOS specification to a Galileo net to obtain, from the analysis of the resulting net, meaningful information about the LOTOS specification.

1. INTRODUCTION

LOTOS [Bolognesi 87], [ISO 87] is a formal specification language for concurrent systems. It is composed of two parts: behaviour derived from CCS [Milner 80] and CSP [Hoare 85], and functionality based on Act-One [Ehrig 85]. The behaviour specification is based on the temporal ordering of actions that are sequentially observable by an external observer. As a result of that, the "concurrency" is modelled by "non determinism". If two process "a;A" and "b;B" can evolve in parallel, being "a" and "b" different actions, the occurrence order of these actions is not determinate: $a; A||b; B = a; (A||b; B)[]b; (a; A||B)$. The behaviour specification is based on strong communication. If two or more processes "a;A" and "a;B" communicate by the "a" action, this action appears simultaneously in both processes: $a; A||a; B = a; (A||B)$. The functionality part deals with the description of data structures and value expressions. It takes the approach of equational specification of data types with initial algebra semantics.

Galileo [Sanchez 86] is a specification and design language for concurrent systems. It is composed by two parts: control based on Petri nets [Peterson 81], [Petri 84], [Silva 87] and functionality derived from Pascal data types. The control specification is based on a condition (control place) and event (transition) model, such that two or more events can occur simultaneously. If two process A and B can evolve in parallel, the events "a" and "b" are causally independent and may occur in either order or at the same time.

This kind of concurrence model is useful to observe the internal behaviour of a system, and to analyze its properties [Lopez 87], [Silva 87]. Galileo extends the Petri net model with: data places (they are places with data types associated), and functions associated to the transitions. When a transition fires, its associated function is executed. The firing of a transition may depend on conditions on data places. The control part of the Galileo can be analyzed using the Galileo Petri Net Analizer [Sanchez 86a] [Sanchez 86b]. The functionality part of Galileo cannot be analyzed with nets related techniques, but it can be validated using the Galileo simulator.

As a consequence of the comparison of the two models and the necessity of analyzing a LOTOS specification, the idea of the transformation from LOTOS specifications to Galileo nets came up. There are some works trying to combine ideas from CCS [Gold 86], CSP [Gold 86], [Degano 87] or ACP [Glabbeek 87] with Petri nets; however, nobody paid attention to LOTOS semantics and the necessity of analyzing a LOTOS specification. Most of them define the transformation using occurrence nets; this kind of nets are interesting as a basic semantics net model but it is not interesting for our practical purposes.

In section 2 we present the basic objectives of the transformation. In section 3 we define the transformation from the LOTOS behaviour expressions to Galileo nets in a constructive way. In section 4 we introduce the transformation from LOTOS functionality to Galileo functionality. The conclusions and future work are presented in section 5. Due to lack of space a complete example and almost all the proofs have been omitted. For these issues we refer to the full paper [Marchena 87]. As an example of application of the conversion method described in this paper, an alternating bit protocol specification has been analized [Leon 88].

2. TRANSFORMATION FROM LOTOS TO GALILEO

Functional and behavioural parts have been differentiated both in LOTOS and Galileo. So the transformation from LOTOS specifications to Galileo nets is performed in two steps: first, the transformation from LOTOS behavioural part to Galileo control part, then, from LOTOS functional part to Galileo functional part. The goal is to define such transformation as an homomorphism according to the following requirements:

- It must be possible to reason about the Galileo specification in a similar way to that used about the LOTOS specification. To achieve that, the structure of the LOTOS specification must be preserved by the transformation.

- If the sequential firing model is accepted in the Galileo net, the behaviour of the net must be isomorphic to the behaviour of the LOTOS specification.

- The analysis and simulation of the net must give us meaningful information about the LOTOS specification.

This kind of transformation requires to give a new semantics to the parallel operator of LOTOS, accepting the possibility of true parallelism of actions. The realization of this transformation suppose a constructive approach, for doing that an equivalence between the basic processes and operators in LOTOS and the basic nets and operators in nets must be defined.

The transformation from LOTOS functionality part to Galileo functionality part can be achieved only partially at a syntactic level. To get a complete transformation the user must supply a Pascal implementation of the functions defined in the abstract data types.

3. TRANSFORMATION FROM LOTOS BEHAVIOUR TO GALILEO CONTROL

In order to define a formal transformation, it is necessary first to introduce the basic mathematical models for LOTOS processes and Galileo nets. Then a mathematical model for the transformation is presented.

3.1 LOTOS behaviour: Process Algebra

In this section we present a language for reasoning about LOTOS processes in an algebraic way. Let I a process identifier set, F a functionality set {exit, noexit}, G a gate set, L a gate list set, "i" the unobservable action, $A = (G \cup \{i\})$ an action set, E a gate subset set, BE a boolean expression set. The signature of the formal language is defined:

```
sort:        P                        (* process set *)
             BH                       (* behaviour expression set *)
based on:    I                        (* process identifier set *)
             F                        (* functionality set *)
             G                        (* gate set *)
             L                        (* gate list set*)
             A                        (* event set *)
             E                        (* event subset set*)
             BE                       (* boolean expression set*)
const:       stop :       BH          (* stop behaviour expression *)
             exit :       BH          (* exit behaviour expression *)
funct:       _;_ :        (A,BH)BH        (* prefix operator *)
             _[]_ :       (BH,BH)BH       (* choice operator *)
             _|[_]|_ :    (BH,E,BH)BH     (* parallel operator *)
             _>>_ :       (BH,BH)BH       (* enabling operator *)
             _[>_ :       (BH,BH)BH       (* disabling operator *)
             hide_in_ :   (E,BH)BH        (* hiding operator *)
             [_] → _ :    (BE,BH)BH       (* guarding operator *)
             process
                _[_] : _ := _
             endproc :    (I,L,F,BH)P     (* process definition *)
             _[_] :       (P,L)BH         (* process instantiation
                                             non-recursive *)
```

A more detailed study including the axioms of these types, can be found in [Rodriguez 88] and [Ehrig 86]. In LOTOS, it is possible to define a recursive process E whose behaviour expression Bh is function of a set of recursive subprocesses $\{X1, \ldots, Xn\}$:

```
process E [...]: f :=
    Bh
where
    process X₁ [...]: f := Bh₁ endproc (* X₁ *)
    ...
    process Xₙ [...]: f := Bhₙ endproc (* Xₙ *)
```

endproc (* E *)

The recursion is achieved in LOTOS by process instantiation and it is used to express infinite behaviours. The behaviour of a process is expressed by the action tree obtained applying the transition system defined as dynamic semantic of LOTOS [ISO 87], [Bolognesi 87].

3.2 Galileo Control: Petri Nets

Let A an alphabet. A Petri net is a 5-tuple $N = (S, T, F, M_i, L)$ where:

- S place set, $S \neq \emptyset$
- T transition set, $S \cap T = \emptyset$
- F arcs set, $F \subset (S \times T) \cup (T \times S)$
- M_i initial marking, $M_i : S \rightarrow$ Nat
- L labelling function, $L : T \rightarrow A$

For $x \in (S \cup T)$ $.x = \{y | (y, x) \in F\}$ is called the *preset of* x, and $x. = \{y | (x, y) \in F\}$ is called the *postset of* x. $S_i = \{s | s \in S, M_i(s) \neq \emptyset\}$ is called the *initial place set*, and $S_f = \{s | s \in S, s. = \emptyset\}$ is called the *final place set*.

A transition t is enabled for a marking M_i, if for all $s \in .t : M(s) \geq 1$. If the transition t is enabled for a marking M, the marking M' follows M, results from firing t, and it is defined as:

$$M'(s) = \begin{cases} M(s) - 1 & \text{if } s \in .t - t. \\ M(s) + 1 & \text{if } s \in t. - .t \\ M(s) & \text{otherwise} \end{cases}$$

The state of the net is the set of marking places. The firing of a transition makes the net evolve from a state S to another state S'. The reachability tree is the tree of reachables states from the initial state. If the transitions cannot be fired concurrently, the reachability tree represents the total behaviour of the net.

In order to characterize the following transformation development we are going to introduce three special labels: "i", "exit" and "stop", and to extend the definition of a net as a 10-tuple $N = (S, Si, So, T, F, Mi, L, f, Ci, Co)$ where:

- S place set
- S_i input place set (= *initial place set*)
- S_o output place set ($S_o = \{s \in S_f | t \in .s, L(t) = "exit"\}$)
- T transition set
- F arcs set
- M_i initial marking
- L labelling function
- f functionality (if $S_o \neq \emptyset$ then f="exit" else f="noexit")
- C_i input conectivity ($C_i = Cardinal(S_i)$)
- C_o output conectivity ($C_o = Cardinal(S_o)$)

The new sets S_i and S_o are fundamental to define net operators; they define how the net can be connected by these operators. The net functionality is a concept equivalent to the

LOTOS functionality; it says if a net can be sequentially composed as prefix of other net. For the proper definition of some of the net operators, we need to work with nets which have acyclic roots (the initial places have no incoming arcs). It is necessary to define a special operation in net "root-unwinding" such as it takes a net and results in an acyclic root net. The definition of this operation can be found in [Glabbeek 87].

3.3 Transformation: mathematical model

A LOTOS behaviour is defined in a constructive way, starting from the basic processes and actions and composing them by the LOTOS operators. To obtain an equivalent net, it is necessary to preserve the same constructive approach. First the basic nets equivalent to the basic processes, and second the net operators equivalent to the LOTOS operators must be defined.

The transformation "tr" for each LOTOS process and operator is defined as an homomorphism in the following way: let two LOTOS processes P_1, P_2, and a binary LOTOS operator "opl". Let $N_1 = tr(P_1)$, $N_2 = tr(P_2)$ and $opr = tr(opl)$ the processes and operator transformed. Let "$\rightarrow$" an equivalence relation between processes LOTOS and nets.

$$P_1 \text{ opl } P_2 \rightarrow N_1 \text{ opr } N_2$$
$$\Downarrow \qquad\qquad\qquad \Downarrow$$
$$P \quad\rightarrow\quad N$$

The transformation "tr" is well defined if the P process result of the composition of P_1 and P_2 by "opl" operator, is equivalent to the N net result of the composition of N_1 and N_2 by the "opr" operator. If the equivalence between the basic processes and basic nets, and LOTOS operators and net operators are demonstrated, the result net N is equivalent by construction with the result process P.

The equivalence relationship "$\rightarrow$" that satisfies the requirements presented in section 2 is the isomorphism between the LOTOS behaviour tree and the net reachability tree. This equivalence can be demonstrated verifying that the transformation "tr" satisfies the axioms and inference rules of the operational LOTOS semantics [Bolognesi 87] [ISO 87].

3.4 Transformation: basic LOTOS process

(a) *Inaction*: stop

It is the inactive behaviour expression. The equivalent net is composed of an input place "s_0", a transition "t_0" labelled with a special label "stop", and a final place "s_1" that cannot be connected to any transition.

$$S = \{s_0, s_1\}, S_i = \{s_0\}, S_o = \emptyset$$
$$T = \{t_0\}, F = \{(s_0, t_0), (t_0, s_1)\}$$
$$M_i = \{(s_0, 1)\}, L = \{(t_0, stop)\}$$
$$f = \text{"noexit"}, C_i = 1, C_o = 0$$

Other possibility is to model the process "stop" as the state "s_1" only. Perhaps it is a more intuitive approach, but this requires the modification of the basic net model introducing labels on the places.

Equivalence. No axiom or inference rule is associated with the behaviour expression "stop". The equivalent net can fire transition "stop" and no more transitions.

(b) *Successful Termination:* exit

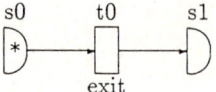

It is a behaviour expression that performs a successful termination action in order that a new behaviour expression can be enabled by the "$\gg$" operator. The equivalent net is composed of an input place "s_0", a transition "t_0" labelled with a special label "exit", and an output place "s_1" that can be connected to some transition.

$S = \{s_0, s_1\}$, $S_i = \{s_0\}$, $S_o = \{s_1\}$
$T = \{t_0\}$, $F = \{(s_0, t_0), (t_0, s_1)\}$
$M_i = \{(s_0, 1)\}$, $L = \{(t_0, exit)\}$
$f = \text{"exit"}$, $C_i = 1$, $C_o = 1$

Equivalence. The behaviour expression "exit" performs the successful termination action (exit $-\& \to$ stop). The action "&" plays a key role in the sequential composition. The equivalent net can fire the transition "exit". Transition "exit" defines the connectivity of the net.

(c) *Action Prefix:* g;B i;B

The behaviour expression B is prefixed by the observable "g" or unobservable "i" action. The equivalent net N is the composition of the net $N_a = N_g$ or $N_a = N_i$ equivalent to the action "g" or "i" respectively, and the behaviour expression N_b.

The action ("g" or "i") must be performed before the behaviour expression B. The equivalent net N_a of the action is composed by an input place "s_0", a transition "t_0" labelled with the label "g" or a special label "i", and an output place "s_1" that can be connected to some transition. $N_a = \{S_a, S_{ia}, S_{oa}, T_a, F_a, L_a, f_a, C_{ia}, C_{oa}\}$ where:

$S_a = \{s_0, s_1\}$, $S_{ia} = \{s_0\}$, $S_{oa} = \{s_1\}$
$T_a = \{t_0\}$, $F_a = \{(s_0, t_0), (t_0, s_1)\}$
$M_{ia} = \{(s_0, 1)\}$, $L_a = \{(t_0, "a")\}$ where "a" is ("g" or "i")
$f_a = \text{"exit"}$, $C_{ia} = 1$, $C_{oa} = 1$

If $N_b = \{S_b, S_{ib}, S_{ob}, T_b, F_b, M_{ib}, L_b, f_b, C_{ib}, C_{ob}\}$, the composed net $N = (N_a; N_b)$ is defined as:

$S = (S_a - S_{oa}) \cup (S_b - S_{ib}) \cup (S_{oa} \times S_{ib})$, $S_i = S_{ia}$, $S_o = S_{ob}$
$T = (T_a \cup T_b)$
$F = (F_a - \{(t_a, s_a) | (s_a \in S_{oa})\}) \cup (F_b - \{(s_b, t_b) | (s_b \in S_{ib})\}) \cup$
$\quad \{(t_a, (s_a, s_b)) | (t_a, s_a) \in F_a, (s_a, s_b) \in S\} \cup \{((s_a, s_b), t_b) | (s_b, t_b) \in F_b, (s_a, s_b) \in S\}$
$M_i = M_{ia}$, $L = (L_a \cup L_b)$
$f = f_b$, $C_i = C_{ia}$, $C_o = C_{ob}$

Equivalence. The semantics of the action prefix behaviour expression (x;B) is captured by the axiom (x;B $-x \to$ B). The behaviour expression is capable of performing action "x" and transforms into process B. The equivalent net must perform action "x" before enabling the net B.

Example: $a; B = a; (b; exit |||c; exit)$

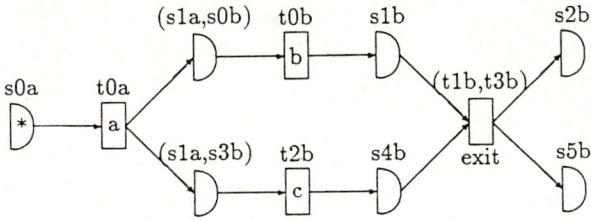

(d) *Choice:* A [] B

If A and B are behaviour expressions, $A[]B$ is a new behaviour expression that behaves either like A or like B. Let N_a and N_b the equivalent nets of A and B respectively, such that they are root-unwinding, the composition net $N = (N_a[]N_b)$ is defined as:

$$S = (S_a - S_{ia} - S_{oa}) \cup (S_b - S_{ib} - S_{ob}) \cup (S_{ia} \times S_{ib}) \cup (S_{oa} \times S_{ob})$$
$$S_i = (S_{ia} \times S_{ib}), S_o = (S_{oa} \times S_{ob})$$
$$T = (Ta \cup Tb)$$
$$F = (F_a - \{(s_a, t_a) | (s_a \in S_{ia})\} - \{(t_a, s_a) | (s_a \in S_{oa})\}) \cup$$
$$\quad (F_b - \{(s_b, t_b) | (s_b \in S_{ib})\} - \{(t_b, s_b) | (s_b \in S_{ob})\}) \cup$$
$$\{((s_a, s_b), t_a) | (s_a, t_a) \in F_a, (s_a, s_b) \in S\} \cup \{((s_a, s_b), t_b) | (s_b, t_b) \in F_b, (s_a, s_b) \in S\} \cup$$
$$\{(t_a, (s_a, s_b)) | (t_a, s_a) \in F_a, (s_a, s_b) \in S\} \cup \{(t_b, (s_a, s_b)) | (t_b, s_b) \in F_b, (s_a, s_b) \in S\}$$
$$M_i = \{((s_a, s_b), 1) | (s_a \in S_{ia}), (s_b \in S_{ib})\}, L = (L_a \cup L_b)$$
$$f = \text{if } (f_a = f_b) \text{ then } f_a \text{ else "exit"}$$
$$C_i = (C_{ia} \times C_{ib}), C_o = (C_{oa} \times C_{ob})$$

Equivalence. The behaviour of the choice behaviour expression $(A[]B)$ is captured by two inference rules $(A - x \rightarrow A'$ implies $A[]B - x \rightarrow A')$, $(B - x \rightarrow B'$ implies $A[]B - x \rightarrow B')$. It behaves like A or like B. N_a and N_b are enabled in the equivalent net, but if a transition from N_a or N_b fires only N_a or N_b remains enabled, respectively.

Example: $A[]B = (a; exit)[](b; exit |||c; exit)$

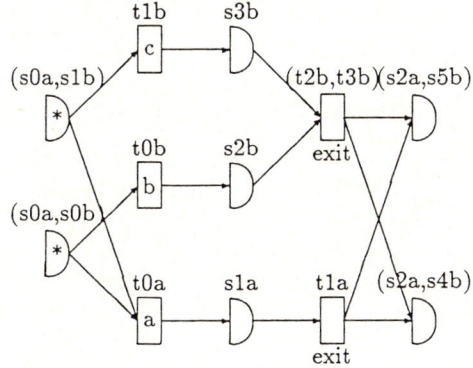

3.5 Transformation: more complex operators

(a) *Parallel:* $A|[E]|B$

If A and B are behaviour expressions, $A|[E]|B$ is a new behaviour expression that is able to perform any action that either behaviour expression is ready to perform at a gate not in E, or any action that both expressions are ready to perform at a gate in E. Let N_a and N_b the equivalent nets of A and B respectively, the composition net $N = (N_a|[E]|N_b)$ is defined as:

$S = (S_a \cup S_b), Si = (S_{ia} \cup S_{ib}), So = (S_{oa} \cup S_{ob})$
$T = (T_a - T_{xa}) \cup (T_b - T_{xb}) \cup$
$\quad \{(t_a, t_b)|(t_a \in T_{xa}), (t_b \in T_{xb}), (L(t_a) = L(t_b)), possible(t_a, t_b)\}$
$\quad where \;\; T_{xa} = \{t_a|(t_a \in T_a), (L(t_a) \in E \cup \{exit\})\}$
$\qquad\qquad T_{xb} = \{t_b|(t_b \in T_b), (L(t_b) \in E \cup \{exit\})\}$
$F = (F_a - \{(s_a, t_a), (t_a, s_a)|(s_a \in S_a), (t_a \in T_{xa})\}) \cup$
$\quad (F_b - \{(s_b, t_b), (t_b, s_b)|(s_b \in S_b), (t_b \in T_{xb})\}) \cup$
$\quad \{(s_a, (t_a, t_b))|(s_a, t_a) \in F_a, (t_a, t_b) \in T\} \cup \{((t_a, t_b), s_a)|(t_a, s_a) \in F_a, (t_a, t_b) \in T\} \cup$
$\quad \{(s_b, (t_a, t_b))|(s_b, t_b) \in F_b, (t_a, t_b) \in T\} \cup \{((t_a, t_b), s_b)|(t_b, s_b) \in F_b, (t_a, t_b) \in T\}$
$M_i = M_{ia} \cup M_{ib}$
$L = (L_a - (t_a, L(t_a))|(t_a \in T_{xa})) \cup (L_b - (t_b, L(t_b))|(t_b \in T_{xb})) \cup$
$\quad \{((t_a, t_b), L(t_a))|(t_a, t_b) \in T\}$
f = if $(f_a = f_b)$ then f_a else "noexit"
$C_i = (C_{ia} + C_{ib}), C_o = (C_{oa} + C_{ob})$

The predicate *possible(ta,tb)* decides wheter both transitions are simultaneously reachable in the nets N_a and N_b. This predicate eliminates the transitions not reachables in the composed net in order to simplify it. When the set of synchronization gates E is empty, the parallel operator "$|[E]|$" is equivalent to the interleaving operator "$|||$". The composed net $N = (N_a|||N_b)$ is the union of nets N_a and N_b.

Equivalence. The semantics of the parallel behaviour expression $(A|[E]|B)$ is defined by the following inference rules: $(A - x \to A'$ and $x \notin E$ implies $A|[E]|B - x \to A'|[E]|B)$, $(B - x \to B'$ and $x \notin E$ implies $A|[E]|B - x \to A|[E]|B')$, $(A - x \to A'$ and $B - x \to B'$ and $x \in E \cup \{\&\}$ implies $A|[E]|B - x \to A'|[E]|B')$. The equivalent net can fire any enabled transition not in E of N_a or N_b, or any enabled transition in E that both nets Na and Nb are ready to fire.

Example: $\qquad A|[a]|B = (a; exit)|[a]|(a; exit|||c; exit)$

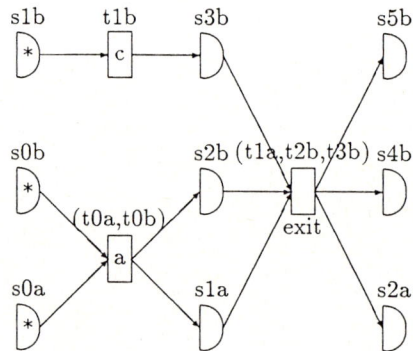

(b) *Enabling:* $A \gg B$

If the behaviour expression A terminates successfully then the behaviour expression B is enabled. This operator is similar to the prefix operator. Let Na and Nb the equivalent nets of A and B respectively, the composition net $N = (Na \gg Nb)$ is defined as:

$S = (S_a - S_{oa}) \cup (S_b - S_{ib}) \cup (S_{oa} \times S_{ib}), S_i = S_{ia}, S_o = S_{ob}$
$T = (T_a \cup T_b)$
$F = (F_a - \{(t_a, s_a)|(s_a \in S_{oa})\}) \cup (F_b - \{(s_b, t_b)|(s_b \in S_{ib})\}) \cup$
$\quad \{(t_a, (s_a, s_b))|(t_a, s_a) \in F_a, (s_a, s_b) \in S\} \cup \{((s_a, s_b), t_b)|(s_b, t_b) \in F_b, (s_a, s_b) \in S\}$
$M_i = M_{ia}, L = (L_a \cup L_b)$
$f = f_b, C_i = C_{ia}, C_o = C_{ob}$

Equivalence. The semantics of the sequential composition expression $(A \gg B)$ is captured by two inference rules $(A - x \to A'$ implies $A \gg B - x \to A' \gg B)$ and $(A - \& \to A'$ implies $A \gg B - i \to B)$. First N_a is enabled in the equivalent net, and when a transition "exit" from N_a is fired, the control is transferred from N_a to N_b.

Example: $\quad A \gg B = (a; stop[]b; exit) \gg (c; exit)$

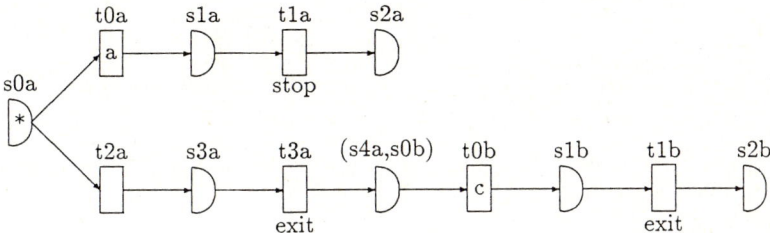

(c) *Disabling: $A[> B$*

The behaviour expression A can be interrupted by the initial actions of the behaviour expression B. When the behaviour expression A is interrupted, the control is transferred from A to B, and cannot return to A. Let N_a and N_b the equivalent nets of A and B respectively, N_b must be root-unwinding, the composition net $N = .(N_a[> N_b)$ is defined as:

$S = (S_a - S_{oa}) \cup (Sb - S_{ib} - S_{ob}) \cup (S_{oa} \times S_{ob}), S_i = S_{ia}, S_o = (S_{oa} \times S_{ob})$
$T = T_a \cup (T_b - T_{ib}) \cup (ST_a \times T_{ib})$
$\quad \text{where} \quad T_{ib} = \{t_b|(t_b \in T_b), (.t_b \in S_{ib})\}$
$\qquad \qquad ST_a = \{X|(X \subset P(S_a)), reachable(N, X)\}$
$\qquad \qquad P(S_a) \text{ is the power-set of } S_a$
$F = (F_a - \{(t_a, s_a)|(t_a \in T_a), (s_a \in S_{oa})\}) \cup$
$\quad (F_b - \{(s_b, t_b)|(s_b \in S_{ib})\} - \{(t_b, s_b)|(t_b \in T_{ib})\} - \{(t_b, s_b)|(s_b \in S_{ob})\}) \cup$
$\quad \{(t_a, (s_a, s_b))|(t_a, s_a) \in F_a, (s_a, s_b) \in S\} \cup \{(t_b, (s_a, s_b))|(t_b, s_b) \in F_b, (s_a, s_b) \in S\} \cup$
$\quad \{(s_a, (X, t_b))|(X \in ST_a), (s_a \in X), (X, t_b) \in T\} \cup$
$\quad \{((X, t_b), s_b)|(X \in ST_a), (t_b \in T_{ib}), (t_b, s_b) \in F_b\}$
$M_i = M_{ia}, L = (L_a \cup L_b)$
$f = \text{if } (f_a = f_b) \text{ then } f = f_a \text{ else } f = \text{"exit"}$
$C_i = C_{ia}, C_o = (C_{oa} \times C_{ob})$

The predicate *reachable(N,X)* decides whether the state set X is reachable in the net N. This predicate eliminates the transitions not reachables in the composed net, in order to simplify it.

Equivalence. The semantics of the disabling behaviour expression $(A[> B)$ is captured by the following inference rules $(A - x \to A'$ implies $A[> B - x \to A'[> B), (A - \& \to A'$

implies $A[> B - \& \to A')$ and $(B - x \to B'$ implies $A[> B - x \to B')$. N_a and N_b are enabled in the equivalent net, if a transition of N_b fires, the control is irreversibly transferred from N_a to N_b.

Example: $\quad A[> B = (a; stop[]b; exit)[> (c; exit)$

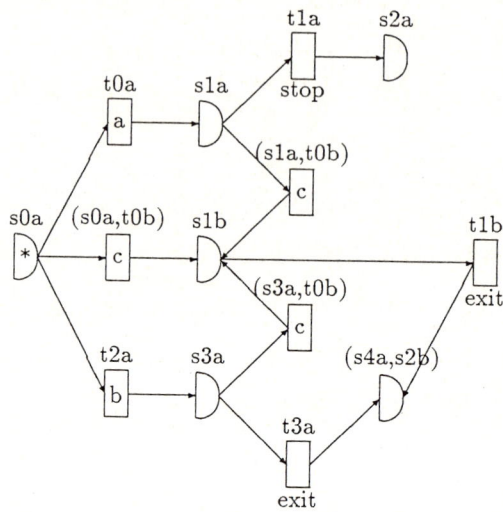

(d) *Hiding*: hide E in A

Hiding allows one to transform the observable actions of the behaviour expression A included in a set E, into unobservable ones. These actions are thus made unavailable for synchronization with other processes. If N_a is the equivalent net of A, the resulting net N = (hide E in N_a) is the same as N_a with a new labelling function L defined as:

$$L = \begin{cases} (t_a, i) & (t_a \in T_a), (t_a \in E) \\ (t_a, L_a(t_a)) & \text{otherwise} \end{cases}$$

Equivalence. The transformation is a relabelling function, the equivalence is trivial.

3.6 Transformation: Process definition and instantiation

(a) *Process Definition*: process $I[G] : f := BH$ endproc (* I *)

Process definition P allows to define a behaviour expression in terms of a process identifier I and a formal gate list $G = \{g1, ..., gn\}$. The goal is that a process instantiation occurs in the behaviour expression defining some other process, or the process I itself. The equivalent net N is the equivalent net of the behaviour expression BH, extended with a gate list GN defined as $\quad GN = \{((g_1, t)|(t \in T), L(t) = g_1), ..., ((g_n, t)|(t \in T), L(t) = g_n)\}$

(b) *Process Instantiation*: $I[G]$

Process instantiation is formed by a process identifier I (associated to a process definition P, which must exist somewhere in the specification) with a actual gate list $G = \{g_1, ..., g_n\}$.

The behaviour of instantiation is defined as the behaviour expression BH of the associated process definition P with formal gates replaced by actual gates. The equivalent net N is the same as the equivalent net (N_p, GN_p) of the definition process P with a new labelling function L defined as:

$$L = \begin{cases} (t_p, g) & (g_p, t_p) \in GN_p, (g, g_p) \in RL \\ (t_p, L_p(t_p)) & \text{otherwise} \end{cases}$$

where $RL = \{(g_1, g_{p1}), \ldots, (g_n, g_{pn})\}$ is the relabelling relation.

Equivalence. The transformation is a relabelling function, the equivalence is trivial supposed the bijection of this function.

3.7 Transformation: Recursion

Recursion is achieved in LOTOS by process instantiation, and it is used to express infinite behaviour. There are two kinds of recursion, simple recursion when a process A invokes itself, and composed recursion when a set of processes mutually invoke each other. Well formed recursion is only considered, meaning that all recursions are prefixed by the ";" prefix operator. In nets, this kind of infinite behaviour can be achieved only by cyclical nets.

(a) *Simple Recursion:* process A := ...; A endproc (* A *)

Let N_a the equivalent net of the process A without recursion, and $S_x = \{s_a | (s_a \in S_{fa}), (t_a \in .s_a), (L(t_a) \neq "exit"), (L(t_a) \neq "stop")\}$ is the output recursive place set. The recursive net is defined as:

$S = (S_a - S_x),\ S_i = S_{ia},\ S_o = (S_{oa} - S_x)$
$T = T_a$
$F = (F_a - \{(t_a, s_a) | (t_a, s_a) \in F_a, (s_a \in S_x)\}) \cup \{(t_a, s_a) | (t_a \in .S_x), (s_a \in S_{ia})\}$
$M_i = M_{ia},\ L = L_a$
$f = f_a,\ C_i = C_{ia},\ C_o = .Cardinal(S_o)$

(b) *Composed Recursion:* process A_0 := ... where
$\qquad\qquad\qquad$ process A_1 endproc (* A_1 *)
$\qquad\qquad\qquad\qquad$ ...
$\qquad\qquad\qquad$ process A_n endproc (* A_n *)
$\qquad\qquad$ endproc (* A_0 *)

Let the recursive process A_0 function of a set of recursive processes $A_1, \ldots, A_n$, and $N_{a0}, N_{a1}, \ldots, N_{an}$ the equivalent net without recursion respectively. S_{xi} and R_{xi} sets are defined for each process A_i in the following way:

$S_{xi} = \{s_a | (s_a \in S_{oai}), (t_a \in .s_a), (L(t_a) \neq "exit"), (L(t_a) \neq "stop")\}$
$R_{xi} = \{(s_a, a_j) | (s_a \in S_{xi}), (a_j \in Id)\}$
$\qquad$ where $Id = \{A_0, A_1, ..., A_n\}$ is the process identifier set

The composition net N is defined as:

$$S = (S_{a0} - S_{x0}) \cup (S_{a1} - S_{x1}) \cup \ldots \cup (S_{an} - S_{xn})$$
$$S_i = S_{ia0}, \; S_o = (S_{oa0} - S_{x0}) \cup (S_{oa1} - S_{x1}) \cup \ldots \cup (S_{oan} - S_{xn})$$
$$T = (T_{a0} \cup T_{a1} \cup \ldots \cup T_{an})$$
$$F = (F_{a0} - \{(t_a, s_a) | (t_a, s_a) \in F_{a0}, (s_a \in S_{x0})\}) \cup$$
$$(F_{a1} - \{(t_a, s_a) | (t_a, s_a) \in F_{a1}, (s_a \in S_{x1})\}) \cup$$
$$\ldots \cup$$
$$(F_{an} - \{(t_a, s_a) | (t_a, s_a) \in F_{an}, (s_a \in S_{xn})\}) \cup$$
$$\{(t_a, s_a) | (t_a \in .S_{x0}), (s_a, a_j) \in R_{x0}, (s_a \in S_{iaj})\} \cup$$
$$\{(t_a, s_a) | (t_a \in .S_{x1}), (s_a, a_j) \in R_{x1}, (s_a \in S_{iaj})\} \cup$$
$$\ldots \cup$$
$$\{(t_a, s_a) | (t_a \in .S_{xn}), (s_a, a_j) \in R_{xn}, (s_a \in S_{iaj})\}$$
$$M_i = M_{ia0}, \; L = (L_{a0} \cup L_{a1} \cup \ldots \cup L_{an})$$
if (f_{a0} = "exit" or f_{a1} = "exit" or ... or f_{an} = "exit")
  then f = "exit" else f = "noexit"
$$C_i = C_{ia0}, \; C_o = Cardinal(s_0)$$

Example: process $A[a, b, c]$: noexit :=
            $a; A[a, b, c]$ [] $c; B[a, b, c]$
        where
            process $B[a, b, c]$: noexit :=
                $b; B[a, b, c]$ [] $c; A[a, b, c]$
            endproc (* B *)
        endproc (* A *)

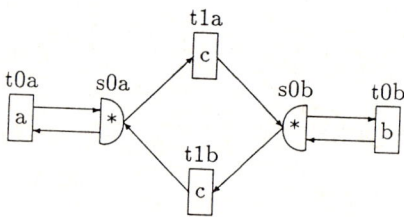

In LOTOS it is possible to introduce recursion in a parallel expression in order to define a process dynamic activation. The equivalent net in general is infinite and cannot be represented, see the counter example in [Milner 81]. In other cases it is unlimited and cannot be correctly analyzed.

Example: process $A[a]$: noexit := $a; (A|||B)$
        where
            process $B[b]$: noexit := $b; stop$ endproc (* B *)
        endproc (* A *)

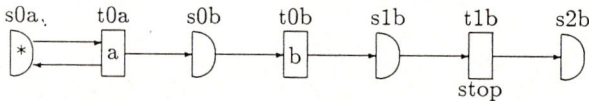

4. TRANSFORMATION FROM LOTOS FUNCTIONALITY TO GALILEO FUNCTIONALITY

The definition of sorts, variables and functions associated to actions are equivalent to data types, data places and transition types in Galileo respectively. The axioms of the functions defined in the LOTOS algebraic specification convey the semantics of the data types. This is provided in Galileo by the Pascal implementations of the functions associated to the transition types. To get a complete transformation the user has to supply a Pascal implementation of the functions and sorts defined in the LOTOS type definitions. A more detailed study can be found in [Marchena 87].

5. CONCLUSIONS

A transformation from LOTOS specifications to Galileo nets has been presented such as the meaning of the specification is preserved. Only the transformation of the behavioural part of LOTOS can be well defined as an homomorphism. It can be demonstrated by verifying that the transformation satisfies the inference rules that define the LOTOS operational semantics.

Some examples have been presented, but due to the lack of space a real size example has been omitted. Now, we are working on the implementation of a conversor from LOTOS to Galileo based on this transformation, to make this work applicable in an industrial setting. Some problems have been found in the transformation, specially with the dynamic activation of processes.

The future work is centered in two lines: study of the meaning and application to a LOTOS specification of properties that can be analyzed in the corresponding net, and study of the relation between functional and behavioural part of LOTOS, and the transformation form one to the other preserving the meaning.

6. REFERENCES

[Bolognesi 87] T. Bolognesi & E. Brinksna, "Introduction to the ISO Specification Language LOTOS", 1987.

[Degano 87] P. Degano, R. Gorrieri & S. Marchetti, "An Exercise in Concurrency: A CSP Process as a Condition/Event System", Proceeding of 8 European Workshop on Application an Theory of Petri Nets, Spain June 87.

[Ehrig 85] H. Ehrig & B. Mahr, "Fundamentals of Algebraic Specification 1. Equations and Initial Semantics", EATCS Monographs on Theoretical Computer Science, Springer 1985.

[Genrich 84] H.J. Genrich et al, "Elements of General Net Theory", Springer LNCS 84, 1984.

[Glabbeek 87] R. Glabbeek and F. Vaandrager, "Petri Nets Models for Algebraic Theories of Concurrency", Springer LNCS 259, 1987.

[Goltz 86a] U. Goltz & A. Mycroft, "On the relationship of CCS and Petri Nets", Springer LNCS 172, 1986.

[Goltz 86b] U. Goltz & W. Reisig, "CSP-Programs as Nets with Individual Tokens", Springer LNCS 188, 1986.

[Hoare 85] C.A.R. Hoare, "Communicating Sequential Processes", Prentice Hall 1985.

[ISO 87] ISO - Information Processing Systems - "LOTOS - A Formal Description Technique Based on the Temporal Ordering of Obsevational Behaviour", Dis 8807, 1987.

[Leon 88] G. Leon, S. Marchena - "Formal Conversion between LOTOS specifications and Galileo Nets", EUROMICRO88.

[Lopez 87] I. Lopez, "Experiences in the Use of Galileo to Design Telecommunication System", Proceeding of 8 European Workshop on Application and Theory on Petri Nets. Spain 1987.

[Marchena 87] S. Marchena & G. Leon, "Transformacion de una Especificacion LOTOS en una Red Galileo", Internal Report 87-TR- 84.11, Alcatel Standard Electrica 1987.

[Milner 80] R. Milner, "A Calculus of Communicating Systems", Springer LNCS 92, 1980.

[Peterson 81] J.L. Peterson, "Petri Net Theory and the Modelling of Systems", Prentice-Hall, 1981.

[Petri 84] C.A. Petri, "Introduction to General Net Theory", Springer LNCS 84, 1984.

[Rodriguez 88] F. Rodriguez, G. Leon, C. Delgado, "Development of a LOTOS Algebraic Semantic Oriented to the Generation of Transformation Rules", Submitted to FORTE88.

[Sanchez 86a] C. Sanchez, "Galileo Model Language and Tools", Electrical Communications Vol. 60, no. 3-4, 1986.

[Sanchez 86b] C. Sanchez, "Galileo: Model Definition", Alcatel SESA internal report, 86-TR-8403, April 1986.

[Silva 87] M. Silva, "Toward a Synchrony Theory for P/T Nets, Concurrency and Nets", Springer 1987.

SPECIFYING ROSE IN LOTOS

David FREESTONE   and   Sukhvinder S. AUJLA

Formal Methods Group
Research and Technology/Information Services Standards Division
British Telecom
St Vincent House
Ipswich, United Kingdom

Remote Operations Service Element (ROSE) is one of the reusable components of the Application Layer of Open Systems Interconnection (OSI). Its natural language definition has been developed in CCITT and ISO. LOTOS is a Formal Description Technique developed within ISO, especially for use with OSI. The authors began to specify ROSE in LOTOS in May 1987. Through the several versions produced since then, many facets of ROSE have been revealed - including omissions and ambiguities in the natural language definition. Also many lessons have been learnt about how to produce correct specifications in LOTOS. This paper reports on the results of the exercise.

1.   INTRODUCTION

Formal descriptions of systems are sometimes thought impenetrable by engineers inexperienced in formal techniques. Advocates of formal methods must ease their path as much as possible. As part of that endeavour, this paper presents a formal description of a real system. It also records the authors' experiences of developing a correct specification and of the latest tool technology.

The example employed is the Remote Operations Service Element (ROSE) [1], one of the reusable components of the Application Layer of Open Systems Interconnection (OSI). The Formal Description Technique (FDT) used is LOTOS [2]. ROSE has been developed in CCITT and ISO, and LOTOS has been developed in ISO. Our work began in May 1987, initially using a version of LOTOS (*Temporal LOTOS*) developed within the FORMAP project [3] and latterly using standard LOTOS. Through the various versions, several facets of ROSE have been uncovered, including omissions and ambiguities, and much has been learnt about producing correct specifications using tools.

Space does not permit us to include the complete specification here. Therefore, our aim has been to present enough of the specification to allow a practising protocol engineer to understand its structure thoroughly, and enough guidance to read the complete specification without further assistance. Section 2 outlines the functionality of ROSE, section 3 discusses the specification development, and section 4 presents the specification itself.

We do not present a tutorial on LOTOS itself, but satisfactory tutorial material is available elsewhere (eg [2] [4]). The complete ROSE specification in LOTOS can be obtained from the authors on request.

2. OVERVIEW OF ROSE

The *Upper Layer Architecture* (ULA) [5] of OSI is being designed to provide modularity and re-usability in Application Layer Standards. This is a recent innovation which is gradually being introduced with components such as *Association Control*, *File Transfer Access and Management*, *Transaction Processing* and *Reliable Transfer*. Each component comprises two standards, *service element* and *protocol machine*, which are analogous to *service* and *protocol* in lower OSI layers. For any particular application, a specific collection of service elements forms an *application context*, under the control of a *Single Association Control Function* (SACF).

Remote Operations is a component of ULA, and ROSE is its service element. A possible application context for its execution is Association Control Service Element (ACSE), Reliable Transfer Service Element (RTSE) and ROSE itself. Figure 1 illustrates the configuration. The definition of ROSE we have used [1] was current when the work started, but has since been revised.

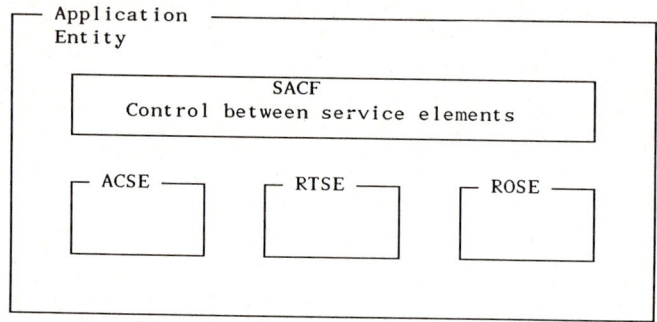

FIGURE 1

The purpose of ROSE is to allow the execution of operations on remote systems. The local system sends invocations to the desired remote system, setting out the operations it wishes executed. The (successful) results or the errors (ie unsuccessful results) of the operations may be reported, or user faults may be reported – discovered either by the remote system or by the underlying service of ROSE (the *ROSE provider*).

There are five ROSE primitives to carry out the service:

invoke	requests the execution of an operation
result	reports the (successful) result of an operation
error	reports the reason for failure of an operation
user rejection	reports a user fault found by the receiving ROSE user in an *invoke*, *result* or *error* primitive
provider rejection	reports a user fault found by the ROSE provider in any primitive.

Each operation is allocated an operation class. There are five classes defined. Operation class 1 is synchronous, ie further operations can be invoked only after a reply is received. Operation classes 2 – 5 are asynchronous, ie further operations can be invoked immediately. Also, operation classes 1 and 2 report both success and failure; class 3 reports only failures; class 4 reports only successes; class 5 does not report any outcome.

Operations are independent except for a *linked invocation* facility, where the invocation receiver can invoke sub-operations from the originator before replying.

It is the responsibility of the SACF to initiate and terminate the ROSE. An association between *association initiator* and *association responder* must already exist when ROSE is initiated, and ROSE continues to function until it is externally terminated.

There are three classes of association for ROSE operation. They determine which user can invoke operations: in class 1 only the association initiator can invoke; in class 2 only the association responder can invoke; and in class 3 both users can invoke independently.

The number of provider rejections permitted is limited at each entity. If this limit is exceeded no further communication is allowed and all existing requests which have not been sent are provider rejected (to give the maximum information possible to the service user). When one user of the association has reached its maximum, the other user soon follows, because all primitives initiated there are necessarily provider rejected.

3. DEVELOPMENT OF LOTOS SPECIFICATION AND LESSONS LEARNT

3.1. Issues Arising from the Informal Description

Typically, producing a formal description from an existing informal description exposes ambiguities and omissions in the latter. ROSE was no exception and the points uncovered were resolved in discussion with engineers involved in ROSE standardisation. Where necessary, the points were relayed to the standardisation committee.

One ambiguity in the informal description of ROSE concerned linked operations. We have assumed that the facility may occur only in association class 3. However, there still seems to be an identification problem. Operations in a sequence of linked operations all bear the *invoke_id* of the original invocation; the subordinate invocations are distinguished by another parameter, *linked_id*. Yet *linked_id* is not a parameter of the response primitives, and so responses cannot be matched with invocations with certainty.

The informal description states that each invocation may optionally include an operation class, but does not say which operation class to assume if it is omitted. We have assumed that the operation class of the previous invocation is to be used in this case, with an initial value supplied at ROSE instantiation.

The informal description also does not make clear what is meant by swapping between asynchronous and synchronous operation classes. We have assumed that a synchronous operation must be completed before another invoke request may occur, but any outstanding asynchronous operations continue unaffected.

One aspect of ROSE that LOTOS cannot express is elapsed time. Timeouts have had to be modelled by an internal event i, annotated informally. This approach isolates the places where the problem impinges, and illustrates how much specification can be done without it. But the lack was a motivation for developing the companion ROSE specification in *Temporal LOTOS* [3].

3.2. Structure

An aim of this work was to explore stylistic objectives, especially the so-called *constraint oriented* style championed in eg [6]. Its features include using LOTOS parallel combinators to reduce constructive detail, common behavioural components to ease analysis, and relatively small process definitions and parameter spaces to ease readability. In particular, we strove to express the structure as "expected" behaviour, *constrained by* exceptional behaviour, and we believe we have succeeded in this.

An example of *separation of concerns* to make the specification more lucid is provided by the treatment of operation classes (see below), where structural aspects (synchronous vs asynchronous) are separated from functional aspects (which replies are required).

The treatment of non-determinism is always important in service descriptions. For example, in ROSE each primitive may be rejected by the ROSE provider instead of the "expected" behaviour occuring. But notice that the choice between the two branches of behaviour must be made by the service element and not by the user. Therefore the choice must be specified as a *non-deterministic choice* between the two branches – and in LOTOS that is achieved by guarding with internal events i.

Typically for LOTOS specifications, the split of information between data types and processes required subjective judgement. An interesting case here was how to represent optional parameters. We decided not to introduce variant parameter structures for all the different possibilities (2^n variants for n optional parameters), nor to make extensive use of boolean guards in the processes, but instead to introduce a special value *absent* to represent omission. For sorts which are used entirely for mandatory parameters or entirely for optional parameters, this is enough. However, for sorts which are used both for optional and for mandatory parameters, it introduces a small problem: the value *absent* is available for mandatory parameters, which it should not be. The problem arises in only one case in ROSE, and we have solved it by using two sorts, one for the mandatory case and the other for the optional case. The two sorts are entirely distinct semantically, but the latter is syntactically a relabelled copy of the former, together with *absent*.

We found in general that the issues to be resolved in data types had different characteristics from those in processes. With data types in ROSE there were a few technical problems to solve, which were replicated through many different types. With processes, the technical problems tended to be more specific – and therefore the solutions were useful once only.

As the specification developed we were able successively to make it simpler and more elegant, using ever fewer technical devices. These properties are to some extent subjective, but we believe their achievement to yield a specification text that is easier to read and less likely to cause misunderstandings, thus reducing product development costs. We also found that the basic structure was increasingly resilient to minor quirks of ROSE that we introduced, which gave us added confidence in our structure.

3.3. Use of Tools

Towards the end of developing the specification we acquired a state-of-the-art LOTOS toolset comprising a syntax checker, a static semantic checker and a simulator.

We ran the ROSE specification through all three utilities with beneficial, sometimes spectacular, results. All three revealed trivial typographical mistakes, a source of potential confusion to readers. In addition, the syntax checker revealed our retention of syntax from an earlier version of LOTOS (the second Draft Proposal). The static semantic checker helped us recognise a subtle point of detail in LOTOS which we had misunderstood – the prohibition of mixing boolean expressions with simple equations in boolean guards. This point has its roots deep in the semantics of the language, but it is important for specifiers to understand. The simulator revealed misplaced brackets which altered the behaviour described.

There is a qualitative difference between the properties of the two checker utilities and the properties of the simulator. The first two yield exact results – a specification is either syntactically and static-semantically correct or it is not. Therefore we were safe to use them in an automatic manner, to achieve clerical neatness. However, like product testing, no amount of simulation can guarantee that the specification captures its requirements correctly.

Being very conscious of the dangers of relying too heavily on simulation results, giving a false sense of security, we tried to devise a sensible strategy for using the simulator. There was not enough time to devise an extensive set of trials, but we devised short experiments to check the main paths through ROSE. We used unexpected outcomes purely as spurs to analytical thinking, and we were pleasantly surprised at the success of this approach. Most of the mistakes discovered were trivial to correct, eg misplaced brackets, but one was more serious. It was a boundary value problem − *invoke_req*uests could occur after the maximum number of provider rejections had occurred but before the fact had been signalled within the specification. It required a change (in fact a straightforward simplification) to the top level behaviour expression.

Following these successful experiences of using tools to support the development of formal descriptions, we intend to continue using them in future work, and we look forward to the more powerful and more robust tools now being planned.

4. OVERVIEW OF FINAL LOTOS SPECIFICATION

4.1. Architectural Decisions

We chose to model ROSE as an integral service with one gate, *rose*. All communication with ROSE is via this gate and users (application entities) are distinguished by values of sort *seap*, representing *service element access point*. Figure 2 illustrates the arrangement, which means that a consistent interface can be maintained and a consistent architecture used to describe the different service elements in ULA.

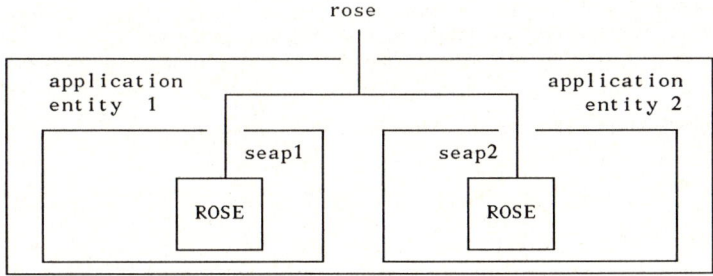

FIGURE 2

Figure 3 shows the skeleton of the specification text. It follows the normal LOTOS pattern of *global data types*, *top level behaviour* and *subordinate definitions*.

Notice the parameters to the specification − the fact that they are parameters captures the requirement for them to be established before ROSE begins. x and y identify the association initiator and responder respectively. *assoc* indicates the association class, and *seed* an initial default value for the operation class. *max* indicates the maximum number of provider rejections allowed for this instantiation (to reduce the number of parameters, we have taken this number to be the same for both users, but it could easily be made different).

Notice also the *noexit* which captures the requirement for ROSE to be terminated only by external interruption.

```
specification          REMOTE_OPERATIONS        [rose]   (x,y:seap, assoc:assoc sort,
                                                seed:op_class_sort, max:Nat) : noexit
    global data types
behaviour
    top level behaviour
where
    subordinate processes and local data types
endspec
```

FIGURE 3

4.2.   Global Data Types

The distribution of data items among different data types is a matter of presentation. Our groupings are intended to highlight the different kinds of data in the specification. There are seven: *basic_data, invokes, results, errors, user_rejects, provider_rejects, functions*. Two types are imported from the library, *NaturalNumber* and *Boolean*.

basic_data, sketched in Figure 4, introduces data sorts and operations (but no equations) which are elementary to the specification and whose internal structure is irrelevant at this level of abstraction. The identifiers given to the sorts are intended to be self-explanatory in relation to the service primitives and their parameters. Some sorts (marked * in figure 4) are used for optional parameters, the rest for mandatory parameters. *absent* values are provided for these sorts, and named base cases (eg *s_1* for *seap*) for the rest. All sorts have constructors to generate new values from old (eg *mk_seap : seap -> seap*). Constant values are declared for the three association classes and the five operation classes. Also, two *undefined* values are declared, for a reason explained below.

```
type basic_data is Boolean

    sorts       seap,                  assoc_sort,              *op_class_sort,
                op_value_sort,         *argument_sort,          invoke_id_sort,
                *absent_id_sort,       *linked_id_sort,         *priority_sort,
                *result_sort,          err_value_sort,          *err_parameter_sort,
                reject_u_reason_sort,  reject_p_reason_sort,    returned_params_sort

    opns        s_1      :        ->  seap
                    etc.
                absent   :        ->  op_class_sort
                    etc.
                mk_seap : seap    ->  seap
                    etc.

                undefined         :   ->  reject_p_reason_sort
                undefined         :   ->  returned_params_sort

                A1, A2, A3        :   ->  assoc_sort
                O1, O2, O3, O4, O5:   ->  op_class_sort

endtype
```

FIGURE 4

The next five data types correspond to the five service primitives, declaring the appropriate sorts, constructors and selectors. For illustration, we present here (figure 5) the data type for *provider_rejects*, which happens to be the most complicated.

> **type** provider_rejects **is** basic_data
>
> **sorts**   RO_rejectp_ind
>
> **opns**
> ```
>         mk_rejectp_ind     :    rejectp_reason_sort,
>                                 absent_id_sort              ->   RO_rejectp_ind
>
>         mk_rejectp_ind     :    returned_params_sort,
>                                 absent_id_sort              ->   RO_rejectp_ind
>
>         get_rprs           :    RO_rejectp_ind     ->   rejectp_reason_sort
>         get_rps            :    RO_rejectp_ind     ->   returned_params_sort
>         get_iis            :    RO_rejectp_ind     ->   absent_id_sort
>
>         is_rps             :    RO_rejectp_ind     ->   Bool
> ```
>
> **eqns**   **forall**   a:rejectp_reason_sort,
>   b:returned_parmeters_sort,
>   c:absent_id_sort
>
>   **ofsort** rejectp_reason_sort
>   get_rprs(mk_rejectp_ind(a,c))   = a;
>   get_rprs(mk_rejectp_ind(b,c))   = undefined;
>
>   *etc.*
>
> **endtype**

FIGURE 5

There is only one kind of provider-reject primitive, the *indication* (ie there is no *request*), and the set of all possible *indication*s is denoted by the sort *RO_rejectp_ind*. However, there are two different forms of *RO_rejectp_ind*, depending on whether the rejection is local or remote. Two operations, both with the name *mk_rejectp_ind*, construct the two forms - the construction involving *returned_params_sort* is for local rejection. Notice the usefulness of operation overloading here (ie using the same name for different operations, and disambiguating by context). *is_rps* discriminates between the two forms.

The three remaining operations (*get_rprs, get_rps* and *get_iis*) select parameters from primitives. The values of *get_rprs* and *get_rps* depend on the form of *RO_rejectp_ind*. However, both values must be defined for both forms, because all functions (operations) in LOTOS must be total - ie must be defined for all values of *RO_rejectp_ind*. It was for this reason that the two special values *undefined* were introduced in *basic_data*: *undefined* is the value of a selector applied to the wrong form of *RO_rejectp_ind*.

Notice that *absent_id_sort* is used for the invoke identifier parameter, indicating that the parameter is optional in this primitive.

In LOTOS data typing, no two values are equal unless an equation (or a succession of equations) says so. Therefore, the equations for the selector functions operate on explicitly constructed RO_rejectp_inds. The *ofsort* statement disambiguates between operations with the same name but different argument or result sorts. It also provides a convenient way of grouping the equations.

The final global type, *functions*, does not define any new sorts. Instead, it groups together operations which show relationships between *request* and *indication* primitives, and also those functions which construct *returned_params_sort*. Figure 6 sketches it. Notice that *mk_rps* is not defined. The standard allows implementation freedom and this is captured in LOTOS by the absence of equations and, informally, by an acknowledgement in the process commentary.

```
    type    functions is invokes, results, errors, user_rejects

    opns    mk_ii       :   RO_invoke_req   ->  RO_invoke_ind
            mk_ri       :   RO_result_req   ->  RO_result_ind
            mk_ei       :   RO_error_req    ->  RO_error_ind
            mk_rui      :   RO_rejectu_req  ->  RO_rejectu_ind

            mk_rps      :   RO_invoke_req   ->  returned_params_sort
            mk_rps      :   RO_result_req   ->  returned_params_sort
            mk_rps      :   RO_error_req    ->  returned_params_sort
            mk_rps      :   RO_rejectu_req  ->  returned_params_sort

    eqns    forall      a:op_value_sort,
                            etc.

            ofsort RO_invoke_ind
            mk_ii(mk_invoke_req(a,j,b,c,d,e)) = mk_invoke_ind(a,b,c,d)
                etc.

            (* there is complete implementation freedom for mk_rps *)

    endtype
```

FIGURE 6

4.3. Top Level Behaviour

The (top level) behaviour of ROSE is described by two fully synchronised processes – both must agree every action. Figure 7 shows the structure.

```
    behaviour
                RO_BEHAVIOUR [rose] (x,y,assoc,seed)
        ||
                RO_COUNTER_CONSTRAINT [rose] (max,x,y)

    where       ........(subordinate processes and data types)
```

FIGURE 7

RO_BEHAVIOUR describes the regular behaviour of ROSE – the behaviour before either user has received the maximum permitted number of provider rejects. That behaviour is constrained by RO_COUNTER_CONSTRAINT, which counts the number of provider rejects. While the number is less than the maximum, it allows the exchange of any primitive. But when the maximum is reached, only local provider rejections are allowed.

4.4. Counter Constraint

Consider first RO_COUNTER_CONSTRAINT. It is defined as two fully interleaved processes, one for each user, figure 8.

```
process RO_COUNTER_CONSTRAINT [rose] (max:Nat,x,y:seap): noexit :=
         RO_CONSTRAINT [rose] (0,max,x)
    ||| RO_CONSTRAINT [rose] (0,max,y)

where

process RO_CONSTRAINT [rose] (pcount,max:Nat,z:seap): noexit :=
         [pcount lt max] -> RO_NORMAL_MODE [rose] (pcount,max,z)
    []   [pcount ge max] -> RO_ABORTED_MODE [rose] (z)
where  ...
```

FIGURE 8

Initially, each individual process RO_CONSTRAINT counts provider rejects while allowing any primitive to occur - RO_NORMAL_MODE, figure 9. Once the maximum has been reached, it allows only local provider rejections - RO_ABORTED_MODE. (NB The Remote Operations protocol makes it clear that a counter exists, although it is not mentioned in the ROSE standard. We have assumed that the counter should also be in the service.)

```
process RO_NORMAL_MODE [rose] (pcount,max:Nat,z:seap): noexit :=
           rose!z?d:RO_invoke_req   ; RO_CONSTRAINT [rose] (pcount,max,z)
    []     ...
    .
    .
    .
    []     rose!z?d:RO_rejectu_ind  ; RO_CONSTRAINT [rose] (pcount,max,z)
    []     rose!z?d:RO_rejectp_ind  ; RO_CONSTRAINT [rose] (succ(pcount),max,z)
endproc


process RO_ABORTED_MODE [rose] (z:seap): noexit :=
           rose!z?d:RO_rejectp_ind[is_rps(d)] ; RO_ABORTED_MODE [rose] (z)
endproc
```

FIGURE 9

4.5. Regular Behaviour

The top level of RO_BEHAVIOUR (figure 10) shows how different behaviours are specified for the different association classes, using boolean guards to decide which branch should be followed.

Recall that x, y, *assoc* (and *seed*) are all parameters of the whole specification: x is the association initiator, y the association responder, and *assoc* the association class. The process RO_ASSOC describes the steady state behaviour within an association in a single direction. Notice how the order of x and y in the instantiation of RO_ASSOC signifies the direction of invocations, capturing the requirements set out in section 2.

```
process RO_BEHAVIOUR     [rose]
                          (x,y:seap,assoc:assoc_sort,seed:op_class_sort) :noexit :=
      [assoc = A1]  ->   RO_ASSOC[rose](x,y,seed)
   [] [assoc = A2]  ->   RO_ASSOC[rose](y,x,seed)
   [] [assoc = A3]  ->   ( RO_ASSOC[rose](y,x,seed) ||| RO_ASSOC[rose](x,y,seed))

where      .....
```

FIGURE 10

RO_ASSOC (figure 11) is the central process of the regular behaviour of ROSE, and understanding it is essential to understanding the regular behaviour as a whole. It describes the steady state operation of invokes from x to y (its parameters).

```
processs RO_ASSOC [rose] (x,y:seap,op_class:op_class_sort): noexit :=
   rose!x?ir:RO_invoke_req ;
      (  let op:op_class_sort = new_op(op_class, get_ocs(ir)) in
              [op = O1]  ->  (       RO_OP1[rose](x,y,ir)
                                >>   RO_ASSOC[rose](x,y,op)   )
           [] [op = O2]  ->  (      (RO_OP2[rose](x,y,ir) >> exit)
                               ||| RO_ASSOC[rose](x,y,op) )
           [] [op = O3]  ->  (      (RO_OP3[rose](x,y,ir) >> exit)
                               ||| RO_ASSOC[rose](x,y,op) )
           [] [op = O4]  ->  (      (RO_OP4[rose](x,y,ir) >> exit)
                               ||| RO_ASSOC[rose](x,y,op) )
           [] [op = O5]  ->  (      (RO_OP5[rose](x,y,ir) >> exit)
                               ||| RO_ASSOC[rose](x,y,op) )
      )

where      .....
```

FIGURE 11

RO_ASSOC begins with an *RO_invoke_req* at *x*, and then its behaviour depends on the required operation class. LOTOS combinators proved ideal for capturing the structural requirements set out in sections 2 and 3. Operation class 1 requires that the current invocation is completed before another can begin, but outstanding invocations continue; this behaviour (called *synchronous* in the standard) is captured precisely by >> in LOTOS. In all other operation classes, further invocations can proceed independently; this behaviour (called *asynchronous* in the standard) is captured precisely by the LOTOS |||.

Recall that the differences between the various operation classes are both structural (synchronous vs asynchronous) and functional (which replies are required). We have separated these two concerns, making the service easier to reason about. The functional differences are embodied in the individual subprocesses relating to the operation classes (figure 14).

Determining which operation class applies is bundled – for textual convenience – into a local operation (function) *new_op*, defined within the *where* clause of RO_ASSOC. Its definition is sketched in figure 12. If a value is given in the *RO_invoke_req*, then that value is used, otherwise the previous value is used (passed by parameter and initialised by *seed*). The assumptions made here, to resolve the ambiguities of the informal description in the standard, were discussed in section 3. For technical reasons, the LOTOS definition necessarily includes definitions of *eq* (equal) and *neq* (not equal) between *op_class_sort* values.

```
type new_op_class is basic_data, invokes

    opns      new_op       :    op_class_sort,
                                op_class_sort           -> op_class_sort

              eq ,
              neq          :    op_class_sort,
                                op_class_sort           -> bool

    eqns      forall  x,y: op_class_sort

              ofsort op_class_sort
              new_op(y,absent)         =     y;
              x neq absent             =>    new_op(y,x) = x;

              ofsort bool
              x eq x                   =     true;
              x neq y                  =     not(x eq y);

              O1 eq absent             =     false;
                    etc.

endtype
```

FIGURE 12

Processes RO_OP1 – RO_OP5 (figure 13) describe the behaviour of ROSE during a single invocation cycle in the respective operation class. We have chosen to set out the text in a way that emphasises the structural similarities and highlights the functional differences between them. Notice in particular that separating structural concerns from functional concerns has revealed explicitly the identical functional behaviour of classes 1 and 2.

```
process RO_OP1[rose](x,y:seap,ir:RO_invoke_req) :exit :=
       RO_REJECT_P[rose](x,get_iis(ir),mk_rps(ir))
    [] i ; rose!y!mk_ii(ir) ;
            (    RO_RESULT[rose](y,x,mk_ii(ir))
              [] RO_ERROR[rose](y,x,mk_ii(ir))
              [] RO_REJECT_U[rose](y,x,get_iis(ir))
            )
endproc

process RO_OP2[rose](x,y:seap,ir:RO_invoke_req) :exit :=
       RO_OP1[rose](x,y,ir)
endproc

process RO_OP3[rose](x,y:seap,ir:RO_invoke_req) :exit :=
       RO_REJECT_P[rose](x,get_iis(ir),mk_rps(ir))
    [] i ; rose!y!mk_ii(ir) ;
            (    RO_ERROR[rose](y,x,mk_ii(ir))
              [] RO_REJECT_U[rose](y,x,get_iis(ir))
              [] i ; exit     (* timeout *)
endproc

process RO_OP4[rose](x,y:seap,ir:RO_invoke_req) :exit :=
       RO_REJECT_P[rose](x,get_iis(ir),mk_rps(ir))
    [] i ; rose!y!mk_ii(ir) ;
            (    RO_RESULT[rose](y,x,mk_ii(ir))
              [] RO_REJECT_U[rose](y,x,get_iis(ir))
              [] i ; exit     (* timeout *)
endproc

process RO_OP5[rose](x,y:seap,ir:RO_invoke_req) :exit :=
       RO_REJECT_P[rose](x,get_iis(ir),mk_rps(ir))
    [] i ; rose!y!mk_ii(ir) ;
            (    RO_REJECT_U[rose](y,x,get_iis(ir))
              [] i ; exit     (* timeout *)
            )
endproc
```

FIGURE 13

In each process, the "expected" behaviour is an *RO_invoke_ind* at *y*, followed by result or error primitives to communicate the successful or unsuccessful outcome of the remote operation. Notice how the result and error options appear only in the operation classes required by the standard, and that timeout options are provided where one or other outcome option is absent.

At each stage, however, a primitive may be rejected by the ROSE provider or, in certain cases, by the other ROSE user. These options are specified systematically in RO_OP1 - RO_OP5. But notice that wherever there is choice between "expected" behaviour and rejection, both branches are guarded by internal events *i*. (Sometimes a level of process text has to be unwrapped to discover the *i*, but it is always there.) This captures the requirement that ROSE itself (and not the ROSE user) determines which branch should be followed, a point discussed in section 3.

Processes RO_RESULT and RO_ERROR are structurally identical, and so we present only RO_RESULT here (figure 14). To represent the possibility of reordering requests (in relation to their priorities) the internal event has been used. It ensures that the result primitive contains the correct *RO_invoke_id*. Controlling the uniqueness of *RO_invoke_id*s (and *RO_linked_id*s) is the responsibility of the ROSE user, not ROSE.

The first event in RO_RESULT is an *RO_result_req*. This can be rejected by the ROSE-provider within a time limit, else an *RO_result_ind* can occur with the same parameters.

```
process RO_RESULT [rose] (x,y:seap,ii:RO_invoke_ind) :exit :=
    rose!x?rr:RO_result_req[get_iis(ii) = get_iis(rr)] ;
        (   RO_REJECT_P[rose](x,get_iis(rr),mk_rps(rr))
        [] i ; rose!y!mk_ri(rr) ;
            (   RO_REJECT_U[rose](y,x,get_iis(rr))
            [] i ; exit       (*  timeout  *)
            )
        )
endproc
```

FIGURE 14

RO_REJECT_U differs in structure from RO_RESULT and RO_ERROR only in that it cannot itself be user rejected.

The event sequences specified in RO_REJECT_P (figure 15) are all *RO_rejectp_ind* followed by exit. The choice construct and the cascade of boolean guards just select valid parameter combinations: the *invoke_id* must be correct and, if the *RO_rejectp_ind* is local, then the *returned parameters* must also be correct. Recall that the *RO_rejectp_ind* is the event that increments the counter in the relevant RO_COUNTER_CONSTRAINT.

```
process RO_REJECT_P [rose]
                 (x:seap,iids:invoke_id_sort,rps:returned_params_sort) :exit :=
    choice rpi:RO_rejectp_ind []
       [get_iis(rpi) = iids]
         ->     ( ([is_rps(rpi)] -> [get_rps(rpi)=rps]
                          -> i ; rose!x!rpi ; exit
                )
                []
                  ([not(is_rps(rpi))] -> i; rose!x!rpi ; exit )
                )
endproc
```

FIGURE 15

5. CONCLUSIONS

ROSE has proved a useful specification on which to explore development techniques with LOTOS. It is reasonably small for industrial specifications but it is not trivial. The relative smallness meant that the entire specification could be included in the exercise, and the non-triviality meant that realistic problems needed to be solved.

Among the lessons learnt, the exercise reinforced the need for good structure – to aid understanding and analysis, and also to facilitate modifications when new versions of the informal specification appear. It also showed the benefits to be gained from support tools, even the early tools currently available. Syntax and static semantic checks reveal elementary mistakes which can be confusing to the reader. Simulation can reveal other classes of typographical mistakes (eg misplaced brackets). Beyond that, simulation gives some added confidence that the functionality has truly been captured in the specification – although the technique can never give a guarantee of correctness, and misplaced trust must be avoided.

Specification is necessarily a creative process, but it should be guided by design discipline and by past experience. We hope that our work will add to that body of knowledge for LOTOS specifications.

ACKNOWLEDGEMENTS

The work reported in this paper was performed under FORMAP, a collaborative project between British Telecommunications plc and the General Electric Company plc, within the UK Alvey programme (SE/051).

Thanks are extended to Peter Ingram and Keith Rayner, British Telecom engineers involved in standardising ROSE, for many useful comments on the evolving LOTOS descriptions. Thanks are given also to Rob Booth and Jim Lynch for providing the tools environment.

Acknowledgement is made to the Director of Research and Technology of British Telecom for permission to publish this paper.

REFERENCES

[1] CCITT Draft Recommendation X.ros0; ISO Working Document for DIS 9072/1; [Version 4, Munich, February 1987]: Remote Operations[Part 1]: Model, Notation and Service Definition.

[2] ISO/DIS 8807 – Information Processing Systems – Open Systems Interconnection – LOTOS – A Formal Description Technique Based on the Temporal Ordering of Observational Behaviour; July 1987.

[3] A Library of Specification Modules and Their Application; Report No 5 to the Alvey Directorate; UK Alvey FORMAP Project (SE/051); November 1987.

[4] Tommaso Bolognesi, Ed Brinksma: Introduction to the ISO Specification Language LOTOS; Computer Networks and ISDN Systems; Vol 14 No 1; 1987.

[5] ISO/DP 9545 – Information Processing Systems – Open Systems Interconnection – Application Layer Structure; November 1987.

[6] ISO/IEC JTC 1/SC 21/WG 1 N556 – Formal description of a Transport protocol in LOTOS for the ISO/CCITT Guidelines on the application of Estelle, LOTOS and SDL; January 1988.

ON THE USE OF LOTOS FOR THE FORMAL DESCRIPTION OF A TRANSPORT PROTOCOL

Jeroen van de Lagemaat and Giuseppe Scollo

University of Twente, Department Informatica
PO Box 217, 7500 AE Enschede, The Netherlands
phone: + 31 53 893684, 893768 - telex: 44200 thtes nl
e-mail (uucp): mcvax!utinu1!lagemaat, mcvax!utinu1!pippo

ABSTRACT As part of the work to stimulate the use of formal description techniques, we developed a formal description in LOTOS of a simplified transport protocol. Not surprisingly numerous deficiencies were discovered in the informal description of this protocol and solutions were generated: an account of this work is presented and discussed. The formal description illustrates the suitability of LOTOS for well-structured and complete descriptions of fairly complex protocols. In this paper we exemplify this for a few architectural concepts of the protocol, some of which are of general OSI nature. As a conclusion, it appears that the effort needed to develop the formal description was well invested. The use of LOTOS tools was found very helpful both for aligning the specification with the LOTOS language definition and for checking the specification w.r.t. the desired behaviour as given in the informal description.

1. INTRODUCTION

As a joint effort of ISO/IEC and CCITT (the standardization bodies internationally responsible for the OSI standards) guidelines for the application of standard FDTs are being produced [T 88]. Major objectives of this cooperative work are to favour the introduction of Formal Description Techniques (FDTs), to encourage their use (with special attention to the production of Formal Descriptions (FDs) of OSI standards) to illustrate errors and ambiguities that can arise when using natural language descriptions (NLDs), and to illustrate the use of FDTs to describe architectural concepts.

As part of this work we produced a FD in LOTOS of an example transport protocol which was derived from [C 84]. The NLD of this protocol and its FDs in Estelle, LOTOS, and SDL, are in chapter 11 of [T 88]. For the sake of brevity, in this paper we term the NLD of this protocol simply "the NLD", its three aforementioned FDs "the FDs", and its FD in LOTOS "the FD", all as presented in [T 88]. Some knowledge of OSI architectural concepts [IC 84] and of LOTOS [I 87] is assumed. A good tutorial on LOTOS can be found in [BB 87].

Not surprisingly, the production of the FDs led to the detection of several deficiencies in the NLD. In section 2 we summarize the most significant of these deficiencies and their resolutions as adopted in [T 88], but in a more general setting of the discussion of protocol NLDs.

As we argue in section 2.2, an interesting class of deficiencies that affect some protocol NLDs, including our subject example, has its origin in a poor understanding of architecture and of related basic concepts. For this reason we have chosen to present in this paper (see section 3) a few architectural concepts of the example protocol and an illustration of the use of LOTOS to represent these concepts.

On the other hand, the presentation of technical issues relating only to the representation of basic, simple concepts might induce in the unaware reader the feeling that formal description in LOTOS is a simple and inexpensive exercise in all cases, which is not the case [BSV 87]. We find it useful therefore to also present an evaluation of the effort needed to obtain the FD (see section 4). We report on the use of LOTOS tools and give an estimation of the related investment of time.

Conclusions are drawn in section 5.

2. PROTOCOL DESCRIPTION IN NATURAL LANGUAGES

It is fairly commonplace to admit, especially by FDT experts, that the usage of natural languages for complex technical descriptions such as protocol standards favours ambiguities, errors and specification gaps, collectively termed *deficiencies*. These appear also difficult to *discover* in large descriptions presented in natural languages, and often even to *fix* without inadvertently introducing new deficiencies.

Below, without aiming at being exhaustive, we mention a few typical problems of this kind, that we illustrate further with reference to the NLD. Since we dislike commonplaces, however, we start with problems that do *not* derive (or at least do not derive *only*) from the informal nature of the description language.

2.1 The seven sins of the specifier

The following list of classes of deficiencies is found by [M 85] to be both common and particularly damaging to the quality of requirements: *Noise* ("The presence in the text of an element that does not carry information relevant to any feature of the problem"), *Silence* ("The existence of a feature of the problem that is not covered by any element of the text"), *Overspecification* ("The presence in the text of an element that corresponds not to a feature of the problem but to features of a possible solution"), *Contradiction* ("The presence in the text of two or more elements that define a feature of the system in an incompatible manner"), *Ambiguity* ("The presence in the text of an element that makes it possible to interpret a feature of the problem in at least two different ways"), *Forward reference* (The presence in the text of an element that uses features of the problem not defined until later in the text")[1], *Wishful thinking* ("The presence in the text of an element that defines a feature of the problem in such a way that a candidate solution cannot realistically be validated with respect to this feature").

This classification proves useful for its quite wide generality. We illustrate (see 2.4) occurrences of some such flaws in the NLD and their resolutions. In detail: *Silence* deficiencies are addressed in 2.4.1 and 2.4.2, *Overspecification* in 2.4.3, combinations of *Noise* and *Silence* in 2.4.4.

2.2 Peculiar sins of protocol specifiers

No matter how much sympathy is given to the use of formal methods for protocol standard definitions, the historical origin of interesting deficiencies in such standards lies in two facts which have nothing to do with languages, and much instead with the subject of these definitions.

In the first place the well-known *lack of recognition of the service concept*. This is thoroughly debated in [VL 85], to which we refer the interested reader. It is clear that the deficiencies referred to in 2.4.1 below follow from this fundamental mistake.[2] Fortunately, it seems that the recognition of the service concept is generally gaining ground.

In the second place, but strongly related, is a basic *misunderstanding of the protocol concept*, such as that of a set of rules on exchanges of messages or Protocol Data Units (PDUs) via a "virtual" medium rather than via the Service Primitives (SPs) of an underlying service which may also show some initiative of its own. This misunderstanding is perfectly consistent with the opinion that service interactions are irrelevant to protocols. However protocol procedures do often need reference to the interactions with the underlying service. Silence about the latter therefore, often entails silence about important relationships and dependencies between protocol procedures (see 2.4.2 below).

On the other hand, the emphasis on the PDU concept is frequently pushed beyond necessity. The presentation of abstract PDU structures is dismissed for their concrete encoding as bitstrings need be given anyway ("assuming" transparent user data transfer by the underlying service). As a consequence, PDU encoding is often only referred to in procedures to which it actually proves irrelevant (see 2.4.4 below).

2.3 Natural (language) sins

The notion of nondeterminism draws a fundamental distinction between specification and programming. While determinism is an inherent property of programs (if it defines a (partial, recursive) *function* on its input domain [S 77]), specification allows *possibilities* and prescribes *necessities* about implementations [M 81]. Therefore modal constructors (such as *may*, *must*, *shall*, etc.) naturally populate specification sentences in NLDs.

Unfortunately, as pointed out in [VS 88], misuse of modal constructors, especially in combination with negation and/or quantifiers (such as *some*, *all*, the often dubious *any*, etc.), is one of the most powerful sources of ambiguity in NLDs.

The only recipe that comes to our mind is that of adopting a *uniform* and *essential* style of representing modality and nondeterminism. Such a style should facilitate (automated) checks to ensure that the above sins are not committed. It stands to reason that essentiality and uniformity apply as well against many other well-known troubles favoured by natural languages. But where may one find good sources for such virtues? In the case of the English language we refer the reader to the valuable [G 87]. It is certainly interesting to mention that the problem is tackled also in [I 86], where preferred terms are recommended for the statement of requirements in standards (for both English and French).

2.4 A few deficiencies in the NLD of a transport protocol

We present the most significant defects, together with their resolutions for the representation of the NLD by the FDs. Here "significant" has a somewhat statistical flavour: experience with FDs of standard protocols indicates that the blend of deficiencies selected in this section is very likely to be found in many other real-world situations.

2.4.1 Lack of (reference to) service definitions

The example specifies a connection-oriented transport protocol. However, the NLD makes no reference to existing transport and network services. The historical origin of such a kind of deficiency was pointed out in section 2.2 above.3

The deficiency is resolved by inserting in the NLD proper references to the connection-oriented transport service [IC 85], of which a subset is defined to be provided by the protocol, and to the connection-oriented network service [IC 86], of which a subset is defined to be made use of by the protocol.[4] The SPs and their parameters that are relevant to the protocol are introduced, as well as the relation between SPs and PDUs.

2.4.2 Unspecified relationships between protocol procedures

The NLD refers to the connection phases (viz. establishment, data transfer, termination) in terms of related procedures, but describes neither the termination procedure[5], nor any relation between such procedures. The former *silence* is most probably to be attributed to the fact that such procedures make use of no PDU, but only of SPs, which used to be viewed as irrelevant to protocols (cf. arguments in 2.2 above). The latter *silence* is less harmful, but still instructive, because relationships between PDUs *are* defined, so that relationships between procedures can be derived insofar as they are determined by those between PDUs.

The deficiency is resolved by extending the NLD consistently with the basic class of the standard OSI transport protocol [IC 87].

2.4.3 Overspecification

The NLD refers to several functions that are not relevant to the protocol, e.g. multiplexing, sequence control, etc. These functions may well be supported by implementations that comply with the protocol, viz. whenever the implementation supports other classes of the OSI protocol. An NLD that includes such superfluous information *should* result in valid implementations, but may lead to confusion and consequently to an incorrect specification.

These deficiencies are left in the NLD, as they do not affect the possibility of producing the FDs. However, for the sake of clarity, the statement is added that only the OSI transport class 0 [IC 87] (with class negotiation and interoperability) is catered for by the NLD.

2.4.4 Scope errors

We consider the misplacement of definitions to be *scope errors*. This sort of deficiency damages the readability of a NLD for two reasons: 1) the information appears to be irrelevant in the place where it is presented, i.e. it is (local) *Noise*, and 2) the information is absent in the place where it should be, i.e. (local) *Silence* is found.

An instructive example of this sort is found in the NLD: it concerns the concatenation of PDUs in the same network service data unit (SDU). The NLD presents a list of transport protocol functions in one of the early sections, but neither does it define these functions nor does it tell which of them are supported by the specified transport protocol. The concatenation function is not in this list: it is not supported by the protocol, but this is not sufficient to justify the absence (see 2.4.3). In fact the function is mentioned later, in the context of the NLD of PDU formats (to which it is irrelevant), saying that it is not supported. For the sake of interoperability, the NLD should also say (in the proper place) what to do with incoming PDUs that are concatenated. The NLD amendment corrects this someway.

Indeed, in this example we very frequently find that protocol requirements that relate to the abstract structure of PDUs are often intermingled with the definition of concrete PDU encoding. The simple fact that the PDU concept is an architectural concept is not clear to everybody.

3. ARCHITECTURAL CONCEPTS AND THEIR REPRESENTATION IN LOTOS

We present a few architectural concepts of the example transport protocol, together with fragments of the FD that relate to those concepts. Our presentation aims at illustrating aspects of the use of LOTOS that occur in FDs of complex protocols and services, such as those of the OSI architecture. In this section, the LOTOS text is in italics.

3.1 Service Access Points and Addresses

Service access points (SAPs) are abstract means of interaction between service users and a service provider.[6] A transport protocol entity uses the network service to provide the transport service. It accesses one or more transport SAPs and one or more network SAPs.[7]

Addresses identify SAPs. In the case of a connection oriented service, different connections at one SAP are distinguished at that SAP by means of connection endpoint identifiers (CEIs).

A simple way of representing SAPs in LOTOS is to employ one gate to represent a whole service boundary. This is in fact necessary whenever an unspecified number of SAPs form the service boundary, for no language facility is available to support other representations.[8]

In the FD, the *t* and *n* gates respectively represent the transport and network service boundary accessed by the entity. The specification is parameterized with sets of transport addresses and network addresses (*tas* and *nas*). Proper cooperation between entities of adjacent layers within one open system is ensured by assigning the same set of addresses to the subsystems to which those entities belong.[7] This implies that a transport entity cannot interact with a session entity if they reside in different open systems.

Abstractness of specification requires the possibility to distinguish any number of SAPs, and therefore of addresses, even without specifying any particular address structure.[9] In the FD, the following definition represents an infinite number of transport addresses.[10]

```
type       TransportAddress       is Boolean
sorts      TAddress
opns       SomeTAddress : -> TAddress
           AnotherTAddress : TAddress -> TAddress
           _eq_ , _ne_ : TAddress, TAddress -> Bool
eqns       forall a,a1 : TAddress ofsort Bool
           SomeTAddress eq SomeTAddress              = true     ;
           SomeTAddress eq AnotherTAddress(a)        = false    ;
           AnotherTAddress(a) eq SomeTAddress        = false    ;
           AnotherTAddress(a) eq AnotherTAddress(a1) = a eq a1  ;
           a ne a1                                   = not(a eq a1) ;
endtype (* TransportAddress *)
```

Similar constructions in the FD specify network addresses, as well as transport and network CEIs, to which the abstractness requirement obviously applies as well.

3.2 Service Interactions.

In most specifications of OSI standards in LOTOS, the following event structure represents service interactions:

service-gate ad:address cei:connection-endpoint-identifier sp:service-primitive

The reason for representing a whole service boundary by a single gate was already explained (see 3.1). In the sequel we propose a few elements of discussion about the other items of representation of service interaction.

3.2.1 SAP identification

The representation is adequate insofar as every address corresponds at any given time to one SAP. Planned extensions of the OSI reference model however, cater for so-called 'generic' addressing - viz. where an address identifies a set of SAPs. Under such an extension, an additional, possibly local mechanism for SAP identification (e.g. in the scope of the given generic address) would be required. The corresponding extension of the event structure is straightforward.

3.2.2 Connection Endpoint Identification.

The representation has two important implications:

1) abstraction is made from assignment of responsibility, viz. to either the service user or the service provider, in the selection of connection endpoints; and
2) no particular structure of connection endpoints is assumed.

Both issues fall in the scope of implementation decisions.

3.2.3 Atomicity of service primitives.

The issue is old-dated, and we would not like to readdress it except to add the following remarks.

1) The atomicity assumption is harmless in the representation of services, but critical in that of protocols; we made it in the FD only for the sake of simplicity.
2) There are ways of relaxing the atomicity assumption in protocol FDs in LOTOS that preserve related service FDs where that assumption is made (see [S 87] and [SRL 87] for one such example).

3.3 Service Primitives

SPs are the main elements of interaction at SAPs.[11] In LOTOS the definitions of SPs can use the following outline:

a) construction of the basic SP data type;
b) definition of "SP subsort" constants, corresponding to the "SP types" found in the Service definition: the difference in terminology is due to our wish of avoiding confusion with the (algebraic) concept of type in LOTOS;
c) enrichment of the basic SP type with boolean functions, termed "classifiers", that tell whether or not a given SP is of a given subsort;[12]
d) enrichment of the type with functions, termed "parameter selectors", that tell whether a given value is the value of a certain parameter of a given SP (this indirect representation is convenient, for the sake of completeness of the equational definition, as generally a SP parameter is defined only for some - not all - SPs).
e) enrichment of SPs with boolean functions representing equality and inequality;
f) definitions relating to individual parameters of SPs: each definition includes basic construction and equality enrichments;
g) enrichments with other functions that prove convenient to the formulation of requirements in process definitions; these definitions are best presented locally, in the scope of the process where they are invoked.

A few fragments of the description of transport SPs in the FD are presented below, to exemplify the approach. For the sake of brevity, we simplify here the example to the case of T-CONNECT SPs only.

Step a) gives the following definition:

```
type      BasicTSP   is TransportAddress
sorts     TSP
opns      TCONreq, TCONind   : TAddress,TAddress   -> TSP
          TCONresp, TCONconf :                      -> TSP
endtype (* BasicTSP *)
```

In step b) the *TSPSubsort* constants are introduced. Equality of constants is specified in a concise way by means of the auxiliary function *h*, which injectively maps the constants to the natural numbers.[13] Furthermore we term 'Request' any request or response SP and 'Indication' any indication or confirm SP. This yields a much improved regularity of the type structure and favours conciseness of process specifications.[14] We assume an enrichment of the standard [I 87] type *NaturalNumber* with the boolean functions *Even* and *Odd*, having the obvious meaning.

```
type      TSPSubsort            is NaturalNumber
sorts     TSPSubsort
opns      TCONNECTrequest, TCONNECTindication,
          TCONNECTresponse, TCONNECTconfirm : -> TSPSubsort
          h : TSPSubsort -> Nat
          IsRequest, IsIndication : TSPSubsort -> Bool
          eq, ne : TSPSubsort, TSPSubsort -> Bool
eqns      forall s,s1:TSPSubsort, n:Nat ofsort Nat
          h(TCONNECTrequest)         = 0                                    ;
          h(TCONNECTindication)      = succ(h(TCONNECTrequest))             ;
          h(TCONNECTresponse)        = succ(h(TCONNECTindication))          ;
          h(TCONNECTconfirm)         = succ(h(TCONNECTresponse))            ;
        ofsort Bool
          IsRequest(s)    = Even(h(s))     ;    IsIndication(s)    = Odd(h(s))     ;
          s eq s1         = h(s) eq h(s1)  ;    s ne s1            = not(s eq s1)  ;
endtype (* TSPSubsort *)
```

In step c) the outcome of the first two steps are merged and TSP classifiers are introduced. Notice the top-down equational specification of these functions.

```
type      TSPClassifiers        is BasicTSP, TSPSubsort
opns      Subsort : TSP -> TSPSubsort
          IsTCON,IsTCON1, IsTCON2,IsTCONreq, IsTCONind,
          IsTCONresp, IsTCONconf, IsTReq, IsTInd : TSP -> Bool
eqns      forall a,a1:TAddress, t:TSP      ofsort TSPSubsort
          Subsort(TCONreq(a,a1))     = TCONNECTrequest                      ;
          Subsort(TCONresp)          = TCONNECTresponse                     ;
          Subsort(TCONconf)          = TCONNECTconfirm                      ;
        ofsort Bool
          IsTCON(t)       = IsTCON1(t) or IsTCON2(t)                        ;
          IsTCON1(t)      = IsTCONreq(t) or IsTCONind(t)                    ;
          IsTCON2(t)      = IsTCONresp(t) or IsTCONconf(t)                  ;
          IsTCONreq(t)    = Subsort(t) eq TCONNECTrequest                   ;
```

```
              IsTCONind(t)           = Subsort(t) eq TCONNECTindication        ;
              IsTCONresp(t)          = Subsort(t) eq TCONNECTresponse          ;
              IsTCONconf(t)          = Subsort(t) eq TCONNECTconfirm           ;
              IsTReq(t)              = IsRequest(Subsort(t))                   ;
              IsTInd(t)              = IsIndication(Subsort(t))                ;
endtype (* TSPClassifiers *)
```

In step d, the construction of Transport SPs presented above is enriched with functions that allow for determining the value of individual parameters of TSPs. As an example, the selection of addresses is given. The address parameter selectors are defined as boolean functions. As mentioned above, reason for this indirect representation is the completeness of the equational definition.

```
type     TSPParameterSelectors              is TSPClassifiers
opns         _IsCallingOf_, _IsCalledOf_ : TAddress, TSP -> Bool
eqns     forall a,a1,a2:T_Address, t:TSP       ofsort Bool
              a IsCallingOf TCONreq(a1, a2)               = a eq a1   ;
              a IsCallingOf TCONind(a1, a2)               = a eq a1   ;
              not(IsTCON1(t)) => a IsCallingOf t          = false     ;
              a IsCalledOf TCONreq(a1, a2)                = a eq a2   ;
              a IsCalledOf TCONind(a1, a2)                = a eq a2   ;
              not(IsTCON1(t)) => a IsCalledOf t           = false     ;
endtype (* TSPParameterSelectors *)
```

In step e), equality of SPs is specified as the conjunction of TSP subsort equality and of equality of TSP parameters.

```
type     TSPEquality              is TSPParameterSelectors
opns         _eq_, _ne_ : TSP, TSP -> Bool
eqns     forall a1, a2, a3, a4 :TAddress, t1,t2:TSP        ofsort Bool
              Subsort(t1) ne Subsort(t2) => t1 eq t2 = false ;
              TCONreq(a1,a3) eq TCONreq(a2,a4) = (a1 eq a2) and (a3 eq a4) ;
              TCONind(a1,a3) eq TCONind(a2,a4) = (a1 eq a2) and (a3 eq a4) ;
              TCONresp eq TCONresp = true ;
              TCONconf eq TCONconf = true ;
              t1 ne t2 = not(t1 eq t2);
endtype (* TSPEquality *)
```

In This example, step f), definition of individual parameters including equality enrichments, consists of the definition of transport addresses (see 3.1).

Step g) is generally 'distributed' over the process definitions that require new functional enrichments of the type. In the FD one such enrichment is already present in the service FD. It introduces the function *IsValidTCON2For* that is used in the formulation of the local ordering constraints on TSPs expressed in process *TCEP* (see 3.5).

```
type     TransportServicePrimitive         is TSPEquality
opns         _IsValidTCON2For_ : TSP, TSP -> Bool
eqns     forall t,t1,t2 :TSP        ofsort Bool
              t2 IsValidTCON2For t1 =
                  (IsTCONconf(t2) and IsTCONreq(t1)) or (IsTCONresp(t2) and IsTCONind(t1))
endtype (* TransportServicePrimitive *)
```

The outline illustrated above for the definition of SPs enables a clear separation of different aspects of the SP structure in a modular, top-down fashion. Furthermore, it assumes no specific implementation model or language, thus reflecting the desired level of abstraction for the definition of SPs.

3.4 Protocol Data Units.

PDUs convey information between protocol entities in different open systems. PDU transfer takes place by embedding PDUs into SDUs of the underlying service, that are transferred *transparently* as SP parameters.The specification of PDUs therefore includes their encoding into octetstrings.
The same outline as given above for the definition of SPs can be followed also for the definition of PDUs, with a further enrichment of:

h) definitions that specify the encoding of PDUs as octetstrings.

Notice that encoding is specified only at the latest stage, when all aspects are already described. This is convenient in the first place because the equational specification of encoding proves quite a burden. Conceptually it is not difficult, but we found it tedious and dull, after all. Besides this psychological motivation, there is also a methodological reason to defer the specification of encoding as much as possible. Most of the requirements associated with PDUs are really concerned with the abstract PDU structure (see the last paragraph in 2.4.4). Having the encoded PDU structure not yet available at the time of the formulation of these requirements may be of help in avoiding the reference to irrelevant information.[15]

We will not re-exemplify the method for the case of PDUs. It is just the same except for the new step h. Moreover, since we happened to hear doubts about the 'possibility' of specifying PDU encoding in such an abstract technique as LOTOS is, we refer the reader to the FD (see [T 88]) where a reasonably complex example of equational specification of PDU encoding is presented.[16]

3.5 Protocol

The FD is designed on the basis of two major requirements which together provide the appropriate framework for the formal representation of the protocol architecture by way of the formal specification of a generic transport protocol entity:

a)   the formal specification is to be provable consistent with the FD in LOTOS of the OSI connection-oriented transport service [IC 85] as available in [S 87], assuming a correct FD in LOTOS of the OSI connection-oriented network service [IC 86],
b)   the specification applies to any transport entity that implements the protocol.

The structure chosen for the specification considerably simplifies the formal description. This structure is based on a 'constraint-oriented' specification style [T 86], where conjunction of independent constraints on events at a gate (set) is described by the parallel composition of corresponding processes synchronized at that gate (set). This style facilitates the reflection of the architectural features of the protocol in the decomposition of the formal specification.

The main features of this specification style are:

- reduction of the amount of constructive detail by means of the LOTOS "parallel composition" operators;
- reduction of the average size of process definitions;
- reduction of the average parameter space of process abstractions.

For protocol FDs, the additional benefit is obtained of an increase of commonality with the FDs of the related services.

The structure of the example FD enables a clear separation of concerns between

- independent constraints on the provision of transport connections,
- independent constraints on the usage of network connections,
- dependencies between provision of transport connections and usage of network connections, such as those relating to assignment of transport connections to network connections, generation of outgoing blocks from occurred TSPs, etc.

The manner in which the constraints on the protocol entity behaviour is first decomposed is based on the first requirement above (see Figure 1). Some of the components describe constraints that apply to, and depend upon, the behaviour of the protocol entity at only one of the two service boundaries. These constraints will be referred to as service constraints, whereas the term protocol constraints will refer to those which are described by the other components. Notice that, in subsequent decomposition steps, the description of a protocol constraint may reveal further service constraints among its own components.

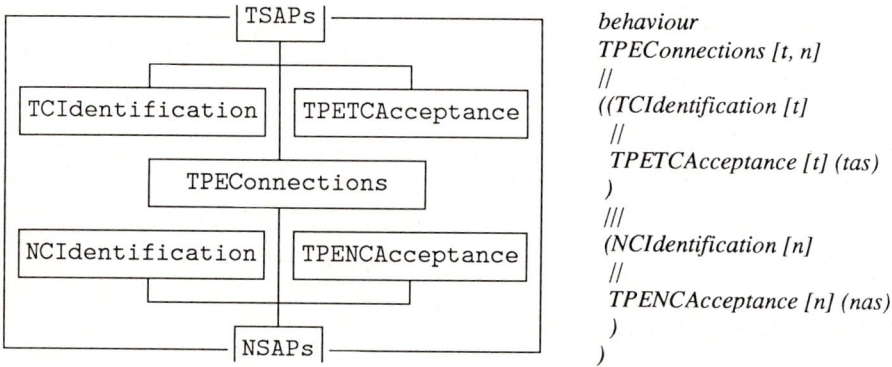

Figure 1 : Constraint-oriented decomposition of the protocol entity

Process *TCIdentification* ensures that a unique identification is used for every transport connection. Process *TPETCAcceptance* ensures that only transport addresses are used that belong to the set of addresses assigned to the entity (*tas*) and that at least one transport connection is always accepted. Processes *NCIdentification* and *TPENCAcceptance* enforce similar constraints at the network service boundary. All of these processes are shared with the corresponding service FD. They enable part of the verification of the so called "integration property" [V 83], that is the requirement that an (N)-Protocol together with the (N-1)-Service provides the (N)-Service.

The definition finds its most complex component in process *TPEConnections* which describes the constraints on provision of transport connections in relation to usage of network connections. Process *TPEConnections* consists of an unspecified number of unsynchronized parallel instances of process *TPEConnection* that are all synchronized with a process which ensures that unique references are assigned to different transport connections.

process TPEConnections [t, n] : noexit :=
(TPEConnection [t, n] ||| TPEConnections [t, n]) |[n]| UniqueLocalReferences [n]
endproc (* TPEConnections *)

The definition of process *TPEConnection* is illustrated in Figure 2. It enables a further separation of concerns between

a) service constraints relating to a transport connection endpoint which are considered in isolation to ensure that the same identification is used at the transport service boundary (pair TAddress-TCei) and to enforce the required local temporal ordering of primitives,
b) service constraints relating to a network connection endpoint which are considered in isolation similar to the requirements at the transport service boundary.

Also the processes representing constraint a) and b) above are shared with the corresponding service FDs.

c) Protocol constraints between TSPs and NSPs, i.e. the relation between TSPs and NSPs directly (e.g. TConReq -> NConReq), the relation between TSPs and blocks, and the relation between blocks and NSPs, and
d) constraints on the local temporal ordering of blocks.

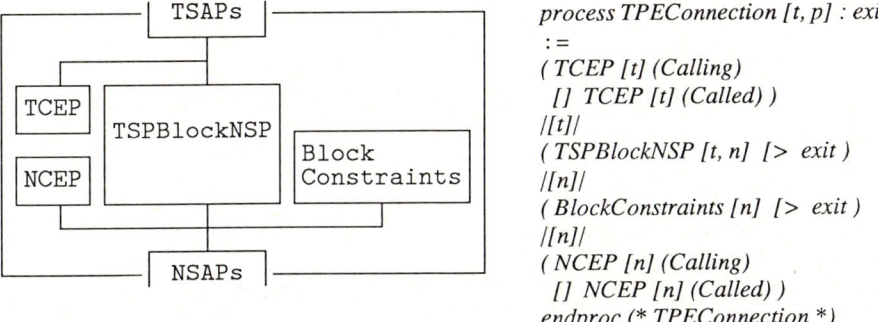

process TPEConnection [t, p] : exit
:=
(TCEP [t] (Calling)
[] TCEP [t] (Called))
/[t]/
(TSPBlockNSP [t, n] [> exit)
/[n]/
(BlockConstraints [n] [> exit)
/[n]/
(NCEP [n] (Calling)
[] NCEP [n] (Called))
endproc (* TPEConnection *)

Figure 2 : Decomposition of Process TPEConnection

The resulting definition clearly separates the independent requirements. Requirements on single connections are separated from requirements on multiple connections and requirements on one interaction point are separated from requirements on another or more interaction points.

We note at this point an autocritical remark concerning our former terminological distinction between service constraint and protocol constraints. According to that distinction, process BlockConstraints would represent (network) service constraints. This is misleading, as the notion of PDU is irrelevant to the service (transparency). In fact, the constraints represented by the process in question refer to the *usage* of the underlying service in the (asynchronous) peer-to-peer interaction. Hence they only characterize the protocol and only the protocol. Obliged to revise our terminology, we get an improved understanding of the protocol concept.

4. EVALUATION OF SPECIFICATION EFFORT

A first draft of the FD referred to in this paper was derived from a draft FD in LOTOS of the ISO connection-oriented transport protocol [IC 87], covering classes 0 to 3. The example protocol is less complex hence a restructuring was needed, e.g. since neither multiplexing nor splitting are supported the definition could be simplified. Furthermore some functions, like protocol error handling, differ from the corresponding functions in [IC 87]. Therefore parts of the specification needed to be re-specified.

In all it took about 8 man-month to develop the formal description in LOTOS of the example protocol. The effort can be decomposed into:

- study of the informal description, 0.5 man-month,
- detection and resolution of deficiencies in the NLD, 1 man-month (from our side),
- interaction with other experts to agree on NLD deficiencies and resolutions, and to harmonize style and notation of the FDs (written using different FDTs) of the same NLD, 2 man-months
- production of formal text, 2 man-months
- production of explanatory text, 1 man-month
- use of tools, 1 man-month.

We did check an intermediate version of the FD using LOTOS tools. A syntax checker (SCLOTOS) and a static semantics checker (LISA) were employed to align the FD with the language definition [I 87]. Also a LOTOS simulator (HIPPO) was made use of to determine whether the described behaviour does fulfil the requirements stated in the (amended) NLD. This tool proved very useful to check properties of the description. However, due to machine memory restrictions, it was possible to simulate only one connection.

5. CONCLUSIONS

The value of reliability of protocol definitions can hardly be underestimated. Usage of formal methods for this purpose is not free from problems. The technical maturity of today's standard FDTs, however, seems to deliver more solutions than new problems. This is an encouraging perspective, which this paper has tried to justify by a swift glance both at well-known problems of informal definitions and at some of the possible solutions that are made available by the use of LOTOS.

In the first direction we found, and had to point out, that sometimes problems arise from poor understanding of architecture rather than from the informal nature of the definitions. This preliminary conclusion motivated our preference, in the second direction, for illustrating the application of LOTOS on basic architectural concepts. The resulting solutions are neither unique nor necessarily the best possible ones. They seem good solutions however (and *are* solutions anyway).

Finally, solutions are not inexpensive. Formal specification only gets industrial attention if it is cost-effective. We have presented some approximate figures drawn from a single, limited experience. What seems more important in our opinion is that costs will decrease by improving familiarity with formal methods and effectiveness of specification tools. The future looks promising.

ACKNOWLEDGEMENTS

The authors wish to thank Vijaya Chari and Toshihiko Kato, who produced the tutorial descriptions of the protocol example referred to in this paper in the FDTs Estelle and SDL respectively, for their helpful co-operation towards the identification and resolution of deficiencies in the natural language description of the protocol example.

This work was partly supported by the Commission of the European Communities under project ESPRIT ST 410 (SEDOS: Software Environment for the design of Distributed Open Systems).

NOTES

(1) Actually we do not consider *explicit* forward references as deficiencies. We consider that a *Forward reference* deficiency occurs when a concept defined later in the text is made use of without any explicit reference to that definition.

(2) *Silence* is not always accidental, one might observe.

(3) Strictly speaking, the NLD under consideration seems to present a "Basic Transport Service", according to the title of section 11.1.2.3 of [T 88]. The expectation is disappointed, however, because the content of that section refers to "Blocks" (that is, PDUs) only, not to transport SPs.

(4) Most of these simplifications are introduced for the tutorial nature of the example, but some are inherent to the example itself, e.g. no provision of transport expedited data and no usage of network expedited data.

(5) Actually the NLD says what the termination procedure *is not*, viz. an explicit termination procedure (relying on the assumption that one reads "explicit" as "by PDU exchange"), but doesn't say what it *is*. A case of *silence by negation* is easily recognized here. A warning is in place about the deceptive nature of such cases: they *seem* to cater for their subject, yet really they do not. In other words, they are cases of *hidden silence*, which - intriguing enough - is often combined with *noise*.

(6) That the SAP *concept* is *abstract* is almost a tautology, yet many still fail to catch this simple point. Consider for example the following statement, probably due to an anonymous OSI architect, that we quote from [A 88]:

> " (...) *Network Service Access .Points within the End System (...) are not to be known by other End Systems, i.e. a remote End System is not required to be aware of the internal organization of this End System (...)*"

(7) The fact that a transport entity may access two or more network SAPs has been criticized in [I 87a] for it entails a lack of robustness of the protocol. On the other hand, limitation of the access of an entity to a service boundary to one SAP only is not restrictive w.r.t. implementations because several (N)-entities may run concurrent in the same OSI ends-system. Indeed, the collection of them is termed "(N)-subsystem" in [IC 84].

(8) For instance gate structures, or functions to construct the specification gate set. In the design of LOTOS this choice was dictated mainly by the criterion of parsimony.

(9) Work is underway by the technical committees responsible for OSI in order to standardize the network address structure, and to extend the OSI reference model [IC 84] to deal with naming and addressing, throughout the OSI architecture, in a consistent and uniform way. We have made no reference to this work in the FD, however, mainly for the sake of simplicity.

(10) Other, more concise constructions could be employed, e.g. renaming the *NaturalNumber* data type defined in the standard library of LOTOS ADTs [I 87]; one would get extra operations, however, thus we preferred the construction reported in this paper.

(11) With reference to the event structure presented in section 3.3, one may see the SP as telling 'what' of the interaction, while the SAP address and the CEI together tell the 'where' of it.

(^{12}) Notice that we define SPs as values of the same sort. This choice favours conciseness of the specification of processes that have to engage in *all* of the SP interactions but are actually only concerned with *some* of them. The case frequently occurs that this *"some"* is: "those which result from application of a given (class of) constructor(s)", such as TCONreq, TCONind, etc. The notion of subsort yields straightforward representations of such situations, thus we have adopted it to the extent allowed by LOTOS.

Subsorts were originally introduced in the context of order-sorted algebras [F 85], where the partial ordering on (sub)sorts is intended to denote set inclusion on the corresponding carriers. Thus, in that approach, the subsort concept is built in the semantics of the specification language. The semantics of LOTOS ADTs is simpler and does not possess that concept, hence the obvious escape is to build the concept in the language pragmatics. This calls for a sufficiently general and possibly elegant usage of the available language facilities. The approach presented in this paper has been successfully applied to the much larger ADTs of standard services such as the Session service primitives [SAC 88], with considerable simplification of equality enrichments. Another way of looking at this style has to do with the 'propositions as types' slogan. Type polymorphism is absent in LOTOS, but we mimic it by the multiplicity of boolean classifiers; one could refer to this practice by reverting the slogan to read "types as propositions' or more precisely 'subsorts as propositions'.

(^{13}) This idea results from our modification of a suggestion by P. van Eijk, who aimed at improving the efficiency of the interactive simulation of the specification by means of the LOTOS simulator HIPPO. We found the combination of his idea with our 'subsorts as propositions' practice fruitful for both efficiency and conciseness. The criticism can be raised, however, that one needs an auxiliary function to achieve this, that introduces a descriptive 'mechanism' where only inherent 'properties' should be referred to. We find that the gain in conciseness largely outweighs the (debatable) loss of elegance.

(^{14}) To the best of our knowledge, this simple but very effective idea was proposed by K. Turner, in one of the earliest attempts to describe the network service in (an earlier version of) LOTOS.

(^{15}) One may call this a 'lazy specification' strategy.

(^{16}) Consistently with the preceding note, this reflects a 'lazy presentation' style.

REFERENCES

[A 88]   AFNOR, *Use of Network Layer addressing by the Transport Layer,*, ISO/IEC JTC 1/SC 6/WG 4 N 375, January 1988.

[BB 87] T. Bolognesi, E. Brinksma, *Introduction to the OSI Specification Language LOTOS*, Computer Networks and ISDN Systems 14, North Holland, 1987, pp. 25-59.

[BSV 87] E. Brinksma, G. Scollo, C.A. Vissers, *Experience with, and future of, LOTOS as a specification language*, in: R. Saracco, P. Tilanus (Eds.), "SDL '87 State of the Art and Future Trends", Proceed. Int. Third SDL Forum, The Hague, NL, April 3-10, R. Saracco, P.A.J. Tilanus (Eds), 1987; North-Holland, 1987, pp. 439-450.

[C 84]   CCITT, *Recommendation T70, Network Independent Basic Transport Service for the Telematic Services* (Red Book), CCITT, Geneva, 1984.

[F 85]   K. Futatsugi, J.A. Gogien, J.-P. Jouannaud, J. Moseguer, *Principles of OBJ2*, Proceed. 12th Symp. on Principles of Programming Languages, ACM, 1985.

[G 87]   Sir E. Gowers, *The Complete Plain Words*, rev. by S. Greenbaum and J. Whitcut, Penguin Books, England, 1987.

[I 86]   ISO, *Rules for the drafting and presentation of International Standards (1986)*, 1st Edition, ISO Central Secretariat, Geneva, 1986.

[I 87]   ISO, *Information Processing Systems - Open Systems Interconnection - LOTOS - A Formal Description Technique for the Temporal Ordering of Observational Behaviour*, ISO Draft International Standard 8807, October 1987.

[I 87a]   ISO, *A problem relating to usage of more than one NSAP by a Transport Protocol Entity,* ISO/TC 97/SC 6/WG 4 N 323, October 1987.

[IC 84]   ISO, *Basic Reference Model for Open System Interconnection*, International Standard ISO 7498, Geneva, 1984, also CCITT Recommendation X.200.

[IC 85]   ISO, *Information Processing Systems - Open Systems Interconnection - Transport service definition*, ISO International Standard 8072, Geneva, 1985, also CCITT Recommendation X.214.

[IC 86]   ISO, *Information Processing Systems - Open Systems Interconnection - Network service definition*, ISO International Standard 8348, Geneva, 1986, also CCITT Draft Recommendation X.213.

[IC 87]   ISO, *Information Processing Systems - Open Systems Interconnection - Connection-oriented transport protocol specification*, ISO International Standard 8073, Geneva, 1987, also CCITT Recommendation X.224.

[M 81]   R. Milner, *Modal Characterization of Observable Machine Behaviour*, in: G. Astesiano and C. Bohm (Eds) *CAAP 81 Proceedings,* Lecture Notes in Computer Science, N 112, Springer Verlag, 1981, pp. 25-34.

[M 85]   B. Meyer, On Formalism in Specifications, *IEEE Software*, Vol. 2, No. 1, January 1985, pp. 6-26.

[S 77]   J. Stoy, *Denotational Semantics: The Scott-Strachey Approach to Programming Language Theory*, MIT Press, 1977.

[S 87]   G. Scollo (Ed.), *Formal Description of ISO 8072 in LOTOS*, Proposed Draft Technical Report, ISO/IEC JTC 1/SC 6 N 4870, Guernsey, February 1988; original version in ESPRIT/SEDOS N 119.6, October 1987.

[SAC 88]   M. v. Sinderen, I. Ajubi, F. Caneschi, *The Application of LOTOS for the Formal Description of the ISO Session Layer,* Univ. Twente, NL, and TECSIEL, Pisa, I, April 1988, submitted for publication.

[SRL 87]   G. Scollo, A. Rennoch, J. v.d. Lagemaat, *Formal Description of ISO 8073 in LOTOS*, ISO/IEC JTC 1/SC 6 N 4871, Guernsey, February 1988; original version in ESPRIT/SEDOS N 119.7, October 1987.

[T86]   A.J. Tocher (Ed.), *Formal Specification of ISO 8072 in LOTOS,* ISO/TC 97/SC 6 N 4395, Tokyo, October 1986, original version in ESPRIT/SEDOS/C1/WP/25/IK, ICL, Kidsgrove, GB, August 1986.

[T 88]   K.J. Turner (Ed.), *Guidelines for the Application of Estelle, LOTOS, and SDL*, ISO/IEC JTC 1/SC 21 N 2011, June 1987.

[V 83]   C.A. Vissers, *Architectural requirements for the Temporal Ordering Specification of Distributed Systems,* in: T. Kalin (Ed.), *EUTECO*, North-Holland, 1983, pp. 79-96.

[VL 85]   C.A. Vissers and L. Logrippo, The importance of the service concept in the design of data communications protocols, in: M. Diaz (Ed.), *Protocol Specification, Testing, and Verification, V*, Proceed. 5th IFIP 6.1 Int.l Workshop, Toulouse-Moissac, F, June 10-13, 1985; North-Holland, 1986, pp. 3-17.

[VS 88]   C.A. Vissers, G. Scollo, The Architecture of Interaction Systems, Course Lecture Notes, Univ. Twente, NL, March 1988.

THE APPLICATION OF LOTOS FOR THE FORMAL DESCRIPTION OF THE ISO SESSION LAYER

Marten van Sinderen (*), Ibrahim Ajubi (*), Fausto Caneschi (**)

In November 1985, ISO/TC97/SC21 installed an ad-hoc working group of WG6 with the purpose of formally describing the Session standard by application of the formal description technique LOTOS. This paper explains the background of this decision, discusses the design principles of the Session Layer specification in LOTOS, and presents the formal description of the Session Service and Protocol on basis of a number of specification samples. Finally, some conclusions are drawn from this large-scale specification experience.

1. INTRODUCTION

Protocol standards must be defined unambiguously in order to ensure that implementations derived from them by different manufacturers are able to interwork. Also for obtaining mutual consistency of two adjacent protocols, interrelated through a service definition, precise and unambiguous definitions are indispensable. The need for accurate definitions was particularly felt by ISO/TC97/SC21, the subcommittee responsible for the Open Systems Interconnection (OSI) standards development. It initiated the standardization of two formal desciption techniques (FDTs), viz. LOTOS [3] and ESTELLE [4], that were to be used for the formal definition of OSI standards.

This paper reports on the application of LOTOS for the formal description of the OSI Session Service (SS) and Session Protocol (SP) [9, 10]. It is not the objective of this paper to further introduce LOTOS, nor to explain the technical details of the Session Layer. The interested user is referred to [1] for a tutorial presentation of the language. An overview of the Session Layer functionality can be found in [7].

An ad-hoc group of WG6 for the formal description of the Session Layer was established in November 1985. At that time, the status of the LOTOS definition was that of a Draft Proposal while the SS and SP documents had reached the Draft International Standard status. The ad-hoc group therefore faced the problem of adapting to any changes made to these documents. This problem is no longer present today. An International Standard (IS) of Session became available in 1987; LOTOS is expected to become an IS in the course of 1988. The Session formal description, which is necessarily lagging in status as compared to the documents it uses as its basis, is currently being progressed as a set of two Technical Reports, one for the service and one for the protocol [5, 6].

The paper is structured as follows: In the next section an overview is given of the background on the overall Session formal description. Then, the general principles that have driven the style of

---

(*) Twente University, PO Box 217, 7500 AE Enschede, The Netherlands
(**) TECSIEL, Via St. Maria 19, 56100 Pisa, Italy
All three authors are member of the ISO/SC21/WG6 ad-hoc group for the formal description of the Session Layer.

the formal description are outlined. Subsequently, the structure of the service and protocol formal descriptions (FDs) is discussed, exemplified by some LOTOS specification samples. Finally, our conclusions are drawn with respect to our experience, and some future activities related to the further progression of the FDs are sketched.

2. BACKGROUND ON THE SESSION FORMAL DESCRIPTION

The background for the application of FDTs to OSI standards is formed by a number of drawbacks of the current informal descriptions. A distinction can be made between the informal natural language description and the semi-formal state table description. Both are used in most OSI standards, including the Session standard.

The drawbacks of a natural language description are pretty obvious. OSI services and protocols are complex definitions, and a natural language is not fit to express such definitions in a concise and, at the same time, precise way. Voluminous definitions written in a natural language are hard to comprehend, and, therefore, verifying the internal consistency and completeness of such a definition is very difficult. Lack of preciseness leads to ambiguous descriptions. Moreover, a natural language can be (intentionally or unintentionally) misused to "solve" differences of opinion between experts developing a standard by adopting a formulation which conceals the controversies. Finally, consistency between a service and the underlying protocol is difficult to obtain and to verify.

State table descriptions were introduced both as an expedient for developers and users of standards. It helped to keep a definition manageable. Nowadays, state table descriptions are very prominent in OSI standards. They often became the authoritive description of a standard, which means that in case of conflicts between a natural language description and the corresponding state table description the latter takes precedence (for example, this is the case for the Session Protocol). State tables, however, do not constitute a formal definition. They are not interpreted in terms of an underlying mathematical model but on informal (albeit, straightforward) grounds. In addition, some aspects of a service and protocol cannot be represented at all by means of state tables. For example, a state table description of a service is limited to the description of the local behaviour at the two endpoints of a connection. The end-to-end relation between service events is not representable. Also multiplicity of connections and identification of connections at the same access point is not described. A state table description of a protocol does not describe the mapping of the protocol data units on the underlying service. Another notable drawback of protocol state table descriptions is that their precribed ordering of protocol events is often not exhaustive (i.e. a finer granularity is possible), and thus unnecessarily restrictive with respect to implementations.

The drawbacks mentioned above may disappear when a FDT is used for the definition of a standard. Naturally, the extent to which this approach is successful depends on the FDT and on the quality of its application. By definition, any FDT enables a precise and unambiguous definition. A FDT, however, must also be expressive in order to keep the definitions concise and to define all aspects of services and protocols without being too restrictive for implementations. Furthermore, the application of the FDT should be suitable for human reading. This implies that the FDT should offer structuring facilities by which reading, understanding and maintaining a FD is facilitated. FDTs and their related tool environment should also support verification, implementation and testing, thus improving the productivity of standards and standard products development.

LOTOS seems to offer many of the desirable characteristics of FDTs [8]. Its application to the Session standard formed a proper testbed in which its suitability for large-scale specifications could be demonstrated.

3. STYLE OF THE LOTOS SPECIFICATION

3.1 Specification Design Principles

LOTOS specifications are definitions of externally observable behaviour. The definition of behaviour is based on process algebras, in particular CCS, while data values are defined with abstract data types based on ACT-ONE. The characterization "externally observable" stems from the fact that the behaviour of a system is described in terms of possible interactions of that system with its environment. The atomic form of interaction is called an event. LOTOS definitions of dynamic behaviour consist of collections of events which are ordered in time.

A LOTOS specification can be organized in many ways. For the formal description of the Session standard a "constraint-oriented" style of specification is adopted. With this style of specification we consider the definition of dynamic behaviour as being the synthesis of constraints with respect to different aspects of that behaviour. Each individual constraint can be specified in LOTOS by a separate process, and instances of these processes can be properly composed (with the parallel-composition operator) to define the total behaviour. The constraint-oriented style, as compared to a less structured approach, has a number of advantages (for more information about this and other styles, see [12]). First, the decomposition results in a "divide et impera" strategy: the complexity of a system becomes manageable so that its specification and the maintenance of the specification becomes easier. Also, with a "smart" decomposition it is possible to use process abstractions more than once, thereby making the specification more concise. The specification is also easier to understand, provided that the decomposition is "natural", that is, corresponds with the intuition of the human user. In the Session standard specification, decomposition is used at several levels.

Another strategy which is followed, and which influenced the presentation of the specification, is to emphasize the commonalities between the service and the underlying protocol. The effort with this strategy was to identify as much as possible data and process abstractions which can be used in both the SS and the SP specification. The constraint-oriented style links up very well with this approach whose main purpose it is to facilitate the verification of the consistency between service and protocol.

3.2 Global Structure of the Specification

The Session standard specification consists of a service specification and a protocol specification. The service specification describes the behaviour which is observable at the Session Service boundary. This FD has no parameters and represents the whole service boundary by a single interaction point, or gate, *s*. Events at *s* consist of three values, of sort *SAddr*, *SCEI* and *SSP* respectively: *s ?sa:SAddr ?si:SCEI ?p:SSP*. The first value identifies the Session Service Access Point (SSAP) where the event occurs, the second value identifies the Session Connection Endpoint Identifier (SCEI) within that SSAP, and the third value represents the Session Service Primitive (SSP) executed in the event. The service FD represents the possibility of multiple concurrent and consecutive Session Connections (SCs). The behaviour described is therefore that of a non-terminating SS-provider.

The top-level decomposition of the service, according to the constraint-oriented approach, shows a structuring of the global service constraints, i.e. the constraints which concern the multiplicity of SCs (see figure 1):
(1) the dynamic behaviour of all potential SCs;
(2) the correct allocation of SCEIs;
(3) the possibility of refusing new SCs;
(4) the backpressure flow control exerted on existing SCs.

Constraint (1) is further decomposed into a set of identical constraints, each one related to the dynamic behaviour of a single SC.

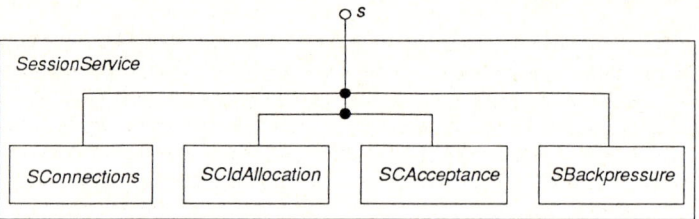

Figure 1: Constraints on the Session Service behaviour.

The protocol specification describes the behaviour of a single SP entity. It is parameterized with an implementation options parameter which indicates which of the available protocol options are supported by this entity. Two external gates, *s* and *t*, are used to interact with the environment, respectively to represent the SS boundary and the Transport Service boundary. The specification describes the support of multiple concurrent and consecutive SCs with a non-terminating behaviour.

The top-level decomposition of the protocol is identical to that of the service, except that here the constraints relate to two different (adjacent) service boundaries (see figure 2). The constraints on the dynamic behaviour of all potential SCs is again decomposed into single SC constraints. From this level on, the structuring of the service and protocol diverge: the protocol constraints are concerned with the provision of the Session Service on basis of the use of the Transport Service. The protocol structure is therefore particularly based on the recognition of separate protocol procedures whose composition in "cascade" is responsible for the service enhancement.

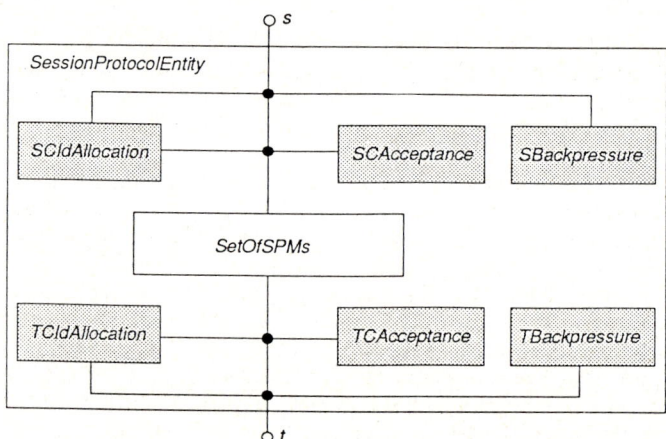

Figure 2: Constraints on the Session Protocol entity behaviour. The shaded boxes represent the processes which are already defined in the Session and Transport Service specifications.

In the next sections we will discuss the structure of the FDs in more detail, restricting ourselves to the discussion of the provision of a single SC (for the service) and the use of a single Transport Connection (TC) (for the protocol).

4. SESSION SERVICE SPECIFICATION

4.1 A Single Session Connection

Specification sample S.1 illustrates the top-level decomposition of the single connection behaviour. Here, "local" and "end-to-end" constraints are recognized, where local means local to a SCEP and end-to-end is related to the exchange of data via the SS-provider. The local constraints are represented by two instances of process *SCEP*, which are distinguished by their actualization with *calling* and *called* (of sort *SSUserRole*), respectively, to indicate the role of the user associated with the local endpoint. The end-to-end constraints are represented by an instance of process *SCAssociation*. The termination of this instance is determined by one or both instances of process *SCEP* (that is, *SCEPAssociation* can at any time be disabled by **exit** which must synchronize with the other components). It may occur that a connection attempt is prematurely aborted (by the calling user or by the provider) or refused (by the provider) and no behaviour can be observed at the called endpoint. This possibility is represented by the choice offered between the instance of *SCEP*, actualized with *called*, and **exit**.

process SConnection [s]: **exit** :=
(SCEP [s] (calling) ||| (SCEP [s] (called) [] **exit**)) || (SCAssociation [s] [> **exit**)
endproc

   Specification sample S.1

The distinction between local and end-to-end constraints also gives rise to a grouping of data type definitions. We distinguish, apart from "ad-hoc" data types, "interface" and "association" data types. Interface data types are used in the specification of local constraints, and are to be shared with FDs that may interwork with the SS specification, viz. the SP and Presentation Protocol FDs. Association data types are used in the specification of the end-to-end constraints; they abstract from the SP behaviour and can for that reason probably not be reused in other FDs.

4.2 Interface Data Types

The interface type definitions relate to the representation of SSAP addresses, SCEIs and SSPs. The definitions for the construction of a SSAP address and a SCEI are relatively simple since the Session standard does not define an internal structure for these identifiers. The only requirement which has to be satisfied is the representation of an infinite number of distinguishable identifiers.

The specification of a SSP data type is more complex because of the great number of SSPs, some of which have many parameters, and the optionality of some of the parameters. The specification is therefore not accomplished in a single type definition, but by way of a number of hierarchical type definitions:
- type *SSPConstant*, which defines a set of constants, each constant corresponding with a "type" of SSP;
- type definitions for each individual SSP parameter;
- type *SessionServicePrimitive*, which imports the forementioned types and defines functions for the construction of SSPs, for the recognition of SSP "types", for testing whether a parameter value is carried by a SSP, and for testing equality of SSPs;
- type *ValidSSP*, which is an enrichment of type *SessionServicePrimitive* with functions that test the validity of SSPs with respect to static parameter restrictions (e.g. user data length) and the relation between request (response) and indication (confirm) primitives.

type SessionServicePrimitive **is** STokens, SData, SSPConstant **sorts** SSP
opns
SPTreq,SPTind: STokens, SData -> SSP   IsSPTreq, IsSPTind: SSP -> Bool
IsTokensOf: STokens, SSP -> Bool   _IsDataOf_: SData, SSP -> Bool
k: SSP -> SSPConstant   _eq_: SSP, SSP -> Bool
eqns forall p,p1:SSP, ts,ts1:STokens, d,d1:SData
ofsort SSPConstant
k(SPTreq(ts,d)) = S-TOKEN-PLEASE-request;
k(SPTind(ts,d)) = S-TOKEN-PLEASE-indication;
ofsort Bool
IsSPTreq(p) = k(p) eq S-TOKEN-PLEASE-request;
IsSPTind(p) = k(p) eq S-TOKEN-PLEASE-indication;
ts1 IsTokensOf SPTreq(ts,d) = ts1 eq ts;   ts1 IsTokensOf SPTind(ts,d) = ts1 eq ts;

(* IsTokensOf yields false when applied to a SSP which does not carry a Tokens parameter; these equations are omitted here since we consider only two SSP "types". Similar comments apply to IsDataOf. *)

d1 IsDataOf SPTreq(ts,d) = d1 eq d;   d1 IsDataOf SPTind(ts,d) = d1 eq d;
p eq SPTreq(ts,d) = IsSPTreq(p) and (ts IsTokensOf p) and (d IsDataOf p);
p eq SPTind(ts,d) = IsSPTind(p) and (ts IsTokensOf p) and (d IsDataOf p);
endtype

Specification sample S.2

Specification sample S.2, illustrates the definition of type *SessionServicePrimitive* on the basis of one service element, viz. Please Tokens:
- *SPTreq* and *SPTind* are constructor functions, which build a S-PLEASE-TOKEN request and a S-PLEASE-TOKEN indication, respectively, from a given set of parameters. The SS FD defines similar functions for the other SSPs. The function names correspond with the names used in the state tables of the SS standard. In the following, we will refer to SSPs by way of these abbreviated names;
- *k* is a mapping function that maps a given SSP to its corresponding constant. Constants (of sort *SSPConstant* and defined by type *SSPConstant*) have names corresponding with the full SSP names, as defined in the standard;
- *IsSPTreq* and *IsSPTind* are classifier functions that tell whether a given SSP is a SPTreq or a SPTind respectively. Similar functions are defined for the recognition of other SSP "types";
- *IsTokensOf* and *IsDataOf* are selector functions that test whether a given value is the value of a Tokens parameter (of sort *STokens*) or a User Data parameter (of sort *SData*), respectively, carried by a given SSP. Similar functions are defined for the selection of the other SSP parameters;
- *eq* is a boolean function for testing equivalence of two given SSPs.

4.3 Local Constraints

Two components of the local constraints are separated in the definition of *SCEP*, shown in specification sample S.3: those of the identification of a SCEP and those concerning the local behaviour in terms of SSP events at that endpoint. The latter constraints are specified by process *SCEPBehaviour*; it presents the formulation, in LOTOS, of the state tables in the SS standard. Process *SCEPIdentification* specifies the constraints on the SSAP address and SCEI used in SSP events at the SCEP: both identifiers are established in the first event and are thereafter constant for the duration of the SC.

The SC establishment phase is specified as the sequence of an instance of process *SCEPConnectPropose* and the choice of instances of *SCEPConnectAccept* and *SCEPConnectReject*. Process *SCEPConnectPropose* describes the execution of a first SSP, that is, a SCONreq or a

SCONind. *SCEPConnectAccept* describes the acceptance of the SC by the second SSP; *SCEPConnectReject* describes the rejection of the SC by the second SSP. The second SSP must be a SCONrsp or a SCONcnf with the Result parameter indicating acceptance or rejection.

In case of acceptance of the SC, the data transfer phase, specified by process *SCEPDataTransfer*, is entered. The negotiated values of a number of Session variables are passed to an instance of this process: the set of selected functional units (of sort *SFUs*), the local assignment of tokens (of sort *SLTsState*), and the initial Synchronization Point Serial Number (SPSN) (of sort *SSPSN*; the value *absent* is used if no SPSN is selected).

The behaviour discussed sofar may be disrupted at any time after the execution of the first event by a SUABreq or SPABind. This possibility is specified in process *SCEPAbort*.

The constraints on the data transfer phase are decomposed as follows:
- restrictions on the available set of service elements and associated primitives as a function of the selected functional units are specified by process *SCEPServices*;
- the constraints on the primitive parameters which depend on the Session variables (tokens, Vact, Vrsp, Vrspnb, V(A), and Vsc) are specified by process *SCEPVariables*; and
- the constraints on valid orderings of primitives as a function of the local state are specified by process *SCEPSPOrdering*.

An instance of process *SCEPSPOrdering* successfully terminates after the affirmative (local) completion of the Orderly Release service element, and thereby disables the instances of *SCEPServices* and *SCEPVariables*. It is actualized with a boolean indicating the local assignment of the data token (*dk* is a constant representing the data token), and the role of the local user. The first parameter is relevant for the ordering of SSPs after the execution of a SUERind or a SPERind; the user role is used in the resolution of a Release collision.

process SCEP [s] (role:SSUserRole): **exit** := SCEPIdentification [s] || SCEPBehaviour [s] (role) **endproc**

process SCEPBehaviour [s] (role:SSUserRole): **exit** :=
SCEPConnectPropose [s] (role) >> **accept** p:SSP **in**
((SCEPConnectAccept [s] (role,p) >>
        accept fus:SFUs, lts:SLTsState, sn:SSPSN **in** SCEPDataTransfer [s] (fus,lts,sn,role)
    [] SCEPConnectReject [s]
)   [> SCEPAbort [s]
)
endproc

process SCEPDataTransfer [s] (fus:SFUs, lts:SLTsState, sn:SSPSN, role:SSUserRole): **exit** :=
    ((SCEPServices [s] (fus) || SCEPVariables [s] (fus,lts,sn,role)) [> **exit**)
|| **let** dkOwned:Bool = (dk IsIn MyTokens(lts)) **in** SCEPSPOrdering [s] (role, dkOwned)
endproc

   Specification sample S.3

4.4 Association Data Types

The specification of end-to-end constraints is based on maintaining a history of the service behaviour at each endpoint, which is relevant for deriving the behaviour at the other endpoint. Therefore, the most important data type for this part of the FD is one for the construction of a history of service events.

Two definitions are introduced for this purpose, shown in specification sample S.4. Type *BasicSEventHistory* provides the basic construction, by way of the functions *empty* (the empty history) and *AddLast* (to update the history with the latest event). Only requests and responses, and indications locally generated by the SS-provider, at a SCEP, have to be recorded in an associated history (the functions *IsReq* and *IsProvGenerated*, which are used to express this condition, are not defined here). For brevity, we will hereafter refer to these events as "Requests", and to indications and confirms as "Indications".

Type *SEventHistory* enriches the first definition with the following functions which are needed to formulate the end-to-end constraints:
- *Tops*: has a history as result consisting of those Requests in the argument history which may lead to an immediate next Indication. The result history also depends on the type of control (i.e., extended control or not) which is exerted by the SS-provider, and forms the second argument of this function;
- *ReduceHistory*: updates an argument history given the fact that a Request, indicated by the second argument, has led to the execution of a corresponding Indication;
- *ResynTops* and *ExcepTops*: these functions are similar to *Tops*, except that different rules are used for deriving the result history, corresponding to two special states of the SS-provider.

The above functions take into account the fact that the SS-provider does not necessarily preserve the order in which Requests are executed. For example, a Request pr2 may lead to a corresponding Indication pi2 before an earlier Request pr1 leads to a corresponding Indication pi1. Moreover, depending on pr2, pi1 may never occur once pi2 is executed. SSPs can therefore be categorized according to their relative precedence. This categorization, defined by type *SSPGrouping*, is made use of in type *SEventHistory*. A SUABreq, for instance, is of higher precedence than a SRSYNrsp, which, in turn, is of higher precedence than a SDTreq (both with and without extended control).

Further association types are needed for the representation of the type of control exerted by the SS-provider (of sort *SFlowControl*), the state of the SS-provider (of sort *SProviderState*), and the global assignment of the data token (of sort *SGDkState*).

type BasicSEventHistory **is** SessionServicePrimitive **sorts** SEventHistory
opns
empty: -> SEventHistory   AddLast: SSP, SEventHistory -> SEventHistory
eqns forall p:SSP, h:SEventHistory **ofsort** SEventHistory
not (IsReq(p) or IsProvGenerated(p)) => AddLast(p,h) = h;
endtype

type SEventHistory **is** BasicSEventHistory, SSPGrouping, SFlowControl
opns
Tops, ResynTops, ExcepTops: SEventHistory, SFlowControl -> SEventHistory
ReduceHistory: SSP, SEventHistory -> SEventHistory
(* Equations are omitted. *)
endtype

Specification sample S.4

4.5 End-to-End Constraints

After the execution of the first Request associated with a SC (i.e., a SCONreq) the connection identification at the calling end is known and that of the called end is to be established. Process *GetCalledSCId* specifies the possible SSP events after the initial Request until the SC identification at the called end is also known or until the connection attempt fails. The latter occurs when a SUABreq, or a provider generated SPABind or SCONcnf is executed at the calling end and prevents any further behaviour. The instance of *SCEPAssociation* will then be disabled by **exit** synchronized with the instance of *SCEP* actualized with *calling*.

If the identification at the called endpoint is established, two instances of process *SCHalf* are enabled, each one specifying the relation between Requests and Indications for a different direction of transfer. These relations comprise the SS-provider's nondeterminacy, i.e. the ability of the SS-provider to autonomously generate Indications, change parameter values, and re-order or destroy Requests.

```
process SCEPAssociation [s]: noexit :=
s ?cgA:SAddress ?cgI:SCEI ?p:SSP [IsReq(p)];
let cgH:SEventHistory = AddLast(p,empty), a:SGDkState = InitialGDkStateOn(p) in
(    GetCalledSCId [s] (cgA,cgI,cgH) >>
     accept cdA:SAddress, cdI:SCEI, cgH:SEventHistory in
     (    SCHalf [s] (cgA,cdA,cgI,cdI,cgH,basicCtl,normalState,a)
       || SCHalf [s] (cdA,cgA,cdI,cgI,empty,basicCtl,normalState,a)
     )  )
endproc

process SCHalf [s] (frA,toA:SAddress, frI,toI:SCEI, c:SFlowControl, h:SEventHistory, s:SProviderState, a:SGDkState): noexit :=
(    [s eq normalState] -> SSPEvent [s] (frA,toA,frI,toI,Tops(h,c),h,c,s,a)
[]   [s eq excepState] -> SSPEvent [s] (frA,toA,frI,toI,ExcepTops(h,c),h,c,s,a)
[]   [s eq resynState] -> SSPEvent [s] (frA,toA,frI,toI,resynTops(h,c),h,c,s,a)
) >> accept h:SEventHistory, c:SFlowControl, s:SProviderState, a:SGDkState in
     SCHalf [s] (frA,toA,frI,toI,c,h,s,a)
endproc
```

Specification sample S.5

The two instances of *SCHalf* are synchronized and therefore not independent. Each of the instances "observes" the SSP events for the direction associated with the other instance, which is necessary to keep track of some variables which influence the end-to-end constraints. *SCHalf* is parameterized with these variables: the type of flow control (initial value: *basicCtl*), the SS-provider state (initial value: *normalState*), and the assignment of the data token (initial value derived from the SCONreq with function *InitialGDkStateOn*).

The definition of *SCHalf* is that of a simple tail-recursion. At any time, the process *SSPEvent* specifies the constraints on the next observable event. The fifth parameter of *SSPEvent*, indicating the "top" Requests, is the keystone to the requirements relating to end-to-end nondeterminacy. The value of this parameter is derived with either one of the functions *Tops*, *ExcepTops* or *ResynTops*, the choice of which depends from the value of the SS-provider state *s*. After execution of the next event, a new instance of *SCHalf* is enabled with updated parameters.

5. SESSION PROTOCOL SPECIFICATION

5.1 A Single Session Protocol Machine

We will now present the specification of a single "Session Protocol Machine" (SPM) that makes use of a TC in order to support one or, in the case where the TC is reused, multiple consecutive SCs. The LOTOS description of the SPM behaviour may profit from the availability of the local constraints definitions of the SS and the (assumed) Transport Service specification. This is reflected in specification sample P.1, presenting the formalization of an SPM as process *SPM* (a graphical representation is shown in figure 3). Process *EitherSCEPs* defines the local constraints at endpoint *s*, which results from a sequential composition of instances of *SCEP* (see 4.3). It terminates when the TC is not to be reused, specified by *SPM0*, in which case synchronization on *exit* occurs following an instance of *SCEP*. Similarly, proces *EitherTCEP* defines the local constraints at endpoint t, however corresponding to the use of a single TC (process *TCEP* is assumed to form a component process in the Transport Service specification). The remaining constraints that relate the events at s with those at t such that one or more SCs can be provided, using a single TC, are specified by process *SPM0*. As we mentioned in 3.2, the SP specification is parameterized with an implementation options parameter; its value (of sort *SPEOptions*) is passed to process *SPM*, which in turn passes it to *SPM0*.

process SPM [s,t] (peo:SPEOptions): **exit** := (EitherSCEPs [s] ||| EitherTCEP [t]) || SPM0 [s,t] (peo) **endproc**

process EitherSCEPs [s]: **exit** := (SCEP [s] (calling) [] SCEP [s] (called)) >> (EitherSCEPs [s] [] exit) **endproc**

process EitherTCEP [t]: **exit** := TCEP [t] (calling) [] TCEP [t] (called) **endproc**

Specification sample P.1

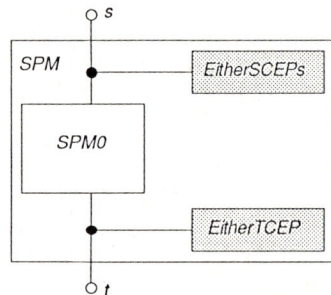

Figure 3: Structure of process SPM. The shaded boxes represent the processes which are partially defined in the Session and Transport Service specifications.

5.2 Protocol Data Types

The SP specification can make use of the interface data types, not only those of the SS specification but also those of the Transport Service specification. The protocol data types which remain concern Session variables and Session Protocol Data Units (SPDUs). The Session variable data types are actually merely extensions to the variable definitions in the SS specification, and will not be discussed here. The SPDU data type, however, is different in nature from the other data types since it also requires the definition of encodings, in addition to an abstract representation of a set of values.

The elements of procedure related to SPDUs can be described separately from the encoding of SPDUs, as is in fact done in the SP standard. The LOTOS description therefore distinguishes between "abstract" SPDUs and encoded SPDUs. The abstract SPDU type is defined in very much the same way as the SSP data type, that is, through:
- the definition of SPDU constants (type *SPDUConstant*, cf. *SSPConstant*), that correspond with the "types" of SPDUs;
- the definitions relating to the individual parameters of SPDUs.
- the basic construction of an abstract SPDU data type (type *AbstractSPDU*, cf. *SessionServicePrimitive*) from (abstract) SPDU parameters, with similar functions as defined by type *SessionServicePrimitive* (see 4.2);

The definitions that specify the encoding of the abstract SPDU are included in type *SPDUEncoding*. Specification sample P.2 illustrates the chosen approach by example of the encoding of the PLEASE TOKENS SPDU. *SPDUEncoding* imports the types *AbstractSPDU*, *OctetString* (from the standard library of data types), and *NatValOctetString* (an auxiliary type). The latter type defines a function *NatNum* which yields the natural number represented by a given octet string when interpreted as a bitstring with the leftmost bit being the most significant bit, and a function *E* which yields the shortest octet string which represents a given natural number. Two principal functions are defined by *SPDUEncoding*, viz. *Encodes*, an infix boolean function which yields true when its lefthand argument - an octet string - is the correct encoding of its righthand argument - an abstract SPDU; and *Decodes*, a boolean function which tests the inverse relation.

The definition of function *Encodes* reflects the general structure of a SPDU as defined by the standard (see figure 4). The first, leftmost part of an encoding is the SI field which identifies the type of SPDU. It consists of a single octet that encodes, as a binary number, a natural number value that is unique for the type of SPDU (e.g., 2 for PLEASE TOKENS). The second part, called the LI field, indicates the length of the following encoding of the SPDU parameters. In case the length, in octets, is within the range 0-254, one octet is used to encode the length value as a binary number. A length within the range 255-65535 comprises three octets, the first coded 1111 1111 and the second and third encoding the length value as a 16-bit binary number (with the first bit of the second octet being the most significant bit). Only if the SPDU may carry one or more parameters, a Parameter field can be present, forming the third part of the encoding. The Parameter field consists of PGI units and/or PI units. A PGI unit contains a PGI field, a LI field, and, optionally, a Parameter field. The PGI field identifies a parameter group, and is encoded in the same way as the SI field. The Parameter field, if present, contains a single parameter value or one or more PI units. A PI unit contains a PI field, a LI field, and, optionally, a Parameter field. The PI field identifies a parameter, encoded in the same way as the SI field. The Parameter field, if present, consists of a single parameter value. A SPDU encoding may additionally contain a user information field, following the Parameter field of the SPDU, if user information is defined and present for that SPDU.

To test the above constraints on the encoding of a SPDU, the following auxiliary functions have been defined:
- *EncodesTypeOf*: tests the encoding of the SI field;
- *EncodesLengthOf*: tests the encoding of the LI field of a SPDU, PGI unit or PI unit;
- *EncodesParsOf*: tests the encoding of the Parameter field of a SPDU; and
- functions for testing the encoding of PGI and PI units, such as:
    . *EncodesTokensOf*: tests the encoding of the Token Item PI unit, and
    . *EncodesDataOf*: tests the encoding of the User Data PGI unit.

Some additional functions have been defined for the handling of invalid encoded SPDUs; they are not discussed here.

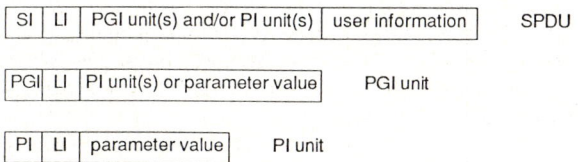

Figure 4: Structure of SPDUs.

type SPDUEncoding **is** AbstractSPDU, OctetString, NatValOctetString **sorts** SPDU
opns
Encodes, _EncodesLengthOf_, _EncodesParsOf_, _EncodesTokensOf_, _EncodesDataOf_:
    OctetString, SPDU -> Bool
EncodesLengthOf: OctetString, OctetString -> Bool
Decodes: SPDU, OctetString -> Bool
eqns forall p:SPDU, o:Octet, s,si,li,pgi,pi:OctetString **ofsort** Bool

(* ++, Length, Octet and <> are standard library functions, defined by type OctetString. ++ is an infix function that concatenates two given strings; Length yields the length of a given octet string; Octet constructs an octet from 8 bit values; and <> is a constant denoting the empty octet string. *)

(si ++ li ++ s) Encodes p = (si EncodesTypeOf p) and (li EncodesLengthOf s) and (s EncodesParsOf p);

(* The following equations are restricted to PLEASE TOKENS SPDUs; function IsPT, defined by type AbstractSPDU, yields true when its argument (abstract) SPDU is a PLEASE TOKENS SPDU. *)

IsPT(p) => si EncodesTypeOf p = (si eq E(2));
Length(s) le 254 => li EncodesLength of s = li eq E(Length(s));
(Length(s) ge 255) and (Length(s) le 65535) =>
    li EncodesLength s = li eq (Octet(1,1,1,1,1,1,1,1) + E(Length(s)));
IsPT(p) =>
    (s2 ++ s1) EncodesParsOf p = (s2 EncodesTokensOf p) and (s1 EncodesDataOf p) and
        ((s2 eq <>) implies (s1 eq <>));

(* Function Bit8, defined by type OctetString, yields the value of the rightmost bit of its argument octet; this is bit 1 according to the conventions of the protocol standard. Bit 1 = 1 indicates that the data token is requested in the SPDU. Bit7, Bit6, etc. yield the values of bit 2, bit 3, etc. *)

(ts IsTokensOf p) and (ts ne {}) =>
    (pi ++ li ++ Octet(o)) EncodesTokensOf p = (pi eq E(16)) and (li eq E(1)) and
        ((Bit2(o) eq 1) iff (tr IsIn ts)) and ((Bit4(o) eq 1) iff (ma IsIn ts)) and
        ((Bit6(o) eq 1) iff (mi IsIn ts)) and ((Bit8(o) eq 1) iff (dk IsIn ts));
(ts IsTokensOf p) and (ts eq {}) =>
    (pi ++ li) EncodesTokensOf p = ((pi eq E(16)) and (li eq E(0))) or ((pi ++ li) eq <>);
(d IsDataOf p) and (d ne <>) =>
    (pgi ++ li ++ d) EncodesDataOf p = (pgi eq E(193)) and (li EncodesLengthOf d);
(d IsDataOf p) and (d eq <>) =>
    (pgi ++ li) EncodesDataOf p = ((pgi eq E(193)) and (li eq E(0))) or ((pgi ++ li) eq <>);
p Decodes s = s Encodes p;

(* The definition of the natural number constants 2, 16 and 193 is omitted. *)
endtype

Specification sample P.2

5.3 Session to Transport Boundary Relation

The relation between two adjacent layer boundaries, as defined by a protocol, is generally far more complex than the relation between two endpoints of the same boundary, being the subject of a service definition. This is certainly true for the Session Layer. Intuitively, the constraint-oriented approach alone seems insufficient to tackle the complexity of a SP entity. However, when protocol functions could be identified that can be composed in cascade [11], the output of one being the input to another, the "distance" between adjacent layer boundaries may be "bridged" more easily. The "bridge segments" which result from this structuring can then be structured further by conjunction of related partial constraints according to the constraint-oriented approach. Note that function cascading can be seen as a structuring approach oriented towards resources, instead of constraints, with the functions in cascade representing resources.

The top-level decomposition of process *SPM0* is illustrated in specification sample P.3. Two components are composed in cascade, *SPMTop* and *SPMBottom*, interacting at an internal, i.e. hidden, gate *p*. Process *SPMTop* defines the relation between SSP and (abstract) SPDU events, including queuing and dequeuing of SPDUs, and segmenting and reassembly of data or typed data SSDUs. Process *SPMBottom* specifies the relationship between SPDU and Transport Service Primitive (TSP) events. Here, encoding and decoding, concatenation and separation, and the related error handling is included. Two further processes are introduced. Some TSPs do not carry SPDUs, but can be directly related to an SSP. Such direct mappings are specified by process *DirectMapping*. The constraints related to the state tables of the SP standard, that is, concerning the ordering of SPDUs and the parameter values contained in SPDUs, are defined by process *SPDUConstraints*.

```
process SPM0 [s,t] (peo:SPEOptions): exit :=
(     DirectMapping [s,t] (peo)
||    hide p in ( SPMTop [s,p] (peo) |[p]| SPMBottom [p,t] |[p]| SPDUConstraints [p] (peo) )
)     [> exit
endproc
```

Specification sample P.3

The structure of process *SPM0* is such that at gate *p* (abstract) SPDUs and related information are exchanged. The format of the events at the *p* gate is:

p ?pd:ASPDU ?f:TFlow ?d:Dir ?v:Val ?s:SPMState

where *pd* is the abstract SPDU, *f* the transport flow option which is used (i.e., normal or expedited), *d* the transfer direction of the SPDU (i.e., send or receive), *v* the validity of the SPDU (only relevant if the SPDU is received), and *s* the state of the SPM (only relevant if the SPDU is received, and determined by *SPDUConstraints*). The need for variables *v* and *s* results from the fact that none of the processes interacting at *p* can independently decide whether a SPDU which is received on the TC is valid in all respects or not. For example, *SPMBottom* detects invalid encodings and incorrect concatenations, and *SPDUConstraints* determines whether the receipt of a SPDU in the present state and with the present variable settings is allowed. Variable *v* indicates the validity of a SPDU, or the type of invalidity of the SPDU, with contributions from any of the processes. The reason for communicating the state *s* of the SPM in interactions at *p* is that in some cases the (in)validity of a SPDU can only be determinated when also *SPMBottom* is aware of the SPM state which is monitored by *SPDUConstraints*.

5.4 Internal Protocol Constraints

Process *SPDUConstraints*, presented in specification sample P.4, models the core of the SPM. We can use the constraint-oriented approach again to obtain a further structuring in parallel processes, interacting at gate *p*:
- process *SPMImplementation* specifies the constraints which are derived from the implementation options parameter. For example, it determines the maximum TSDU size to be used on the TC;
- process *SPMVariables* is concerned with the variables related to the predicates and actions described in the state tables w.r.t. protocol events. *SPMVariables* defines the constraints imposed on SPDU exchanges which depend on these variables, and specifies the assignment of new values to the variables due to SPDU exchanges;
- process *SPDUParRelations* specifies the constraints on parameter values carried by a SPDU insofar these depend on the values carried by an earlier exchanged SPDU (e.g. such a dependency exists between a CONNECT and an ACCEPT SPDU);

- process *SPDUOrdering* defines the temporal ordering of SPDUs, but explicitly does not constrain the contents of the SPDUs nor does it specify conditions, other than those concerning ordering, for sending or receiving SPDUs.

In the specification sample, the process parameters, except the implementation options parameter, are deliberately omitted, since they relate to the internal structure of these processes which is not discussed here.

process SPDUConstraints [p] (peo:SPEOptions): **noexit** :=
SPMImplementation [p] (peo) || SPMVariables [p] || SPDUParRelations [p] || SPDUOrdering [p]
endproc

Specification sample P.4

6. REFLECTION ON EXPERIENCES

The Session specification in LOTOS describes the standard of the 1987 version, that is, without extensions such as unlimited user data, connectionless, and symmetric synchronization. However, the specification can be used as it is as a basis for developing test suites and specification of higher level protocols. Besides, the specification work has already proved useful by disclosing a number of errors and inconsistensies in the standard that have been documented as Defect Reports and submitted to the WG6 Session group. Last, but probably most important, a significant experience has been gained on large-scale specifications in LOTOS.

The design of the Session FDs has evolved from a mere translation of the existing state tables to a more structured specification based on the constraint-oriented approach (compare, for example, the report on an intermediate version of the FDs in [11]). The development of the FDs took a considerable amount of time for the following reasons:
- LOTOS itself has evolved during the last few years;
- there were but a few LOTOS experts when the specification work within ISO started. It is hoped for that due to the availability of a stable LOTOS definition and due to the early specification work, LOTOS will gain more familiarity among protocol developers;
- the Session specification was one of the first large-scale specifications in LOTOS, and little experience was available with respect to suitable specification styles when the work started (a number of styles which evolved from past experience are evaluated in [12]);
- as mentioned above, the Session documents were not free of errors and interpretation problems, the resolution of which had to precede the specification work;
- only in the course of the specification work, prototype tools to support the specification in LOTOS became available. So far, the use of these tools has been very limited.

From this we may conclude that the effort and time spent on the Session FDs is not representative and could be considerably reduced should the work now start from scratch. Also, our experience suggests that FDs can better be developed during the standardization process instead of being based on existing (draft) standards. Technical solutions can then be evaluated on basis of their formal description and can be unambiguously documented.

A large-scale specification, such as that of the Session Layer, forms a good testbed both for the language and the tools that support the application of the language, as has been demonstrated in the European ESPRIT/SEDOS Project 410. The tools developed by this project [2] could only have been made limited use of so far. Nonetheless, it is the intention to check the syntax and static semantics (i.e. the scope and type rules) of the FDs and to perform a limited functional analysis using available tools, before registering them as a TR. We would stress however, that tools should normally be applied at an early stage of developing a FD so as to improve productivity.

7. ACKNOWLEDGEMENTS

We like to acknowledge the other members of the Session Formal Description ad-hoc group, Claude Mahy, Isabelle Sicot, Grenville Taylor and Eddie Michiels, for their contributions to progress the work to the current level of completeness. Especially, their profound knowledge of the Session Layer and their experience with the former specification of the Session in ESTELLE was of great value.

The work on the Session Layer formal description in LOTOS would not have been possible without the support from ESPRIT/SEDOS. In particular, we like to thank Giuseppe Scollo his comments on, and contributions to the documents originated from this project.

REFERENCES

[1] E. Brinksma, A Tutorial on LOTOS, Proc. of the IFIP WG6.1 5th Int. Workshop on Protocol Specification, Testing, and Verification, Toulouse-Moissac, June 1985 (North-Holland 1986) 171-194.

[2] M. Diaz, C. Vissers, S. Budkowski: ESTELLE and LOTOS Software Environments for the Design of Open Distributed Systems, in: ESPRIT '87 - Achievements and Impact, Proc. of the 4th Annual ESPRIT Conf., Brussels, Sept. 1987 (North-Holland 1987) 543-558.

[3] ISO DIS 8807, Information Processing Systems - Open Systems Interconnection - LOTOS - A Formal Description Technique Based on the Temporal Ordering of Observational Behaviour.

[4] ISO DIS 9074, Information Processing Systems - Open Systems Interconnection - ESTELLE - A Formal Description Technique Based on an Extended State Transition Model.

[5] ISO DTR 9571, Formal Description of the Basic Connection Oriented Session Service in LOTOS (also: ESPRIT/SEDOS 119.8).

[6] ISO DTR 9572, Formal Description of the Basic Connection Oriented Session Protocol in LOTOS (also: ESPRIT/SEDOS 119.9).

[7] W.F. Emmons, and A.S. Chandler, OSI Session Layer: Services and Protocols, Proc. of the IEEE, Vol. 71, No. 12, Dec. 1983, 1397-1400.

[8] P. Gelli, Evaluation and Comparison of three specification languages: SDL, LOTOS and ESTELLE, in: SDL '87: State of the Art and Future Trends, Proc. of the 3rd SDL Forum, The Hague, April 1987 (North-Holland 1987) 211-231.

[9] ISO 8326, Information Processing Systems - Open Systems Interconnection, Basic Connection Oriented Session Service Definition.

[10] ISO 8327, Information Processing Systems - Open Systems Interconnection, Basic Connection Oriented Session Protocol Specification.

[11] G. Scollo, and M. van Sinderen, On the Architectural Design of the Formal Specification of the Session Standards in LOTOS, Proc. of the IFIP WG6.1 6th Int. Workshop on Protocol Specification, Testing, and Verification, Montreal, June 1986 (North-Holland 1987) 3-14.

[12] C. Vissers, G. Scollo, and M. van Sinderen, Architecture and Specification Style in Formal Descriptions of Distributed Systems, to appear in: Proc. of the IFIP WG6.1 8th Int. Symp. on Protocol Specification, Testing, and Verification, Atlantic City, June 1988.

LOTOS supported system development.

Kees Bogaards

Department of Informatics
Tele-Informatics Group
University of Twente
Enschede, The Netherlands

1. Introduction

This paper presents an example of the use of the Formal Description Technique LOTOS [ISO8807] in the design of a complex concurrent system.

The work presented here is carried out in the within the PANGLOSS project, which is a ESPRIT funded cooperative project of CAP (UK), University of Twente, University of Liege, 7-Technologies, University of Sterling, University of Reading and YARD. The objectives of the PANGLOSS project are:
  the development of a systematic design and development methodology for distributed and concurrent systems.
and
  to prove this methodology by designing a high performance networking gateway according to the principles of OSI
Thus, the project emphasizes the use of design methods, including formal methods, by application in a large realistic problem in which also performance plays an important role.

The key theme in this paper is that, the design of a complex, open ended system demands a systematic approach in which formal and non-formal methods are combined. The need for creativity in the development of design steps as well as the usefulness of formalization will be illustrated.

The structure of this paper is as follows:
First the design approach is described in Chapter 2. The methods used in this approach clearly identify a number of description levels.
Within the scope of this paper, two of these descriptions, namely the so called Gateway Architecture and the Reference Architecture, which both are fully formalized, are of interest as an example of LOTOS supported design. The development of these descriptions are described in more detail in the chapters 3 and 4.
In the last Chapter some conclusions and recommendations are given.

2. Formal Descriptions of intermediate design.

2.1 top down design process

We view the design as a process. It starts with input data and delivers a result. (fig 2.1)

For PANGLOSS the required result is the implementation of a high performance gateway. With this we mean a complete, unambiguous blueprint for the realization of a gateway. As an a-priori quality requirement, we demand that the notation system used for the description of the blueprint is a formal language with formalized semantics, thus avoiding ambiguity.

Input to the design process is a set of informal requirements, probably incomplete and vague.

The end-product, the Gateway implementation, not only differs from the informal requirements in its level of abstraction, it also uses a formal language allowing an unambiguous and precise description.

The task of the designer is to transform this set of informal requirements to the formal precise implementation. To achieve this, the designer may have a number of tools at his disposal such as software engineering methods, formal languages, compilers, verification methods.

Since the task is too large to arrive in a single step at the desired result, the design process is split up into a number of subsequent steps. Each step intends to lower the abstraction level by adding more detail in the description, hence the term top-down design method. (fig 2.2)

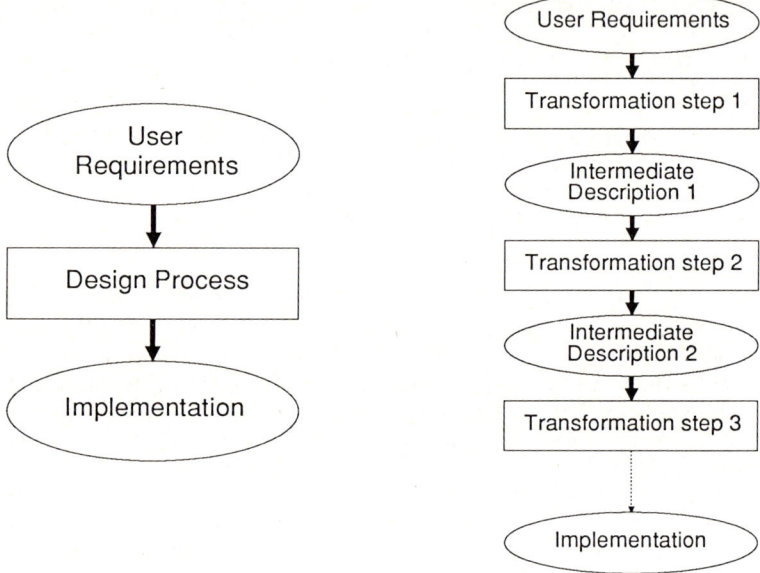

figure 2.1 figure 2.2

We can characterize a top-down step now as the transformation of the specification of an object that is expressed at a certain level of abstraction, into another specification that is expressed at a lower level of abstraction. At the same time, the transformation intends to achieve more formality.

2.2 design criteria

Top-down design steps may be performed in a variety of ways. From that variety, the designer will have to make a choice. In order to make a proper selection, he must be guided by criteria.

These criteria are already formulated in the informal requirements. They constrain the set of possible implementations to those implementations that conform to quality criteria such as modularity, extendability, adaptability etc.

Technical design criteria for the PANGLOSS gateway [PAN86] are:

- High Performance
- Subnet adaptability.
  concerns the adaptation to new sub-network technologies. Introduction of new network technology may not effect the required effort for hardware and software development by more than 15%.
- Generality
  states the capability to accommodate a variety of internet protocols. Both Connection-Oriented(CO) and Connection-Less (CL) as well as Stream-Oriented (SO) (such as video and voice) protocols must be supported.
- Enhanceability
  refers to the requirement to extend the total gateway throughput by hardware and software increments without meeting performance bottle-necks. To be achieved by:
  Increase of the number of connections.
  Increase of throughput per connection.
- Product life time
  Product life time must extend at least 10 years after the project finishes.
- Portability
  Refers to the requirement to port the gateway design to other hardware and possibly to other software.
- Cost/ Efficiency
  Clearly a relationship between the delivered performance and the cost must exist.

Evaluation of these criteria leads to an ordering that will be of use in the design process (see section 3). The most important criteria have been identified as:

- high performance, and

- generality

The fact that high performance is a major concern can be understood by observing that a methodology which is only applicable for the development of systems in which performance does not play a role, is <u>not</u> a very convincing methodology in the area of concurrent systems.

Generality is equally important since acceptance of non-general solutions may lead to a number of unrelated designs thereby allowing to split up the PANGLOSS project in multiple smaller, independent projects.

2.3 iteration

Although the number of possible implementations is constraint by the informal requirements, multiple implementations still be may feasible. Moreover, substructuring of the design process in various transformation steps can be accomplished in many ways, because the nature of the transformations will in general differ in different designs, whereas also the order in which the transformations are applied may have a decisive effect on the quality of the implementation. Therefore the design cannot be carried out in a strictly top-down fashion, but transformations are iterated to obtain a satisfactory implementation.

2.4 global description levels

In the PANGLOSS design approach 4 descriptions (fig 2.3), differing from each other in level of formality and abstraction, can be identified, namely:

- the Informal Requirements
  the first and informal definition of the gateway functions and requirements, the user requirements.

- the Gateway Architecture
  the first formal specification at the highest level of abstraction.

- the Reference Architecture.
  This is an intermediate formal specification, which has a specific meaning in the PANGLOSS design approach.

- The implementation.
  a complete blueprint for the realization of the gateway.

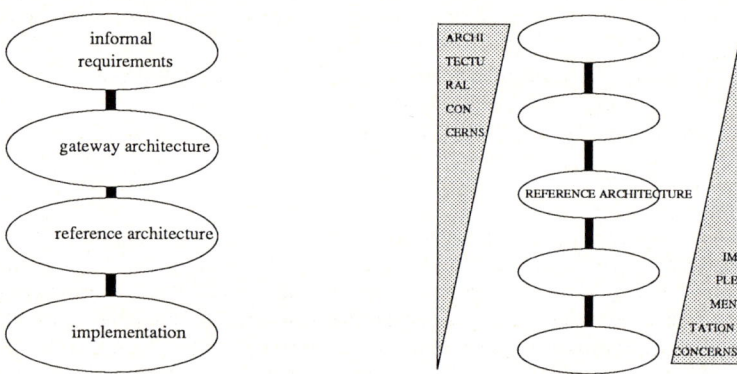

figure 2.3   figure 2.4

The implementation will not be further considered as it is outside the scope of this paper. In the following the (nature) level of abstraction of the first 3 description will be briefly explained.

2.5 informal gateway definition

The informal gateway definition captures all requirements the gateway is supposed to fulfil in an informal description. This description is based on the description(s) for standard network interconnection protocol(s), augmented with network management requirements and other user requirements such as performance and installation or maintenance criteria. These descriptions are usually in English, augmented with illustrations such as tables, diagrams, etc. They are generally loosely related and given in terms of lists of requirements which strongly appeal to the designers knowledge of the technical area of concern. Therefore they are usually incomplete, vague, and ambiguous. These descriptions represent, however, the ideas that people have of what a gateway should be able to achieve.

2.6 gateway architecture

Requirements engineering is the art of formulating the requirements in an unambiguous and complete way. A dedicated tool to achieve this goal is an FDT such as LOTOS. In the formal description of an object, e.g. the PANGLOSS gateway, its externally observable behaviour is completely specified.

A specification of externally observable behaviour should be "implementation independent", i.e. refrain from specifying internal behaviour. This requirement, however, touches a principally difficult conflict between observability and clarity for the reader. In order to make (complex) specifications perspicuous, they inevitably need to be structured. Since structuring can be done in an infinite number of ways, and since it will be practically impossible for the reader (or implementor) to detach from this structure, there is inevitably the danger that the specification is interpreted as prescribing internal behaviour. Therefore, even if this cannot be completely avoided, the specification should be interpreted as a black box. Of interest in this type of specification is 'what' happens, not 'how' it happens.

No formal description technique is currently known in which it is possible to completely specify all requirements formally. Performance requirements, for example, cannot be expressed formally in LOTOS . As a consequence, the LOTOS formal description has to be annotated with text, either informal or using other formalisms, explaining the requirements that are not formalizable (yet) in LOTOS.
The description at this level, when complete, can be regarded as the most precise and most abstract description of the gateway, hence called "Gateway Architecture (G.A)". This description is used as input to the transformation delivering as output the Reference Architecture.

2.7 reference architecture

The validity of the above described top-down approach is influenced by the pragmatic limitation that expertise required for the various transformations will differ. Expertise necessary in early transformations require mainly knowledge of user requirements and architectural structuring techniques, whereas later transformations require more thorough knowledge of implementation structures, programming languages, operating systems and hardware technologies. (fig 2.4)
This differing expertise is reflected in the PANGLOSS project organization by identifying 3 Tasks in which the different expertise are concentrated:

- An Architectural Task,
  This task is responsible for the establishment of the user requirements for the Gateway, the formal definition of the Gateway in terms of a formal GA, and the initial design steps that lead to the Reference Architecture
- an Implementation Task,
  This task is responsible for producing the Gateway Implementation starting from the Reference Architecture, and
- an Performance Analysis Task
  This task is responsible for assessing the performance of the specifications, including the Reference Architecture in an as early as possible phase.

Thus the Reference Architecture is defined as that intermediate specification which is the last specification of the Architecture Task, and the starting point for the Implementation Task.

The remainder of this paper will concentrate on the contents of the Gateway Architecture (GA) and the Reference Architecture (RA). The Gateway Implementation is outside the scope of this paper.

A major advantage of the formal description is that one can formally reason about a specification and about the relationship between two different specifications. This formal reasoning can, in turn, be machine supported. It opens the possibility to transform this description into another formal description which is more implementation oriented, and verify, or validate the second one (possibly automatically) against the first one.

One could well ask what the meaning is of a "more implementation oriented description", since the FDT descriptions were supposed to be implementation independent. The answer lies in the structuring of a formal description with the intention to express implementation requirements.
This structuring of an implementation oriented description is achieved by composing the description out of a number of interacting processes. We require that each of these processes is described in terms of its externally observable behaviour in the same way as the GA is described. We further require that these processes, and their events of interaction, have a mapping on implementation structures.

We define an implementation oriented description to be a "decomposition" of a source description if the composite behaviour of the component processes of the implementation oriented description has an equivalent observable external behaviour as the description in which no components were identified.

The implementation orientedness of the RA is intended to be still at a quite high level of abstraction. The intention is to define the RA in terms of a composition of architectural components that can be recognized in any implementation of the gateway. This mapping of the GA on still abstract architectural components however should make it easier to assess whether or not a valid gateway implementation exists or not.

3. Gateway Architecture

In this section the methods used in to obtain the Gateway Architecture are presented. The amount of

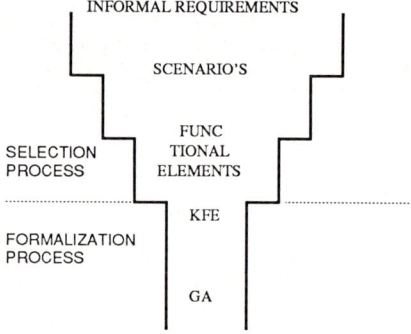

figure 3.1

informal requirements for the PANGLOSS gateway is so large that it prohibits a straightforward formalization of all details. This difficulty not only arises in the PANGLOSS project, but occurs as a rule in the development of any other concurrent system of some size. Hence attention must be paid to methods for obtaining a formalized description and the impact that these methods have on the contents and structure of the GA.

To get control over the requirements, the designer is forced to use mental tools such as abstraction and structuring. Use of these tools leads to the concepts of incremental design, scenario's and functional elements. These concepts will be explained in more detail in the following subsections. (fig 3.1)

3.1 incremental design

The possibility to use formal reasoning is a major advantage of formalized descriptions. It can help to obtain control over requirements. Hence the method in PANGLOSS is geared to obtain as early as possible a formalized description (GA), which then can be transformed into an implementation.

Formalization of requirements is a time consuming task. Under the constraint of limited manpower being available, a strategy is chosen to produce the GA in an incremental way: a GA is established based on a subset of the informal requirements and this GA is extended and refined in next iterations. There are at least three reasons for the incremental approach:

1) Requirements do not have the same relevance for the end product. They even can be conflicting. Therefore a structure is chosen based on those requirements that are qualified by the users as most relevant for the implementation. The merits of this structure can be assessed. Details, which have less relevance for the users of the end-product, and which happen to have a minor impact on the structure of the implementation, can then be incrementally added, whereas less relevant details that have a large impact on the structure can be better evaluated with respect to the work necessary in restructuring the implementation.

2) The sheer amount of details in a complete specification, will prohibit the architects to obtain an overview over all requirements.

3) In a commercial environment the time to introduce a product on the market may be limited. A complete specification of all functions that eventually are going to be required, will demand a large effort in manpower in the initial phase. The outcome of the effort is a set of detailed requirements, of which it is not known in advance, how they will be implemented. In the meantime, no work can be done in producing an implementation that conforms to some (the most relevant) requirements and is a marketable product in its own right.

Thus the problem reduces to establishing a subset of informal requirements which will serve as a basis for a formalized GA. The methods used in this project to filter the informal requirements are:

- Establishment of Scenario's
- Identification of Functional Elements
- Selection of Key Functional Elements

3.2 scenario's

A scenario is the description of a typical situation in which the gateway will be used. It informally specifies which subnetwork technologies, which internetwork protocols and what management functions, will be supported and in what mix. It also presents typical topologies and applications that will be using the internet functions. The selection criteria are mainly dictated by the market.

Scenario's show the relationship and dependencies which can exist between the various protocols.

3.3 functional elements

A next step to reduce the amount of detail, is to classify all functions within the protocols which are supposed to be supported. By identification of the same, or similar functions, double specification work can be avoided and the total effort can be reduced.

In the identification of similarity of the diverse functions, the designer will abstract away minor differences in the protocol functions. The result of this process is a list of informally described functional elements.

Definition and identification of functional elements is possible in various ways. Architectural principles, such as orthogonality of functions, generality, simplicity, dependency and separation of concerns, can be applied to establish the quality of the definition of the functional elements. [Vis88]

3.4 key functional elements

After having defined a list of functional elements, the architect may still find himself in the position of having to specify a too large amount of details. It means that a selection of functional elements and other requirements has to be accomplished, reducing the functions to a manageable, comprehensible set of features.

In making the reduction of the functions for the GA, the architect must anticipate what purpose the limited (reduced functions) RA will serve. It allows to highlight certain aspects of the total problem, find implementations and quickly evaluate them. Reduction of the functionality is achieved by reducing both the formalizable and the non-formalizable requirements.

3.5 GA outline

[ISO8648] mentions 3 approaches to the interconnection of subnetworks. They are:

- Interconnection of OSI Subnetworks.
- Hop-by-hop harmonisation over the individual subnetworks; and
- The use of an internetworking protocol approach over more than one subnetwork.

Following the latter approach, 3 different service levels can be identified within the network layer of an internetwork.

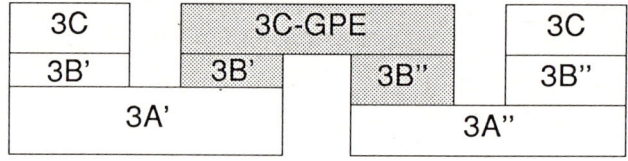

figure3.2

1) A subnetwork or 3A service provided by the SubNetwork Access Convergence Protocol (SNACP) offering connectivity to other users of the subnetwork.
2) An internet or 3C service, provided by the SubNetwork Independent Convergence Protocol (SNICP) offering connectivity among the users of all interconnected subnetworks.
3) An enhancement/de-enhancement or 3B service provided by the SubNetwork Dependent Convergence Protocol (SNDCP) which is delivered by operating a protocol on top of the subnetwork service, such that the capabilities assumed by the SNICP are fulfilled.

Within PANGLOSS it is assumed that protocol entities supporting the subnetwork technologies are available and implementable, or will be in the near future. The PANGLOSS project focuses on interconnection and not on the development of new subnetwork technologies; if subnetwork technologies are not available, there is no reason to consider their interconnection. As a consequence, a subnetwork service is assumed to be present and the subnetwork protocol entities are not further considered for design.

Thus, the objects to focus our attention on in the development of the gateway, are the internet protocol entity, which will be referred to as the 3C Gateway Protocol Entity (3C-GPE) and the 3B enhancement\de-enhancement protocols necessary to harmonize the services of the subnetworks.

The actual choice of KFE's in the first iteration of the project is constraint by the non-availability of standardized internetting protocols supporting Connection-Oriented and Stream-Oriented (Continuous Bit Streams e.g. voice traffic) traffic. This has led to the situation that only KFE's from the Connection-Less Internetting Protocol (CLIP) [ISO8473] have been selected. In the meantime efforts are undertaken to develop internetting protocols supporting CO and SO services.

Currently the GA contains an almost complete specification of CLIP . It is specified in LOTOS as one process.

specification Gateway [sn] (c:context):**noexit**
  library ...
  endlib
  type context *is*
    .....
  endtype
  behaviour
    CL_3C_GPE[sn](c)
  where .....

endspec

The structure that is present within this specification uses the constraint oriented style for clarity of expression and understandability. No further meaning should be attached to the internal structure as it is irrelevant for the implementation.

4. Reference Architecture

4.1 level of abstraction

The RA is an intermediate design that defines the PANGLOSS gateway at an abstraction level which is not as much implementation independent as the Gateway Architecture (GA), but also not so implementation specific as the final implementation. At the abstraction level of the GA, no direct relation exists between structures in the description and implementation structures. The implementation, on the other hand is a complete blueprint for the realization of the gateway, specifying exactly what hardware and software will be used. The RA is described at an abstraction level in between, which means that a certain relationship between the structure of the RA and the final implementation structures will exist.

The structure, that is created in the RA, is achieved by decomposing a global specification in two or more component specifications. Again the specification of the components only prescribes the external behaviour; internal structure is incidental and is only used for readability.
Clearly the composite behaviour of the components must be equivalent to the behaviour of the original, global specification.

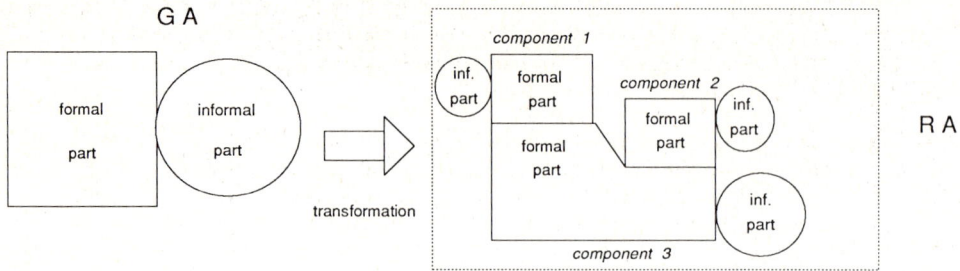

figure 4.1

The specification of the GA consist of a formalized and a non-formalized part. Equally, the components of the RA will consist of a formalized and a non formalized part. (fig 4.1)

The introduced structure can serve the purpose of formalizing one or more non-formalized requirements from the source specification, and/or to restrict the freedom of implementation choices.
For example, the GA may contain the non-formalized requirement of modularity. The RA could possess a modular structure, thus expressing this non-formal requirement of the GA in a formal way. At the same time it restricts the designers from creating other modular structures.

In the successive transformations of stepwise refinement freedom of design is incrementally restricted and non-formalized requirements are realized.

The concept of iterative design assumes that with each next iteration the structure will be incrementally updated and refined while maintaining an overall stable structure.

Special attention must be given to those requirements that were rated as most relevant in the previous chapter namely: generality and high performance.
Both requirements have their own impact on the structure of the specification. They also require their own levels of abstraction, to demonstrate meaningful that the structure of the specification conforms to them.

The P and A in the acronym PANGLOSS stand for Parallel Architectures. It suggests that high performance can be achieved through the use of parallel hardware architectures and concurrency.

A method to support this structure is to distinguish two types of processes in the RA, namely a Processing Function (PF) and a Communication Function (CF).
CF's are characterized as functions that only transport information between interaction points transparently, whereas PF's are allowed to read and modify the information.

To summarize, the structure of the RA must conform to the following constraints:

- It is a composition of cooperating processes.
- Each process is formally described in an implementation independent way, and is annotated by non-functional requirements.
- Each process represents either a Processing Function (PF) or a Communication Function (CF). CF's transport information between interaction points transparently.

- The identification of CF's represents a design decision, taken by the AT. to help the implementors in mapping the functions on a loosely coupled processor network. The next sections will clarify why these design decisions are still in the realm of the Architecture Task.
and 4.2and 4.2and 4.2and 4.2and 4.2and 4.2and 4.2and 4.2

4.2 Decomposition

The actual decomposition of the GA into the RA, based on the performance criteria discussed in the previous section, is discussed in the next sub-section from an engineering viewpoint. This approach results in a decomposition which seems desirable. The feasibility of this decomposition is explained in the next sub-section.

4.2.1 heuristic decomposition

In this section we present an intuitive, heuristic, engineering like approach towards the decomposition of the 3c-GPE (fig 3.2). This approach is particularly guided by the requirement to create parallel operating components for the gateway.

We consider the most dominant function of the gateway, viz. to route data from any service access point to any other service access point i.e. a communication function.
Since this function requires interconnectivity between any service access point, it implies that this function is central, i.e. each service access points is either directly or indirectly connected to it. This also implies that any function that performs operations on data have to be kept outside this communication function. We will call this function the Interconnection Function (IF).

An advantage of such a design step is that the proposed interconnection function, which would be equally usable for connectionless or connection oriented protocols, as well as for continuous bit streams, is central to the gateway. Thus it conforms to the requirement of generality: general functions are centralized, providing a common service to all its users, and functions which are required only for particular protocols, are layered on top of this service.

Analysis, in short, of the main operations that have to be carried out on the service primitives that are available at the 3b service access points, imply:

- the engaging in 3b enhanced subnetwork service operations (e.g. in a connection oriented enhanced subnetwork this means setting up, maintaining and closing down of a subnetwork connection),
- the unwrapping of 3c-internet PDUs from 3b-SDUs,
- the analysis of these PDUs, in particular the detection of the destination and QoS,
- other operations on these PDUs, like segmentation, reassembly and the like,
- the setting up of a route to the 3b-SAP via which the destination can be reached and the reservation of the bandwidth resources along the path to this SAP,

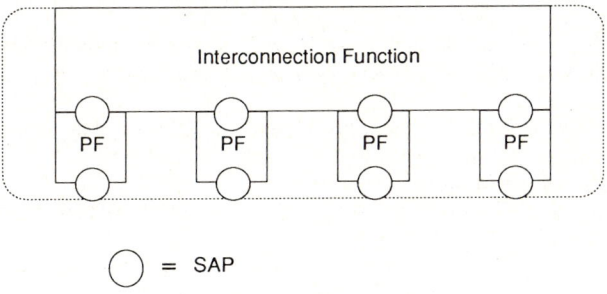

fig 4.2

- the forwarding of data along this path,
- the above operations in the reverse direction.

These operations have to be carried out before or after the related results are transported across the IF, and thus the functions implementing these operations are located between the 3c-SAPs and the IF, in the periphery of the 3c-GPE.

The nature of these functions is that they all require a certain degree of processing capability, hence can be specified by Processing Functions (PF). Since in an implementation of these PF's, processing is relatively slow compared to communication, multiple PFs can be placed in parallel to accommodate for performance.

In high-performance gateways, where high data rates have to be realized, the implementation of the interconnection function will not be trivial. Examples of communication elements, which conform to the functional specification of the interconnection function, permitting full interconnectivity, are various types of buses and rings. These interconnection structures rate different performances, including throughput rates in the order of hundreds of megabits per second.

4.2.2 Architectural decomposition

In this section we try to answer the question whether it will be possible to decompose the gateway in the above described way, and what functions must be assigned to the components of the RA. This question is answered by developing a structure for the RA following an architectural methodology of equivalence relations, decomposition, hiding etc. This development is described in detail elsewhere [BPPS88] and is beyond the scope of this paper. We just present here the result.

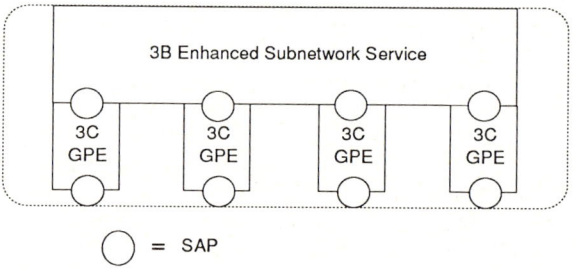

figure 4.3

In figure 4.3 the single 3C-GPE is replaced by an interconnection function having a 3B subnetwork service functionality, and n processing functions having similar functionality of the original 3C-GPE.

The result of this exercise seems counterproductive at first glance: rather than having a single 3c-GPE we have now n, and there is an extra 3b enhanced subnetwork. It seems that we multiplicated the functions of the gateway.

However, looking in more detail we have achieved the following simplifications and clarity:
- the 3c-GPEs in the RA are defined from one 3c-SAP to one IF-SAP, rather than between multiple 3c-SAPs, which is a drastic simplification with respect to its implementation,
- an enhanced 3b subnetwork service is used to interconnect IF-SAPs, rather than a 3c-GPE interconnecting 3c-SAPs,
- the enhanced 3b subnetwork service need not to be implemented with a large geographical distribution, but only within the geographical constraints of the gateway, which again is a drastic simplification with respect to its implementation,

- the approach allows us in a quite analytic way to characterize the functions of the IF and PF's components in the RA.

4.3 RA Outline

The 3B- Enhanced Subnetwork Services can be further decomposed in 2 types of functions, resulting in a total decomposition of the 3C-GPE in:
- An Interconnection Function, IF,
- An enhancement function, called the Harmonized IF (HIF) ,and
- A 3C Gateway Protocol Entity function, termed the Partial Internetting Entity (PIE).

This decomposition is structured in a similar way, as [ISO8648] decomposes the total gateway. Thus, an Interconnection Function is identified, which in ISO terms has the role of 3A subnetwork. Also the PIE functions are comparable to the 3C internet protocol entities and finally the HIF functions adapting the interconnection functions to the requirements of the PIE functions are similar to the functions in the 3B enhancement layer.

It should be noted that similarity to ISO8648 does not imply that the interconnection function can be regarded in all respects as an arbitrary subnetwork. On the contrary, the interconnection function is a subnetwork with very specific characteristics, which will be exploited in the consecutive steps of the development of the RA.

The overall structure of the RA behaviour looks like:
behaviour
hide hifg,ifg **in**
CL_PIE_Set[sn,hif](env,ConfigTable1(env))
|[hifg]|
HIF_PE_Set[hifg,ifg](env,ConfigTable2(env))
|[ifg]|
IFService[ifg](env)

where
       process HIF_PE_Set[hifg,ifg](env:Environment,con:ConfigTable2):**noexit** :=
         choice hifsap_id:HIFAddr []
         [ExistingEntry (hifsap_id,con]-
          let ce: ConfigEntry=SelectedEntry(hifsap_id,con) **in**
          HIF_PE[hifg,ifg](ConfigTable2(env))
           |||
          HIF_PE_Set[hifg,ifg](env,Remove(ce,con))
       where ...
       endproc
       process CL_PIE_Set[sn,hifg(env:Environment,con:Configtable1):**noexit**:=
       similar to HIF_PE_Set
       endproc

The SAP's depicted in figure 4.4 correspond with the 3B SAP's that the original 3C-GPE has with the various 3B enhanced subnetwork services.
One important observation is that the PIE functions only contain 2 SAP's. One SAP is the interface to the subnetwork. The other SAP is the interaction point with the HIF function. Compared with the arbitrary number of SAP's of the 3C-GPE this leads to a considerable reduction of complexity.

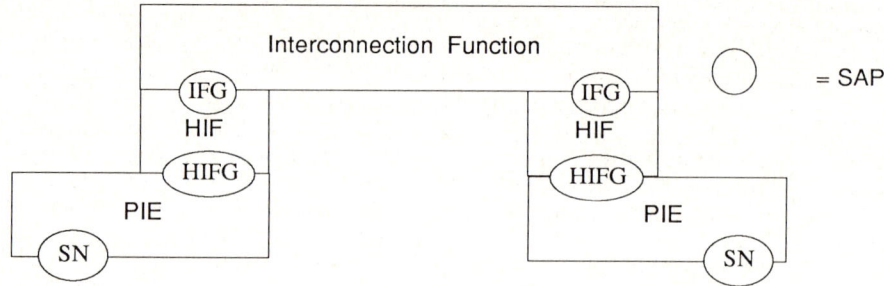

figure 4.4

In the presented decomposition only the question of feasibility was posed. It was established that indeed such a decomposition was feasible. In section 4.2.1 it was established that decomposition into a number of protocol entities and an interconnection function was desirable.

It was not shown that duplication of the internet protocol entities is a decomposition which is easily mapped on an efficient implementation. In fact it is not. The merit of decomposing the 3C-GPE in this way, is that it is an easily verifiable correct decomposition and it is taken as the starting point for further refinements.

In the elaboration of the PIE-function, optimization's are incorporated, taking advantage from the Qos parameters that are assumed to be realistic in an implementation of the IF. Since a realization of the IF resembles in many respects a bus system or other type of internal interconnection structure in a computer, similar error rates and other qos can be expected. This has for example the effect that a PDU is subjected to CRC checking in only one PIE function. Similar reasoning leads to significant reduction of the functions.

Although these simplifications can be applied, it leaves the generic character of the decomposition intact.

5. Conclusions

In this section, some preliminary observations can be made. Since the project is not finished, definitive conclusions have to await the final evaluation. Nonetheless, some trends can be identified:

Precision
The use of LOTOS as a specification technique for intermediate designs has proved to be of good use to improve the precision of the specification. Both in the GA to express the overall requirements, as well as in the RA serving as an interface document between the project tasks.
However, numerous discussions have taken place between the project tasks as for the abstraction level of the RA: What do the abstract components represent and in what way do they constrain further implementation ? Answering this question represents one of the challenges of this project.

Formal Methods
The use of LOTOS has permitted application of various tools, such as syntax and static semantic checkers, as well as in the RA serving as a simulator which allows an initial test for the designs.
A special group within the project is assigned to the development of methods to establish relationships between the various levels of descriptions. These methods have up till now not been applied to the GA and RA. However, the descriptions are formalized and the least that this allows is some form of testing, which is not possible with informal designs.

Informal Transformation Methods
Although usage throughout the project of a formal language suggests a compiler for the transformations from specification to implementation, the current state of art is still far away from achieving this. The transformation of the GA into the RA exemplifies how difficult such a compiler will be. For this transformation a number of interesting observations can be made:

- The type of transformation was guided by performance arguments. These arguments assume knowledge of technologies and may even be different for different technologies.
- The form of the transformation was guided by architectural principles, implying knowledge of network protocols.
- The initial transformation initially led to almost doubling the functions of the gateway.
- Reduction of this functions could be achieved by anticipating what Q.o.s. parameters in the Interconnection Function are reasonable to expect from an implementation.

It seems that these observations support the viewpoint that human reasoning will still be required in transformations in the coming years.

Reduced Formalization
The PANGLOSS project exemplifies that LOTOS is only able to formalize a subset of all informal requirements. This is partly due to the limitation of LOTOS not to capture quality aspects, such as performance, modularity etc, and partly due to the work involved in formalization, which with an open-ended problem statement soon may become prohibitively large.

Early Performance Evaluation
The performance requirements for each process in the RA are indications for both Implementation and Performance Analysis Tasks. With these figures, the PAT. can assess the performance of the gateway in an early stage. The IT provides more details on the implementation of the RA processes, and as a consequence provides more accuracy for the PAT., as well as feed back for the AT.

Rapid Prototyping
Leaving intact what was remarked in the subsection on Informal Transformation Methods, the use of a formal language allows quick and even automated transformations to implementations of limited functions that may be used in rapid prototyping. Work on these type of transformations is currently been done in the Implementation task, investigating the transformation of LOTOS to a suitable implementation language.

References:

[**BPPS88**] Bogaards K, Pires L, Pras A, Schot A 'The PANGLOSS Method' to be published in Proceedings of ESPRIT Conference 88, North Holland
[**ISO8473**] ISO:'Draft International Standard 8473 - Information Processing Systems - Data Communications - Protocol for providing the Connectionless-mode Network Service' International Organization for Standardization, Geneva, 1986
[**ISO8648**] ISO:'International Standard 8648-Information Processing Systems- Open System Interconnection- Internal Organization of the Network Layer' International Organization for Standardization, Geneva, 1987
[**ISO8807**] ISO:'Draft International Standard 8807 - Information Processing Systems - Open Systems Interconnection - LOTOS A formal description technique based on the temporal ordering of observational behaviour' International Organization for Standardization, Geneva, 1987
[**PAN86**] PANGLOSS Technical Annex 1986
[**VIS88**] Lecture Notes 'Architecture of Interaction Systems' Spring 1988 University of Twente, Enschede

Abbreviations

AT- Architecture Task
CF- Communication Function
CL- ConnectionLess
CO- Connection Oriented
FDT- Formal Description Technique
FE- Functional Element
GA- Gateway Architecture.
GPE- Gateway Protocol Entity
HIF- Harmonized Interconnection Function
IF- Interconnection Function

IT- Implementation Task
KFE- Key Functional Element
PANGLOSS- Parallel Architecture for Networking Gateways Linking OSi Systems
PAT- Performance Analysis Task
PE- Processing Element
PF- Processing Function
PIE- Partial Internetting Function
RA- Reference Architecture
SO- Stream Oriented

Application of Formal Description Techniques to Conformance Evaluation

Jean-Philippe Favreau
Richard J. Linn, Jr.
Philip Gaudette

U. S. Department of Commerce
National Bureau of Standards
Institute for Computer Sciences and Technology
Gaithersburg, MD 20899, USA

Abstract. Formal description techniques, and software tools based on them, are applied successfully in the development of test systems for OSI protocols. The test system architecture uses reference implementations augmented with test features in a manner that facilitates multi-layer testing and minimizes the effort necessary to develop test cases. The designs for test systems in general and for a specific gateway are described, focusing on the use of Estelle and ASN.1.

Keywords: Multi-layer conformance testing, OSI communication protocols, formal description techniques, Estelle, Abstract Syntax Notation One (ASN.1), application-layer gateways, electronic mail, file transfer.

1. Introduction

Within the International Organization for Standardization (ISO), three significant activities have matured regarding data communication protocols: (1) the development of protocols for Open Systems Interconnection (OSI), (2) the development of conformance testing methodology for OSI protocols [7], and (3) the development of Formal Description Techniques (FDTs) for OSI protocols and services [6] [11].

This paper introduces a new approach in the design of test systems. It is based on reference implementations derived from formal descriptions of protocols, extended with testing features. Test systems are described using Estelle and ASN.1. They are designed to be used as components of a multi-layer test system, just as protocol entities are used in the basic OSI reference model.

This work is a contribution of the National Bureau of Standards and is not subject to copyright.

Disclaimer: Certain companies and their products are mentioned in order to adequately describe the application of international standards in different environments. In no case does such identification imply recommendation or endorsement by the National Bureau of Standards.

Estelle [6] is a formal description technique developed within ISO for the description of OSI protocols and services, and is based upon a set of extensions to ISO Pascal. Estelle provides the facilities to specify a hierarchy of modules that communicate by exchanging messages, to specify an abstract message interface for each module, to describe message contents (but not syntax or encoding), and to define behavior of modules. The control structure of modules is based upon an extended finite-state machine model.

Abstract Syntax Notation One (ASN.1) [5], is a nonprocedural language for the abstract description of the syntax of messages between the Application and Presentation Layers of the OSI Reference Model. It includes rules, known as the *Basic Encoding Rules*, for machine-independent encoding of messages for transfer by lower layers. ASN.1 was derived from X.409 [1], which was developed within the International Telegraph and Telephone Consultative Committee (CCITT) for the specification of the syntax and encoding of electronic mail in X.400 Message Handling Systems.

Estelle and ASN.1, and tools supporting them, are applied wherever possible in the definition of the test systems. Indeed, Estelle is used extensively in the test systems' specification and ASN.1 is the formalism used for the definition of the syntax of protocol data units, the test language, the test results language, and the test-management protocol data units. Executable test cases are specified as ASN.1 values. The operational semantics of the test language are realized by the actions of an Estelle module called a test processor. Estelle and ASN.1 translators developed at the National Bureau of Standards (NBS) aid in automating the implementation of the test systems.

OSI Conformance Testing Methodology, which is based on abstract test methods and test cases, is applied whenever possible. Executable test systems based on these abstractions must be provided by implementors. Our work demonstrates a path to get from OSI abstract test methods and test systems to executable test methods and test cases.

Our test system design has been applied to two application-layer gateways. NBS is implementing and testing these gateways as part of a planned transition by the Department of Defense (DoD) from military standard protocols to Open Systems Interconnection (OSI) protocols. One gateway exchanges mail between two networks employing different protocols for electronic mail; the other transfers and accesses files between two networks employing different file transfer protocols. The electronic mail protocols are called Message Handling Systems (MHS) [1] and Simple Mail Transfer Protocol (SMTP) [2-3]. The file transfer protocols are called File Transfer Protocol (FTP) [4] and File Transfer, Access and Management (FTAM) [8]. Since the facilities of SMTP and FTP are functional subsets of MHS and FTAM, test systems for the gateways are also functional subsets of test systems for the full protocols. Nevertheless, these systems are extensible, so that a full MHS or FTAM test system can be derived from the initial investment.

In the following sections, we introduce the design of test architectures based on the use of Estelle and ASN.1. Then, we present a concrete application: the MHS/SMTP gateway test system. Annex 1 contains a test case expressed as ASN.1 print values drawn directly from a test suite for the MHS/SMTP Gateway Test System. Annex 2 contains fragments of a test processor written in Estelle to process test cases; it is extracted directly from the Test Processor specification. system.

2. Layered Test System Design

Multi-layer testing concerns methods to test an implementation composed of a stack of protocol entities, on a layer basis, without access to the intermediate interfaces. Structuring of test suites is a major problem in multi-layer testing, because the focus of testing must move among the layers repeatedly as confidence levels are built up together for all layers by increasingly sophisticated test cases at each layer. The problem is particularly difficult when a universal test language is used. Each test case must contain all the alternatives and complex behaviors of several layers of protocols, which are interleaved in complicated ways. The test architectures described below offer a simpler solution, largely because they follow the layered structure of the OSI reference model.

2.1. Gateway Tester Top-level Design

Each gateway test system design begins with the OSI Reference Model concept of protocol layers in a stack, joined by service interfaces *(see Figure 1)*. The Lower Tester replaces a protocol implementation as the peer entity for the Implementation Under Test (IUT).

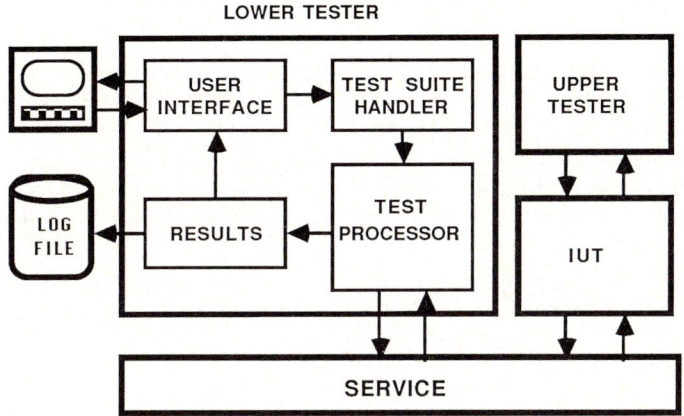

Figure 1. Components of a Coordinated Test System.

Instead of providing a normal service, the test system provides a test service, monitors results of individual test steps, and builds a results log. A test entity must detect and report abnormal behavior of the IUT regardless of test purpose. It may behave normally or abnormally to induce error recovery on the part of the IUT.

A protocol-independent user interface is part of the Lower Tester. The User Interface module provides convenient syntax for manipulating tests, and on-line monitoring of test results for test selection and control via a Test Suite Handler.

A test system uses an underlying service, which is assumed to work correctly, or at least well enough to perform a test. A test case consists of a sequence of test steps that, if completed successfully, demonstrates some desired behavior on the part of the IUT. The test purpose specifies the expected behavior of an IUT when a test case is executed. A test system specification gives an overview of an executable test system for the Lower Tester, including all necessary constraints on the test environment and a detailed behavioral specification for the Upper Tester.

The usual assumption that each layer is fully tested from the bottom layer to the current layer under test, is convenient but inadequate. It implies that all interfaces are exposed, whereas frequently they are not. Many protocols have sub-layers with implied interfaces, and a multi-layer approach is beneficial even for a single protocol of that kind. Indeed, the MHS/SMTP gateway has sub-layers without interfaces, and a full test system for that software requires a multi-layer approach. We assume that the unmodified layers below an exposed interface are fully interoperable. These assumptions allow a solution because the gateway software itself is implemented above an exposed interface high in the OSI stack [9]. Test systems were designed and implemented according to these assumptions.

2.2. Formal Specifications for Multi-Layer Testing

Our design of a test system starts with the complete description of the protocol entities in Estelle and of the messages exchanged by the entities in ASN.1. Test implementations of the corresponding layers are derived from the formal descriptions of the protocol entities, which may involve one or more layers of the OSI Basic Reference Model. Test entities differ from the protocol implementations in the following ways.

- Minimally, logic is added to the specifications in all layers (or sublayers) of test implementations to detect and report invalid behavior on the part of the IUT. This may include:
- invalid encoding of messages,
- inopportune transmission of validly encoded messages, or
- duplication or loss of PDUs containing sequence information.
- Logic is added to allow the test entity to test for error recovery on the part of the IUT. Examples include:
- transmission of valid messages at the wrong phase of the protocol,
- the wrong response to a message sent by the IUT (inopportune PDUs),
- use of optional facilities after negotiation which prohibits their use, or
- invalid encoding of PDUs.
- Desirable features include:
- automated test coordination procedures and results reporting,
- automatic generation of test verdicts,
- minimal human intervention in test results analysis,
- automated generation of reports for clients, and
- transfer of test log files and reports between test centers and client sites.

2.3. Application of ASN.1

Within ISO, ASN.1 is applied to the description of Protocol Data Units (PDUs) in the Application and Presentation Layers. However, ASN.1 is applicable to the description of a wider class of data structures. Furthermore, because ASN.1 defines a grammar for description of user defined data types and a syntax for values associated with user defined types, both type definitions (ASN.1 modules) and values may be processed by software [14]. That is, lexical analysis and parsing of both type definitions and values are possible because of the underlying grammar. Both aspects are important when defining a language for a test system. Since CCITT and ISO have used ASN.1 to define PDU syntax, and since test cases frequently include ASN.1 values as components of PDUs, it is quite natural to use these standardized definitions as the basis for a test language.

The ASN.1 translator developed at the NBS defines eight operations on values associated with ASN.1 types, and allows the arbitrary combination of these operations within a program *(see Figure 2)*. The central node, labeled "Value Desc", is a general-purpose tree-structured representation of values. Behind it lies a shaded area labeled "Type Desc" that corresponds to the output of our translator for a set of user defined types. The nodes labeled "print value" and "transfer value" correspond to values in the syntax defined by the standard for printable values in the defined value notation and encoded values for transfer by lower layers. The node labeled "local values" corresponds to values of data structures in the memory of a communicating protocol entity. Representation of local values is not specified in the standard; they may be stored in any fashion convenient to the implementor of a protocol entity. The node labeled "filed value" corresponds to values stored on a peripheral device. Again, this is not defined in the standard; use of this form will be described later.

This translator is applied to processing test cases for the test system. The first step is to preprocess test cases, which are stored in files as print values. Each contains a sequence of

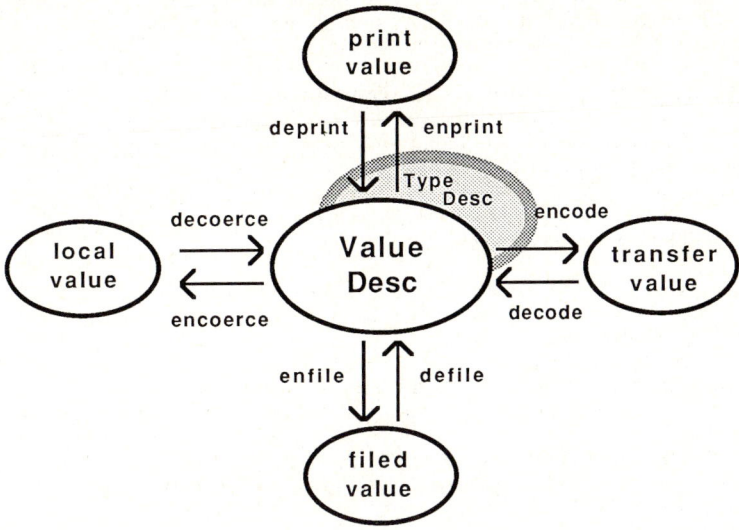

Figure 2. Value Processor Model.

test directives from the test language, including any necessary PDUs. A lexical analyzer and parser that are generated by the translator automatically perform syntactic and static semantic checking while transforming print values to value trees stored in the value descriptor node. Those values are then saved on disk as filed values. We call such a filed value an executable test case.

The second step occurs when a test case is executed. When an operator selects a test case for execution, a file is opened containing filed values which are then coerced into local values. In this test system, the local data structures are Estelle interactions. Each test directive is enqueued in the Test Processor module which is the part of a test system that interprets the test directives as commands to be executed. Parameters of test directives are passed to the Estelle module as parameters of interactions. These are the actions of the Test Suite Handler described in section 3.

2.4. Application of Estelle

Estelle is used to specify the dynamic behavior of the major components of the Upper and Lower Testers while trying not to constrain unduly other implementors. Thus, many functions are specified as primitive functions and procedures in Estelle, with the implication that an implementor may choose to implement them in any appropriate manner. Implementations are semi-automatically realized using translators [10] [15].

The Test Processor module is specified in sufficient detail to define the operational semantics of the test language, to log specific data as processing of a test case progresses, and to define actions necessary to coordinate the Upper and Lower Testers. Estelle interactions are defined for every interface between modules, but the actions of the Test Suite Handler and operator interface modules are largely specified using ASN.1 and LEX augmented with actions embedded in the grammars.

In the gateway test systems, Estelle is also used to specify FTAM and MHS protocols. These descriptions are augmented with functions necessary for testing, such as recovery from reception of unexpected PDUs, complete activity logging, implementation of the semantics of test directives (service primitives), and detection of invalid test cases. The logged data reflects the data flow in the protocol. The minimum information logged identifies the module instance, determines the type of behavior (normal or abnormal), identifies the transition executed, and produces a complete ASN description for the input and output events for the transition executed as print values. Test language directives supported by the test entities realize the transmission of invalid or inopportune PDUs, matching of specific PDUs or checking of specific fields contained in the PDUs received.

3. Detailed Design of the MHS/SMTP Gateway Test System

3.1. Components of the Test System

When ISO's Coordinated Test Method is adapted for gateway testing, the entire gateway and non-OSI system must be treated as the IUT *(see Figure 3)*. If an Upper Tester with sufficient capability is available, then this method can provide adequate testing in both directions. However, most of the complexity remains in the Lower Tester. The MHS/SMTP gateway test architecture *(see Figure 4)* relies on Estelle specifications for the Lower and Upper Testers.

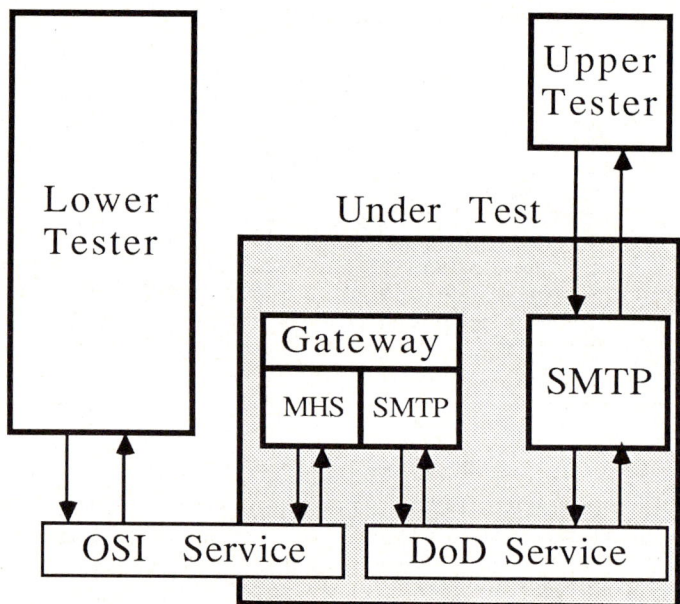

Figure 3. MHS/SMTP Gateway Testing.

The Lower Tester is an entity which reads test cases from a test suite as directed by an operator. Each test case contains a set of test directives; each directive is described in the ASN.1 data value notation. The semantics for each test directive define the logic associated with a test case. A test case is mapped into a sequence of Estelle interactions. This process results in the encoding and transmission of test data and Test Management Protocol Data Units

(TMPDUs) for delivery to the Upper Tester, or the reception and decoding of test data and TMPDUs received from the Upper Tester. TMPDUs carry information to realize coordination procedures between Upper and Lower Testers and data such as reports from the Upper Tester. TMPDUs are embedded as data in MHS and SMTP mail messages for the test system being described. The contents of TMPDUs received from the Upper Tester are analyzed by the Lower Tester and compared with the expected results; results are reported to the test-log-file.

The Lower Tester is subdivided into five Estelle modules: the Lower Tester Manager, Terminal Interface, Test Suite Handler, Test Processor and Message Transfer Agent (MTA) interface modules. Each module of the Lower Tester is assigned a specific role, described below. The Upper Tester is an entity using the MHS/SMTP gateway under test.

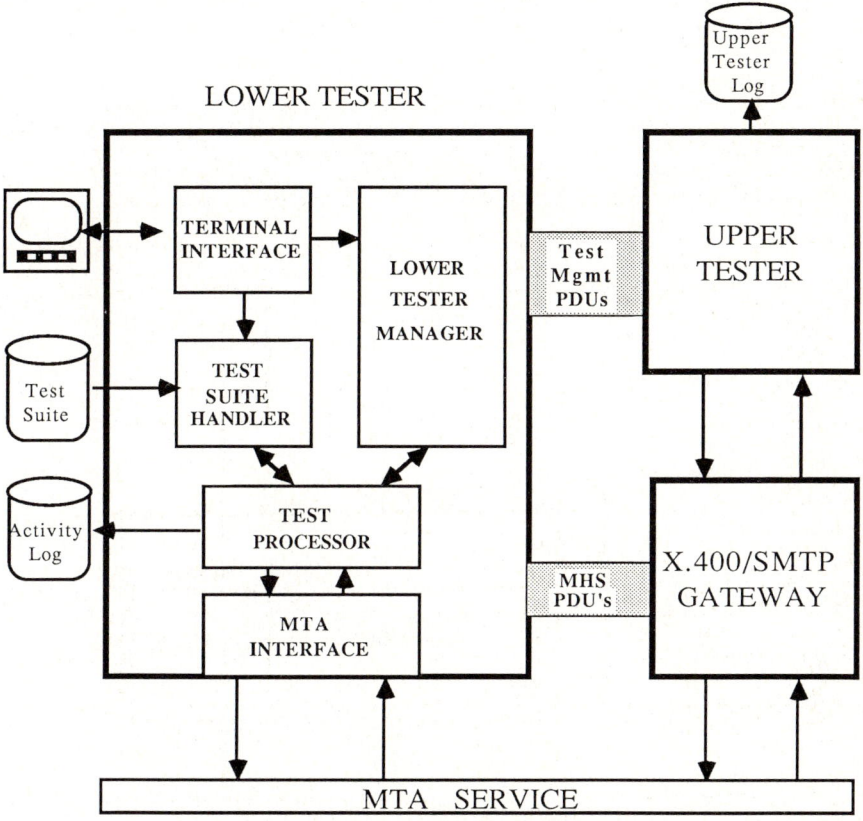

Figure 4. Lower Tester for MHS/SMTP Gateway

After initialization by an operator, actions of the Upper Tester are directed by TMPDUs sent by the Lower Tester. The Upper Tester receives and generates mail messages containing test data or TMPDUs. Test control and result reporting are centralized in the Lower Tester.

3.2. Components of the Lower Tester

The Lower Tester Manager (LTM) module is the root of a hierarchy of modules in the subsystem composing the Lower Tester. It has the responsibility for synchronizing other modules and taking global actions. These actions include modification of global variables and requesting periodic reports from the Upper Tester. The LTM is the operator's primary source of information.

The Terminal Interface module is the only interface between the operator and the Lower Tester. Its Estelle description is composed of a module header and an empty body. The header allows: (1) definitions of Estelle interactions to be generated by a lexical analyzer of operator commands; and (2) connections to the LTM and Test Suite Handler modules. Most of the body of the terminal interface module is specified with a LEX grammar. An operator command is analyzed and interpreted, and an Estelle interaction is enqueued in either the LTM or the Test Suite Handler modules.

The Test Suite Handler (TSH) module transforms directives within test cases into Estelle interactions. When the operator selects a test case, an Estelle interaction is sent to the TSH module. It directs the TSH to read a test case from a peripheral device. Each test directive in a test case is mapped into an Estelle interaction that is enqueued in the Test Processor module. This mapping of test directives into Estelle interactions is called coercion.

The Test Processor (TP) module contains all the logic necessary to execute a test case. When coercion of a test case has been completed by the TSH module, the TP module processes the interactions. The TP sends TMPDUs or test data to the Upper Tester, analyzes and interprets both TMPDUs and test data received from the Upper Tester and judges the results of test cases. The TP writes data to the test-log-file as processing proceeds.

The Message Transfer Agent (MTA) Interface module is the only module which depends upon the OSI services offered by the host system environment. Its role is to submit messages to the message encoder and to receive and decode messages.

4. Conclusions

Our methodology for the specification of test systems for OSI protocols is based on specifications of the protocols using formal description techniques, preferably, standardized descriptions of the protocols. If they do not exist, they may be written using Estelle and ASN.1. Given this foundation, reference specifications may be augmented with features necessary for testing. Because the dynamic behavior of a protocol entity is inherent in the reference specification, it is the default behavior in a test entity specification. The reference specification need only be augmented with actions to initiate error recovery on the part of the IUT, to detect and report invalid behavior on the part of the IUT, and to log the stimulus and responses of the IUT.

Because a test entity contains all the logic of a reference implementation of a protocol entity, test cases need not focus on detailed behavioral descriptions. Test cases consist of specifying stimulus to the test entity in the form of abstract service primitives. The test entity responds to the stimulus, composes PDUs containing valid or invalid parameters and stimulates the IUT by transmitting PDUs (including inopportune PDUs). The test entity logs the stimulus, the PDU transmitted and the response of the IUT.

These ideas may be extended to the construction of multi-layer test systems from single layer test entities. Adjacent entity exchange service primitives. Thus, the "default test script" for a lower layer entity is simply the service primitives a pair of adjacent reference entities would exchange during normal operation. However, test-specific service primitives are tagged with a layer identification. Thus, a test case may be composed of test-service primitives for several layers, and each test entity passes on service primitives destined for lower layers.

Several conclusions can be drawn from the experience reported. Estelle and ASN.1 are appropriate tools to define a solution to multi-layer testing. They fit the problem domain well and relate formal descriptions of protocol entities and the syntax of the PDUs to test systems for the protocols. Test cases are correspondingly simpler: (1) they need not express dynamic behaviors — only stimulus, and (2) ASN.1 print values are a natural way to express the values of protocol control information and data for PDUs whose syntax is defined in ASN.1. Either ASN.1 transfer syntax or print values may be used to log PDUs transmitted; the latter has the advantage that it is human readable. Given ASN.1 descriptions of other objects (e.g., service primitives, verdicts), the trace of all activities may be written to a log file in a form that is inherently machine processable because of the underlying grammar. Thus, tools may be constructed to process log files in an automated way. Finally, since the methodology is based upon machine processable languages (Estelle and ASN.1), realization of test implementations from formal descriptions of test entities may be automated by use of translators for the languages.

We have found that the methodology presented is technically sound and improves productivity. Lower layer services may be simulated by writing a service specification in Estelle. Thus, it is feasible to simulate a distributed system in a single CPU. Given the debugging and trace facilities found in the support library for the NBS Estelle compiler, design errors may be detected well before testing an IUT commences.

Acknowledgements

The authors acknowledge the support of the team of people who participated in the gateway test system development. They include John Garguilo, John Lindley, Akira Iwabuchi, Len Gebase and Jony Chang. Each contributed to formal specifications and implementation of the test systems described.

References

[1] Consultative Committee for International Telegraph and Telephone (CCITT). *Message Handling Systems — Recommendations X.400 series, Geneva, 1984.* Geneva, 1984.
[2] Postel, J. B. *Simple Mail Transfer Protocol, RFC 821.* DDN Network Information Center, SRI International, 333 Ravenswood Ave., Rm. EJ291, Menlo Park, CA 94025, 1982.
[3] Crocker, D. H. *Standard for the Format of ARPA Internet Test Messages, RFC 822.* DDN Network Information Center, SRI International, 333 Ravenswood Ave., Rm. EJ291, Menlo Park, CA 94025, 1982.
[4] *Military Standard File Transfer Protocol, MIL-STD-1780.* USA, 1984.
[5] International Organization for Standardization ISO/TC97/SC21. *Open Systems Interconnection — Abstract Syntax Notation One (ASN.1).* IS 8824 and 8825, 1987.
[6] ISO/TC97/SC21. *Open Systems Interconnection — Estelle: A Formal Description Technique Based on an Extended State Transition Model.* DIS 9074, 1987.
[7] ISO/TC97/SC21. *Open Systems Interconnection — Conformance Testing Methodology and Framework, Parts 1 - 5.* ISO/IEC JCT1/SC 21 N517, N518, N519, N520, N521, 1988.
[8] ISO/TC97/SC21. *Open Systems Interconnection — File Transfer, Access and Management, Parts I-IV.* IS 8571, 1987.
[9] *A Test System for Implementations of MHS/SMTP Gateways, Final Report, Parts 1 - 3.* Report ICST/SNA - 87/5, National Bureau of Standards, Institute for Computer Sciences and Technology, Sep. 1987.
[10] *Users Guide for the NBS Prototype Compiler for Estelle.* Report ICST/SNA - 87/3, National Bureau of Standards, Institute for Computer Sciences and Technology, Oct. 1987.
[11] Linn, R. J. *A Revised Tutorial on the Features and Facilities of Estelle.* Report ICST/SNA - 87/6. National Bureau of Standards, Institute for Computer Sciences and Technology, Aug. 1987.
[12] Linn, R. J.; Favreau, J-P. "Application of Formal Description Techniques to the Specification of Distributed Test Systems". in *Proc. of Infocom 88.* IEEE, March 1988.
[13] Favreau, J-P.; Garguilo J.; Lindley J.; Chang J. *A Test System for Implementations of FTAM/FTP Gateways, Parts 1 - 3.* Report ICST/SNA - 88/6, National Bureau of Standards,

Institute for Computer Sciences and Technology, 1988 (in preparation).
[14] Gaudette, P.; Trus S.; Collins S., "An Object-Oriented Model for ASN.1". in this volume.
[15] Garguilo, J.; Favreau, J-P.; Hobbs, M.; Linn, R. J. *Automated Protocol Development Through the Use of the NBS Prototype Estelle Compiler*. Report ICST/SNA - 87/2, National Bureau of Standards, Institute for Computer Sciences and Technology, January 1987.

Annex 1: Test Case Example

This annex presents a test cases example from a set of test cases for the NBS MHS/SMTP gateway implementation.

A test suite for a protocol is composed of a set of test cases each of which is designed to achieve a test purpose. A test case is composed of a sequence of executable test steps (directives/commands). Consequently, test suites, test cases and test directives are related classes of data types which can be represented as ASN.1 values.

Although test cases and test directives have a data structure representation, instances of these objects also have operational semantics within the context of a test system. The Test Suite Handler translates the ASN.1 values representing individual test cases into interactions and their parameters which are interpreted and acted upon by the Test Processor. Thus, the operational semantics of the test language are defined by the formal description of the Lower Tester module in Estelle (see Annex 2). The following is an *executable test case* derived from an *abstract test case* written in TTCN [7].

```
<t40.1.1.1> TestCase ::=
  {
    test {
      test-identifier      {"40.1.1.1"}  },

    --summary of test purpose:
      --Test whether the gateway under test transforms the
      --IPMessageId part of the delivered IM-UAPDU into
      --the corresponding part of a SMTP message. The
      --printable string form of the IPMessageId is used.

    --role-of-IUT (Gateway):
      --Accept the MHS message.  Create and send a
      --corresponding SMTP message to the Upper Tester

    --role-of-Lower-Tester:
      --Submit an MHS message with the IPMessageID
      --part of the content parameter set.

    --role-of-Upper-Tester:
      --Receive the SMTP message, extract specified
      --parts from this message, and send these parts
      -back to the Lower Tester as the data of an
      -SMTP message.

  -- log the following comments:
    log  {"Test Id: 40.1.1.1"},
    log  {"Test name: orig-indication/MHS-initiated/valid/1"},
    log  {"summary: P2.IPMessageID using printable string"},

    synchronize -- the Upper and Lower Testers with a
              -- test management protocol data unit (TMPDU):
        acknowledge {
          loop-counter       1,
```

```
                    smtp-fields    { messageId }
                        },
-- send an MHS message with the following message contents:
   send { { submit-req
           {
             recipient-O-R-names   { ut-recip1 },
             originator-O-R-name   lt-recip1,
             primary-recips { { ut-name ut-recip1 } },
             content  { { {
                           "40.1.1.1-id"
                           }
                         },
                         {{ "message" }}
                       },
             content-type    p2,
             priority   normal,
             disclose-recipients TRUE
           } } },

-- direct the Test Processor to wait for delivery of:
   match { deliver-ind { } },
   -- containing a message from the Upper Tester.

-- direct the Test Processor to check for:
   check { check-type   bodypart,
           bodypart-token messageId,
           operand       "40.1.1.1-id"
         },
   -- in the message received
   -- when judging the results of the test.

   endTest {"40.1.1.1"} }
```

Annex 2: Test Processor Module in Estelle

This annex contains fragments of the Test Processor module as an example of the application of Estelle to the formal specification of a test system. For a better understanding of Estelle, the following references are suggested [6] [11]. The Test Processor module defines the operational semantics of the test language.

The test directives and test service primitives defined in Annex 1 are interpreted, in part, by the module definition below. The TP module header definition below includes interaction points by which interactions are exchanged with other modules. Transitions below are ordered so that they follow the processing of interactions resulting from the execution of the test case of Annex 1.

```
module Test_Processor_Header process;
   ip   { external interaction points between
                    the Test Processor and:}
      TSH: TP_TSH(TPoutputs);{ Test Suite Handler    }
      MTA: TP_MTA(User);     { Message Transfer Agent }
{ exported variable declarations ... }
end { of header for test processor; its body follows: }

body Test_Processor for Test_Processor_Header;
{variable declarations ... and initialize Test Processor ...}
```

The Test Processor is in the START state when it is not processing a test case. Each test case begins with the TSH.Test directive. Transition 1 processes it, saves the test case identifier and logs it via the LogTestid primitive. RUNTEST is the next state.

```
transition 1:
from START
  to RUNTEST
    when TSH.Test(testid) { start of test case}
      begin
        TP_Log_result := LogTestid(testid);
        { initialize for this test case }
      end;
```

Transition 2 processes a log-comment test directive (TSH.Log_ts_pm). Comments in a test case are saved in the log file.

```
transition 2:
from RUNTEST { Log comment }
  to RUNTEST
    priority low
    when TSH.Log_ts_p(comment)
      begin
        TP_Log_result:= Logcomment(comment);
      end;
```

Transition 3 processes a synchronize-and-acknowledge test directive. A synchronize-and-acknowledge TMPDU must be sent to the Upper Tester via the Message Transfer Agent interface which forwards it to the Upper Tester. The synchronize-and-acknowledge TMPDU directs the Upper Tester to acknowledge receipt of specific test data. SYNC_SUBREQ is the next state.

```
transition 3:
from RUNTEST
    priority high
    to SYNC_SUBREQ
    when TSH.Sync_ackn(TMPDU)
      begin
        TP_Synch := ACKNOWLEDGE;
        TP_Log_result := LogacknSync(TMPDU);
        build_ack(TMPDU); {build and save expected fields}
        output MTA.SubReq(TMPDU);
      end;
```

Each time the Test Processor requests the MTA to send a message, it waits for the MTA to indicate success or failure after submitting a message. If success is indicated, the Test Processor goes to the SYNC_DELIVERY state where it waits for the Upper Tester to confirm synchronization.

```
transition 4:
from SYNC_SUBREQ
   priority medium
   to SYNC_DELIVERY
     when MTA.SubConf(Succ_Ind)
     provided  Succ_Ind

       begin
         { synch correctly sent by MTA }
         TP_Log_result := LogSubConf();
       end;
```

In transition 5, the Test Processor waits for the Upper Tester to send a synchronize TMPDU of the correct type with the correct test case identifier. When a Delivery indication is received, the message is parsed via the primitive Parse_content and then the test id and TMPDU type are checked. If the TMPDU type and test id are OK, synchronization between the Upper and Lower Testers is complete. Otherwise, the TP waits.

```
transition 5:
from SYNC_DELIVERY
  priority medium
  to SYNC_DELIVERY
    when MTA.DelivInd(TMPDU)
      begin
        TP_Log_result := LogDelInd();
        { verify the TMPDU correctness in the bodypart }
        TP_Sync_complete := Parse_content (TMPDU,...);
      end;
```

If TP_Sync_complete is true, the Test Processor module returns to the RUNTEST state and is ready to process the next test directive.

```
transition 6:
from SYNC_DELIVERY  {priority lowest }
  to RUNTEST
    provided TP_Sync_complete {Set in transition 5}
      begin
        { no action; return to RUNTEST state }
      end;
```

Transition 7 processes a Submit-Request test directive (TSH.S_SubReq), which directs the Test Processor to compose and send one or more mail messages to the Upper Tester via the MTA. The MTA forwards the messages to the Upper Tester and acknowledges each Submit Request with a submit confirmation. The Test Processor waits in the SENDSUBREQ state for a submit confirmation.

```
transition 7:
from RUNTEST
  to SENDSUBREQ
    priority high
    when TSH.S_SubReq(Count, ...)
      begin
        TP_Log_result := LogSubReq(Count, ...);
        build_SubReq (message);
        for i:= 1 to Count do
          output MTA.SubReq(message);
      end;
```

In the SENDSUBREQ state, the Test Processor waits for a Submit Confirmation from the MTA (MTA.SubConf) which indicates success or failure in sending a message.

```
transition 8:
from SENDSUBREQ
 priority medium
  when MTA.SubConf(Succ_Ind)
    provided  Succ_Ind
    to SENDSUBREQ
      begin
        TP_Log_result := LogSubConf(Succ_Ind);
        Count := Count-1
      end;
```

When all expected submit confirmations are received, the Test Processor returns to the RUN-TEST state and waits for the next test directive.

transition 9:
from SENDSUBREQ
  priority high
  to RUNTEST
    provided (Count = 0)
    begin
    { no action; all messages were sent }
    end;

Transition 10 processes Match-Delivery test directives (TSH.M_Delivery), which direct the Test Processor to wait for a given number of messages to be delivered by the MTA. Each message is saved in a list which is subsequently checked. The Test Processor goes to the MDELIVERY state and waits for delivery indications.

transition 10:
from RUNTEST
  to MDELIVERY
    priority medium
    when TSH.M_Delivery(Count)
      begin
      TP_Log_result= Log _()
        { Save count, initialize list }
      end;

When a Delivery Indication is received from the MTA interface (MTA.DelivInd), the body of the message is parsed (primitive Parse_content). If the test case identifier is the same as the current test case id, the delivery indication belongs to the current test. When they match, the contents of the Delivery indication are saved and the delivery counter is decremented.

transition 11:
from MDELIVERY
  priority medium
  to MDELIVERY
    when MTA.DelivInd(TMPDU)
      begin
        TP_Log_result := LogDelInd(TMPDU);
        testid := Parse_content (TMPDU, ...);
        { check the testid in the TMPDU;
          add appropriate ones to the list }
        Count :=Count-1
      end;

When all expected Delivery indications arrive, the Test Processor goes to the RUNTEST state and waits for the next test directive.

transition 12:
from MDELIVERY
  to RUNTEST
    priority high
    provided (Count = 0)
      begin
      { checking begins with the next directive}
      end;

Transition 13 processes Check test directives (TSH.Check). A specific field of a message and its value are identified using the "field" and "what" parameters of the Check directive. Checks are made against the contents of previous messages saved by actions associated with the previous Match directive. The pair of directives and the list of messages saved provide enough information to pass judgment on the results of the test case. Verdicts may be PASS, FAIL, ABORTED (for a variety of reasons). If the verdict differents from PASS on any check, checking ceases.

```
transition 13:
from RUNTEST
 priority low
 to RUNTEST
   when TSH.Check(field, what)
     begin
       { check to confirm values received
         are identical to the value expected }
       TP_Log_result := LogCheck(field, what);
     end;
```

Transition 14 processes an End-of-Test directive (TSH.EndTest). The test verdict is sent to the operator; the test case context and results are written on the log file in case additional analysis is required. EndTest is output to the Test Suite Handler module which initiates coercion of the next test case when running in automatic mode. The Test Processor module goes to the START state and waits for the next set of test directives or a request from the Lower Tester Manager.

```
transition 14:
from RUNTEST
  to START { end of test case }
    when TSH.EndTest
      begin
        TP_Log_result := LogtcContext();
        TP_Log_result:= LogEndTest(TP_result, TP_testid);
        showverdict (TP_result, TP_Testid); {to the operator}
        output TSH.EndTest(TP_Testid);
      end;
```

Derivation of Useful Execution Trees

from LOTOS Specifications by Using an Interpreter

Renaud Guillemot and Luigi Logrippo

University of Ottawa
Protocols Research Group
Computer Science Department
Ottawa, Ont., Canada K1N 9B4
e-mail: LMLSL@UOTTAWA.BITNET

A contribution towards the development of formal methodologies for testing protocol implementations is presented. We report on a system that is able to execute the specification of a protocol or service written in LOTOS and to derive an execution tree of the entity specified. Several heuristics are used in order to eliminate impossible or uninteresting execution paths. The tree obtained can then be used as a basis for the derivation of test suites.

1. Introduction

1.1. Generating Test Suites from Formal Specifications

Current test methods for protocols and services usually derive test suites manually from informal descriptions or semi-formal ones. The methodology towards which this paper intends to be a contribution assumes instead that the behavior of the entity to be tested has already been specified precisely in LOTOS [ISO1][BB] and derives test suites automatically or semi-automatically from this specification.

Several results have already been reported on generating test suites from formal specifications. Some recent references are [DEM][FL][SBMS][UR][URS][BSS]. Eertink and Brinksma [EB] have developed an algorithm, based on a formal theory, for deriving "canonical testers" for a specification written in a restricted version of "pure LOTOS" (i.e., LOTOS without data). The slant of our paper is more pragmatic. We deal with full LOTOS specifications, and we obtain execution sequences from specifications by using an existing tool, i.e. our LOTOS interpreter. As we shall see, the interpreter generates a great number of sequences that are either unfeasible, in the sense that they relate to logically impossible paths, or redundant, in the sense that they differ the ones from the others only by the placement of nonrelevant internal events. Of course, eliminating all impossible paths and taking out all nonrelevant internal events involves unsolvable problems. Therefore, these execution sequences are simplified by using various heuristics in order to make them useful for testing purposes.

This technique does not constitute (yet) a methodology for the derivation of test suites. Apart from the several possible improvements to be discussed later, the remaining steps, which are the selection of test sequences and the formulation of test sequences in a test specification language, must still be done by hand using ad hoc methods.

1.2. Labelled Symbolic Trees (LSTs)

By LOTOS semantics, given a behavior expression B one can find the set of actions a and the set of resulting behavior expressions B' such that: B -a-> B' , meaning that process *B* can execute action *a* and transform into *B'*. In other words, given a behavior expression, one can find its behavior tree. In the absence of an environment, actions that depend on guards or selection predicates which cannot be evaluated because this involves the knowledge of values that have to be provided by the environment must be listed, together with their guards. Such trees will be called Labelled Symbolic Trees *(***LST**s*)*.

Our LOTOS interpreter [GHL] is able to systematically generate LSTs for a given process up to given maximum lengths and widths. Such trees show all possible execution sequences for the entity specified. When the maximum specified length along a path is exceeded, this is indicated by closing the path with a "continue". Paths exceeding the specified width, instead, are simply ignored, but the user is informed of this (of course, the user must be aware of the fact that, if some paths are ignored, some of the procedures discussed in this paper may yield incorrect results). A realistic example is shown in Section 2.1 of the Annex.

1.3. Overview of The Method

Unfortunately, the practical usefulness of LSTs is greatly reduced by the many unfeasible, redundant, or uninteresting paths that they contain. This is especially true for specifications written in the constraint-oriented style, where each action is subject to a number of logical constraints originating from different processes. Heuristics can be used in order to obtain more useful trees by detecting and eliminating some such paths.

- The first step is to obtain a *Significant Symbolic Tree* (or **SST** for short), where input variable values are represented by symbols derived from the variable's name. Some unfeasible paths or actions are detected and removed by using techniques similar to "symbolic evaluation".
- Loops in behavior are identified.
- Some non-significant internal events are detected and removed.
- All the previous steps are executed dynamically as the tree is generated by the interpreter. In a final step, the stored tree is scanned in order to eliminate some remaining redundant internal events or duplicate paths.

Needless to say, the resulting tree is by no means optimal, in any possible meaning for this word. However it will usually be much more manageable than the original LST.

2. Obtaining a Significant Symbolic Tree

2.1 Contextual Symbolic Trees

Actions specified for a process may contain variables to be bound by the environment, values to be offered to the environment, and conditions on the variables and values (guards and selection predicates).

We use a symbolic representation for the variables which allows us to relate several occurences of the same variable with different external names. A renaming scheme is used. Each occurrence of a variable is replaced by an identifier (a "symbol") which consists of:

- the variable's sort,
- a symbol which expresses how the value was bound, i.e. @ for a variable bound at a gate, and % for a variable bound in a *choice*, an *exit(any)*, or an initial process parameter.
- an identifier that shows the depth in the tree of the variable's first occurrence.
- a second identifier to distinguish different variables of the same sort and the same nesting level (if needed).

Example:

> g?x:Nat ; exit(x) >> accept y:Nat in   g!y ; stop

The value of variable x is exported (by means of *exit* and *enable* operators) to become bound to variable y. By the renaming process, both variables get the indentifier $Nat@1$, which stands for variable of sort Nat bound at level 1.

The LST is:

```
1 g?x:Nat
| 1 i(enable:exit(x))
|  | 1 g!y
```

while the SST is:

```
1 g?Nat@1
| 1 i(enable:exit(Nat@1))
|  | 1 g!Nat@1
```

Example:

> choice x:Nat []   g? y [y lt x] ; stop

Value y bound at gate g must be less than value x chosen arbitrarily by the environment. Since a *choice* is not an action, we use the symbol % and represent x by $Nat\%1$.

The LST is: 1 g?y:Nat [y lt x]

The SST is: 1 g?Nat@1 [Nat@1 lt Nat%1]

2.2. Feasible Symbolic Trees

One may eliminate certain paths that are not feasible, by trying to evaluate symbolically guards and selection predicates [BJ]. Predicates that cannot be evaluated to false and are not in contradiction with others previously assumed to be true are assumed to be true. Each action is associated with a list of predicates, which gives all the constraints that must be satisfied for the action to be executed (these are the combined selection predicates of all action offers cooperating in the action). We call these *action predicates*. It is also associated with the list of predicates that occurred ahead of it on the same path, in guards or other predicates. We call these *path predicates*.

During the tree building process, an action is reduced to a *stop* if a contradiction is detected in its path predicates. It is checked in the following order whether:

A) One of the action predicates can be evaluated to false.
B) A contradiction can be detected in the action predicates
C) A contradiction can be detected in the path predicates.
D) A contradiction can be detected between path predicates and action predicates.

The detection of contradictions in the general case is of course an undecidable problem. Some heuristics are needed. Contradictions such as ($q(x)$ and $p(x)$), where $q(x) = not(p(x))$ appears in the list of axioms, are detected automatically. Upon finding a predicate such as this one, the system scans the list of axioms looking for such immediate contradictions. In specifications we have studied [ISO2], such cases are frequent.

In addition, our system allows the user to establish a data base of contradictions. A user-defined contradiction can involve several terms.

Example:

```
( in?x:Nat [x gt 3] ; out?y:Nat [y gt x] ; exit
[]
   in?x:Nat [x le 3] ; out!3 ; exit   )
||
( in?x:Nat; (out?y [y lt 3] ; exit
           []
              out?y [y eq x] ; exit   )  )
```

Assume that the data base of contradictions contains:

(1) [x gt y] # [x eq y]
(2) [x gt y] & [y gt z] # [x lt z]

Before simplification, the tree is:

```
1 in?Nat@1 [Nat @1 gt 3]
| 1 out?Nat@2 [Nat@2 gt Nat@1] [Nat@2 lt 3]
| | 1 exit      EXIT
| 2 out?Nat@2 [Nat@2 gt Nat@1] [Nat@2 eq Nat@1]
| | 1 exit      EXIT
2 in?1Nat@1 [Nat@1 le 3]
| 1 out!3 [3 lt 3]
| | 1 exit      EXIT
| 2 out!3 [3 eq Nat@1]
| | 1 exit      EXIT
```

- Branch 1.1 is pruned because of D(2) (it implies 3 < 3).
- Branch 1.2 is pruned because of B(1).
- Branch 2.1 is pruned because of A (the predicate contains no variables and can be evaluated to false).

The SST is:

```
1 in?Nat@1 [Nat@1 gt 3]    DEADLOCK
2 in?Nat@1 [Nat@1 le 3]
| 1 out!3 [3 eq Nat@1]
| | 1 exit      EXIT
```

2.3 Towards a Limited Tree

Trees generated by this method are usually infinite. This is the normal case when recursion is involved. Two methods of dealing with infinite paths are detecting recursion, and ignoring some paths under user control.

a) **Detecting Recursion**

Recursion can be detected automatically at least in some cases. For example, a unique identifier can be associated with an occurrence of a behavior expression in a tree. Later occurences of the same behavior expression or of an equivalent one in the same path are then replaced by the identifier preceded by the word "again". This can be done to a certain extent while building the tree, by comparing each behavior obtained against the ones obtained previously. The currently used comparison criterion is strict character-by-character identity. Although this may appear to be an overly simple criterion, we have found that it is useful in many cases. This is shown in Annex 2.2.

Example:

```
process P[a,d]:exit :=   a ; P[a,d]
                         []
                         d ; exit
```

The LST is: while the SST is:

```
1 a
| 1 a                          bh0  1 a      ==> again bh0
  ...                               2 d
| 2 d                               | 1 exit   EXIT
| | 1 exit     EXIT
2 d
| 1 exit       EXIT
```

Also, according to our criterion a behavior expression such as *P[a](x)* is considered identical to *P[a](succ(x))*, while *P[a](0)* would be considered different from *P[a](succ(0))*. This is because in the second case some predicates will be yielding different values for *0* and *succ(0)*, while in the first case, predicates involving the variable *x* would not be evaluated and would therefore all be considered to be true, unless they contain some contradiction independent of the value of *x*.

While equivalence of behavior expressions is an undecidable problem, more sophisticated criteria of behavior equivalence could be added to our system, also in consideration of the needs of the application. For example obviously behavior *a [] b* can be considered to be identical to behavior *b [] a*. Furthermore, it is well-known that for testing purposes it may be appropriate to consider equivalent behaviors that cannot be considered to be equivalent from other points of view.

b)   **Ignoring Some Paths**

In generating behavior trees for complex systems, it is normal that the user may wish to ignore certain paths. For example, this can happen for paths relating to error conditions, or for paths relating to the creation of several connections if it is wished to consider the case of one connection only. Such paths are usually guarded by internal actions. Our system allows one to specify that the entire subtree following a certain internal action be ignored.

3. The Treatment of Internal Events

A process in LOTOS is described in terms of its actions, which can be of two types: observable actions or internal actions. Internal actions occur in execution sequences either because they are specified explicitly (an *i* in the specification) or because they result from the dynamic behavior of the system (we call this implicit specification). This is the case for example when the enable (>>) operator is used together with the *exit* statement.

Internal events, especially those due to enable operations, are a major cause of complexity in the symbolic tree. Hence the importance of eliminating them when possible.

3.1. Internal Events and Implementations

Internal actions introduce nondeterminism. Implementations may differ by the way they reduce this nondeterminism. Thus, for a given specification, one can obtain several valid implementations [BSS]. For instance, consider the following process:

```
process Connection[ConReq,DisInd,ConConf] : exit :=
   ConReq ; ( ConConf ; exit
              []
              i ; DisInd ; exit )
endproc
```

This is the connection phase of a protocol that always accepts a disconnection indication after a connection request, but may refuse the connection confirmation. The choice between these two alternatives is left to the implementation. Therefore, there are three possible implementations for this specification. One is the specification itself. The other two are:

- ConReq ; (ConConf ; exit [] DisInd ; exit)
- ConReq ; (DisInd ; exit)

The first alternative always offers *ConConf,* while the second nevers offers it.

Internal events designating implementation choices cannot be eliminated from the tree.

3.2. Simplification by Congruence Rules

In some cases, internal events can be removed by applying congruence rules. This removal does not in any way change the semantics of the specification. In this experiment, we implemented only the following rules:

1	a;i;B	is simplified to	a;B
2	B [] i;(B[]C)	is simplified to	i;(B[]C)
3	B[]B	is simplified to	B

Note that the second rule is a stronger version of the well-known congruence $B[]i;B = i;B$. It is more useful than the latter, especially when disable is present.

The most obvious way to perform reduction by congruence rules is to generate the whole tree, to store it in memory, and then to scan it bottom-up to find places where congruence rules can be applied. However, memory can be saved if congruence rules are applied as far as possible, by using a look-ahead mechanism, already while the tree is being generated. The stored tree is then scanned bottom-up to further simplify it.

a) **Application of Congruence Rules While Building the Tree**

The interpreter is unable to directly apply rules 1 to 3 above. All it can do is to to compute sets of possible next actions with resulting behavior expressions. Situations where these simplifications can be applied are detected by a "look-ahead" mechanism. Consider for example rule 2. When the interpreter finds that the set of possible "next actions" is of the form N = {a1,...,am,b1,...,bn,i}, if the set of next behaviors is respectively {A1,...,Am,B1,...,Bn,D}, the set of next actions for D is computed. If this set includes {b1,...,bn}, with next behaviors {B1,...,Bn} respectively, then the tree is simplified by using only the actions in {a1,...,am,i} and their successors. Again, two behavior expressions are considered to be the same only if they are the same character by character.

A corresponding criterion is used in testing for equivalence for rule 3.

These rules are applied recursively while possible. Therefore, an expression such as

```
a ; b ; (c ; d ; stop
        []
        i ; c ; d ; stop)
```

is reduced to

```
a ; b ; c ; d
```

by applying first rule 2, and then rule 1. Annex 2.2. shows an extended example.

b) **Application of Congruence Rules on the Resulting Tree**

The tree resulting from the simplification process described above is stored in memory and further simplified by an algorithm that is able to detect other cases in which rules 1 to 3 can be applied. Consider for example the following behavior expression:

```
a ; b ; (c ; d ; stop
        []
        i ; c ; d ; stop)
[]
a ; b ; c ; i ; d ; stop
```

By using the "look-ahead" mechanism, the following tree will be saved:

```
    a ; b ; c ; d ; stop
[]
    a ; b ; c ; d ; stop
```

By scanning the tree according to this algorithm, it is simplified to:

```
a ; b ; c ; d ; stop
```

3.3. The Enable Operator.

In our study of realistic examples, it soon became obvious that some method had to be found to manage the complexity generated by internal events due to enables. This can be seen by a study of Annex 3.2. For example, consider the following behavior expression:

```
(a; exit >> b; exit)
||
(a; exit >> b; exit)
```

If we call $i1$ and $i2$ the internal actions resulting from the first and second enable respectively, the resulting **LST** shows both mutual orderings of these actions, i.e.

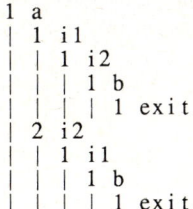

The tree of observable actions instead is simply

```
1 a
| 1 b
| | exit
```

By applying the simplification rules discussed in **3.2.a)** we get:

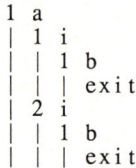

```
1 a
| 1 i
| | 1 b
| | | exit
| 2 i
| | 1 b
| | | exit
```

This tree cannot be simplified further by the look-ahead mechanism because the behavior expression resulting from the execution of *i1* is
$$(b; exit) \parallel (exit >> b; exit)$$
while the behavior expression resulting from the execution of *i2* is
$$(exit >> b ; exit) \parallel (b; exit)$$
and unfortunately these two behavior expressions are not textually identical.

The internal events will be completely eliminated by using the algorithm in 3.2.b) (and, of course, could be eliminated by the look-ahead mechanism if we informed it that $p \parallel q = q \parallel p$).

Internal events could be eliminated at the source by using modified inference rules, such as (in simplified form):

exit -exit-> stop

A >> B -a-> A' >> B   if A-a-> A' and name(a) =/= exit

A >> B -a-> B'   if A -exit-> A' and B-a-> B'

Unfortunately, these rules do not work in some cases. For example, suppose that the *exit* statement appears as the first action as in the following example:

```
process p[a,b] :=  exit >> a ; stop
                  []
                   b ; stop
endproc
```

this behavior is equivalent to: *i ; a ; stop [] b ; stop*. By eliminating the internal event according to the rules above, we obtain the behavior:
a ; stop [] b ; stop.
This expression is not equivalent to the previous one. The semantics of the original specification give priority to *b* while the semantics of the second specification don't. The modified rules for the exit can only be used if constructs such as the one in the example do not occur in the specification, and this can be checked statically.

The question of the treatment of internal events due to enabling for testing purposes deserves further study.

4. Considering Values

After obtaining the simplified tree according to the procedure described above, execution sequences can be derived by the following steps:

- identifying, for every action in all remaining paths, all the values that can be accepted
- and then constructing the expanded tree.

Concerning the first step, this consists in replacing every symbolic action, containing or not a guard, by values. The set of values that can be accepted by an action is usually infinite.

Example:

For the LOTOS specification :

$$g?x:Nat \; ; \; g?y:Nat \; [y \; gt \; x] \; ; \; exit$$

the SST obtained is:

```
1   g ?Nat@1
|   1   g ?Nat@2  [Nat@2  gt  Nat@1]
|   |   1  exit
```

Values for *Nat@1* and *Nat@2* must be chosen before this sequence can be used as a test case. Possible values belong to the set of all pairs (x,y) of natural numbers such that $x<y$. Strategies for choosing such test values have been studied in the testing literature and will not be discussed in this paper [MY].

5. Conclusions and Future Work

The work presented in this paper is an effort towards a methodology for generating test suites from LOTOS specifications. We showed that useful execution trees can be generated by using existing interpreters and some basic simplification rules. More sophisticated heuristics could be added to the system. Similarly, other congruence rules could be added to the very basic list given in Section 3.2. As a further step, we are envisaging the use of theorem-proving methods to enhance the methods for detecting contradictions and equivalences.

Furthermore, this method should be related to the existing theory on generating test suites from LOTOS specification [EB][BSS]. And then, there is the problem of obtaining real test specifications with values, mentioned in Section 4.

Finally, while the main emphasis of this paper is on testing, it sould be noted that trees are also interesting in verification. Therefore, application of similar techniques in verification appears to be possible.

Acknowledgment. The interpreter was written by J.P. Briand, M.C. Fehri, R. Guillemot, and M. Haj-Hussein. We are indebted to A. Obaid for many useful discussions, and we have also used some ideas due to H. Elgendy. This work was supported in part by the National Science and Engineering Research Council of Canada and Bell-Northern Research.

References

[BB] Bolognesi, B. and Brinksma, E. Introduction to the ISO Specification Language LOTOS. Computer Networks and ISDN Systems 14 (1987) 25-59.

[BJ] Brand, D., and Joyner, W.H. Jr. Verification of Protocols Using Symbolic Execution. Computer Networks 2, 4/5, 351-360.

[BSS] Brinksma, E., Scollo, G., and Steenbergen, C. LOTOS Specifications, their Implementations, and their Tests. In: B. Sarikaya and G.v. Bochmann (eds.) Protocol Specification, Testing, and Verification, IV. North-Holland, 1987, 349-360.

[DEM] de Meer, J. Derivation and Validation of Test Scenarios Based on the Formal Specification Language LOTOS. In: B. Sarikaya and G.V. Bochmann (eds.) Protocol Specification, Testing, and Verification, VI. North-Holland, 1987, 203-216.

[EB] Eertink, E., and Brinksma, E. Implementation of a Test Derivation Algorithm. Technische Hogeschool Twente, Oct. 1987 (SEDOS/C2/N82).

[FL] Favreau, J.P., and Linn, J.R. Automatic Generation of Test Scenario Skeletons from Protocol Specifications written in Estelle. In: B. Sarikaya and G.V. Bochmann (eds.) Protocol Specification, Testing, and Verification, VI. North-Holland, 1987, 191-202.

[GHL] Guillemot, R., Haj-Hussein, M., and Logrippo, L. Executing Large LOTOS Specifications. University of Ottawa, Department of Computer Science, Technical Report 88-03 (Jan. 1988).

[ISO1] International Organisation for Standardization. Information Processing Systems. Open Systems Interconnection. LOTOS - A Formal Description Technique Based on the Temporal Ordering of Observational Behavior (ISO DIS 8807), 1987.

[ISO2] International Organization for Standardization. Formal Description of ISO 8072 in LOTOS. (ISO/TC 97/SC 6/WG 4/N 317), 1987.

[LP] Logrippo, L. and Probert, R.L. Protocol Specification-Level Validation. In: Sunshine, C. (ed.) Protocol Specification, Testing, and Verification North-Holland, 1982, 303-304.

[MY] Myers, G.J. The Art of Software Testing. Wiley, 1979.

[SBMS] Sarikaya, B., Bochmann, G.v., Maksud, M., and Serre, J.M. Formal Specification Based Conformance Testing. In: Communications Architectures and Protocols, SIGCOMM '86 Symposium, 236-240.

[UR] Ural, H. A Test Derivation Method for Protocol Conformance Testing. In: H. Rudin and C.H. West (eds.) Protocol Specification, Testing, and Verification, VII. North-Holland, 1987, 347-358.

[URS] Ural, H., and Short, R. An Interactive Test Sequence Generator. In: Communications Architectures and Protocols, SIGCOMM '86 Symposium, 241-250.

[VE] Van Eijk, P. Software Tools for the Specification Language LOTOS. University of Twente, 1988.

ANNEX. An Example: Transport Connection

We give an extended example showing some aspects of our method. Because of the length of the trees obtained, only certain sample sections may be shown.

1. Specification
The specification is a simplified formal description of the OSI Transport Service, based on [ISO2].
The simplifications relate to the end-to-end constraints:
- only one connection is provided,
- queues of requests, lost requests and provider-generated indications are not specified.

```
  2   specification    SimplifiedTransportService [t] : noexit

       (* data part *)

721   behaviour TConnection[t]
722   where
723
724   process TConnection[t]:noexit:=        TCEPs[t]  ||  TCEPAssociation[t]   endproc
725
726   process TCEPs[t]:exit:=     TCEP[t](CallingRole) |||  TCEP[t](CalledRole)   endproc
727
728   process TCEP[t](role:TSUserRole):exit:= TCEPAddress[t]||TCEPSFOrdering[t](role) endproc
729
730   process TCEPAddress[t]:exit:=              t?ta:TAddress?tsp:TSP ; ConstantTA[t](ta)
731                                              [> exit         endproc
732
733   process ConstantTA[t](ta:TAddress):noexit:= t!ta?tsp:TSP; ConstantTA[t](ta) endproc
734
735   process TCEPSFOrdering[t](role:TSUserRole):exit:=
736      TCEPConnect1[t] (role) >> accept tsp:TSP in
737      (  (  TCEPConnect2[t](tsp) >> accept x:TEXOption in TCEPDataTransfer[t] (x)
738      )  [> TCEPRelease[t] )
739      []
740      [role = CalledRole] -> exit
741   endproc
742
743   process TCEPConnect1[t](role:TSUserRole):exit(TSP):=
744      [role=CallingRole] -> t?ta:TAddress?tcr:TSP[IsTCONreq(tcr) and (ta IsCallingOf tcr)]; exit(tcr)
745      []
746      [role=CalledRole] -> t?ta:TAddress?tci:TSP[IsTCONind(tci) and (ta IsCalledOf tci)]; exit(tci)
747   endproc
748
749   process TCEPConnect2[t](tc1:TSP):exit(TEXOption):=
750      t ?ta:TAddress ?tc2:TSP [tc2 IsValidTCON2For tc1] ;
751      ( choice x:TEXOption [] [x IsTEXOptionOf tc2] -> exit (x) )
752   endproc
753
754   process TCEPDataTransfer[t](x:TEXOption):noexit:=
755      TCEPNormalDataTransfer[t]  |||  [x = UseTEX] -> TCEPExpeditedDataTransfer[t]
756   endproc
757   process TCEPNormalDataTransfer[t]:noexit:=
758       t ?ta:TAddress ?tsp:TSP [IsTDT(tsp)] ; TCEPNormalDataTransfer[t]  endproc
759
760   process TCEPExpeditedDataTransfer[t]:noexit:=
```

```
761    t ?ta:TAddress ?tsp:TSP [IsTEX(tsp)] ; TCEPExpeditedDataTransfer[t]
762    endproc
763
764    process TCEPRelease[t]:exit:=   t?ta:TAddress?tsp:TSP[IsTDIS(tsp)]; exit  endproc
765
766    process TCEPAssociation[t]:noexit :=
767    t ?ta:TAddress ?tsp:TSP [IsTReq(tsp)] ;
768    (  TAssoc1[t] (ta,CallingRole,CalledRole,tsp)
769      |||
770       TAssoc1[t] (ta,CalledRole,CallingRole,NoTReqs) )
771    endproc
772
773    process TAssoc1[t](ta:TAddress,from,to:TSUserRole,rh:TSP):noexit:=
774    ( TCEPReq[t](ta,from) ||| TCEPInd[t](ta,to) )  || TCReqToInd[t](rh)
775    endproc
776
777    process TCEPReq[t](ta:TAddress,role:TSUserRole):noexit:= TReq[t]||GetCalledTId[t](ta,role) endproc
778
779    process TReq[t]:noexit:= t?ta:TAddress?tsp:TSP[IsTReq(tsp)]; TReq[t]  endproc
780
781    process TCEPInd[t](ta:TAddress,role:TSUserRole):noexit:= TInd[t]||GetCalledTId[t](ta,role) endproc
782
783    process TInd[t]:noexit:=    t?ta:TAddress?tsp:TSP [IsTInd(tsp)]; TInd[t]  endproc
784
785    process GetCalledTId[t](ta:TAddress,role:TSUserRole):noexit:=
786    ( [role = CallingRole] -> exit(ta)
787      []
788      [role = CalledRole] -> t?ta1:TAddress?tsp:TSP [ta1 ne ta] ; exit(ta1)
789    ) >> accept ta:TAddress in ConstantTA[t](ta)
790    endproc
791
792    process TCReqToInd[t](rh:TSP):noexit:=
793    TSPEvent[t](rh) >> accept rh1:TSP in TCReqToInd[t](rh1)
794    endproc
795
796    process TSPEvent[t](rh:TSP):exit(TSP):=
797    [NonEmpty(rh)] ->
798     ( choice tspi:TSP [] [tspi IsIndicationOf rh] -> i;t?ta:TAddress!tspi;exit(NoTReqs))
799    []
800    [Empty(rh)] -> t ?ta:TAddress?tsp:TSP [IsTReq(tsp)] ; exit(tsp)
801    endproc
802
803    endspec (* SimplifiedTransportService *)
```

The numbers on the left-hand side are line numbers.

These numbers appear in the following trees between square brackets to indicate the action offers which cooperate to yield the actions shown.

2. Process TCEPSPOrdering (role: User Role): Local ordering of primitives at a calling endpoint

2.1 Labelled Symbolic Tree (depth = 7)
```
1 [role=CallingRole] t ?ta ?tcr [and(IsTCONreq(tcr),IsCallingOf(ta,tcr))]  [744]
| 1 i (enable: exit !tcr )  [744]
| | 1 t ?ta ?tc2 [IsValidTCON2For(tc2,tc1)]  [750]
| | | 1 [IsTEXOptionOf(x,tc2)] i (enable: exit !x:TEXOption)  [751]
| | | | 1 t ?ta ?tsp [IsTDT(tsp)]  [758]
| | | | | 1 t ?ta ?tsp [IsTDT(tsp)]  [758]
| | | | | | 1 t ?ta ?tsp [IsTDT(tsp)]  [758]       => continue
| | | | | | 2 [x=UseTEX] t ?ta ?tsp [IsTEX(tsp)]  [761]     => continue
| | | | | | 3 t ?ta ?tsp [IsTDIS(tsp)]  [764]      => continue
| | | | | 2 [x=UseTEX] t ?ta ?tsp [IsTEX(tsp)]  [761]
| | | | | | 1 t ?ta ?tsp [IsTDT(tsp)]  [758]       => continue
| | | | | | 2 t ?ta ?tsp [IsTEX(tsp)]  [761]       => continue
| | | | | | 3 t ?ta ?tsp [IsTDIS(tsp)]  [764]      => continue
| | | | | 3 t ?ta ?tsp [IsTDIS(tsp)]  [764]
| | | | | | 1 exit ** EXIT SUCCEED **  [764]
| | | | 2 [x=UseTEX] t ?ta ?tsp [IsTEX(tsp)]  [761]
| | | | | 1 t ?ta ?tsp [IsTDT(tsp)]  [758]
| | | | | | 1 t ?ta ?tsp [IsTDT(tsp)]  [758]       => continue
| | | | | | 2 t ?ta ?tsp [IsTEX(tsp)]  [761]       => continue
| | | | | | 3 t ?ta ?tsp [IsTDIS(tsp)]  [764]      => continue
| | | | | 2 t ?ta ?tsp [IsTEX(tsp)]  [761]
| | | | | | 1 t ?ta ?tsp [IsTDT(tsp)]  [758]       => continue
| | | | | | 2 t ?ta ?tsp [IsTEX(tsp)]  [761]       => continue
| | | | | | 3 t ?ta ?tsp [IsTDIS(tsp)]  [764]      => continue
| | | | | 3 t ?ta ?tsp [IsTDIS(tsp)]  [764]
| | | | | | 1 exit ** EXIT SUCCEED **  [764]
| | | | 3 t ?ta ?tsp [IsTDIS(tsp)]  [764]
| | | | | 1 exit ** EXIT SUCCEED **  [764]
| | | 2 t ?ta ?tsp [IsTDIS(tsp)]  [764]
| | | | 1 exit ** EXIT SUCCEED **  [764]
| | 2 t ?ta ?tsp [IsTDIS(tsp)]  [764]
| | | 1 exit ** EXIT SUCCEED **  [764]
| | 3 [role=CalledRole] exit ** EXIT SUCCEED **  [740]
```

2.2 Simplified Symbolic Tree

This is the resulting tree after the simplification rules discussed in the paper are applied.

Congruence rule 1 was applied twice, while rule 2 was applied once.

```
bh0 * 1 [CallingRole=CallingRole] t ?ta ?tcr[and(IsTCONreq(tcr),IsCallingOf(ta,tcr))]  [744]
bh1 *  | 1 t ?TAddress@0 ?TSR@0[IsValidTCON2For(TSR@0,[])]  [750]
bh2 *  | | 1 [IsTEXOptionOf(TEXOption%2,TSR@0)] t ?TAddress@1 ?TSR@1[IsTDT(TSR@1)]  [758]
bh3 *  | | | 1 t ?TAddress@2 ?TSR@2[IsTDT(TSR@2)]  [758]           => again bh3
         | | | 2 [TEXOption%2=UseTEX] t ?TAddress@2 ?TSR@2[IsTEX(TSR@2)]  [761]
bh4 *  | | | | 1 t ?TAddress@3 ?TSR@3[IsTDT(TSR@3)]  [758]         => again bh4
       *  | | | | 2 t ?TAddress@3 ?TSR@3[IsTEX(TSR@3)]  [761]      => again bh4
       *  | | | | 3 t ?TAddress@3 ?TSR@3[IsTDIS(TSR@3)]  [764]
bh5 *  | | | | | 1 exit ** EXIT SUCCEED **  [764]
       *  | | | 3 t ?TAddress@2 ?TSR@2[IsTDIS(TSR@2)]  [764]
       *  | | | | 1 exit ** EXIT SUCCEED **
       *  | | 2 [IsTEXOptionOf(TEXOption%2,TSR@0)][TEXOption%2=UseTEX]
               t ?TAddress@1 ?TSR@1[IsTEX(TSR@1)]  [761]           => again bh4
       *  | | 3 [IsTEXOptionOf(TEXOption%2,TSR@0)] t ?TAddress@1 ?TSR@1[IsTDIS(TSR@1)]  [764]
       *  | | | 1 exit ** EXIT SUCCEED **
       *  | 2 t ?TAddress@0 ?TSR@0[IsTDIS(TSR@0)]  [764]
       *  | | 1 exit ** EXIT SUCCEED **
```

3 Process TConnection

3.0 Data Base of contradictions
(1) IsTReq(@1) # IsTInd(@1)
(2) IsTReq(@1) # IsTCONind(@1)
(3) IsTReq(@1) # IsIndicationOf(@2,@1)
(4) IsValidTCON2For(@2,@1) & IsTReq(@1) # IsTReq(@2)
(5) IsValidTCON2For(@2,@1) & IsTInd(@1) # IsTInd(@2)
(6) IsIndicationOf(@2,@1) & IsTDIS(@1) # IsTDT(@2)

3.1 (Part of) the Contextual Symbolic Tree
The applicable rules of section 2.2 are shown after reaching node [1.1.1.1].

```
1 [CallingRole=CallingRole] t ?TAddress@1 ?TSR@1
  [and(IsTCONreq(TSR@1),IsCallingOf(TAddress@1,TSR@1))]
  [IsTReq(TSR@1)]    [730,744,766]
| 1 i (enable: exit !TSR@1) [744]
| | 1 [CallingRole=CallingRole] i (enable: exit !TAddress@1) [786]
| | | 1 [NonEmpty(TSR@1)] [IsIndicationOf(TSP%4,TSR@1)] i (specified explicitly) [798]
| | | | 1 [CallingRole=CallingRole] i (enable: exit !TAddress@1) [786]
| | | | 2 t !TAddress@1 !TSP%4
          [IsValidTCON2For(TSP%4,TSR@1)]
          [IsTReq(TSP%4)]    [733,750,779,733,798]              ** rule C(4) **
| | | | 3 [CalledRole=CalledRole] t !TAddress@1 !TSP%4
          [IsValidTCON2For(TSP%4,TSR@1)]
          [IsTInd(TSP%4)]
          [ne(TAddress@1,TAddress@1)]    [733,750,783,788,798]  ** rule A **
| | | | 4 [CalledRole=CalledRole] [Empty(NoTReqs)] t !TAddress@1 ?TSR@5
          [IsValidTCON2For(TSR@5,TSR@1)]
          [IsTReq(TSR@5)]
          [ne(TAddress@1,TAddress@1)]
          [IsTReq(TSR@5)]    [733,750,779,788,800]              ** rule A **
| | | | 5 t !TAddress@1 !TSP%4
          [IsTDIS(TSP%4)]
          [IsTReq(TSP%4)]    [733,764,779,733,798]              ** rule C(3) **
| | | | 6 [CalledRole=CalledRole] t !TAddress@1 !TSP%4
          [IsTDIS(TSP%4)]
          [IsTInd(TSP%4)]
          [ne(TAddress@1,TAddress@1)]    [733,764,783,788,798]  ** rule A **
| | | | 7 [CalledRole=CalledRole] [Empty(NoTReqs)] t !TAddress@1 ?TSR@5
          [IsTDIS(TSR@5)]
          [IsTReq(TSR@5)]
          [ne(TAddress@1,TAddress@1)]
          [IsTReq(TSR@5)]    [733,764,779,788,800]              ** rule A **
| | | | 8 [CalledRole=CalledRole] t !TAddress@1 !TSP%4
          [and(IsTCONind(TSP%4),IsCalledOf(TAddress@1,TSP%4))]
          [IsTReq(TSP%4)]    [730,746,779,733,798]              ** rule B(2) **
| | | | 9 [CalledRole=CalledRole] [CalledRole=CalledRole] t ?TAddress@5 !TSP%4
          [and(IsTCONind(TSP%4),IsCalledOf(TAddress@5,TSP%4))]
          [IsTInd(TSP%4)]
          [ne(TAddress@5,TAddress@1)]    [730,746,783,788,798]  ==> continue
| | | | 10 [CalledRole=CalledRole] [CalledRole=CalledRole] [Empty(NoTReqs)] t ?TAddress@5 ?TSR@5
           [and(IsTCONind(TSR@5),IsCalledOf(TAddress@5,TSR@5))]
           [IsTReq(TSR@5)]
           [ne(TAddress@5,TAddress@1)]
           [IsTReq(TSR@5)]    [730,746,779,788,800]             ** rule B(2) **
```

3.2 (Part of) the Feasible Symbolic Tree

```
     * 1 [CallingRole=CallingRole] t ?TAddress@1 ?TSR@1
         [and(IsTCONreq(TSR@1),IsCallingOf(TAddress@1,TSR@1))]
         [IsTReq(TSR@1)]      [730,744,766]
     * | 1 i (enable: exit !TSR@1)  [744]
     * | | 1 [CallingRole=CallingRole] i (enable: exit !TAddress@1)  [786]
bh1  * | | | 1 [NonEmpty(TSR@1)] [IsIndicationOf(TSP%4,TSR@1)] i (specified explicitly) [798]
     * | | | | 1 [CallingRole=CallingRole] i (enable: exit !TAddress@1) [786]
     * | | | | | 1 [CalledRole=CalledRole] [CalledRole=CalledRole] t ?TAddress@6 !TSP%4.2
                   [and(IsTCONind(TSP%4),IsCalledOf(TAddress@6,TSP%4))]
                   [IsTInd(TSP%4)]
                   [ne(TAddress@6,TAddress@1)]    [730,746,783,788,798]
     * | | | | | | 1 i (enable: exit !TSP%4)  [746]
     * | | | | | | | 1 i (enable: exit !TAddress@6)  [788]
     * | | | | | | | | 1 i (enable: exit !NoTReqs)  [798]
     * | | | | | | | | | 1 [Empty(NoTReqs)] t !TAddress@6 ?TSR@10
                             [IsValidTCON2For(TSR@10,TSP%4)]
                             [IsTReq(TSR@10)]
                             [IsTReq(TSR@10)]   [733,749,779,733,800]
     * | | | | | | | | | | 1 [IsTEXOptionOf(TEXOption%11,TSR@10)] i (enable: exit !TEXOption%11) [751]
     * | | | | | | | | | | | 1 i (enable: exit !TSR@10)  [800]
     * | | | | | | | | | | | | 1 [NonEmpty(TSR@10)] [IsIndicationOf(TSP%13,TSR@10)]
                                   i (specified explicitly)  [798]
     * | | | | | | | | | | | | | 1 t !TAddress@1 !TSP%13
                                     [IsValidTCON2For(TSP%13,TSR@1)]
                                     [IsTInd(TSP%13)]  [733,749,783,733,798]
     * | | | | | | | | | | | | | | 1 [IsTEXOptionOf(TEXOption%15,TSP%13)]
                                       i (enable: exit !TEXOption%15)  [751]
     * | | | | | | | | | | | | | | | 1 i (enable: exit !NoTReqs)  [798]
     * | | | | | | | | | | | | | | | | 1 [Empty(NoTReqs)] t !TAddress@1 ?TSR@17
                                           [IsTDT(TSR@17)]
                                           [IsTReq(TSR@17)] [IsTReq(TSR@17)] [733,758,779,733,800]
     * | | | | | | | | | | | | | | | | | 1 i (enable: exit !TSR@17)  [800]
     * | | | | | | | | | | | | | | | | | | 1 [NonEmpty(TSR@17)] [IsIndicationOf(TSP%19,TSR@17)]
                                               i (specified explicitly)  [798]
     * | | | | | | | | | | | | | | | | | | | 1 t !TAddress@1 !TSP%19
                                                 [IsTDT(TSP%19)]
                                                 [IsTInd(TSP%19)]  [733,758,783,733,798]    ==> continue
             ... ... ...

     * | | | 2 [CallingRole=CallingRole] i (enable: exit !TAddress@1)  [786]           ==> continue
     * | | | 2 [NonEmpty(TSR@1)] [IsIndicationOf(TSP%3,TSR@1)] i (specified explicitly) [798] ==> continue
     * | | 3 [CallingRole=CallingRole] i (enable: exit !TAddress@1)  [786]
bh2  * | | | 1 [CallingRole=CallingRole] i (enable: exit !TAddress@1)  [786]           ==> continue
     * | | | 2 [NonEmpty(TSR@1)] [IsIndicationOf(TSP%4,TSR@1)] i (specified explicitly) [798] ==> continue
     * | 2 [CallingRole=CallingRole] i (enable: exit !TAddress@1)  [786]
     * | | 1 i (enable: exit !TSR@1)  [744]                                             ==> again bh1
     * | | 2 [NonEmpty(TSR@1)] [IsIndicationOf(TSP%3,TSR@1)] i (specified explicitly) [798] ==> continue
     * | | 3 [CallingRole=CallingRole] i (enable: exit !TAddress@1)  [786]
bh3  * | | | 1 i (enable: exit !TSR@1)  [744]                                           ==> continue
     * | | | 2 [NonEmpty(TSR@1)] [IsIndicationOf(TSP%4,TSR@1)] i (specified explicitly) [798] ==> continue
     * | | 3 [NonEmpty(TSR@1)] [IsIndicationOf(TSP%2,TSR@1)] i (specified explicitly) [798] ==> continue
     * | 4 [CallingRole=CallingRole] i (enable: exit !TAddress@1)  [786]
     * | | 1 i (enable: exit !TSR@1)  [744]                                             ==> again bh2
     * | | 2 [CallingRole=CallingRole] i (enable: exit !TAddress@1)  [786]              ==> again bh3
     * | 3 [NonEmpty(TSR@1)] [IsIndicationOf(TSP%3,TSR@1)] i (specified explicitly) [798] ==> continue
```

The last part shows the complexity introduced by enables, since there are as many branches as there are possible permutations of successive enables. Note for example that [1.1.1] and [1.2.1] lead to the same behaviour labelled bh1.

Node [1.1.1.1.1.1] corresponds to node [1.1.1.1.1.9] in the tree of Annex 3.1. Its subtree was not explored there.

SDS: A LOTOS BASED TOOL FOR SYMBOLIC DEBUGGING

Francesco COSTA, Daniela NARDI, Roberto RINALDI

Olivetti Systems & Networks
Networking & Communication Division
Ivrea, Italy

The Symbolic Debugging System, currently under development, is intended to support the activities of testing and debugging of communication software, through the generation of an execution trace which can be analyzed inside the notational framework of the specification language LOTOS.
Different applications of the tool can be foreseen, depending on the relationship between a LOTOS specification, used as reference, and the architecture of implemented software.

1. INTRODUCTION

Among the main objectives of FDTs there is the improvement of protocol implementation process, which can be achieved giving a formal basis [11]:
- for determining conformance of implementations to specifications, and
- for implementation support.

In this paper an implementation support tool is described, which is based on LOTOS [12]. The system is being developed by the group in charge of defining, implementing, and testing the communication software of Olivetti products (PCs, Minis). After introducing the main problems which arise in communication software validation, the general architecture of the system is described. Then, the basic functions of the tool are explained, through an elementary example, and its possible utilizations for testing and debugging of communication software are discussed.
A basic knowledge of LOTOS is assumed.

2. VALIDATION OF COMMUNICATION SOFTWARE

Software validation is the process of evaluating the results of the software development process, to determine compliance with the requirements [10].
The problem of validation can be summarized as follows: given that a program P is correct with respect to all features which can be tested by the language support, it must be assured that it calculates what it was written for [7].
The solution to this problem can be searched using two distinct approaches: formal verification and testing.
FORMAL VERIFICATION leads to a demonstration of program correctness, expressed by logical assertions on input and output data.
TESTING is based on the execution of the program being validated,

and it is performed through the following steps:

1) Test data collection,
2) Execution,
3) Analysis of output data.

The activity of testing is aimed not only at isolating coding errors; in general it is the attempt to infer certain properties of the program, from the analysis of execution data.
Testing and debugging of COMMUNCATION SOFTWARE, which is characterized by the real-time interaction of many complex distributed entities, can be effectively performed with the support of methodologies and tools, expressly developed for this kind of applications.

3. EXECUTION HISTORIES

The Symbolic Debugging System is intended to support the activity of testing, through the generation of an execution history of the program. History is created by tracing statements which are inserted in the program: at certain points in the execution, a procedure is called, which stores some information in memory for post-mortem examination [9].
These kinds of devices are often informally used by programmers; attempts to formalize these techniques, and to implement tools for history generation and analysis, are described in [8] [2].
The recording of large amounts of data for later examination, can take along some limits and disadvantages, including:

1) The inability of the user to drive the test, through interactions with the executing program, basing himself on partial results,

2) The compilation and execution distortions which may be caused by the history collecting subroutine calls,

3) The potentially large size of the data base.

However, the availability of information about the program evolution, allows a more systematic approach to testing and debugging, giving the following possibilities:

1) The program is tested in its actual usage environment,

2) Data analysis and display is isolated from execution. It can be done off-line, in a separate debugging environment,

3) Properties and conditions to be verified, can be chosen after collecting a complete summary of execution data, without preplanning.

Use of execution histories is especially effective in debugging of communication software: the peculiar problems of testing real-time systems are caused by the subtle interactions which may arise between the various processes in the system. System errors may be time dependent, only arising when the system processes are in a particular state [14]. The exact state of the system processes when the error occurred may be impossible to reproduce, without making use of complete information about the actual system behaviour.

4. THE SYMBOLIC DEBUGGING SYSTEM

The Symbolic Debugging System (SDS) is based on the generation of execution histories, which can be read and analyzed inside the notational framework of the specification language LOTOS.
A LOTOS specification is the description of a system in terms of its ability to communicate with the environment. Interactions take place at a set of gates.
If an implementation of the system is correct, it has the same external behaviour: it must be possible to determine at which points of the execution, observable events of the specification happen. At each of these particular places in the program, a statement can be included, to save the name of the gate at which the interaction takes place, and (some of) the 'passed' values.
At the end of execution, a LOTOS-like trace is available, which can be analyzed, using the specification as reference.

5. OVERALL ARCHITECTURE

In fig.1, the basic elements of the system are shown. Implementation is developed, satisfying the requirements imposed by a LOTOS specification. Produced code is instrumented with calls to trace generation procedures, provided to the programmer as run-time support, which create and update the trace area. The content of this area can be read using a debugger after the end of execution.
In the activities of trace creation and analysis, two basic implementation problems must be solved:

1) Memory occupation should be kept as limited as possible,

2) Values passed in LOTOS interactions do not exist, at least with the same format, in the implementation domain.
For these reasons, execution HISTORY is composed by a sequence of gate names, each followed by some meaningful data: to convert these information into the correct (possibly incomplete) form of the related LOTOS actions, a transformation must be performed, which is directed by a set of action-DECODING INSTRUCTIONS.
By these instructions, the programmer defines the translation of traced data, in terms of LOTOS values.
What is obtained is a LOTOS-like EXECUTION TRACE, wich has the same form of SIMULATION TRACES: the simulation of the LOTOS specification gives the possibility to compare the desired behaviour with the actual behaviour of the system.

6. CODE INSTRUMENTATION

The procedure call which records the occurrence of an action has the form

$$TRACE(E,P,L)$$

where:
    E is the action-identifier,
    P points to memory location where data to be stored begins,
    L is the number of memory locations occupied by data to be stored.

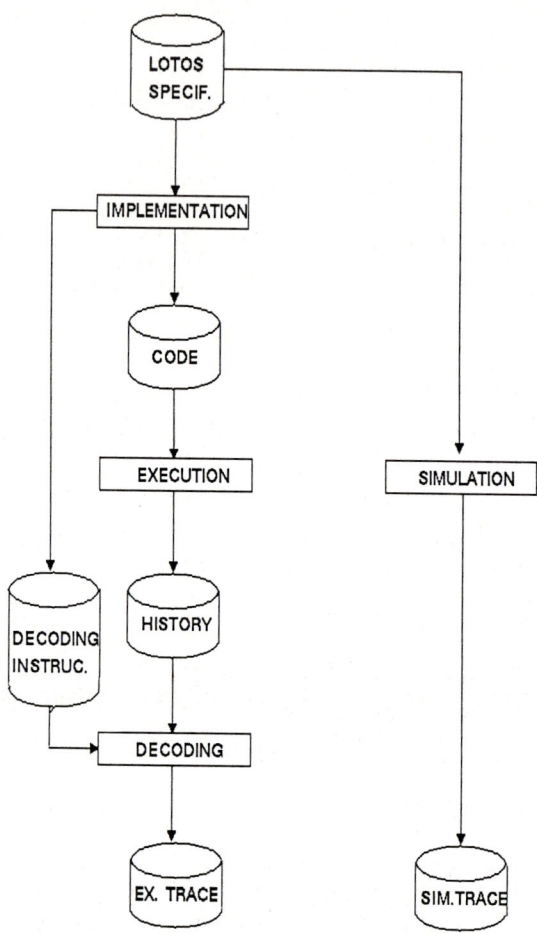

FIG. 1 - SYMBOLIC DEBUGGING SYSTEM: OVERALL ARCHITECTURE

For each gate, the format of stored data can be considered as a Pascal record: actions at the same gate must be always traced with the same format.

Moreover, for each gate, a priority level is defined. Then, using the procedure

                TR_LEVEL(L)

only tracing of events at gates with priority greater then L, is enabled.

7. LOTOS TRACE GENERATION

The generation of a LOTOS-like symbolic trace, from data stored, is directed by a set of decoding instructions.
These instructions describe, for each gate:

1) The format of the actions which occur at the gate, i.e. the name of the gate, and a list of structured parameters;

2) The actual meaning of the content of memory locations in wich data, related to each action occurrence, are stored;

3) Commands which allow to obtain some of the values passed at the gate, from the stored data.

Such instructions, wich are written using a special language, express the choices made by the programmer about:

- which events are to be traced,
- for each event a subset of its passed values which can be effectively stored,
- all implementation-dependent features of stored values.

8. AN INSTRUMENTED IMPLEMENTATION OF THE SLIDING WINDOW PROTCOL

To investigates the advantages of the proposed method an implementation of the Sliding Window Protocol has been developed [6]. The resulting programs have been instrumented to record the actions defined by the LOTOS specification.
The model of the system described by the specification, has been mirrored in the software architecture. Then, for all gates, it is possible to assert at which point of the execution an action occurs, and which are the passed data.

For example, an interaction at gate 'mt' can represent either the transmission of a message from the TRANSMITTER to the MEDIUM, or an acknowledgment given from the MEDIUM to the TRANSMITTER.
Actions at gate 'mt' have the format:

        mt ! primitive_name(p_object)

The 'primitive_name' discriminates between a message-passing (PDT_request), and the receiving of an acknowledgment (PDT_indication).

In case of a PDT_request the 'p_object' is composed with the operation MESS, which has two parameters: the text of the message, and an integer number which is the message-identifier. The 'p_object' of a PDT-indication is made with the operation ACKN, applied to the message-identifier of the message being acknowledged.

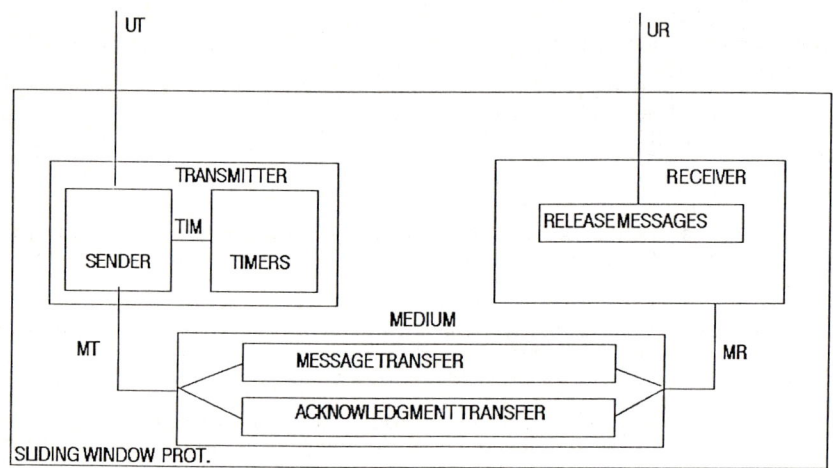

FIG. 2 - SLIDING WINDOW PROTOCOL

A set of data which can be effectively stored, to record the occurence of an action at gate 'mt' is:

       INDIC_PRIMITIVE:BOOLEAN
       MESSAGE_ID:INTEGER

From these data, the LOTOS notation of each action at gate 'mt' can be obtained, using statements which allow to assign actual values to the formal parameters 'primitive_name' and 'p_object'. Such statements, written using a language which is being expressly developed, have a form similar to the following:

```
REPLACE primitive_name WITH
  [INDIC_PRIMITIVE] -> 'PDTindication'
  [NOT INDIC_PRIMITIVE] -> 'PDTrequest'

REPLACE p_object WITH
  [IND_PRIMITIVE] -> 'ACKN(',MESSAGE_ID,')'
  [NOT IND_PRIMITIVE] ->'MESS(',MESSAGE_ID,',_)'
```

In case of a PDTindication, the LOTOS action obtained is complete. On the other end, if the primitive is PDTrequest, only one of the two parameters of the MESS function is known, i.e. the message-identifier: the text of the message is not traced, because it wouldn't be effective in terms of memory occupation. A missing element is indicated by the symbol '_'. Here follow some examples of stored records, and LOTOS actions obtained:

```
FALSE, 8                     mt ! PDTrequest(MESS(8,_))
FALSE, 2                     mt ! PDTrequest(MESS(2,_))
TRUE, 7                      mt ! PDTindication(ACK(7))
```

9. DESIGN SPECIFICATION AND SYMBOLIC DEBUGGING

The analysis of LOTOS-like symbolic traces is performed with different purposes, depending on the available LOTOS specification, which is used as reference.
A correct implementation of a given LOTOS specification, is a system which has the same external behaviour. The implementation can have a completely different internal architecture: in this case what can be accomplished using the SDS is a kind of TESTING of the implementation. Only external actions can be traced, so that it is possible to determine any inconsistency in the system interactions with its enviroment.
The actual goal of the SDS project is to develop a tool which is useful also for DEBUGGING: if the system is not behaving properly, we want to obtain some helpful indications about where the error is located. For this purpose, a specification is needed which reflects, to a certain extent, the implementation architecture. In this case, also some internal actions can be traced: it will be possible to observe the behaviour of internal components of the system and to have indication about the possible reasons of execution errors.
In summary, while testing can be supported by a PROTOCOL SPECIFICATION, for symbolic debugging a DESIGN SPECIFICATION must be available, i.e. a specification which reflects the architectural choices made in the design phase [3].

Experience and studies about the utilization of LOTOS in all stages of protocol development process are needed, especially about:
- the relations between different specifications of the same system,
- utilization of LOTOS to describe a system design.

In fig.3 a general framework is proposed which summarizes the activities of consistence verification between Protocol Specification, Design Specification, and Implementation. While consistence between different LOTOS specifications can be formally defined and verifyed [4] [5], any comparison with a real system must be based on execution trace generation, or other empirical methods.

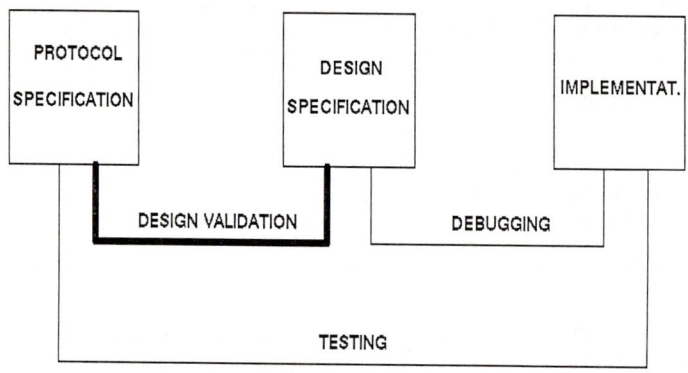

FIG. 3 - DIFFERENT GOALS OF CONSISTENCE VERIFICATION

10. CONCLUSIONS

Effective industrial utilization of FDTs in communication software production depends on the availability of methodologies and tools which allow to go through all phases of the developement process, without leaving a given formal notation.
While the use of LOTOS and other FDTs for Protocol Specification and Service Definition has been studied in depth [15] [13], much is still to be done about the efficent derivation of complete and correct software systems.
The 'black-box' model of LOTOS, and its definition of behaviours as sequences of atomic events, seem to be helpful for arguing about real systems and their relations with abstract specifications.
A prototype of the SDS tool described in this paper is currently under development in Olivetti. The testing fase of the tool is planned for the end of the year. The authors are the persons carrying on the project.

REFERENCES

[1] Abbott J., "Software testing techniques", NCC Pubblications, Manchester 1986

[2] Balzer R., "EXDAMS: Extendable Debugging and Monitoring System", AFIPS Conf. Proc. Vol.34, 1969

[3] Bochmann G. v., "Usage of protocol development tools, the results of a survey", Protocol Specification, Testing and Verification VII, H.Rudin and C.H. West (Editors), Elsevier Science Publishers B.V. (North-Holland), IFIP 1987

[4] Bolognesi T., Smolka S.A., "Fundamental results for the verification of observation equivalence", Protocol Specification, Testing and Verification VII, H.Rudin and C.H. West (Editors), Elsevier Science Publishers B.V. (North-Holland), IFIP 1987

[5] Brinksma E. et al., "LOTOS specifications, their implementations, and their tests", Protocol Specification, Testing, and Verification VI, B. Sarikaya and G.v. Bochmann (Editors), Elsevier Science Publishers B. V. (North-Holland), IFIP 1986

[6] "ESTELLE, LOTOS, SDL: Draft examples", meeting in Turin, 15-19 December, 1986

[7] Dameri E., Simonelli C., "Validazione del software", Franco Angeli Ed., Milano 1986

[8] Farley R., "An experimental program-testing facility", IEEE Trans. on Software Engineering, Vol. SE-1, N.4, Dec.1975

[9] Farley R., "Software engineering concepts", McGraw-Hill Int. Editions, 1985

[10] IEEE Std. 729-1983 "IEEE standard glossary of software engineering terminology", published by the IEEE, New York, N.Y.

[11] ISO/TC 97/SC 21 N 1534, "Revised guidelines for the application of FDT to OSI"

[12] ISO/TC 97/SC 21 N 2157, "Revised Text of 2nd ISO/DP 8807 - LOTOS - A Formal Description Technique Based on the Temporal On Temporal Ordering of Observationial Behaviour"

[13] Scollo G., et al., "Formal description of the OSI connection oriented Transport Protocol in LOTOS", SEDOS/119.7

[14] Sommerville I., "Software engineering", Addison – Wesley Publ., London, 1982

[15] Turner K., "An architectural semantics for LOTOS", Protocol Specification, Testing and Verification VII, H.Rudin and C.H. West (Editors),Elsevier Science Publishers B.V. (North-Holland), IFIP 1987

Validation Of The Ferry Clip Local Testing System Using An Estelle-C Compiler

Son T. Vuong and Wendy Y. L. Chan

Department of Computer Science
The University of British Columbia
Vancouver, BC
CANADA V6T 1W5

ABSTRACT

This paper presents a simulation and validation study of the Ferry Clip local testing system proposed for the conformance testing of data communication protocols. The simulation process involves specifying the testing system in Estelle and translating the specification into an executable C program using an Estelle-C compiler. Validation of the testing system follows by using the ferry protocol as the implementation under test. Tracing is used to observe the behavior of the system under normal testing. This study found the Ferry Clip concept viable and provided us with a better understanding of its application to protocol testing. Estelle and the Estelle-C compiler proved to be useful tools for simulation. In addition, this study confirmed one advantage of automatically generated implementations: they conform to their specifications.

I. INTRODUCTION

Two significant activities within the International Organization for Standardization (ISO) have been the development of Formal Description Techniques (FDTs) [ISO87, ISO87a, CCIT85] for the specification of communication protocols and services, and the development of conformance testing methodologies [ISO87b] for communication protocols.

Formal description techniques, such as Estelle [Linn86] and LOTOS [Brin86], were developed to remove ambiguities in the specification of protocols and services. Significant contributions from around the world have been made toward the development of support tools for FDTs [Boch87]. Specifically, several compilers that automatically generate protocol implementations from their formal specifications have been developed in various countries [Boch87a, BULL87, Kato87, NBS87, Phoe86, Saqu87, Vuon88]. Automatically generated implementations have the advantages of reduced errors and incompatibilities as well as protocol development time. At the University of British Columbia, a new Estelle-C compiler has recently been developed [Vuon88a]. It performs automatic protocol implementation in C from an Estelle protocol specification. This compiler is used in our study for the simulation of the testing system.

Four testing methodologies have thus far been identified by ISO to test protocol implementations for conformance to their specifications. These are the local test method, the remote test method, the distributed test method and the coordinated test method [ISO87b]. Although the local test method has the advantage of having direct access to the upper and lower service boundaries of the Implementation Under Test (IUT), the complexity of the test software required in the System Under Test (SUT) has deterred its use. The proposed Ferry Clip local testing approach [Zeng88] attempts to overcome this problem.

The goal of our study is twofold: to better understand the Ferry Clip local testing system and determine whether it is viable, and to experiment with Estelle and the Estelle-C compiler as simulation tools. We will begin by presenting the Ferry Clip system and the simulation tools, followed by a discussion of the simulation and validation processes. The paper concludes with some afterthoughts on the testing system.

II. THE FERRY-CLIP TESTING SYSTEM

1. Abstract Test Methods

Four abstract test methods for the conformance testing of communication protocols have been identified by ISO. These methods are classified as *external* or *local*, depending upon the location of the lower tester.

The *remote* test method, the *distributed* test method and the *coordinated* test method belong to the external category. Their lower testers are located remotely from the SUT and connected to it via a link or a network. During test execution, synchronization is required between the lower and upper testers. However, only the distributed and coordinated test methods use upper testers, giving them greater testing capabilities than the remote test method. The distributed and coordinated test methods are similar, but they differ in the level of standardization imposed upon the synchronization procedure for their testers, and in their requirements on the access to the layer boundary above the IUT. The coordinated test method uses a set of *test management protocols* to achieve coordination in its testers. The upper tester in the distributed test method directly accesses the upper service boundary of the IUT.

The *local* test method is the only member in the local category. It defines its points of control and observation (PCOs) to be directly at the service boundaries above and below the IUT; hence, it is possible to simulate various protocol and service events during testing. Since upper and lower testers reside in the same SUT, synchronization between these testers is easily achieved. However, this method requires complicated test software to be placed in the SUT, making it difficult to be considered as a general approach.

Figure 1, extracted from [ISO87b], shows an overview of these four abstract test methods. The lower and upper testers are abbreviated to **LT** and **UT** respectively. Protocol data units between peer layers are denoted as **PDUs**. Abstract service primitives exchanged between the service user and the provider are denoted as **ASPs**.

2. The Ferry Concept

Applicability to different SUTs and relatively complete testing capabilities together contribute to the popularity of the distributed and coordinated test methods. However, they suffer from two problems: synchronization between the lower and upper testers, and conflict between the power of the upper tester and its applicability to different SUTs. In 1985, Zeng [Zeng85] introduced the *ferry concept* to overcome these two problems.

The idea is to replace the upper tester in the SUT by a simple "ferry" and move the upper tester to the same machine as the lower tester. Synchronization no longer poses a problem as it can be achieved by inter-process communication within the same testing system. The upper tester may be enhanced without any limitation as it is no longer restricted by the SUT. The test software to be placed in the SUT is reduced to a minimal, simply for the provision of the ferry service.

The *Ferry Approach* [Zeng87] was subsequently proposed to realize the distributed and coordinated test methods. An *active ferry* residing in the same machine as the testers communicates with a *passive ferry* residing in the SUT via a *ferry control protocol*. Test data are transported between the upper tester and the IUT by the ferries through a ferry channel. The approach has been applied to different testing systems. It was found that the same ferry control protocol could be used for testing IUTs in all layers above the network layer.

The ferry concept has been recognized as one way of realizing the upper tester in distributed testing by ISO. Standardization of the ferry control protocol has been suggested.

3. Ferry Clip Local Testing Approach

Although the ferry concept has enhanced the realization of the distributed and coordinated test methods, their testing capabilities remain limited because the lower tester is not in the SUT. Control and observation of the lower service boundary of the IUT is obtained indirectly through a peer Service Access Point (SAP) of the IUT. Some defined state transitions of the IUT invoked by the lower service primitives cannot be executed if these primitives violate the underlying protocol or if they occur before an underlying connection has been established.

The local test method has greater testing capabilities because it has direct access to the service boundaries of the IUT. However, test software required is too complicated to be implemented in the SUT. To overcome this problem, Zeng introduced the *ferry clip* and proposed the *Ferry Clip local testing approach*, an extension of the ferry concept for the local test method.

The passive ferry at the SUT has two arms added to "clamp" onto the SAPs of the IUT, directly accessing its service boundaries. It is assumed that these service boundaries are accessible at the IUT. Test data are again transported between the test center and the SUT by the active and passive ferries using the same ferry control protocol. The means of providing the ferry transfer service is assumed to be reliable and may or may not be the layer below the IUT.

The Ferry Clip local testing approach is depicted in Figure 2. The **ferry controller** establishes and releases the connection of the ferry channel. The **ferry servers** add a header to the test data before transporting them across the ferry channel and remove the header from the test data arriving from the channel. The format of the header is shown in Appendix A. The **ferry protocol machines** implement the ferry control protocol to connect and release a ferry connection, and to transfer test data across the ferry channel. The state transition tables for the active and passive ferries are given in Appendix B. The **mapping** modules perform the mapping between the ferry protocol data units and the ferry transfer service interface data units; hence, its implementation is dependent upon the transfer service provider.

III. SIMULATION TOOLS

1. Estelle

Estelle is a formal description technique developed within ISO for the specification of communication protocols and services. It is based upon a set of extensions to Pascal.

Facilities in Estelle [Budk88] allow the specification of a hierarchy of modules. Parent modules may dynamically create and destroy child modules. Modules contain abstract message interfaces or interaction points that can be connected to form communication channels. These channels can be dynamically connected and disconnected by the parent modules. Messages or interaction primitives may be exchanged across these channels as a means of communication among modules. The control structure of the modules is based on an extended finite state machine model. A state change in a module occurs if the criteria expressed in a set of clauses are met. These criteria include the receipt of messages from other modules and conditions expressed in a predicate. A state change may be accompanied by a set of actions performed by the module. These are specified as Pascal statements.

2. The Estelle-C Compiler

The new Estelle-C compiler developed at the University of British Columbia accepts the 1986 Second DP version of Estelle [ISO86], which is essentially the same as the 1987 DIS version. Unlike other Estelle compilers, this Estelle-C compiler is implemented in C without the aid of any of the UNIX utilities such as LEX and YACC. This removes any restriction that may hinder further development of the compiler in non-UNIX environments. Implementation dependent details in the Estelle specification are directly translated into a compilable C program. A set of pre-compiled, specification independent run-time support routines is linked to the compiled program to produce an executable program. This program is driven by two support routines during execution to produce a dynamic implementation. The compiler is found useful in reducing protocol development time or, in this study, simulation time.

IV. SIMULATION OF THE FERRY CLIP LOCAL TESTING SYSTEM

Although Estelle was developed for specifying communication protocols and services, its modular constructs and simplicity, along with the availability of the Estelle-C compiler suggested it may be useful as a tool for simulating the Ferry Clip local testing system which contains inter-communicating entities. During simulation, we discovered Estelle and the compiler were not only easy to use, they alleviated the burden of programming and provided the translation from our description of the interactions between entities to an executable program that simulates these actions. We were able to completely concentrate on the simulation, leaving the programming to the compiler.

The testing system is specified as a hierarchy of modules, depicted in Figure 3. The three outer modules are the **protocol tester**, PT, **ferry transfer service**, XSLT, and **system under test**, SUT. Within the PT, the TD module represents the **tester drivers** and the AF module represents the **active ferry**. Within the SUT, the PF module represents the **passive ferry** and the IUT module represents the **implementation under test**.

The TD module houses the **tester** module and the **setup** module. The tester module constitutes the interface between the user and the testing system. Since the IUT is to be the ferry protocol machine, complete testing of the IUT can be easily performed by the user interactively without the aid of either upper or lower testers. However, if testers are to be used, they would be placed in this module either together or separately. The establishment and release of the ferry channel is also controlled by the user via this module. Test data to be sent to the upper and lower SAPs of the IUT is sent via the U and L interaction points respectively. Ferry channel control commands are sent via the C interaction point.

The setup module sends the actual establish and release commands to the active ferry via the F interaction point under the command of the tester module. This module uses a timer and reports to the tester module if the ferry channel is not connected within a user-defined interval of time. This is easily simulated using the DELAY feature in Estelle. However, since these are perfect channels between the ferries, the corresponding DELAY clause has not been executed.

The **FSR** module in the active ferry receives test data from the tester, adds a header to it and outputs the data via the **FC** interaction point to the ferry protocol machine. When data arrives from the protocol machine, the FSR module removes the header and passes the data to the tester module via interaction point U or L, depending on the U bit in the header.

The ferry protocol machine, **FPM**, receives interaction primitives in the form of FC-CONN, FC-DISC, FY-CONN, FY-DISC, FY-DATA, FT-DATA or FY-ERROR. Each transition contains a state change and/or an output, specified according to the state transition table shown in Appendix B. The FC-primitives are sent and received via the **F** interaction point, the FY- primitives, intended for the passive ferry, are transmitted via **FP**, and FT-DATA is sent via **FC**.

The mapping function is performed in **AMAP**. This simulation assumes the transport layer is providing the ferry transfer service. Hence, FY-CONN would be mapped to a CONNECT REQUEST and sent out via interaction point **A**. FY-DISC would be mapped to DISCONNECT REQUEST, and FY-DATA mapped to DATA REQUEST. Similarly, a CONNECT CONFIRM would be mapped to an FY-CONN and passed up to the FPM via interaction point FP.

The **XSLT** module models the ferry transfer service provider. Essentially, it converts REQUEST primitives from one end to INDICATION primitives for the other end; similarly for RESPONSE and CONFIRMATION primitives. It provides a perfect ferry channel, which is an assumption made by the testing system. This module communicates with the active and passive ferries via interaction points **XA** and **XP** respectively.

Modules **PMAP**, **FPMP** and **FSRP** correspond to the mapping function, ferry protocol machine and ferry server in the passive ferry respectively. Their functions are essentially the same as their counterparts in the active ferry. The FPMP receives only the FY-CONN, FY-DISC, FY-DATA, FY-ERROR and FT-DATA interaction primitives. The passive ferry cannot initiate a connection, but may initiate a disconnection if it receives erroneous messages. Incidentally, the PMAP is responsible for mapping any error packet received to FY-ERROR. Error packets are anything that does not correspond to a valid interface data unit. The interaction points **M** and **S** connect to the IUT module and they represent the upper and lower SAPs of the IUT respectively. Interaction primitives sent via M are transmitted back to the tester module via interaction point U, similarly for interaction points S and L.

The entire testing system is specified in Estelle. Display statements are inserted to facilitate interactions between the user and the testing system, and for the tracing of the modules during testing. An external file containing procedures referenced by these statements is prepared separately. The specification is then translated to C and compiled with the external file and a set of pre-defined support routines to yield the final executable simulation. This final program thus contains codes generated from the specification as well as specification independent codes. The following is a summary of the amount of code written and code generated by the compiler.

Estelle Specification :	2255 lines	38845 bytes
Compiler Generated C Code :	3624 lines	67911 bytes
External C File :	545 lines	10937 bytes
Object Code :		65536 bytes

V. VALIDATION OF THE FERRY CLIP LOCAL TESTING SYSTEM

1. Validation Via VALIRA

Prior to our validation of the Ferry Clip local testing system, we validated the ferry control protocol using **VALIRA** [Vuon86], a validation tool developed at the University of British Columbia. It validates a given protocol, represented as communicating finite state machines (CFSM), via reachability analysis. Validation of the ferry protocol was done for the connection establishment and release phases, as well as the data transfer phase. Possible errors that can occur were simulated, using modified CFSM, by having the ferries transmit error messages in each phase. These CFSM were validated separately. The resulting CFSM are then combined and shown in Appendix C. Only the interactions between the ferries are shown. Communications among a ferry, its ferry server and the ferry controller are omitted. These are clearly depicted in the state transition tables. Validation results showed the absence of state deadlocks, state ambiguities and unspecified receptions. The ferry protocol was found to be valid in general.

2. Validation Via Testing Of The Simulated System

The simulation was tested with the active and passive ferry protocol machines placed in the IUT module. Events pertaining to the ferry channel controller and the ferry server are treated as upper service access primitives. Events pertaining to the active or passive ferries are treated as lower service access primitives. Parameters in the interaction primitives received at the M and S interaction points from the tester are mapped to the appropriate test event in the form of an interaction primitive and passed to the appropriate protocol machine via one of four internal interaction points **TA**, **TP**, **TAL** or **TPL**. The corresponding protocol machine responds by sending interaction primitives via the appropriate internal interaction point to M or S. The response then travels through the testing system arriving at the tester module for analysis. Each response carries two parameter fields to convey the previous and present states of the responding protocol machine.

Complete testing of the protocol machines was performed by implementing each entry in the state transition table at least once. The machines as IUTs were found to react exactly as stated in the table. Tracings showed the modules in the system to be behaving precisely as expected. Test data were transferred across the system correctly. A test session depicting the establishment of the ferry channel and the responses of the active ferry protocol machine to two consecutive FC-CONN test events is recorded and shown in Figure 4. The "?" marks indicate receipts, "!" marks indicate transmissions. Note that at the test data transfer phase, the FSR receives test data via U, the upper tester driver (UTD), and responds by sending FT-DATA, which is the test data accompanied by a header. At the FSRP, upon receiving FT-DATA, it checks the U bit in the header and determines that it is test data from the UTD. It removes this header and transmits the test data to the upper SAP of the IUT. At the IUT, it receives the test data, maps it to one of the test events intended for the active ferry, and passes it down to the active ferry protocol machine. The first test event sent was FC-CONN. When the active ferry responds with FY-CONN to the passive ferry, it does so through its "lower SAP," which is received at the lower SAP of the IUT and transmitted back to the tester driver via L, representing the lower tester driver (LTD).

So far, we have found the ferry concept proposed by Zeng to be viable in our simulation. It has allowed us to test the IUTs successfully via a ferry channel. As well, since the whole system is specified in Estelle and turned into an executable program with the Estelle-C compiler, this has affirmed the validity of the compiler and the fact that automatically generated implementations such as the ferry protocol machines in here indeed conform to their formal specifications. However, these were simple protocols depicting only their behaviors during implementation. Parameters, options or timing events were absent in their specifications. Nevertheless, their behavior conformance contributes to an increased confidence in automatic implementations. It should be noted that this simulation can be easily converted to a real implementation. Performing the simulation using Estelle and the compiler removed our concern of scheduling and executing the modules correctly during testing, and allowed us to fully concentrate on correctly modelling the system.

3. Some Afterthoughts

In the Ferry Clip testing approach, the mapping modules play significant roles. They must use the exact format of the service access primitives known to the ferry transfer service provider. If the provider requires the length of the data passed down to be specified, such as in the SEND and DELIVER primitives in the Transmission Control Protocol (TCP), then the mapping modules must have some way of obtaining this information, either by means of a counter or by added communication with the IUT and testers directly or indirectly. Options and parameters might be negotiated during connect establishment. These must be supported by the mapping modules. Implementation of the ferries thus depends somewhat on the ferry transfer service provider and must be known by the test center and its client.

With respect to the ferry control protocol, since the ferry channel controller resides in the same machine as the active ferry, theoretically it could be coordinated with the active ferry and should not be sending redundant FC-CONNs to the active ferry during the establishment of a connection or during the data transfer phase. If it does, the active ferry should not need to respond with disconnecting the ferry channel as specified in the state transition tables in Appendix B [Zeng88], since the passive ferry might be at the other side of a network and disconnect-connect sessions could be costly. Instead, the active ferry could use an acknowledging response to inform the controller that it is in the midst of establishing a connection with the passive ferry or that it is transferring data. A timer may be incorporated, as in our simulation, to avoid the transmission of redundant FC-CONNs.

Recall that it is the ferry server who adds and removes the header to and from the test data. In the proposed header shown in Appendix A, the Type field would always be set to 00 since the ferry server only deals with test data. The FY-CONN and FY-DISC control PDUs are not explicitly transmitted but are mapped into the respective primitives for the ferry transfer service provider. Hence, in connection-oriented systems, this Type field may be eliminated. It may be argued that this field is needed if the ferry transfer service provides connectionless service. This way, the ferries could be establishing a virtual connection on top to ensure reliable transmission. But this would imply a complex ferry protocol, contradicting the original intention of the ferry concept to simplify test software in the SUT. It would thus be more reasonable to avoid the connection establishment and disconnection phases, and eliminate the Type field altogether.

The Channel Number is not required at this stage for single layer testing; it was not included in the simulation. Another questionable feature is the Byte Count, which records the number of bytes of user data. This was intended to aid in reassembling a large amount of data that has been segmented prior to transporting it across the ferry channel. However, since the underlying layers provide means of delimiting messages passed down from upper layers, the M bit alone suffices in the reassembly process. Nevertheless, this Byte Count may be used for another purpose: "piggybacking." Certain test cases may require the transmission of consecutive test events via the same SAP or via both SAPs. To reduce transmission cost and increase efficiency, the Byte Count may be used as an indicator that there are more than one test event abroad the incoming ferry boat. Each test event is still accompanied by its own header, the Byte Count merely indicates the length of the current event. If the Byte Count is already in use to meet the needs of the underlying transfer service, then a P (piggyback) bit may be used to indicate multiple test events are present. Piggybacking can also be used to transport multiple responses from the IUT back to the test center abroad the same ferry boat. This is more common as the IUT is frequently required to respond to both its service user and its service provider.

It may be worthwhile to provide an extra D (Data generation) bit in the ferry PDU header to allow the passive ferry to generate data locally at the SUT site. This will avoid the potential excessive delay and cost incurred in the actual ferrying of a large amount of data between the tester and the SUT. Certain X.400 test cases may involve data transfer of as much as megabytes of data to test the Message Transfer Agent's (MTA's) data handling capability. The provision of this data generation feature in the passive ferry calls for an increase in complexity in the passive ferry and an extra Dcount (Data count in units of Kbytes) field of one or two bytes in the ferry PDUs to indicate the amount of data generated. This Dcount field may be absent if the D-bit is turned off. This feature may be made selectable during connection establishment.

It would be interesting to consider the provision of multiple arms at the passive ferry server, to allow the observation of interactions among the layers during testing. Three extra bits can be added to the header to identify the layer under observation, the U bit still used to indicate the upper or lower SAP. Another alternative may be the use of multiple passive ferry servers, but this would require extra resources and multiplexing capabilities either at the protocol machine or the mapping module, which is undesirable if we wish to preserve the applicability of the passive ferry in general. So far, we have considered single layer testing, embedded testing and multi-layer testing may also benefit from this Ferry Clip approach.

VI. CONCLUSIONS

We have presented a simulation and validation study of the proposed Ferry Clip local testing approach. Simulation was done with the aid of Estelle and an Estelle-C compiler. They were found to be useful tools, alleviating the burden of programming and redirecting the user's attention to the specification of the testing system. The ferry protocol was validated with VALIRA and found to be acceptable. The simulated system was validated by placing the ferry protocol machines in the IUT module and tracing through the system during test execution. The Ferry Clip testing system was found to be viable. Various suggestions were offered for changes to the ferry header format and state transition tables. A possible extension of the ferry concept was discussed.

This study has re-affirmed the advantages of using the Estelle-C compiler, that it not only reduces protocol development time, but it is capable of producing implementations that conform to their specifications. These implementations may then be placed in a protocol tester as reference implementations. The simulation study also suggested behavior testing of implementations may be conducted using simulations obtained automatically from their specifications. Tracing could be used and errors can be easily detected and corrected in the specification. The final implementation can then be obtained automatically from the specification. This would not only increase the behavior conformance of the resulting implementation, but the difficult task of tracing and modifying an implementation is made simpler.

Other related projects underway include implementations of the upper layers of an X.400 Message Handling System and developing testing facilities for them. We are also simulating the prototype for this system using the Estelle-C compiler.

ACKNOWLEDGEMENT

The authors would like to thank Dr. H.X. Zeng for a number of fruitful discussions on the ferry testing concept and system.

REFERENCES

[Boch87]   Bochmann, G.v., "Usage of Protocol Development Tools: The Results of a Survey," *Protocol Specification, Testing and Verification, VII,* (IFIP/WG6.1), H. Rudin and C.H. West, Eds., North Holland, 1987.

[Boch87a] Bochman, G.v., Gerber, G.W. and Serre, J.M., "Semiautomatic Implementation of Communication Protocols," *IEEE Trans. on Software Engineering,* SE-13:989-1000, 1986.

[Brin86]   Brinksa, E., "A Tutorial on LOTOS," *Protocol Specification, Testing and Verification, V,* (IFIP/WG6.1), M. Diaz, Ed., North Holland, pp.177-193, 1987.

[Budk88]   Budkowski, S. and Dembinski, P., "An Introduction to Estelle: a Specification Language for Distributed Systems," to appear in *Computer Networks and ISDN System,* 1987

[BULL87]   User Guide for the BULL Prototype Compiler for Estelle, BULL S.A., Corporate Networking and Communication (DRCG), Distributed System Architecture and Standards (ARS), LOUVECIENNES, 1987.

[CCIT85]   CCITT/SGXI, "Functional Specification and Description Language," Recommendation Z101 to Z104, 1985.

[ISO86]   ISO/TC97/SC21/WG1/Subgroup B, "Estelle - A Formal Description Technique Based on an Extended State Transition Model," 2nd DP 9074, 1987.

[ISO87]   ISO/TC97/SC21/WG1/Subgroup B, "Estelle - A Formal Description Technique Based on an Extended State Transition Model," DIS 9074, 1987.

[ISO87a]   ISO/TC97/SC21/N, "LOTOS - A Formal Description Technique Based on the Temporal Ordering of Observational Behavior," DIS 8807, 1987.

[ISO87b]   ISO/TC97/SC21/N, "OSI Conformance Testing Methodology and Framework," 2nd DP 9646-1, 1987.

[Kato87]   Kato, T., Hasegara, T. and Horinchi, H., "Design of Translator from Estelle with ASN.1 to ADA," KDD Kamifukioka R&D Labs., 2-1-15 Ohara, Kamifukuoka-shi, Saitama-Ken 356, Japan, 1987.

[Linn86]   Linn, R.J., Jr., "The Features and Facilities of Estelle," *Protocol Specification, Testing and Verification, V,* (IFIP/WG6.1), M. Diaz, Ed., North Holland, pp.291-296, 1986.

[NBS87]   User Guide for the NBS Prototype Compiler for Estelle, Final Report, Report No. ICST/SNA-87/3, NBS Institute for Computer Science and Technology, October 1987.

[Phoe86]   Estelle Development System, Users Manual, Phoenix Technologies Ltd. (formerly Protocol Development Corporation), 675 Mass Avenue, Cambridge, MA., 1986.

[Saqu87]   Saqui-Sannes, P.D. and Courtiat, J.P., "ESTIM: An Interpretative Tool for the Simulation of Estelle Descriptions," SEDOS Report SEDOS/115, Nov. 1987.

[Vuon86]   Vuong, S., Hui, D.D. and Cowan, D.D., "VALIRA - A Tool for Protocol Validation Via Reachability Analysis," *Proc. of the Sixth IFIP Workshop on Protocol Specification, Testing and Verification,* St Jovite, Montreal, June 1986.

[Vuon88]   Vuong, S.T., Lau, A.C. and Chan, R.I., "Automatic Implementation of Protocols Using an Estelle-C Compiler," *IEEE Trans. on Software Engineering,* March 1988.

[Vuon88a] Vuong, S.T., Chan, R.I. and Chan, W.Y.L., "An Estelle-C Compiler for Automatic Protocol Implementation," submitted to the Eighth International Symposium on Protocol Specification, Testing and Verification, Atlantic City, N.J., June 1988.

[Zeng85]   Zeng, H.X. and Rayner, D., "The Impact of the Ferry Concept on Protocol Testing," *Protocol Specification, Testing and Verification, V,* (IFIP/WG6.1), M. Diaz, Ed., North Holland, pp.533-544, 1986.

[Zeng88]   Zeng, H.X., Li, Q., Du, X.F. and He, C.S., "New Advances in Ferry Testing Approaches," to appear in *Computer Network and ISDN Systems, 1988.*

[Zeng88]   Zeng, H.X., Du, X.F. and He, C.S., "Promoting the 'Local' Test Method with the New Concept 'Ferry Clip'," draft submitted to the Eighth International Symposium on Protocol Specification, Testing and Verification, Atlantic City, N.J., June 1988.

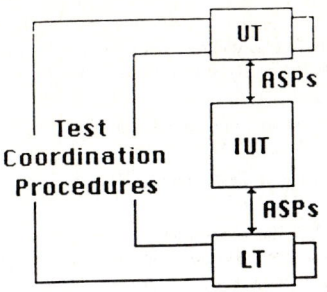

(a) The Local Test Methods

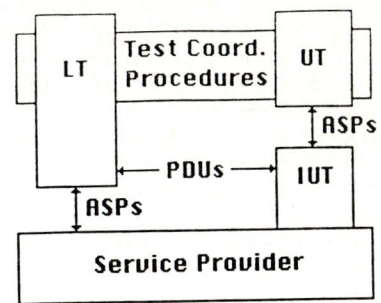

(b) The Distributed Test Methods (external)

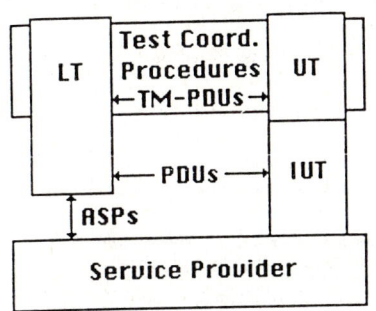

(c) The Coordinated Test Methods (external)

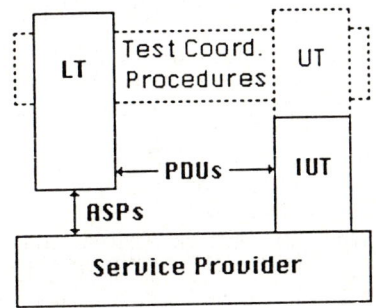

(d) The Remote Test Methods (external)

Figure 1. Overview of Abstract Test Methods

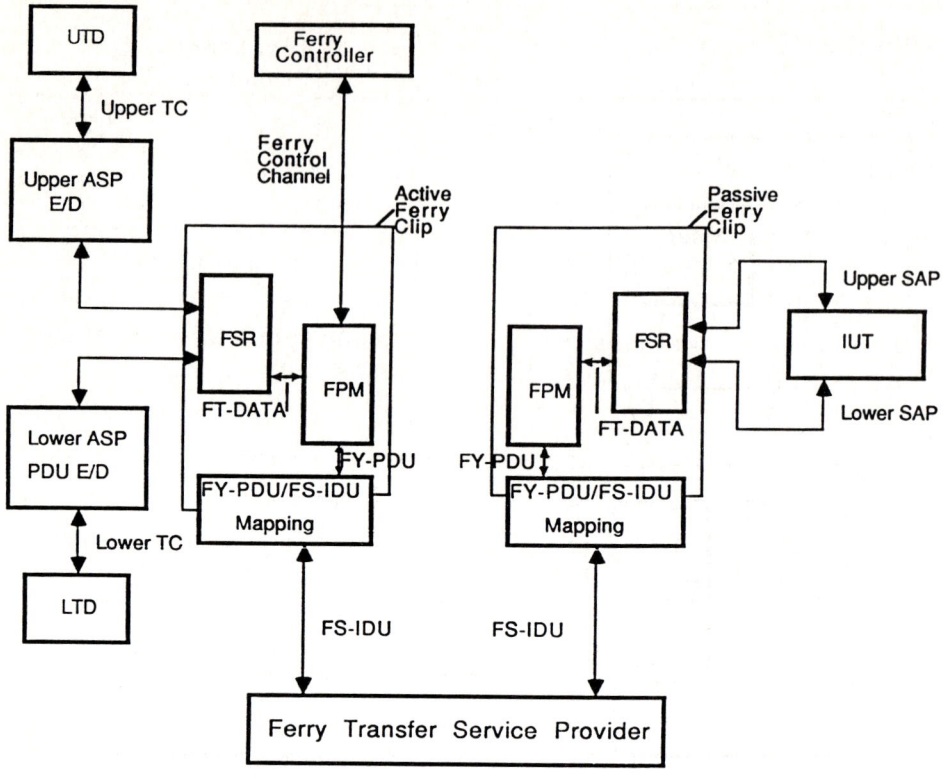

ASP: Abstract Service Primitive
SAP: Service Access Point
TC: Test Channel
FSR: Ferry Server
FPM: Ferry Protocol Machine

FS-IDU: Ferry transfer Service Interface Data Unit
FY-PDU: Ferry Protocol Data Unit
FT-DATA: Test data in a Ferry

Figure 2. The Ferry-Clip Local Testing System

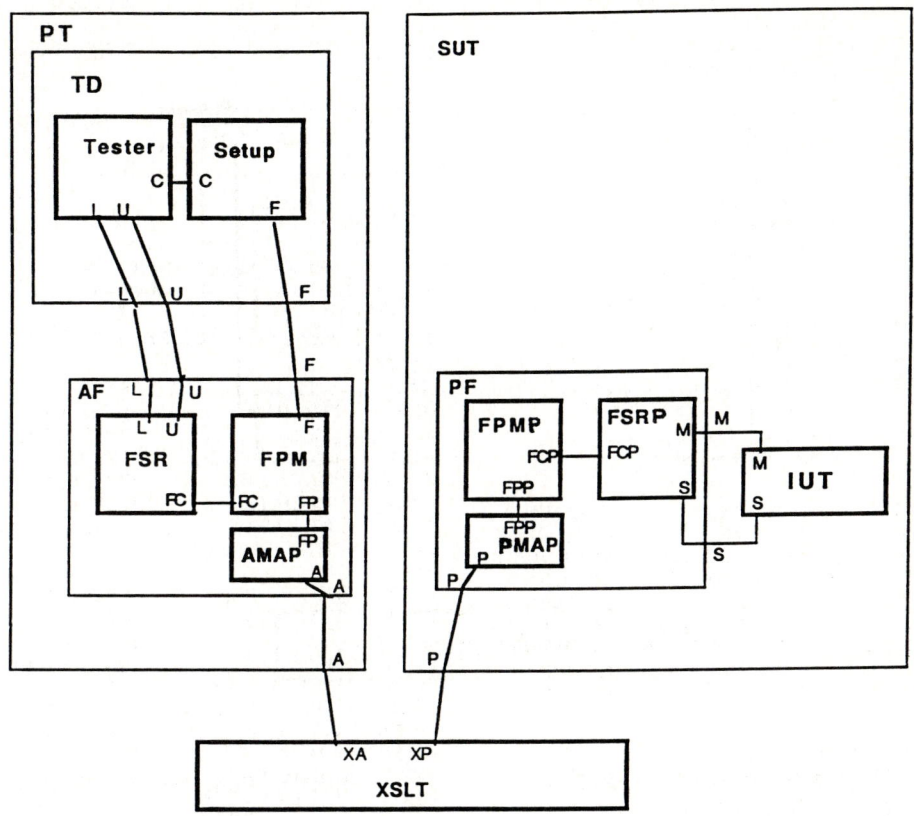

Figure 3. Specification Modules for the Ferry Clip Local Testing System

```
-> 'h' to list user commands, else return: h
    USER COMMANDS:
      -control commands:
          CF : connect ferry channel         AMAP:  ?DATA INDC     !FY-DATA
          DF : disconnect ferry channel      FPM :  ?FY-DATA       !FT-DATA
          SF : send data to IUT              FSR :  ?FT-DATA       !LTD test data
          WA : wait for active ferry
      -test events for active ferry:         Received at LOWER tester driver:
          CC : FC-CONN                       FY-CONN from ACTIVE ferry; from IDLE to WAIT
          CD : FC-DISC
          SA : FY-DATA                       -> 'h' to list user commands, else return:
          DA : FY-DISC                       -> enter code please : SF
          CA : FY-CONN                         *** send data to IUT
          EA : FY-ERROR
          TA : FT-DATA                       -> Please enter transmission packet code:
      -test events for passive ferry:        -> 'h' to list user commands, else return:
          CP : FY-CONN                       -> enter code please : CC
          DP : FY-DISC                         *** FC-CONN to ACTIVE ferry
          SP : FY-DATA
          EP : FY-ERROR                      FSR :   ?UTD test data      !FT-DATA
          TP : FT-DATA                       FPM :   ?FT-DATA            !FY-DATA
                                             AMAP:   ?FY-DATA            !DATA REQU
-> enter code please : CF                    XSLT:   ?PT DATA REQU       !SUT DATA INDC
    *** connect ferry channel                PMAP:   ?DATA INDC          !FY-DATA
                                             FPMP:   ?FY-DATA            !FT-DATA
FPM :   ?FC-CONN        !FY-CONN             FSRP:   ?FT-DATA            !USAP test data
AMAP:   ?FY-CONN        !CONN REQU           IUT :   ?UTD test data
XSLT:   ?PT CONN REQU   !SUT CONN INDC       IUT :                       !UTD test data
PMAP:   ?CONN INDC      !FY-CONN             FSRP:   ?USAP test data     !FT-DATA
FPMP:   ?FY-CONN        !FY-CONN             FPMP:   ?FT-DATA            !FY-DATA
PMAP:   ?FY-CONN        !CONN RESP           IUT :                       !LTD test data
XSLT:   ?SUT CONN RESP  !PT CONN CONF        PMAP:   ?FY-DATA            !DATA REQU
AMAP:   ?CONN CONF      !FY-CONN             FSRP:   ?LSAP test data     !FT-DATA
FPM :   ?FY-CONN        !FC-CONN             XSLT:   ?SUT DATA REQU      !PT DATA INDC
                                             FPMP:   ?FT-DATA            !FY-DATA
                                             AMAP:   ?DATA INDC          !FY-DATA
    *** ferry channel connected.             FPM :   ?FY-DATA            !FT-DATA
-> 'h' to list user commands, else return:   FSR :   ?FT-DATA            !UTD test data
-> enter code please : SF
    *** send data to IUT                     Received at UPPER tester driver:
                                             FC-DISC from ACTIVE ferry; from WAIT to IDLE
-> Please enter transmission packet code:
-> 'h' to list user commands, else return:   PMAP:   ?FY-DATA            !DATA REQU
-> enter code please : CC                    XSLT:   ?SUT DATA REQU      !PT DATA INDC
    *** FC-CONN to ACTIVE ferry              AMAP:   ?DATA INDC          !FY-DATA
                                             FPM :   ?FY-DATA            !FT-DATA
FSR :   ?UTD test data       !FT-DATA        FSR :   ?FT-DATA            !LTD test data
FPM :   ?FT-DATA             !FY-DATA
AMAP:   ?FY-DATA             !DATA REQU      Received at LOWER tester driver:
XSLT:   ?PT DATA REQU        !SUT DATA INDC  FY-DISC from ACTIVE ferry; from WAIT to IDLE
PMAP:   ?DATA INDC           !FY-DATA
FPMP:   ?FY-DATA             !FT-DATA        -> 'h' to list user commands, else return:
FSRP:   ?FT-DATA             !USAP test data
IUT :   ?UTD test data
IUT :                        !LTD test data
FSRP:   ?LSAP test data      !FT-DATA
FPMP:   ?FT-DATA             !FY-DATA
PMAP:   ?FY-DATA             !DATA REQ
XSLT:   ?SUT DATA REQU       !PT DATA INDC
```

Figure 4.   Sample Test Session

Appendix A

Ferry Header

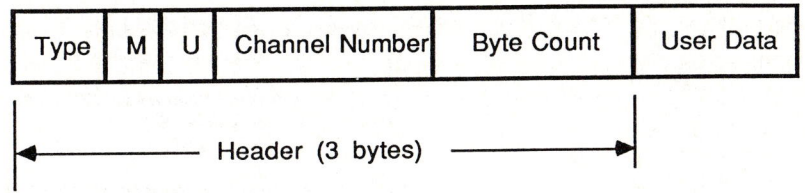

Type (2 bits):   00 - data
              01 - connect
              10 - disconnect
              11 - error

M - More bit: 0 - complete message
              1 - more segments to follow

U - Upper interface bit: 0 - lower interface
                        1 - upper interface

Byte count (2 bytes):   records the length of user data (test data)

Channel Number (4 bits):   1111 - reserved for single test channel case

Appendix B

State transition tables for the Active Ferry and the Passive Ferry

Event \ State	FY-CONN	FY-DISC	FY-DATA	FY-ERROR	FT-DATA
Idle	!FY-CONN -->:Active	-->: R	!FY-DISC -->: R	!FY-DISC -->: R	-->: R
Active	!FY-DISC -->: Idle	-->: Idle	!FT-DATA -->: R	!FY-DISC -->: Idle	!FY-DATA -->: R

(a) Passive Ferry

Event \ State	FY-CONN	FY-DISC	FY-DATA	FY-ERROR	FC-CONN	FC-DISC	FT-DATA
Idle	!FY-DISC -->:R	-->:R	!FY-DISC -->:R	!FY-DISC -->:R	!FY-CONN -->:Wait	-->:R	!FY-DISC -->:R
Wait	!FC-CONN -->:Active	!FC-DISC -->:Idle	!FY-DISC !FC-DISC -->:Idle	!FY-DISC !FC-DISC -->:Idle	!FY-DISC !FC-DISC -->:Idle	!FY-DISC -->:Idle	!FY-DISC !FY-DISC -->:Idle
Active	!FY-DISC !FC-DISC -->:Idle	!FC-DISC -->:Idle	!FT-DATA -->:R	!FY-DISC !FC-DISC -->:Idle	!FY-DISC !FC-DISC -->:Idle	!FY-DISC -->:Idle	!FY-DATA -->:R

(b) Active Ferry

- Event   "FY-" - Ferry Channel PDU event
  - "FT-" - Test message from the UTD or from the IUT (FT-DATA is the only type)
  - "FC -" - Ferry Channel Control message event relevant to the Ferry Channel establishment and release

- Action   "FY-" - Message passed on the Ferry Channel or action taken in the Ferry Channel
  - "FT-" - Message passed on the Test Channel
  - "FC-" - Message passed on the UTD via Ferry Control Channel

- Next state "-->:R" - remain in the original state

Appendix C

CFSM Representing the Ferry Control Protocol

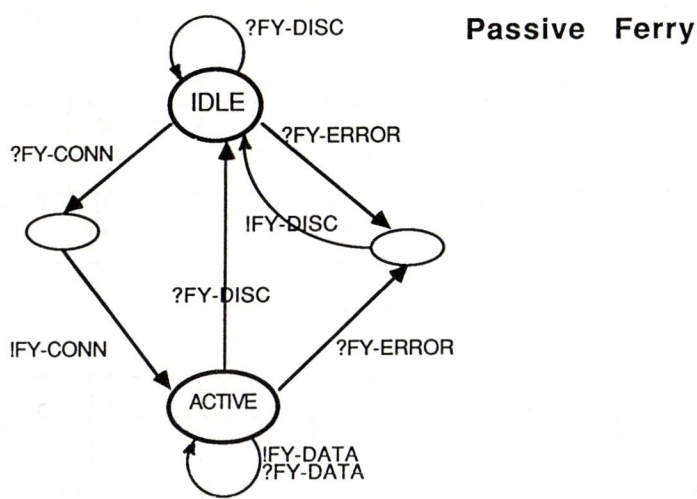

?: Reception
!: Transmission

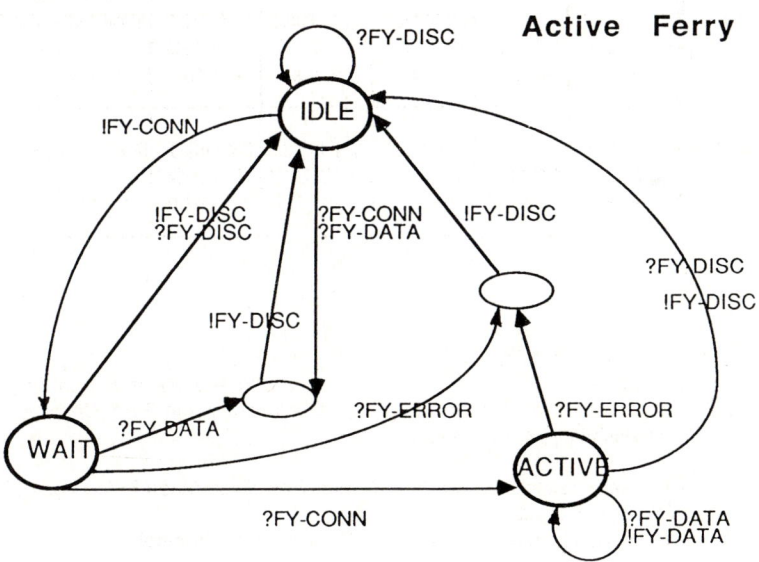

QA 76.6 .I545 1988
International Conference on
 Formal Description
Formal description
 techniques

MAY 0 2 1989